Notes from a Wayward Son

NOTES
from a
WAYWARD SON

A MISCELLANY

Andrew G. Walker

Edited by Andrew D. Kinsey

Foreword by William J. Abraham

CASCADE *Books* · Eugene, Oregon

NOTES FROM A WAYWARD SON
Andrew G. Walker—A Miscellany

Cascade Books
An Imprint of Wipf and Stock Publishers
199 W. 8th Ave., Suite 3
Eugene, OR 97401

www.wipfandstock.com

ISBN 13: 978-1-62564-161-8

Cataloguing-in-Publication Data

Walker, Andrew, 1945–.

Notes from a wayward son : Andrew G. Walker—a miscellany

xviii + 322 p. ; 23 cm. Includes bibliographical references.

ISBN 13: 978-1-62564-161-8

1. Church. 2. Church renewal. 3. Christianity—20th century. 4. Christianity—21st century. 5. Pentecostalism. 6. Orthodox Eastern Church. 7. Christian union. 8. Lewis, C. S. (Clive Staples), 1898–1963. 9. Religion and sociology. I. Kinsey, Andrew. II. Abraham, William J. (William James), 1947–. III. Title.

BV600.3 W355 2015

Manufactured in the U.S.A.   09/03/2015

Colour photography by Matt Boulton

New Revised Standard Version Bible, copyright 1989, Division of Christian Education of the National Council of the Churches of Christ in the United States of America. Used by permission. All rights reserved.

Andrew dedicates this book to Susan his wife
who has loved and supported him with fortitude, forbearance,
and faith throughout the years

Andy dedicates this book to his family
Peggy, Caleb, Hannah, and Grace:
Their love gives strength and hope

CONTENTS

FOREWORD

A ndrew Walker is one of the most remarkable scholars I have met across the years.

We first met by accident. I had been in Dallas for a year or so and had been invited to speak in a series of talks in a small town south of Dallas with the wonderful name of Waxahachie. Earlier in the week I had run into Dr. Bernice Martin, whose husband David Martin had come to an endowed chair at Southern Methodist University. Bernice noted that she had two English academics coming to stay with her on their way to a major conference in sociology in Boston. When she identified them as Dave Docherty and Andrew Walker I immediately recognized the first name, as we had met before. Andrew Walker, however, was new. When she added wistfully that having the two of them together for several days would be a "handful," I suggested that I take Andrew with me to Waxahachie and thus afford her some relief. She agreed immediately. It was a memorable weekend. Before it was over I managed to get Andrew to share in some of the speaking responsibilities. It was a sterling performance on his part, as he was in his element as an intellectual with extraordinary skill in public speaking.

When we met, we hit it off immediately, despite our radical differences in terms of ethnic identity, church membership, and scholarship. We quickly discovered, however, that we had a shared interest in all things American, in Pentecostalism, in Orthodoxy, and in Christianity in Britain. As both of us were new to Texas we were also fascinated by what we encountered in the United Methodist congregation in Waxahachie. Texas is a world of its own. It is not the South but the Southwest of the United States; and sorting out its sense of independence and how that plays out in its religious sensibility and history is a tall order. Aside from sharing our own peculiar journeys into Christianity, then, we found ourselves trying as best we could to get our initial bearings on the new section of planet earth on which we had landed.

As I often drive past the motel on the highway south of Dallas where we stayed, I ponder anew the joys of many years of friendship that started so serendipitously in Waxahachie.

Pursuant to this initial encounter we also developed our relationship as colleagues in the Doctor of Ministry program at Perkins School of Theology. For several years Andrew joined us for intensive courses in the summer. These events were full-scale, no-holes-barred doctoral seminars with a network of first-rate students from across the country. Students read a series of texts in advance, wrote substantive critical reviews, and took their life in their hands in day-long conversation. Andrew was in his element as a teacher. Many of these students have stayed in touch with him and benefited thereafter from his wisdom and erudition, including Andy Kinsey, the editor of this volume.

As a thinker, I would characterize Andrew more as a fox, rather than a hedgehog. His training in sociology was really his point of entry into the life of the mind. Once in, he had a sharp nose for making telling observations on a host of issues that did not initially show up in his training. Changing the metaphor, you never knew where his intellectual ball was going to bounce once he hit it with all the freshness of a new player. However, one followed the ball knowing that a unique new insight would emerge. This made any conversation with Andrew something of an adventure. Readers will see this in the wide-range of issues in the essays that constitute this book. Even on matters that are deeply person-relative he can stand back and survey the landscape in a way that gives us strikingly new perspectives.

On a personal level, then, Andrew always displayed an honesty and even brashness that was stimulating in the extreme. We quickly got to the point in our relationship where we could say absolutely anything to each other. This is rare in academia, and when it happens it is a wonderful antidote to boredom and sterility. Due to personal circumstances over the years, however, we have not been able to keep up the conversation to the degree we would both cherish. We know, though, that whenever and wherever we meet we can pick up exactly where we left off without the usual throat-clearing that is natural in renewed interchange. And yet, on a professional level as an academic, Andrew has displayed amazing fortitude and resilience. The obstacles have been formidable, but the work seems to keep pouring out of his fertile intellect. Whatever subject he tackles somehow becomes the spur to a fresh outburst of energy and imagination.

It is a great pleasure, therefore, to see this collection of essays brought together as a single volume. All of them are fascinating. However, if I were to pick out one for its originality and insight it would be the essay, "The Third Schism." It is worth the price of the whole work. We all know that the divisions within Christianity over the last two hundred years are far from easy to pin down in a non-polemical and illuminating manner. We also know that they cut across standard ecclesial lines, as the current flap over the proposals on divorce and remarriage developed by Cardinal Kasper in the Vatican make clear. It is entirely superficial to see the debate as a debate between conservatives and progressives or between modernists and postmodernists. These are not exactly useless concepts, but they have grown stale and tend to suffocate conversation. The concept of a third schism, however, tackles the problem of naming what is going on in a whole new way. Once it is in place we can then begin to sort out a set of critical questions that we can approach from a whole new angle. We are given a fresh set of proposals to ponder and evaluate. In fact, even if the whole idea is rejected we have been given a new vista from which to look at the present nasty divisions across Christendom.

Those who know Andrew Walker will be delighted to welcome this volume as summing up a lifetime of truly original scholarship presented in a clear and engaging manner. Those who are new to his work are set for a stimulating adventure down trails that will awaken curiosity on topics that deserve extended attention in the current academic arena.

William J. Abraham
Albert Cook Outler Professor of Theology and Wesley Studies
Southern Methodist University

ACKNOWLEDGMENTS

I want to acknowledge those who have assisted me in guiding this project to publication over the last two years. As I quickly discovered, the present volume would have never seen the light of day without the patient and dedicated efforts of Corinne Beyer of Franklin College. Again and again Corrine was invaluable at retyping many of the texts. I appreciate greatly her willingness to assist me. In addition, I also want to thank Sarah Blair of United Theological Seminary and Simon Jenkins of *Ship of Fools* who also helped me to locate pieces Andrew had written over the last forty-five years. I appreciate the time and attention they gave to this project.

And, of course, I want to thank Robin Parry of Wipf and Stock Publishers, who helped at the various stages of this volume and who reviewed the manuscript on the way to the press. It was indeed a learning curve, and taking on this work was a bigger task than I realized. I am grateful to Robin for his words of encouragement and instruction.

And lastly, I would like to thank "Billy" Abraham of Southern Methodist University for writing the Foreword and to Andrew for offering the Afterword. I met Billy and Andrew as a student at Perkins School of Theology in the late 1990s and the relationships we developed over the years have been a means of grace on multiple levels. Their friendships have been enduring and their support a blessing. This book is in many ways a testimony to those friendships and to the gospel we share.

Permissions

The editor thanks the *Encyclopedia of Modern Thought* of Blackwell Publishers with permission to print "Charismatic and Pentecostal Religion"; Mercer University Press, Georgia, for "Pentecostal Power: The 'Charismatic Renewal Movement' and the Politics of Pentecostal Experience" in *Of Gods and Men: New Religious Movements in the West*; MacMillan Press for "Thoroughly Modern: Sociological Reflections on the Charismatic Movement from the End of the Twentieth Century," in *Charismatic Christianity: Sociological Perspectives*; and the *Scottish Journal of Theology* for "Scripture, Revelation and Platonism in C.S. Lewis."

The editor thanks to Basil Blackwell Publishing for permission to print "The Theology of the 'Restoration' House Churches" in *Strange Gifts: A Guide to Charismatic Renewal*.

The editor thanks SPCK for permission to publish "Notes from a Wayward Son" and "The Devil You Think You Know" in *Charismatic Renewal: The Search for a Theology*, and for "The Prophetic Role of Orthodoxy" in *Living Orthodoxy*, "Harmful Religion" in *Harmful Religion*, and "Introduction" in *Different Gospels*.

The editor thanks THE INDEPENDENT Newspaper for the kind permission to reprint the Obituary of Metropolitan Anthony on August 9, 2003.

All other pieces given and used with permission by Andrew G. Walker.

PREFACE

This book is a labor of love. It had its genesis in the hot summer of July 1998 in Dallas, Texas, when I sat around the seminar table with Andrew Walker at Perkins School of Theology. I had no idea who Andrew Walker was, but I found myself captivated by what he taught. At night over dinner we would continue our forays into the vast amount of material he was sharing on theology and evangelism. It was overload, to be sure, but stimulating nonetheless. I made it a point to absorb what Andrew was saying and to glean the implications of his insights into our modern and "postmodern condition," assessing always what it entailed for the church's mission. Little did I realize at the time how much I was gaining, or how much I would come to value Andrew's friendship. This volume of essays and pieces (this "miscellany," as we are calling it) puts readers around the seminar table too and provides a resource to make sense of what Andrew has provided the church over a forty-five year period: wisdom and passion.

I have divided the current volume into five different sections. They do not necessarily follow a distinct chronology, but they do provide a basic outline of where Andrew has traveled and what he has done. The broad interdisciplinary approach to theology and ecclesiology will not go unnoticed, as well as the ecumenical depth. The shorter pieces in particular simply reveal the range and scope of Andrew's passion to engage a wide-range of topics, and the bibliography can definitely provide a way to "wade more deeply" into the currents of what Andrew sought to teach and communicate, especially with respect to the Pentecostal Renewal and the House Church Movements. His use of C. S. Lewis is also relevant, and his journey into Orthodoxy, as the present work reveals, can give helpful direction to the church in its ongoing reflections. It is why I hope the present volume will serve as a steppingstone to further research, as well as a pathway to greater investigation of what Andrew has developed. Introducing Andrew to a wider audience beyond

King's College and Southern Methodist University is a large part of what motivated me to edit these pieces.

Therefore, as readers begin the process of exploring what Andrew has written, they may begin at any point in the present volume: from "Notes from a Wayward Son" to "Harmful Religion" there is ample opportunity to see throughout how the personal, theological, and sociological overlap and reinforce. Even the interviews with Basil Mitchell, Metropolitan Anthony, and Leslie Newbigin are indicative of Andrew's method of integrating disciplines and raising critical questions. This is important, as it all serves as both an explicit and an implicit prolegomena to what C. S. Lewis called "Deep Church"[1] and to what Andrew has built on regarding the kind of "mere Christianity" that can "resource" the church in the days ahead, especially among the Charismatic and Evangelical wings of the church.

There is the old proverb that states that "when the student is ready, the teacher will appear." How true! It is why I would like to share deep words of appreciation to Andrew, as someone who has not only influenced me, but also many along the way, and who appeared when the student was ready. I now believe he also stands ready to help others as well. May we learn from his example!

Andrew D. Kinsey
Grace United Methodist Church
Franklin, Indiana

---

1. See Andrew G. Walker and Robin A. Parry, *Deep Church Rising: The Third Schism and the Recovery of Christian Orthodoxy* (Eugene, OR: Cascade, 2014); and *Remembering Our Future: Explorations in Deep Church* (Milton Keynes, UK: Paternoster, 2007).

JOURNEY INTO THE SPIRIT

Pentecostalism, Charismatic, and Restorationist Christianity

I

PENTECOSTALISM AND
CHARISMATIC CHRISTIANITY
(1993)

Pentecostal and charismatic (or neo-Pentecostal) Christianity mani-
fests religious phenomena that, so its adherents believe, reproduce
or reintroduce the miraculous charismata of the New Testament. To
begin phenomenologically is helpful because—despite difference in organization, style, social class, and doctrine between charismatic Christians—the
experiential dimension of the many Pentecostal movements appears remarkably constant. "Happy clapping," tambourine banging, snake handling,
and leg lengthening are just some of the many sub-cultural and epiphenomenal variations in Pentecostal practice, but essentially it is the conviction
that modern Christians can be infused with the power of the Holy Spirit
in ways similar to the disciples of the New Testament that is the distinctive
flavor of charismatic Christianity. In this respect, whether we are looking at
the classical Pentecostal denominations at the beginning of the twentieth
century, or the so-called renewal movement within the mainline denominations, or again at the many maverick or independent charismatic movements, the experiential hallmarks are much the same.

It is a fascinating fact, though it is impossible to be certain as to why
this should be so, that Pentecostalism and its mutational offshoots are essentially a twentieth-century phenomenon. It is true that *glossolalia* was a
minor feature of the early Shakers in England during the eighteenth century,
and tongues stuttered briefly in North America among the early Mormons

3

in the 1820s and the Millerites in the 1840s. But only the Catholic Apostolic Church, which grew up in the shadow of Edward Irving's ministry (1792–1834) in London, can be said to be a genuine precursor of modern twentieth-century Pentecostalism. And even this fact needs the caveat that Irving was a high-church Calvinist and the Catholic Apostolic Church was in many ways closer to Tractarianism than Evangelicalism.

CLASSICAL ORIGINS OF PENTECOSTALISM

Charles Fox Parham (1873–1929) can claim to be the father of the modern Pentecostal movement. He was deeply influenced by the holiness teachings of Protestant Evangelicalism and late nineteenth-century Adventism. In 1901 at Topeka, Kansas, during a Holy Spirit outpouring highlighted by "speaking in tongues," he formulated what were to become the tenets of classical Pentecostalism, including the "Baptism of the Holy Spirit" as a second blessing subsequent to conversion. By 1905, he also saw the phenomenon of speaking in tongues as the initial evidence of the new experience. However, Parham believed that the outbreak of tongues was evidence of a "Latter Rain" revival that would herald the second coming of Christ. For him the "charismata of tongues" was essentially a miracle of grace whereby Christians could supernaturally evangelize in the mother tongues of the different nations of the world.

Therefore, it is not unfair to say that he confused the *xenolalia* (speaking in foreign languages) of the Day of Pentecost, as recorded in Acts 2, with the ecstatic or unintelligible "language" of *glossolalia* mentioned by Paul in 1 Corinthians 12. This confusion is not unimportant because the dominant features of Pentecostal religion have been *glossolalia*, divine healing, and "sing-along" hymns and choruses, with speaking in foreign languages a marginal and little-recorded activity. This confusion carried over into the burgeoning revivals of the early twentieth century so that, in effect, the word "Pentecostal" as the title of the new enthusiasm is a misnomer. Nevertheless, this exegetical mistake had an important consequence for classical Pentecostalism: it was fervently evangelistic as it believed that the new tongues not only heralded the end-time but would overcome the language barriers created by the debacle of Babel. (Although most present-day Pentecostals no longer see tongues as a major evangelistic tool, and the exegetical mistake is now widely acknowledged, they remain evangelistic in an expansionist way, which is still not a normative feature of renewalist charismatics.)

If Parham can claim to be the father of Pentecostalism, it was one of his followers who really put the new enthusiasm on the map: Joseph William

Seymour (1870–1922). The son of African American slaves and leader of the Parham-inspired Apostolic Faith Mission, Seymour was pastor of the Azusa Street Mission in Los Angeles, California, where in 1906–8 there was an outbreak of Pentecostal revival—with tongues, healings, miracles, and lively singing. The revival was clearly evangelical, Adventist, and deeply under the influence of holiness teaching and the tenets of Parham's own theology. Ironically, Parham, who was racist, was rejected by the Azusa Street elders in 1906; and after public charges of sodomy in Texas in 1907, he never really recovered his leadership of his nascent Pentecostal movement.

The Azusa Street Revival was more than a symbol of Pentecostal origins: more important than providing the raw data of Pentecostal history and hagiography, it was a recapitulation of the abolitionist and integrationist hopes of the Great Awakening of eighteenth-century American enthusiasm. For a short while black and white worked together across the color bar; as one of the early leaders put it, "the color line has been washed away by the blood." Tragically, however, Pentecostalism was soon to develop along segregationist lines and numerous accounts of Pentecostal history have not paid due regard either to the inter-racial characteristics of the Azusa Street Mission or to the separate and somewhat earlier beginnings of black American Pentecostalism.[1]

But if Azusa failed, like the first Great Awakening, to keep black and white together in harmony, it can certainly be claimed as the origin of many a twentieth-century Pentecostal denomination. The Apostolic Faith Church of God (Franklin, Virginia) can trace a direct line to Azusa Street, and both the Pentecostal Assemblies of the World (Los Angeles) and the Assemblies of God (America's largest classical Pentecostal church) claim their origins in part from Azusa. Furthermore, existing denominations became Pentecostal as a result of Azusa Street and its subsequent missions (the Church of God in Christ and the Church of God, Cleveland, Tennessee, would be the most obvious examples).

But the influence of Azusa reached beyond the boundaries of the United States, and there is strong empirical evidence of a rare anthropological and sociological phenomenon—that is, a genuine diffusionism. Azusa was visited by missionaries and curious clergymen from around the world who took back with them both the experience of the "baptism" and the somewhat loose theology of the revivals. In particular, one of the famous "Cambridge Seven," Cecil Polhill (1860–1938), and Thomas Ball Barratt (1862–1940) from Norway, took the Pentecostal message back to Europe. It

---

1. Cf. MacRobert, *The Black Roots and White Racism of Early Pentecostalism in the USA.*

was the revival in Norway under Barratt that encouraged the Anglican vicar Alexander Alfred Boddy (1854–1930) to encounter the new revival first hand, and it was at his church at Monkwearmouth in Sunderland, England, that an interdenominational Pentecostal center began in 1908.

The involvement of these men from the upper classes gives the lie to the simplistic view that Pentecostalism was a religion exclusively of the disinherited.[2] In Britain, however, revivalism soon developed along sectarian and working-class lines and, following the American experience, denominations emerged in opposition to each other. By the mid-1920s, Britain could claim three significant Pentecostal denominations, The Elim Foursquare Gospel Church, which was Presbyterian in structure, the Assemblies of God, which was Congregationalist, and the much smaller Apostolic Church, which, like the earlier Catholic Apostolic Church, could claim to be led by a charismatic apostolate. Other Pentecostal denominations throughout the world (notably the black-led Church of God in Christ) have been Episcopalian along the more traditional lines of the United Methodist Church in North America. In this respect, classical Pentecostalism mirrors the ecclesiastical shape of the Reformation churches of the sixteenth and seventeenth centuries.

Classical Pentecostals may have been the pioneers of twentieth-century charismatic religion, but it would be a mistake to see them as a spent force. Not only do the global figures run into hundreds of millions,[3] but relatively small groups such as the Elim movement in Britain (with some 30,000 to 40,000 members) and the Assemblies of God (with perhaps a further 10,000 adherents) show a stable, though slow, growth. New indigenous Pentecostal sects are springing up in South America at a truly amazing rate as well (see Martin, *Tongues of Fire*). It also holds true that much of the growth of charismatic activity in Eastern Europe, Asia, and Africa can really be understood as an extension of classical Pentecostalism *per se,* and not only as part of the more recent charismatic renewal.

THE CHARISMATIC RENEWAL MOVEMENT

Classical Pentecostalism became intertwined with the fundamentalist movement of the early twentieth century.[4] Consequently there was a separatist, anti-intellectual, and anti-ecumenical air about Pentecostalism. The British Assemblies of God pastor Donald Gee (1891–1966) was one of the

---

2. Cf. Anderson, *Vision of the Disinherited: The Making of American Pentecostalism.*

3. Cf. Barrett, "Statistics Global: Table 1, Column 4," in Burgess and McGee, eds., *Dictionary of Pentecostal and Charismatic Movements,* 812.

4. Cf. Marsden, *Fundamentalism and American Culture.*

few who believed that Pentecostals should be active in the World Council of Churches, but it was a South African-born naturalized American pastor of the Assemblies of God, David Du Plessis (1905–87), "Mr. Pentecost" as he was called, who can claim to have done more than any other individual to encourage dialogue between Pentecostal and mainline churches.

Like the founding leader of the Elim church, Principal George Jeffreys (1889–1962), Du Plessis had always dreamed of a worldwide Pentecostal revival, and from the mid-1960s to the present day it could be claimed that in some respects such a dream has come true. Unlike classical Pentecostalism, it is doubtful whether the same sort of diffusionism marks the beginnings of this "second wave," or phase, of charismatic activity. In fact, throughout the 1950s the somewhat maverick and marginal characters of classical Pentecostalism, such as William Branham (1909–65) and Oral Roberts (1918–2004), had already influenced mainline Christians. Perhaps the declaration in 1959 that the Episcopalian priest of St. Mark's, Van Nuys, California, Dennis Bennett (1917–91), had received the baptism in the Holy Spirit and spoken in tongues, could be said to be one of the triggers of neo-Pentecostalism. But it was only one of many, and soon, remarkably, charismata were being reported in every mainline denomination in the world from Southern Baptist to Roman Catholic.

There was no doubt that itinerants such as Du Plessis played a major role in spreading the word, but the 1960s had an anarchic and spontaneous air about them, and the renewal, as it was increasingly being called, was in no sense orchestrated or manipulated by a single or central organization. No doubt the declaration of support in the early 1970s from such eminent Catholics as Cardinal Suenens (1904–96) gave the movement some respectability. In particular, the Roman Catholics lent a certain amount of doctrinal weight to the somewhat unsystematic and anecdotal method of Pentecostal theology.[5] The Catholics, and many Anglicans, were happy to accept the experiential side of the renewal, but rejected the two-stage, or first and second blessing, theology of classical Pentecostalism. The very presence of the historic churches in Pentecostal territory led to a hands-off stance from many classical Pentecostals who had been led to believe that the older churches were apostate and incapable of genuine spiritual renewal.[6]

From 1970 to 1980, however, it seemed that nothing could stop the bandwagon effect of the renewal. It became increasingly commonplace to see priests dancing in full vestments, praising God in tongues and shouting

---

5. Cf. Gelpi, *Pentecostalism: A Theological Viewpoint*; see also McDonnell, *The Charismatic Renewal and Ecumenism.*

6. Cf. Richards, *Pentecost is Dynamite.*

"Thank you, Jesus." In many ways the decade of 1970 to 1980 was the golden era of the renewal movement, and perhaps the Kansas City Conference of 1977 remains the Woodstock of ecumenical charismatic experience. Some leading evangelical figures[7] attempted some serious theological critique of the movement, but even they were jollied along by the upbeat renewal, even if they were less than sanguine about the charismata *per se*. Without any doubt the songs of the renewal, like the choruses of Pentecostalism before them, and the sounds of the house churches after them, were sung at missions gatherings, conventions, and churches that were not overly charismatic.

No one can say with certainty how many people were caught up in the new Pentecost, though participants at the World Council of Churches' consultation on the renewal at Bossey in Switzerland in 1980 thought that some three to four million people had been affected (though it must be said that the consultation did not always distinguish clearly whether the spectacular growth of the charismatic movement in the Third World was neo-Pentecostalism or old-style sectarianism; recent evidence suggests that it is likely to be a hybrid of both[8]).

Clearly the charismatic renewal in the First World has been a gentrified middle-class version of Pentecostalism. Like its classical cousin it has majored in tongues, healings, new songs, and intense excitement. However, unlike Pentecostalism, and much to the amazement of sociologists,[9] the renewal has not only been middle-class (though not exclusively) but has also appeared to contradict the rules of sociological evidence: charismatics have not automatically become sectarian or separatist; on the contrary, the majority of renewalists remained in their churches (though it might be argued that this amounts to a sectarian implant). In Britain, there was a committed ecumenism throughout the 1970s and 1980s which has remained to this day. No one represents this stream of the renewal better than Canon Michael Harper (1931–2010), who from his days as curate at All Souls, Langham Place, London (until 1965) to the World Conference of Charismatics held in Brighton (in June 1991) has sought to bring together Christians from every denomination.

7. Packer, "Theological Reflections on the Charismatic Movement," 1–2.

8. Cf. Martin, *Tongues of Fire*.

9. Walker, "Pentecostal Power: Charismatic Movements and the Politics of Pentecostal Experience," 89.

INDEPENDENTS AND MAVERICKS

It was Harper, however, who first alerted the British charismatics to the fact that all was not well in the charismatic camp,[10] for in the mid-1970s, beginning in North America and spreading to Europe, a movement known as "shepherding" or "discipling" split the charismatic movement down the middle. In part this split was precipitated by a desire for the charismatic movement to "come of age" and move on to a more committed discipleship.

In any event, this split did not slow down charismatic movements, but it did herald a greater fragmentation of charismatic activity. Henceforth, both classical Pentecostalism and neo-Pentecostalism were both "bled and fed" by numerous independent, and often extremely controversial, movements. It needs to be recognized, however, that the independent maverick is not a new phenomenon in Pentecostalism. Since the days of the Azusa Street Mission there have been numerous men and women who have been either totally independent of or marginally related to Pentecostal denominations.

The roll-call is long and each figure has been involved in some form of scandalous accusation. The so-called "televangelists," for example, follow in a long line of "charismatic stars" who have always rested uneasily within the denominational structures. In this respect, Jimmy Swaggert (b. 1935), Jim and Tammy Bakker (b. 1940 and 1942), and Oral Roberts (1918–2004) are the heirs of Aimee Semple McPherson (1890–1944), William Branham (1909–65), A. A. Allen (1911–70), and T. L. Osborne (1923–2013). Kenneth Hagin (1917–2003) and Kenneth Copeland (b. 1937) continue in this tradition. We might view Pat Robertson (b. 1930) as a more educated and urbane charismatic, but he certainly comes out of the same mold.

In some respects, then, we may see most of these independents as "Bible-Belters" who have influenced Christians beyond the normal boundaries of classical Pentecostalism. But the renewal has also produced its own controversial leaders. One remembers the flamboyant Kathryn Kuhlman (1907–76), and today the former Dominican priest Francis McNutt (b. 1925) and the Californian charismatic John Wimber (1934–97) have in their different ways had considerable impact on both mainline denominations and independent churches. Britain's most well-known charismatic itinerant—from the renewal sector at least—is probably Colin Urquhart (b. 1940).

But the split to which Harper was alluding in the mid-1970s was more than an issue of new independent personalities supplanting the old ones; it was part of the growth of what has become a virtual "third wave"

---

10. See Harper, *Charismatic Crisis*.

of Pentecostal activity. The so-called shepherding ministry, particularly through the instigation of the "Fort Lauderdale Five" of Christian Growth Ministries, has had repercussions throughout America, the Antipodes, Africa, Asia, and Europe.

In Britain, for example, under the influence (amongst others) of two of the Lauderdale Five, Ern Baxter (1914–93) and Bob Mumford (b. 1930), a loose-knit movement composed of "streams" of independent networks combined discipleship teaching with a commitment to the five-fold ministry of Ephesians 4. This ministry was understood in terms of a charismatic apostolate, and throughout the 1980s these "restorationist" fellowships[11] were the fastest growing Christian movements in Britain. Under the leadership of such men as Bryn Jones (1940–2003) these movements have seen the emergence of at least two 10,000-strong formations which begin to have the same denominational solidity as do Wimber's Vineyard churches as they become firmly established in North America and England.

Strictly speaking, the shepherding movement *per se* seems to be a spent force, though the continued growth of independent networks influenced by the five-fold ministries grows apace. The restorationists in Britain, for example, may now be divided into quite distinct networks, but they have been augmented (and to a certain extent have been overtaken) by a mushrooming of independent charismatic churches that can be said to be "fellow travelers." One such group, the Ichthus house church, may have no more than two thousand people in its South London network, but its influence is considerable within the English Evangelical Alliance (founded in 1846) and throughout charismatic circles generally. In this respect they perform a similar function to an earlier "house church movement" in the 1960s and early 1970s in Chard in Somerset.

Many of the restorationist networks, then, independent charismatic fellowships, Ichthus, and others outside the mainline renewal movement and the classical Pentecostal denominations, are increasingly being linked together under the nebulous but popular title of "the new churches."

In North America, too, although the "shepherding" group involved in the Christian Growth Ministries no longer operates and despite the fact that the Fort Lauderdale Five have been disbanded, their influence is still considerable. Charles Simpson (b. 1937), for example, one of the leaders of this group now leads the Fellowship of Covenant Ministers and Conferences with over 350 church affiliations. A much smaller network, with informal links with Bryn Jones in Britain, is led by Larry Tomczak and C. J. Mahaney from their Covenant Life Church in Gaithersburg, Maryland. The largest

---

11. Cf. Walker, *Restoring the Kingdom.*

affiliation of independent charismatic churches is the 350–400 churches of the National Leadership Council founded in 1979, with its strength along the panhandle of Florida and in the southern American states.

A FOURTH STAGE?

Strictly speaking, the notion of a "third wave" of Pentecostalism was coined by the missiologist Peter Wagner (b. 1930) to denote a Pentecostalism that was inclusive, irenic, and harmonious. In practice, however, the third wave has been an eclectic mixture of independent mavericks, renewalists, and indigenous Pentecostals, whose sociological formation may yet end in sectarian denominations, if not new religious movements. Be that as it may, there is strong evidence that the 1990s are witnessing an amalgam of all three stages—or waves—of Pentecostalism.

This is particularly true in Britain. The independent growth of the Spring Harvest Festivals, which can now boast some 80,000 residents during the spring holiday, is infused with renewalists, some classical Pentecostals, new church members, and evangelicals who have no particular charismatic brief. Furthermore, John Wimber, whose influence is perhaps greater in Britain than North America, has performed the remarkable feat of being acceptable to both renewalists and restorationists as well as to other independent groups. The "Make Way" Marches for Jesus, which since 1989 have annually put some 200,000 people on the city streets, have primarily been a new church initiative, with support from many Pentecostals, renewalists, and non-charismatic evangelicals.

As longstanding a Pentecostal denomination as Elim has invited to its Bognor Bible Week an "apostle" from restorationism and a South African evangelist who preaches a similar "health and wealth" gospel to Hagin of Oklahoma. Nothing could be more strange, however, than to see John Wimber (at least temporarily) caught up with some of the prophets of Kansas, who are a throwback to the earlier Pentecostal Holiness movements and the circle of followers connected with Pentecostalism's most controversial figure, William Branham. Paul Cain, the most widely known of these prophets, has had considerable impact on Anglican charismatics and was invited to be the main speaker at Spring Harvest in 1992.

Historical research shows that Pentecostal religion cannot be neatly dissected into three or four stages, even though this is a useful analytic distinction.[12] Charismatic religion is essentially pragmatic: the crowds follow the action, that is, the "stars," regardless of theological or denominational

---

12. Cf. Hocken, *Streams of Renewal.*

affiliation. Nevertheless, it is a remarkable fact that although there have been numerous cults of the personality and clear heretical elements in Pentecostal religion, on the whole Pentecostalism has remained within the bounds of historic orthodoxy in the same sense that we can say Montanism—despite its wildness and messianic pretensions—remained Christian in the early Christian centuries. (Baptizing in Jesus' name only is perhaps the most perennial charge of heresy against some Pentecostals. However, it also crops up in the modalistic "Oneness theology" of classical days, and again with William Branham in the 1940s and in Chard in Britain in the 1960s and 1970s. More recently, charges of Gnosticism and "new thought" metaphysics against Hagin and Copeland have also been made[13]).

It remains to be seen over the next decades, however, whether the separatist trends of charismatic religion will undercut its newfound ecumenism. In Britain, it is already the case that the new church/Wimber alliance is somewhat alienated from a significant section of Catholic charismatics as well as some Anglican and house church groups. Just as the 1970s witnessed a "showdown" between the ecumenical renewal and the discipling movements, so the mid-1990s may see a division between those who stand by an apostolic/prophetic model of Ephesians 4 and those who do not. A truly "fourth wave" would be a long-term alliance of all charismatic groups, for if the third wave provided a new impetus it did not lead in itself to charismatic integration.

Pentecostalism could, of course, go full circle and begin the twenty-first century as it began the twentieth: with schism and discerption. There will, however, be one fundamental difference: charismatic Christianity began as a minority religion of the disinherited, but it has now arguably come into its inheritance and become one of the largest and most potent forces in world Christianity. It has perhaps somewhat recaptured the racial integrationist hopes of Azusa Street (though both African Americans and Afro-Caribbeans feel their separate organizations are necessary in the light of the incipient racism of many white churches). Certainly it has demonstrated that its energy and mutational power is greater than any historian or social scientist could have foreseen when the Apostolic Faith Mission visited Los Angeles in 1906.

13. Cf. McConnell, *The Promise of Health and Wealth.*

2

THE DEVIL YOU THINK
YOU KNOW

Demonology and the Charismatic Movement
(1993)

INTRODUCTION

A t the beginning of *The Screwtape Letters,* C. S. Lewis said:

> There are two equal and opposite errors into which our race can fall about the devils. One is to disbelieve in their existence. The other is to believe, and to feel an excessive and unhealthy interest in them. They themselves are equally pleased by both errors and hail a materialist or a magician with the same delight.[1]

For Christians to disbelieve in demons, and *ipso facto* the devil, is in my view mistaken. Philosophically, it can lead to that sort of monism where God is held responsible for all the suffering and evil in the world as well as all the good. If God were truly the author of evil and confusion as well as order and harmony, it would be legitimate to wonder whether He is not a God of love but a cosmic sadist.

Admittedly, such a monism is more sophisticated and, I think, ultimately more defendable than a metaphysical dualism such as Persian

---

1. Lewis, *The Screwtape Letter,* 9.

Zoroastrianism, which posits that there are two gods of the universe, the good one, and the evil one. If we were to adopt this model and make the Christian devil equal to God, then, of course, there could be no certainty as to the outcome of their eternal opposition. It might also seem that the devil could wield his power to destroy Christians' lives, as witnessed by Blaine Cook's now infamous remark that the devil murdered Canon David Watson.[2]

However, unless one is prepared to override the biblical witness, it is difficult to reject completely the devil and the notion of a spiritual war between the forces of good and evil. Again, I believe that in this matter Lewis is right:

> Real Christianity (as distinct from Christianity-and-water) goes much nearer to Dualism than people think. One of the things that surprised me when I first read the New Testament seriously was that it was always talking about a Dark Power in the universe—a mighty evil spirit who was held to be the Power behind death and disease, and sin. The difference is that Christianity thinks this Dark Power was created by God, and was good when he was created, and went wrong. Christianity agrees with Dualism that his universe is at war. But it doesn't think this is a war between independent powers. It thinks it's a civil war, a rebellion, and that we are living in a part of the universe occupied by the rebel.[3]

This sense of drama and conflict is not only typical of Lewis—we remember how he uses it to good effect in *The Lion, the Witch, and the Wardrobe* —but it also echoes what Gustav Aulen, in his book *Christus Victor,* called "the classical model of atonement." This patristic model draws heavily on the sense of battle or spiritual warfare between God and the devil. The church fathers seemed quite at home with the mythological and conflict language of angels and demons. Perhaps we recall the eighth-century hymn of Saint Andrew of Crete which we sing each Advent:

> Christian doest thou see them on the holy ground,
> How the hosts of darkness compass thee around?
> Christian, up and smite them, counting gain but loss:
> Smite them, Christ is with thee, soldier of the cross.[4]

---

2. Cf. Benn and Burkhill, *A Theological and Pastoral Critique of the Teachings of John Wimber*, 3.

3. Lewis, *Broadcast Talks*, 9.

4. J. M. Neale's translation (1862).

This sort of talk infuriated the liberal theologians of the nineteenth century, for they thought it crude and pre-scientific, but I think the fathers had grasped a central fact of the atonement, which later and more rational theories obscured. That fact is that God's work on the cross included not only the overcoming of death and the ending of enmity between himself and humankind, but also the defeat of the devil. There is strong scriptural warrant for such a view: "Now is the time for judgment on this world; now the prince of this world will be driven out. But I, when I am lifted up from the earth, will draw all men to myself" (John 12:31–32); and again, "The reason the Son of God appeared was to destroy the devil's work" (1 John 3:8).

However, it is precisely at this point that my problems begin. For having sided with Lewis against the liberal and modernist position that there is no devil, and therefore no Christian dualism of any kind, I find myself recoiling from much of the literature, tape ministries, and theology that some modern-day charismatics promote under the broad rubric of "spiritual warfare."

THE PARANOID UNIVERSE

Psychologically speaking, paranoia is that mental state in which we find ourselves abnormally mistrusting and suspecting others. Paranoid people typically see themselves as persecuted by their enemies, and they see their enemies everywhere. In psychotic case-studies enemies range from communists—or capitalists—to extra-terrestrial beings, including demonic angels. Sometimes an extreme sense of persecution is matched by delusions of grandeur, whereby those who are deluded have special powers or attributes which alone can save themselves and others from the evils that will destroy the world.[5]

Paranoia need not only be understood as a medical condition of individuals, for it is catching and can so easily become a group phenomenon. If such groups become dominated by a paranoid worldview that militates against rational and common-sense interpretations of reality, then clearly there is trouble in store. Such groups have a tendency to physical or social isolation where there is little chance that critical and sensible ways of dealing with things will prevail. Obviously, Jonestown in Guyana would be the paradigm of extreme psycho-social paranoia, but cults, sects, holy huddles,

5. See Leon Festinger's now classic treatise *When Prophecy Fails*, full of people with paranoid delusions who can only survive and flourish in a world ambushed by aliens and dangerous powers.

self-selected elite groups, even the "in-crowd," are in danger of becoming both the perpetrators and the victims of a paranoid universe.

A belief in the devil and demonic powers does not in itself entail paranoia, either in the strict medical sense or as a social neurosis. In the third-century writings of Saint Anthony of Egypt, for example, we see ample evidence of a belief in demons, but hardly a blind terror of them. Indeed, stemming from Saint Anthony, and becoming normative in the Christian East throughout the Middle Ages, a sound psychology of the spiritual life developed that distinguished between God's acts, the devil's ploys, and the normal processes of the natural world. The fallen and natural world included the human will, neither yet demonized nor yet redeemed. The Father's insistence that we must discern fallen but natural forces from demonic supernatural ones is one of the great bequests of the patristic era to Christianity. (Demons are fallen angels: they are not intrinsically evil because they were created by God and all that God created was good.)

A Christian worldview that is divided into the tripartite arenas of the divine, the natural, and the demonic is unlikely to fall prey to a paranoia that dissects the world into "us" and "them." Charismatic theologies and methodologies that do tend to divide the cosmos into God's kingdom of light and Satan's kingdom of darkness are in constant danger of first adopting a paranoid worldview, and then becoming entrapped and socialized into the paranoid universe.

Throughout the history of Christianity, if we allow for certain exceptional periods of paranoia—e.g., heretics and the Inquisition during the waning of the Middle Ages, and the witchcraft and the Salem witch-hunts—we will find that beliefs in demons and efficacy of exorcisms rarely gets out of hand. It is true that occasionally hysteria ran riot in monasteries, as one would expect in such socially isolated institutions. And sometimes Christian beliefs in the supernatural world would be adulterated by folk-superstitions such as the evil eye. But on the whole the devil and his works were kept in their place: powerful, yes, but never dominant, and never center stage.

Even today many Catholic, Anglican, and Orthodox traditionalists would agree with the report of the Bishop of Exeter on exorcism in 1972[6] that demonism is a reality, but it is nonetheless rare.

This is in fact my own view—though it is one that, admittedly, satisfies neither a modernist nor a certain kind of fundamentalist. And at this point it is time to ask: when did that kind of fundamentalism arise whereby demons began to break loose from the subterranean moorings of the unconscious

6. Petipierre, ed., *Exorcism: The Findings of a Committee Convened by the Bishop of Exeter.*

and surface in open rebellion with the fury of what the house-church leader Dave Tomlinson has called "charismania?"[7]

One answer might be: "With the birth of the Pentecostal movement at the turn of the century." Now it is true that classical Pentecostalism is primarily dualistic and initially had little room for the natural world, even as a buffer or no-man's land between the kingdoms of darkness and light. But it is a matter of empirical record that Pentecostalism has not been overcome by demonic infestations. On the contrary, and not-withstanding the influence in the 1920s of Jessie Penn-Lewis' blood-curdling book, *War on the Saints*, denominations such as Elim and the Assemblies of God have believed in demons but have kept them firmly under the bed and firmly under control. There has been little interest or fascination in the habits, habitat, or *haute couture* of evil spirits.

I think there are three reasons why, historically, classical Pentecostalism did not capitulate to paranoia. First, unlike much of the charismatic renewal movement, it was essentially evangelistic in nature: its revivalistic impulse was heaven-bent on saving souls. Its evangelism therefore kept it outward-looking and Christ-centered, leaving its demonism in the wake of its excitement and enthusiasm. It was there, all right, but it was peripheral and virtually out of sight. Second, Pentecostalists were too entranced with their own Pentecost—with its tongues, healings, and sing-along songs—to be bewitched by beguiling theories of demonism. And third, Pentecostalists may have been educationally disadvantaged, but they were not stupid. What they lacked in cultural finesse they made up with working-class common sense.

To ask when the paranoid universe came into being is, in fact, to ask for nothing less than a major historical investigation. That work still remains to be done, but let me suggest one line of inquiry that may be worth pursuing.

I think the origins lie in the late 1940s and 1950s in the North American healing movement. It was the time of William Branham, a man who talked with angels, argued with demons, and diagnosed illnesses through the colors of the aura. Two young men associated with him at that time were Ern Baxter, who was later to become a major figure in the so-called "shepherding" or discipleship movement, and Paul Cain, a prophet from a Pentecostal Holiness background who until recently was associated with the Kansas City prophets and the ministry of John Wimber.

Other itinerant charismatics not directly associated with the movement also began to make their mark in the 1950s. Oral Roberts, who was also from the holiness tradition of Pentecostalism, pioneered "slaying in the

---

7 Dave Tomlinson is now a priest in the Church of England.

Spirit" in his tent meetings (though this phenomenon is most closely associated with two women, Maria Woodworth-Etter and Kathryn Kuhlman). Like Branham, Roberts would claim that disease in the sick person's body caused his praying hand to swell and extend. Roberts came from Oklahoma, which has also produced two other controversial Pentecostalists—T. L. Osborn and Kenneth Hagin.[8]

A. A. Allen was the most extravagant maverick of the 1950s and early 1960s. His most infamous claim probably being that on one occasion following prayer God turned dentist and supernaturally filled a man's teeth. And yet, on demonic matters he bears a close resemblance to Branham. He wrote copiously on demonic oppression and possession, and pioneered tape ministries in which he purported to talk with evil spirits. It became fashionable in his churches to talk to the spirits of lust, anger, and jealously. Years later this sort of talk became so established in some charismatic circles that Frank and Ida Mae Hammond could talk of "the spirit of nervousness" and the "demon of heart attack." Allen, it was reported, even talked of the "spirit of nicotine." I am not certain whether he liberalized that old expression "the demon drink," but I do know that he died a hopeless alcoholic in a hotel room in San Francisco.

We could trace the influence of Allen, Hagin, and Roberts on modern charismatics, but I think a more profitable line to follow would be to show the personal and theological link between Branham, Baxter, and the group known as "The Fort Lauderdale Five"; we might even, using language similar to Nigel Wright's, talk of a "psychic trace."[9]

Two members of this group, Don Basham and Derek Prince, not only majored in shepherding and, along with the others, peddled strong views on male leadership, but in the 1970s they also pioneered a belief in the prevalence of witchcraft in our societies and in the danger of amulets and charms, which they saw as demonically infused, or at least under the dominance of Satan. They talked not only of demons as disembodied spirits trying to control individual bodies, but also of "strong men," super-demonic powers that dominated—along with the lesser devils—churches, cities, and whole nations. Prince's work in particular was a major influence on Frank and Ida Mae Hammond and their disturbing deliverance ministry as outlined in their book *Pigs in the Parlor*.

There are echoes of Prince's and the Hammonds' work throughout North America and Great Britain in the 1980s. It resounded and resonated most clearly, however, in New Zealand through the self-deliverance

---

8. Hagin's ministry, like Branham's, is replete with angelic ministrations.

9. Cf. Wright, *The Fair Face of Evil*.

techniques of Graham and Shirley Powell[10] and the ministry of Bill Subritzky. It is probably Subritzky, a lawyer by training, and an Anglican layman, who has had the greatest impact upon Anglican and now independent charismatic church exorcisms in Great Britain in the late 1980s and early 1990s.

It is wrong to make *ad hominem* remarks or pass moral judgments on the integrity and Christian commitment of such people as Bill Subritzky, Derek Prince, and their fellow-travelers, but I do believe that their view of the devil and his powers has helped create—unwittingly—a paranoid universe. For since the 1970s, but with gathering rapidity in the 1980s, demons began to come out from beneath the beds and, like *Gremlins 2: The New Batch*, they got out of control. Their infestation was progressive: at first charismatics tended to see demons only in the world, and thought it better to play it safe and stay in the church. Then, some found that the devil would snipe at you if you left the sanctuary of radically renewed fellowships. (This was a feature of certain restorationist churches for a while.) But then it was found that the demons could get into the sanctuary, and indeed it was really Christians who were in danger of demonization. As Frank Hammond puts it: "Does everyone need deliverance? Personally, I have not found any exceptions!"[11]

The Subritzky model also succeeds in some Christian groups precisely because its supporters believe that the demons will prey on everyone within the local church. In such a context it is difficult for the skeptical believer to oppose the charismatic leader and discerner of evil spirits, for one runs the risk of being said to be under the control of that most hatred of demons, "the spirit of criticism."

In the paranoid universe, not only can Christians become demonized, but so too can whole social groups. For example, other world religions are not simply different, wrong, in error, or as Lewis would prefer to see it, unfulfilled: they are agents of devilish control. And homosexuals are not to be seen as exercising a preference, suffering from a sickness, or living in old-fashioned sin: they are under demonic thrall. It is but a short step from these positions to xenophobia, homophobia, and hate-filled persecution which is the hallmark of the paranoid universe. Fighting back at your supposed enemies entails persecuting your alleged persecutors. This is what happens when spiritual warfare becomes an attempt to match power with power, meet hate with hate of hate, rather than as Jesus commanded, "Love your

---

10. Cf. Graham and Shirley Powell, *Christian Set Yourself Free*.

11. Hammond, *Pigs in the Parlor*, 12.

enemies, do good to those who hate you, bless those who curse you, pray for those who mistreat you" (Luke 6:27–28).

In the paranoid universe women are particularly prone to persecution, especially if they are feminists. Feminism is under the province of the spirit of Jezebel, or so says Don Basham.[12] This spirit's specialty is domination, and feminism is seen as an attempt by women to switch roles with men. Women are apparently particularly prone to domination, which Derek Prince understands to be the essence of witchcraft. For Prince, it is a fact that most witches are women, and what he calls the "Pentecostal witch" is one of the most dangerous kinds. She is the sort of woman who wants to usurp what he sees as the rightful leadership of men, or does not go along with the male "leadership" theology.[13]

One begins to suspect that any woman who becomes critical of men, or is simply a strong personality, is a prime candidate for the dehumanizing label "demonized." This suspicion is somewhat confirmed by one of Don Basham's tapes,[14] in which he unfolds what he sees as the proper role of women and men in creation. What disturbs me about his views is that much of his understanding of female and male roles in society has little to do with the Bible or a thorough grasp of cross-cultural studies, but owes a great deal to his own amateur psychologizing, male prejudices, and somewhat inventive use of gender archetypes.

On this subject, I received a long letter from a "house church" elder in Ireland, who told me:

> Looking at the overall picture I feel that the fundamentalist line of theology that the Americans brought with them led us to see difficulties as black and white issues. This was extrapolated from the early teaching on spiritual warfare, an unhealthy form of "dualism," whereby God and Satan are constantly warring over every trivial issue in our lives. Personal choice and responsibility for our lives seems to be only interpreted in terms of siding with God through an overly superstitious view of "guidance."

He then went on to tell me of the effect that one of Prince's tapes on women and witchcraft had had on the church. Suddenly, he said, men everywhere began to see their wives demonized and in need of deliverance.

---

12. Hear his tape "Spiritual Warfare."

13. For a representative tape of Prince's earlier views listen to "Principalities and Powers" (Anchor Bay: Ministry Messages, undated); for views of his belief in witchcraft, spells, and curses, see also, *Blessing or Curse: You Can Choose!*

14. "Spiritual Warfare," *op. cit.* (n.11).

There was a spirit of fear and suspicion abroad that caused real division within the fellowship.

And it is here that we move to the heart of the problem. Paranoia breeds fear. Ironically, what is demonic about the paranoid universe is not that it is a world that suddenly sees demons everywhere, but that it is a world in bondage to fear. As evangelist Geoff Crocker reminded me, the Scriptures tell us that "perfect love casts out fear" (1 John 4:18), and yet we find that fellowships that see demons everywhere first become fearful, and out of their fear they then become belligerent.

We see what amounts to a fascinated fearfulness in the dramatic details of how demons enter human beings. And it would seem that they can enter any way they choose: through abortion, sexual intercourse, the womb during pregnancy, a traumatic birth, genetic inheritance. Subritzky tells us:

> I prayed with a man, aged 40, who had a spirit of abortion in him and he curled up like a fetus and screamed. As others ministered with me, we saw this man totally delivered. His mother had tried to abort him while he was in the womb; hence the spirit of abortion had entered him.[15]

Again he tells us:

> When sexual intercourse takes place outside of marriage, strong spirits or demons of lust and perverted sex can pass from one body to another during the act of sexual intercourse.[16]

Subritzky is never short of this kind of shock and horror revelation: in fact, he tells us that "On many occasions, demons enter during pregnancy or at birth. Demons can easily enter a fetus where there is shock, fear, or trauma on the part of the mother, particularly where there is disagreement between the parents."[17] Apparently, demons do not always succeed in penetration or infusion: sometimes they just cling on. Subritzky explains that "It is interesting to note that the Bible describes Satan as Beelzebub or 'Lord of the Flies.' On occasions I have seen spirits like flies attached to the back of a person's head."[18]

15. Subritzky, *Demons Defeated*, 3.

16. Ibid., 8. On hearing this statement read out as part of a paper at a recent C. S. Lewis workshop at Sheffield, a "brother" from the Assemblies of God came up with an obvious solution to this demonic penetration: "Wear a condom!"—the eruptions of belly laughter from the 200 people at the conference would have cheered the heart of Luther and Lewis, both of whom believed that jeering and scornfulness, not respect or fearfulness, were the right attitudes toward the demonic.

17. Ibid., 69.

18. Ibid., 66.

The fascination with demonic entrance is matched by an equal fascination with their exit. Vomiting, spitting, foaming—Subritzky calls these the "demonic nests"—and coughing are typical pathways of expulsion. Balls of slime and alien globules have been popular from the days of A. A. Allen. Tom Smail tells us of the time he went to a Pittsburgh charismatic conference organized by Don Basham. It was decided to have a mass deliverance of the spirit of masturbation, and so Kleenex were handed out to the young men (there is no mention of the women) who on the words of deliverance were to cough up the troublesome demon. Tom Smail's reflection on this whole episode must surely be ours: he did not know whether to laugh or cry. It is hard, even with charity, not to laugh when Subritzky tells us that another frequent manifestation of demons leaving is yawning. "Sometimes," he says, "these particular demons can cause people to go to sleep during meetings, particularly when the gospel is being preached. Sometimes yawning is also accompanied by sighing as demons leave a person."[19]

But in the paranoid universe the demons can also reach us indirectly, especially through charms, artifacts, and bracelets. In 1986 Derry Knight managed to extract $500,000 from well-meaning but gullible charismatic Christians. Perhaps the most disturbing aspect of the whole affair was their belief that Knight could seriously dent the devil's power by destroying the old satanic regalia.

Belief in the efficacy of witchcraft and curses now seems to be mandatory in many charismatic fellowships. Demonic influence not only extends to amulets—a strong conviction of Derek Prince—but it can also invade household ornaments. Consider this cautionary tale from the Hammonds:

> While ministering to a nine-year-old girl, the mother told us that the girl awakened every night in the middle of the night. She would be very frightened. They could not account for this. The ministry for the girl turned up nothing that was suspect. We asked that we might inspect the girl's bedroom. Three things were found in the room which we had discovered could attract evil spirits. There was a book about a witch—secured through the public school. Then there was a big, stuffed toy frog, and over the girl's bed was a mobile from which dangled a half dozen little owl images that glowed in the dark.
>
> The family agreed to remove these objects and destroy them. We commanded all demons hiding in the room to leave immediately

in the name of Jesus, and pled the covering of the blood of Jesus over the girl. The girl has slept peacefully ever since.[20]

They go on:

> What about the owls and frogs? These are classified among the creatures mentioned in Deuteronomy 14:7–19 as being unclean and abominable. They are types of demon spirits. My ministry has taken me into many homes, and I have become aware of how many of these unclean creatures are being made into art objects and used for decorations. This is especially true of owls and frogs. It is more than coincidence that both of these are creatures of darkness. They come out at night and hunt their prey. Demons are also creatures of darkness. They cannot operate in the light.[21]

So often we find that paranoia generates its own logic and quirky methods of exegesis. Who says that demons cannot operate in the light? And talking of Deuteronomy 14:7–19, the list on unclean creatures does not actually mention frogs, though they are implied. Of greater significance is the fact that the list of unclean creatures clearly refers to the strict dietary laws of the Israelites and has nothing to do with intrinsically evil beings.

It is time for us to leave the paranoid universe, but before we do, let us leave it with this thought. Paranoid beliefs breed a basic insecurity that is always looking for the men and women of power to show us the way to protect ourselves from danger. After all, a Dungeons and Dragons world, as all modern children know, needs a dungeon-master. Consequently, we should not be surprised that if we live in the paranoid universe we will look for charismatic "strong men" with the gnosis and power—that is, the technique—to protect us and perhaps even turn us, like them, into spiritual warriors.

THE DEVIL, DEVILS, AND THE BIBLE

When we turn from the paranoid universe to the Bible we discover many strange things about the devil. The first thing we discover is that the Old Testament has very little to say about him. Second, we find that the New Testament has a far more developed—although not systematic—treatment of the Dark Power. And third, we cannot find anywhere the sort of fascination

---

20. Hammond, *Pigs in the Parlor*, 141–42.
21. Ibid., 141–42

and detailed accounts of spirit visitations, possessions, and exorcisms that we find in the paranoid universe.

In fact, the word "devil"—meaning enemy, adversary (*diabolos* in Greek)—is not used at all in the Greek translation of the Old Testament. The Hebrew word for adversary or accuser, *satan*, is used, but only ten times and usually as a title (the *satan*; i.e., the accuser), not as a personal name (Satan). Six of these occur in the book of Job.

Satan appears briefly in the Psalms, more as a rhetorical device than as a figure of significance; and Zechariah 3:2, where we read "The Lord rebuke you, Satan!" There is little clue as to why he is introduced into the text or what his role is supposed to be. Indeed, even in the book of Job, Satan is a very curious character. He appears to have more than a nodding acquaintance with God, and it is not clear whether he does God's dirty work for Him, whether he is a sort of cosmic Job's comforter, or whether he is a nasty and irritating opponent of God who nevertheless seems in some way to be His servant or at least subservient to Him.[22]

In the New Testament things are quite different. The devil, either as *Satan* or *Apollyon/Diabolis,* is mentioned well over eighty times. Here we see the sort of dualism that Lewis discovered when he first read the New Testament carefully. The devil appears in multiple guises. He is, among other things, the angel of the pit (Rev 9:11), the god of this world or this age (2 Cor 4:4), the prince of darkness (Eph 6:12), the prince of this world (John 12:31), and the dragon (Rev 12:7).

And yet, there is no exposition of his origins. Christ's enigmatic line, "I saw Satan fall like lightning from heaven" (Luke 10:14), is his only comment, and while it appears to echo Isaiah 14:12, "How you are fallen from heaven, O Lucifer, son of the morning," the Old Testament context would seem to suggest that a historical person is the subject of this description, not a cosmic being. Whatever the case, the New Testament, like the Old, does not fully reveal the nature of the Evil One (though Jesus does tell us that the devil was a murderer and liar from the beginning, John 8:44; cf. 1 John 3:8).

In my opinion, the unsystematic and somewhat haphazard treatment of the devil in the Bible is a signal to us not to attempt to know more. At the very least, we should take note that, in revealing fully to us who Christ is, the canon of Scripture speaks of the devil only in mythological language, often in uncertain and unexplained passages, and sometimes in blunt warnings to have no dealings with him (e.g., Eph 4:27).

---

22. The notion that the devil can be used by God as an instrument of His divine purposes is interestingly discussed in the correspondence between Don Calabria and C. S. Lewis. See *Letters, C. S. Lewis and Don Giovanni Calabria.*

Turning to the devils, we find that they are mentioned only ten times in the Old Testament (though there are nine references to unexplained familiar spirits in the Pentateuch). Excluding the complex use of Paul's nine references to the "powers" in the New Testament, they are mentioned less than thirty times. Most of these references relate to the ministry of Jesus in the Synoptic Gospels (e.g., Matt 4:24; Mark 5:12).

It is the ministry of Jesus that provides the clearest New Testament data for the subject of demonism and exorcism. Some charismatics see such material as providing not merely case studies but inalienable proof texts, because they take it that Jesus as God could not have been mistaken in his spiritual discernment. We might counter such a view on the grounds that such a Christology does not leave room for the full humanity of Christ. To say with the universal church that our Lord never sinned is not the same thing as saying that he knew all things (about sickness, for example) or never made an inaccurate statement. The patristic case for the true divinity of Christ, we should remind ourselves, did not rest on a docetic denial of a free and fallible human will: there was no question that Jesus was gnomically deficient.

We can sidestep these arguments here, for the point at issue is not whether demonization occurs—I affirmed its possibility at the beginning—but whether the New Testament, in believing in demons, is wedded to a paranoid universe. Here, the ministry of Jesus is unequivocal: he clearly believes in demons, but does not see all sickness and evil under devilish control, and he shows no interest whatever in the minutiae and mechanisms of the demonic realm.

This lack of fascination with the demonic, which is the proper antidote to paranoia, is also reflected in the Acts of the Apostles. There are less than ten demonic incidents and allusions in the Lukan apostolic narratives. Similarly, Paul in his epistles has virtually nothing to say about devils, though he warns against worshiping idols and their relationship to the fellowship of demons (1 Cor 10:20).

Although Jesus tells us that eternal fire awaits the devil and his angels (Matt 25:41), the origins of devils are barely mentioned in the Bible. There is of course the war in heaven of Rev 12:7–9, but it is not without irony that many fundamentalist Bible scholars who tend to interpret Revelation as futuristic have no problem in reading this event retrospectively. Indeed, the case for an angelic fall is more a matter of logical necessity, or of its value as a theological hypothesis to help explain suffering and the problem of evil, rather than one with strong biblical warrant (incidentally, a view shared by C. S. Lewis and Evelyn Underhill).

Ezekiel 28:1–17 and Isaiah 12:12–21 are sometimes cited as support for a cosmic fall, but the texts would seem to point to self-exalted human beings rather than angelic ones. At the very least, when Jesus alludes to Isaiah in his description of the fall of Satan he has backing from the Old Testament; but when Jude in his letter talks of the "angels who did not keep their proper domain" (v. 6), he would seem to cross-reference Peter's Second Epistle (2:4), but without any other canonical foundation. Indeed, when in verse 9 he talks of Michael contending with the devil, or mentions the prophecies of Enoch in verse 14 he most clearly is not drawing from the canonical tradition, but is borrowing directly from Intertestamental literature.

Despite these cautionary remarks, I think overall there is enough biblical evidence to support a proper Christian dualism, but it seems to me wise to make modest claims about the origins of devils, the working of the demonic world, and the methodology of exorcisms when the Bible remains virtually silent on these matters (or, at least, if we do speculate about them, we should call our speculations what they really are: not revelations or biblical truths, but daring thoughts that, like those elaborate Chinese kites, we hope will catch the wind and take flight).

It is in this realm of speculative kite-flying that Prince and Subritzky, among many others, do strange things to the biblical texts, and are able to create not only a "topography of hell" but also a fairly detailed plan of the tactics, weapons, and personalities of evil spirits. Let us take one major example: Paul. The apostle Paul, as I have already mentioned, makes nine references to "powers" in the New Testament. Sometimes these are without any evil connotations, such as in Colossians 1:16, "For by him all things were created: things in heaven and on earth, visible and invisible, whether thrones or powers or rulers or authorities; all things were created by him and for him." This contrasts with Ephesians 6:12, where, in the context of putting on God's armor to resist the devil, Paul says, "For our struggle is not against the powers of this dark world and against the spiritual forces of evil in the heavenly realms." Wesley Carr's *Angels and Principalities* and Walter Wink's *Naming the Powers* demonstrate most clearly the difficulty of catching Paul's drift and interpreting his language. There seems to be deliberate ambiguity in the text, whereby we are dealing with power that is both incorporeal and corporal—both invisible and visible.

For what it is worth, I have argued in my book *Enemy Territory* that while not needing to deny the reality of the demonic, we need to understand the dark powers as interpenetrating the power structures of society, so that we fight evil, not in the realm of fantasy or the heavenlies, but in the public world of politics and economics. Hence, I have suggested that we must fight collective evil wherever it is to be found, whether this be organized crime or racism. Wherever we find the oppression of nationalities, social classes, and women, the powers are at work. The same goes for bureaucratic impersonalism, war-mongering, or governmental and societal indifference to poverty and suffering.

Many charismatic specialists on the demonic world interpret Paul's powers and rulers not as negative cosmic influences, nor as social/spiritual power structures, but as superior fiends. But I find their method of biblical interpretation worrying. For example, one becomes suspicious of Subritzky's whole approach when one reads that "demons can be clearly distinguished from angels because angels have wings."[23] He deduces this fact by interpreting literally the phrase "fly swiftly" predicted of Gabriel in Daniel 9:21.

The liberalizing of parable and metaphor becomes an occupational hazard in the paranoid universe. So, for example, when Jesus says in Matthew 12:29, "How can anyone enter a strong man's house and carry off his possessions unless he first ties up the strong man? Then he can rob his house," this is taken by both Prince and Subritzky to indicate that there are demonic strong men. The powers and rulers of Paul now become personified into super-devils, responsible under their general, Satan, for territories and commanding a vast array of demonic forces. This interesting interpretation is reinforced by the Hammonds' conviction that the "Prince of Persia" spoken of in Daniel 10 is a "demonic prince." Given that Daniel, like Revelation, is written in the Jewish apocalyptic genre, with its typically lurid and symbolic language, we might wonder if the text is really capable of such an interpretation. But regarding the Persian reference, the Hammonds tell us: "From this it is clear that there are ruling demon spirits placed by Satan over nations and cities in order to carry out his evil purposes."[24]

However, it is Subritzky who presents us with the most detailed exposition of the strong men, saying that there is in effect a counterfeit unholy trinity of the three strong men—Jezebel, the spirit of antichrist, Death and Hell. (One wonders with what model of the Holy Trinity Subritzky is working.) But let us not get on his ground, for there is no evidence in Scriptures that the spirit of antichrist of 1 John 4:3 is meant to be a cosmic demon. There is even less evidence that it is a so-called strong man. Can one really make out a case that Jezebel, who Subritzky links with the scarlet woman and whore of Babylon, is a superior fiend? It also takes an extraordinary imagination to take the Death and the Hades of Revelation 20:13–14 and amalgamate them into a monophysite strong man of the unholy trinity.

---

23. Subritzky, *Demons Defeated*, 65.

24. Hammond, *Pigs in the Parlor*, 6.

What is most disturbing about this kind of biblical exegesis is that it rests not on sound hermeneutical principles, but on what Nigel Wright in his book *The Fair Face of Evil* calls "inside information"—it is no less than the unholy trinity and the lower angelic hoards that tell Subritzky their names and reveal to him their powers. Indeed, Subritzky admits that he came to realize that Death and Hell were themselves a diabolical Jesus after people became violent when he commanded the spirit Death and Hell of leave them.[25]

This may strike the psychologist as bordering on self-fulfilling prophecy: one predicts that Death and Hell are strong men, and, lo, the demons confirm it. It will certainly strike theologians as unbalanced, for we cannot allow our understanding of the demonic order to be dictated to us by devils, whether real or merely figments of our imagination.

RECHARACTERIZING THE DEVIL AND CHRISTIAN SPIRITUAL WARFARE

Now it is time to conclude, and I want to end with some remarks about the Evil One and about the nature of spiritual warfare.

It strikes me that a presupposition which underlies much charismatic understanding of the demonic is that the devil is a person, with fiendish personality and a brilliant, albeit twisted, rationality. From this it tends to follow that the hosts of hell are *a fortiori* also personal. They are the counterfeits of heaven—fallen angels, like the unfallen ones except that they are committed to evil. Thus, spiritual warfare can be seen in terms of battling against a well-organized and trained army with great powers or detection and destruction.

Such a view facilitates the sort of biblical exposition that we have briefly examined. It fuels the conspiratorial view of the devil that is so essential for the successful maintenance of a paranoid universe: for demons are more fearsome if one knows that they are everywhere, plotting to get us. It also helps facilitate novels such as Frank Peretti's *This Present Darkness*, which, while being a work of fiction, has the unfortunate consequence of being taken too literally.

But evil, I suggest, has no real being of its own, certainly no personal ontology, for God created only that which was good. Lucifer, the morning star of God's creation, was not content to be a creature, but wished to be the Creator. This desire inverted the power of love that sustained him, and the love of power was born. Here, Milton is powerfully convincing in his poetic

---

25. Subritzky, *Demons Defeated*, 35.

insight that Lucifer wished to reign, not to serve; to be a god, not a creature. This craving for ultimate power, C. S. Lewis tells us, was the sin that the devil taught the human race.

So rebellion was born out of a good creature's free choice that turned on its Creator, disfiguring the creature, and, finally, engorging him. Demonized by his own desire, the former angel of light is extinguished by his own darkness and the devil that emerges has no intrinsic life of its own, for it is parasitic on the forces and energies of God's good creation. Therefore, the power of evil ultimately derives from the good power of God, but it is now corrupted power that has fallen away from God's sustaining love. Having cast himself off from this love, that angelic being we call the devil loses not only his relationship with God, but is also out of sorts with himself—his own good nature. He drifts inexorably toward non-personhood, whose only end is nothingness—that existence of non-being which is outside the personal life of God.

As the devil has undergone his depersonalized metamorphosis—the carapace of evil hardening and usurping his good nature—he has become not more rational but irrational, not so much cunning as confused. He is diabolical but disordered, ferocious but fey, fearful but fickle, warlike but whimsical. In short, he has become all that God is not, and its instinct—for think more in terms of a mad beast than a personal agent—is to take as many of us with it as it can.

C. S. Lewis captures something of the eternal life of those who have fallen away from God in his book *The Great Divorce*, where we find that outside the solidity and bright weight of heaven there is the Gray City where there is no substance or depth, only wraiths who cling to their illusions.

Can I furnish biblical verses to substantiate this exposition? I am sorry, but I cannot; for I hope it is obvious that I am just flying a kite: I am speculating on what the Bible chooses not to tell us. However, this is not an arbitrary exercise. I am trying to work through logically certain ideas on an understanding of God's personal revelation, both in Jesus of Nazareth and as the triune God. His self-revelation as perfect love and personal communion also suggest its negations—being (or, more accurately, appearance of being) without communion, hate, and non-personhood. In other words, I am trying to do some serious theology, but only in the realm of legitimate guesswork.

Nevertheless, I am persuaded that the essence of spiritual warfare is not taking on demonic forces by binding strong men, destroying amulets and charms, and banning Halloween. Indeed, the passion with which some charismatics oppose All-Hallows Eve is matched only by their indifference to the celebration which follows it on All Saints' Day!

Perhaps it is only paranoia, but in my weaker moments I have a suspicion that the master Trickster has diverted us away from the battlefield to the games-room, where we indulge ourselves in spiritual fantasies and trivial pursuits while the real evil loosed on the world devours all that is good and decent with the heartlessness and cruelty of the Canaanite god Molech.

We may realize that we can fall prey to our own fantasies, and choose instead to step out from the closed world of our parishes and take to the streets and march for Jesus. Such a move could be a step in the right direction, for "coming out" is a way of "coming clean" with the public about charismatic intentions. But if we do decide to leave our sanctuaries and swarm on to the streets, we must strive to leave the paranoid universe behind, for otherwise we may imagine that by the very act of marching we are "shifting the demonic atmosphere" and "binding the strong men" of the city of Washington, D.C., say, or the Mammon of materialistic America. And if we believe this, we may also come to believe that we can "bind"—and hence solve—unemployment, racism, or environmental decay by a stamp of our feet, a clenched fist in the air, or a shout to the skies.

We need to learn that there is more to exorcising the darkness than exercising our lungs. There is more to spiritual warfare than standing toe-to-toe with the devil and slugging it out. To meet like with like, or as Jesus puts it, evil with evil—or, if you prefer, with more of the same—is to show that we have not really escaped the labyrinth of Dungeons and Dragons, He-Man, and the masters of the paranoid universe. If this were to be our approach to evil in the world, then it would be better if we stayed at home.

If my speculative theology of the parasitic nature of evil is correct, then perhaps attacking demons amounts to a welcoming party for them. Even some of our charismatic services can no longer begin until the demons are first "bound" in prayer. As an American charismatic recently put it: the devils take this as worship and flock to hear themselves addressed! To put it bluntly, belligerence against them is not merely a welcoming, but a feast. (We can almost hear Screwtape telling Wormwood how he can wax fat on human aggression.) At the very least, to behave in this way is to descend to a sub-Christian barbarism. To exercise authority (*exousia* in the New Testament sense) over dark forces is one thing, but this is not the same as striving for greater fire-power to atomize the opposition (*dunamis*, a word rarely used in accounts of Christ's encounters with evil spirits, is over-played in charismatic vocabulary).

The violent comic-strip "blow the enemy away" youth culture of Judge Dread Law Enforcer seems to have found a responsive echo in the triumphalist charismatic camp. At a recent Charismatic Resources Exhibition, for example, there was a hot trade in t-shirts bearing the legend, "Jesus Christ Demon Crusher." I believe that genuine spiritual warfare means quite simply refusing to play the war game: we can only overcome evil with good, for if we appropriate the enemy's weapons we are lost. As Metropolitan Anthony puts it, "The devil does not care who you hate, even if it's himself." Power-seeking is dangerous, and the love of power is nothing less than devilish, for it corrupts Christian virtue.

Paradoxically, there is a more powerful way than power to dispel the gloom of demonic fear: lifting high the burning torch of God's love. How true the children's chorus is. "Jesus bids us shine with a clear, pure light, like a little candle burning in the night." God's love, the self-denying yet bright sacrificial love of Calvary, banishes the darkness as surely as the presence of Aslan melted the snow of Narnia. Jesus, by being nailed to a Roman cross, eschewed the way of violence and submitted to the powers—both human and spiritual. And yet, in his weakness, at his most vulnerable, he revealed God's way of true spiritual resistance to evil: and he rose victorious over sin, death, and the devil.

If we want to be victorious in spiritual warfare, it is not our place, nor is it possible for us, to die for the sins of the world—that battle has been fought and won once and for all by Christ. But the pattern of victory is the same for us, the followers of Jesus, as it was for our Lord. If we take up our cross, we too will discover that God's strength is made perfect in our weakness. We will also find that for us there is glory, but only by the way of the cross.

The love of power is the way of the devil, and it is strong, triumphant, but transient. We can only defeat it with the power of love. Love is meek and lowly, but it is everlasting.

3

PENTECOSTAL POWER

The "Charismatic Renewal Movement" and the
Politics of Pentecostal Experience

(1983)

One of the joys of critical rationalism is that one does not have to be afraid to admit mistakes. Indeed, it is almost a moral imperative to rework previous research material in the light of present experience. Recently, sociologists have been forced into a major rethinking and a clearer understanding of the phenomenon of Pentecostalism. What has happened, in a way, is that it has gotten out of hand: what was once thought by many social scientists to be a sectarian expression of economic and social deprivation[1] has turned out to be a massive social movement beyond sectarian boundaries and incorporating the middle class and the intelligentsia.

In this paper I attempt to chart the emergence of this new Pentecostalism, highlighting its distinguishing features and demonstrating its similarities and differences with the old Pentecostalism. In particular, I want to identify three stages, or phases, of its growth. This identification will concentrate on the power struggles between the Pentecostalists and their opponents within the mainstream churches. Finally, I shall discuss a Pentecostal understanding of Christian practice, the attitude to the secular world, and Pentecostals' future in Christendom.

To begin sensibly, a caveat is needed, for the phenomenon of the new Pentecostalism has been worldwide and has involved between one and a

---

1. Some writers still think the same way. Cf. Anderson, *Vision of the Disinherited*.

half to two million people. No one paper can hope to capture the diversity of practice, the differing theological interpretations by participants, and the national and regional differences that together constitute the movement of charismatic renewal. For the sake of clarity and expediency, therefore, I shall concentrate on the growth of Pentecostalism in the Western world[2] with particular reference to Britain. This affords me not only a manageable package, but allows me to rely on participant observation, personal interviews, and informants.[3] Although it can be argued that this is not the most scientific of methodologies, I contend that it is far more desirable and dependable than having to rely on the idealized versions of Pentecostalism to be found in apologist literature. (For readers who are not familiar with earlier Pentecostalism, I have added a short glossary rather than burden the text with endless definitions.)

CLASSICAL PENTECOSTALISM AS FORERUNNER TO THE CHARISMATIC MOVEMENT

Modern charismatics often say that Pentecostalism is as old as the New Testament and that *glossolalia* is to be found throughout church history. Such statements are contestable as truth statements, but are undeniably powerful as legitimating devices whereby charismatics can demonstrate that Pentecostal experience has always been the lot of the saints of church history. It is true that tongue-speaking—the distinguishing feature of Pentecostal spirituality—has played some part in the life of the historic church. It is more true to say, however, that this was mainly featured among heretical groups, or was an epiphenomenal aspect of the lives of certain saints and a few Protestant sects. Neither the great Methodist upsurgence nor the evangelical and/or holiness movements of the nineteenth century exhibit tongue speaking in any major way. The Irvingites stand out as a distinctive, although small, Pentecostal movement of the nineteenth century, but they prefigure what I believe to be a fascinating yet unexplained fact: Pentecostalism is essentially a twentieth-century phenomenon.

2. This is not meant to imply that the Third World Pentecostal movements are less significant. On the contrary, I believe with Walter Hollenweger that these groups probably have more to contribute to theology and to Christendom as a whole than do Western Pentecostals.

3. This work is in three stages: (1) participant observation among classical Pentecostal and Roman Catholic groups from 1970 to 1975; (2) consultant and/or representative to renewal consultations from 1978 to 1980; and (3) consultation, research, and reporting for British Broadcasting Corporation—television and radio—and London Weekend Television from 1980 to 1982.

Before the Great War has begun in 1914 classical Pentecostalism had emerged in both Europe and the United States of America. The Holiness movements, on both sides of the Atlantic, were the primary crucible for the new sects: their belief in and commitment to the "second experience" soon became the "second blessing," and eventually the more specific Pentecostal doctrine of the "baptism of the Holy Spirit." In America the leadership of the fast-growing sects came from all classes and races, but the bulk of the new ranters and enthusiasts were black or poor urban and rural working class. European Pentecostalism grew from inside Lutheranism and Anglicanism as well as Holiness and Free-Evangelical churches. In Britain, particularly, the role of the aristocracy and the upper classes is far more important in the rise of classical Pentecostalism than is usually realized.[4]

Many Pentecostalists, even after the Great War had given way to the "roaring twenties," wished to remain in their own churches and denominations. They faced great hostility, however, from both the leaders and consumers of mainstream Christianity. Outbursts in tongues or prophecy and the practicing of "divine healing" combined with wildly enthusiastic services, exorcisms, and Adventist eschatology, were too much for traditionalists. Many Christians interpreted this Pentecostalism as blasphemous, demonic, or heretical. Driven out from the mainstream churches, and driven on by the ever-urging Spirit, Pentecostalists soon became "The Pentecostals," forming in groups behind the enclaves of increasingly world-rejecting sects.

The great revivals of classical Pentecostalism continued in bursts throughout Europe and America until the Second World War. Much of the original fervor gave way to ritualized chorus singing and stereotyped extemporaneous prayer and preaching. Standards of education rose, and although classical Pentecostals have remained firmly rooted in fundamentalist Evangelicalism, they look more and more (with their professional pastorate and Bible schools) like established sects and denominations. In the United States, and increasingly in Britain, it is no longer accurate to classify classical groups as disinherited working-classes; like the Methodists before them, Pentecostals have achieved considerable social mobility. (It is also true that Pentecostalism remains a powerful influence among those sections of our society that Marx designated *lumpenproletariat*.)

It is often said by the leaders of the Pentecostals in Britain—notably Jeffreys and Gee—that the essence of Pentecost was experience, not denomination. They looked forward to a time when the Pentecostal experience of the "baptism of the Spirit" would become the birthright of all Christians in the mainstream churches. The classical mode of Pentecostalism would

---

4. Walter Hollenweger rightly insists on this.

wither away—would become redundant—if and when there should be an outpouring of God's Spirit upon the whole church. Their notion of church may have been theologically vague, but they hoped and believed that the *pneuma* of God would revitalize the dying body of Christianity.

Today, many classical Pentecostals are faced with what appears to be the fulfillment of the dream. A vibrant Pentecostalism faces them and assails them from nearly every nook and cranny of Christendom. It is a threat to their very existence, and fear and "sour grapes" are as much part of their reaction as the wonderment and excitement. For many of them the fact that Pentecostalism has taken root in Catholicism and what they would regard as "modernist" churches is more a cause for concern than for rejoicing.

THE PEOPLE OF THE CHARISMATA

Stage 1: Anarchic Pentecostalism

It is important that we do not see the origins and growth of neo-Pentecostalism in terms of crude diffusionism. It is simply not the case (as some charismatics have claimed) that it started in the Church of the Redeemer in Houston, Texas, from whence it spread to the rest of America and Europe. Neither is it the case that it started first in one denomination or one particular country. From the early 1960s—with a noticeable acceleration after mid-decade—here and there, country after country began to experience a form of Pentecostalism similar experientially to the classical mode, but among groups of people within the historic churches and mainstream denominations.

Certainly it was the case that once this unplanned and unorchestrated movement gained momentum, not unnaturally fellow Pentecostals would meet together (often cutting across denominational boundaries), form informal groups, and establish newsletters and journals. It is a well-known phenomenon in science that new discoveries and theories emerge in different parts of the globe even though some of the scientists know nothing of each other's work. I fail to see why it should be so different in the field of religious experience. Once the news is out for all to hear, of course, then collaboration and mutual sharing of information and experience takes place. As the charismatic movement began to spread, many observers wished to write it off as a fad.[5] Such a flimsy judgment looks less than convincing after twenty years of rapid growth.

---

5. The religious correspondent for *The Times* told me in telephone conversation that he saw the renewal as a kind of self-induced therapy.

A more sophisticated and empathetic view of neo-Pentecostalism came from a Catholic professor who attempted to see the new religious movement in the context of the counterculture of the mid and late 1960s:

> These movements belong to a post-literary culture which is ex-perience-oriented, unstructured, spontaneous, inward, almost atomistic in its concern for the now at the expense of history, pursuing illumination, dominated by a sense of presence, sure that somewhere there is ultimate worth. To a greater or lesser degree the movement represents a turning back to recapture the original unstructured experience of the meaning of life at a level which, like tongues, is unutterable.[6]

The period from 1965 to 1975 (which roughly encapsulates what I have called "anarchic Pentecostalism") was a time of old-time revivalism in a new, sometimes alien, setting. Catholics, Episcopalians/Anglicans, Lutherans, the Greek Orthodox Church in America, the Church of Scotland, Baptists, Methodists, Presbyterians—and many other smaller groups—were having to come to grips with a Pentecostalism not burning in some extreme sect, but in their very midst. Many church leaders were pretending nothing was happening; more strange was the fact that neither the national papers nor the trade press really grasped the extent or the fervor of the charismatic renewal movement.

The neo-Pentecostals had three major problems, which, in my opinion, they never really overcame. Their first problem was to demonstrate to their fellow denominationalists that they were not merely Pentecostals, and certainly not classical Pentecostals. They distanced themselves from the latter in a number of ways. First, they preferred the term "charismatic" to the more common substantive, "Pentecostal." For my part, I have yet to be persuaded from the position voiced to me at the World Council of Churches headquarters by a West Indian woman: "Charismatic is just a posh word for Pentecostal." Furthermore, many of the new Pentecostals were middle-class and certainly not fundamentalist in doctrine; for them the classical Pentecostals were admittedly related, but they were either afforded the status of poor cousins or relegated to the undesirable position of skeletons in the closet. The adoption of the word "renewal" as opposed to the more strident "revival" was a further attempt at distancing.

The second problem was more acute and cut across the first problem. What did the Pentecostal experience mean, and how should the new blessing influence worship and liturgy? This was a particularly difficult problem

---

6. Kilian McDonell, quoted in Sullivan, *Can the Pentecostal Movement Renew the Churches?* 5.

for Roman Catholics who had no ready-made-to-hand theology to explain Pentecostalism; nor were they accustomed to the conversion effect of the new experience. I am convinced that Pentecostalism had a strong evangelical and personal appeal to Catholics, more so than to any other denomination. In any event, although it is often forgotten now, many neo-Pentecostals attended (either openly or surreptitiously) classical Pentecostal services. Some fundamentalist theology was adopted and adapted while much of the ritual was taken over. Testifying to conversion and healing remains to this day, but many of the old hymns and choruses have been revamped into a more contemporary style. (Many of the young Catholic and Episcopalian charismatics who pray with their hands uplifted, sing endless repetitions of short choruses, and utter what traditionalists might think to be sentimental phrases about "Je-sus," have no idea that much of "their natural and spontaneous" behavior in the Lord comes directly from classical American Pentecostalism.)

The third problem from the neo-Pentecostals was to demonstrate to their fellow denominationalists who were not charismatics that they were not heretical, psychologically unstable, or dangerous. This was not an easy task. Many of the Pentecostals—in the first flush of their experience—were both lax in their church discipline and unformed in their theology. They were opposed not only by many hierarchs, but by ordinary laypersons who wanted to remain simply Catholic, Baptist, or whatever, without having to take on what appeared to them to be an alien creed and irreverent liturgy. The charismatics responded in two ways: (1) they demonstrated through apologist literature that Pentecostalism belonged to the tradition of their churches, whether Catholic or Protestant, Low or High.[7] (2) Great emphasis was placed on the renewal of the traditional faith. Catholics, for example, insisted that they had a new love for the Mass, a greater desire for the Eucharist, and more time for their rosaries. On the whole, during this phase (despite the very real opposition) the charismatics won more friends than enemies: their enthusiasm, commitment, and certain "controlled wildness" was contagious. The mainstream Pentecostals maintained their denominational commitment, and showed no sign of forming a new sect, or trying to overturn the conventional wisdom. They emerged (and still remain) Catholics, Anglicans, Methodists, Presbyterians, Baptists, who also happen to be Pentecostal by experience.

During this ten-year period, however, there were many experiments that rarely received mention in apologist literature. In America and England,

---

7. For example: O'Connor, C. S.C., *The Pentecostal Movement in the Catholic Church*; Harper, *None Can Guess*.

for example, many charismatic groups dabbled in occultism; there are practices which remain today, such as the holding of hands in a circle, which
seem to owe more to Spiritualism than classical Pentecostalism. Astrology
was popular with some groups, and a general permissiveness seemed part,
for some, of the new frontier in the Spirit: in England, as in America, touching, hugging, and kissing were widespread. Some groups adopted the secular methods of sensitivity training. In England I know of one community
that was closed by the diocesan bishop because of illicit sexual relations.
Indeed, wife swapping and reneging on vows of chastity by priests and nuns
were by no means rare; weird practices of exorcism and excessive emphasis
on demonology were the side effects of anarchic Pentecostalism. Leaders
were often made aware, sometimes painfully, that when the personality is
opened up to its non-rational side, it can reveal the irrational and the dark
shadow-side of life as well as authentic and transfiguring experience.

Stage 2: Consolidation, Broadened Horizons, Official Recognition

By 1975, the charismatics had won even the grudging respect of their an-
tagonists. They had not left the denominations for new cults or sects.

Many of the more embarrassing fellow travelers had left or been forced
out. Furthermore, new, freewheeling forms of liturgy were acceptable to
many of the non-charismatics, who objected to the content, rather than the
form of Pentecostalism: guitars, dancing, and challenging drama were all
becoming commonplace in secular-oriented parishes as well as charismatic
congregations.

Both in Europe and America the charismatics had shown that being
Pentecostal meant more than speaking in tongues: for many it was a new
dimension of spiritual and psychological life. There was a freeing of guilt
and inhibition, an acceptance of the non-rational side of life, and a passion for new experiences. Unlike their classical counterparts, many neo-
Pentecostals were free of fundamentalism: they drank alcohol, went to the
theatre, took an active interest in politics, and in the case of Catholics, still
smoked tobacco. Gradually, even classical Pentecostals became less antagonistic, despite differing cultural and class traits.[8]

Ecumenists began to imagine that Pentecostalism might be an important non-institutional force for church unity. (In fact, Pentecostalism
continues to be interdenominational rather than truly ecumenical.) Church

8. See, for example, Alfred Missen's enthusiastic speech delivered at the united conference of Elim and Assemblies of God, "The Pentecostal Movement in the Eighties."
Missen was the former General Secretary of the Assemblies of God in Britain.

leaders, including two popes, held meetings with charismatics. Encouraging noises were made, and much was said during this time, not only by apologist writers, but also by sympathetic churchmen, to the effect that the new Pentecostalism was the third force in Christendom.[9]

Charismatics did not realize it at the time, but they were enjoying the peak of the renewal movement. England, for example, could boast tens of thousands who could lay claim to the Spirit experience. The mainstream charismatics shared a common life together through conferences, retreats, interdenominational prayer groups, and conventions. Periodicals and tapes sold were everywhere proclaiming the Pentecostal message. *New Covenant*, the American Catholic journal, was so widespread that it could be found in nearly every neo-Pentecostal group in Europe. *Renewal*, the English charismatic magazine, and the Fountain Trust, the interdenominational charismatic organization, not only kept charismatics in touch, but helped to disseminate Pentecostal teaching within the context of traditional Christian practice. Throughout Britain such work—and particularly the leadership of Tom Smail, John Richards, and Michael Harper—did much to calm the fears of anxious Christian leaders.

There was cause for anxiety. The growing number of exorcisms and an increasing emphasis on demonology were permeating the most respectable of charismatic circles. The American practice (stemming from the maverick side of classical Pentecostalism) of "slaying in the Spirit," with its dramatic effect of Spirit recipients swooning to the ground, was becoming established as normal behavior within the renewal. On the whole, however, the people of the charismata, with their clapping, singing in the Spirit, tongue speaking, healings, and unmistakable enthusiasm, had become part of the mainstream of Christian life. They had arrived to such an extent, that around the world all the major denominations were gathering to prepare reports on the charismatics.

While denominational leaders were gathering in their separate consultations, major changes were taking place in the renewal movement. Michael Harper claims in his booklet *Charismatic Crisis* that 1975 was a watershed in the movement because of what he calls the discipleship issue. By the end of that year the renewal was established throughout the Western world. Many of the fringe groups had fallen away, and yet the anarchic spirit was still at work: people refused to do theology, or move beyond the initial Spirit experience. They were prepared to discuss wholeness, Harper claims, but were little interested in traditional notions of holiness. Discipleship became

9. The other two were Catholicism and Protestantism. The Eastern Orthodox churches were hence removed from Christendom by a stroke of the pen.

an issue in an attempt to instill order and seriousness into the movement. Emphasis was placed on growing and maturing in the Christian life. For some, this necessitated living in a community or group under the leadership of "elders,"[10] or spiritual superiors. Catholics in America started their covenanted communities, and in Britain, particularly through the teaching of Harper, there was a growing mood of piety. This mood was not to everybody's taste. Some decided that the "party was over" and left their charismatic congregations; others maintained their links but with a noticeable cooling off towards the renewal.

Although the discipleship issue can be seen as the first real split within the renewal, its initial effects were marginal to the movement as a whole. Many charismatics were now looking to new horizons, not only in terms of evangelism, but also in terms of welfare and social work. Particularly among Catholics and Anglicans (and Presbyterians in America) stands were taken against racism and social injustice. There was a growing interest in ecumenism and a real desire for the renewal of churches that would lead to the unity of Christendom.

Many of the denominational consultation reports tended to underestimate the extent of charismatic involvement in activity other than "tongues talking," prophetic pronouncing, and hand clapping. Between 1974 (the Church of Scotland) and 1981 (the Church of England), all the major denominations of Britain pronounced on charismatic renewal. There was not a single report that could be considered to be really hostile; there were some harsh criticisms, but on the whole they were lukewarm or even favorable.

For me, the 1980 consultation of the World Council of Churches marks the end of the second stage of charismatic renewal. The very fact that the consultation was held at all is witness to the sheer size and significance of worldwide neo-Pentecostalism. Many charismatics were convinced that the leaders of the World Council of Churches would never take notice because of their predilection for social and political concerns. When the General Secretary of the WCC (a self-confessed Methodist socialist) stood up at the consultation and told the assembled company that he had been personally blessed by the charismatic nature of the enquiry, many neo-Pentecostalists

---

10. Orthodoxy was readmitted to the Christian fold by charismatics when they discovered the Eastern tradition of "elders." These men and women were leaders due to their spiritual authority, and were often lay people; their relationship with the official hierarchy was often problematic. Sociologically, the parallel with the modern charismatics is very interesting (and merits serious study), but it is a mistake to make too much of it in religious terms: the spirituality of Orthodox elders is not Pentecostal; see also Harper, *Charismatic Crisis*.

thought (without irony) that this was a miracle. Michael Harper saw it as official recognition; in his words, "an historic occasion."

The supreme irony of the event was this: by the time the consultation was held, the charismatic renewal movement had peaked.[11] By 1980 it had consolidated, become more respectable, serious, and outreaching, but it *had* entered decline. Official recognition was not the cause of the decline, but not only was it the case that many charismatics predicted that official recognition would be the "kiss of death," but it is a well-established convention in sociology that decline in enthusiasm and an increase in official support are often correlated.

Stage 3: Fractions and Factions—1980 to 1985

Projection is a reasonable compromise between prediction and prophecy. What I shall attempt, then, is an informed guess as to the likelihood of future events as well as a description as to what is happening now.[12]

The seeds of stage three were sown between 1975 and 1980. As the renewal movement consolidated, so it began to lose its fervor. Many charismatics left the renewal once the experiential side of the baptism in the Spirit began to wane; even *glossolalia* for some was becoming "vain repetition." Although some denominations were still strong in Pentecostals (the population of Catholics in Ireland grew quite rapidly during this time), the overall trend was either static or slow decline. From its earliest days the renewal had spawned its itinerant evangelists, officially loyal to their denomination, but in reality increasingly loyal to themselves and their organizations. These evangelists maintained an uneasy relationship with the ordinary priests and pastors who were responsible for the day-to-day spirituality of parish life. Sometimes the evangelists (called by one Baptist pastor "professional charismatics") had considerable commercial interests in the charismatic movement; this included their own publishing houses, records, tapes, and videos.

In 1980, the Fountain Trust collapsed. It had rapidly become functionless as the charismatic fire began to lose its sparkle. There was also increasing tension between some of its leaders. The end of what had been the major organization for promotion the renewal message in Britain, came as a great

11. This is not merely my opinion. Tom Smail, former director of the Fountain Trust, said as much as well. So too has Emmanuel Sullivan, *Can the Pentecostal Movement Renew the Churches?*; see also Arthur Wallis of the house church movement's *Restoration* magazine.

12. No sociologist worth his or her salt these days would make such scientific predictions, but I think it is a matter of "bad faith" if we are not prepared "to put our money where our mouth is."

shock to many charismatics, particularly those in the Church of England. Some of the itinerant charismatic leaders began moving away from the mainstream denominational structures. Some formed new "communities" and independent organizations. The fastest growing religious phenomenon in Britain over the last few years is a new classical Pentecostal sect in the making—the house church movement. The restoration church, which is the largest and most structured of these house churches, has been recruiting from the mainstream charismatics. Some of the itinerant evangelists have become increasingly involved in this movement. Furthermore, quite large sections of the Elim and Assemblies of God Pentecostal sects have been defecting to restorationism. It is now clear that a realignment of Pentecostalism (involving both classical and neo-Pentecostals) is taking place in Britain.

The above events signify the growing strain and confusion in the neo-Pentecostal camp. This was highlighted by the debate, in November 1981, of the Church of England's report on the renewal, which was held during the General Synod's annual assembly. The report was bland and seemingly noncontroversial, but to most people's surprise the debate was so vicious and venomous that it had to be abandoned because of heated uproar: the old charges of schism, "triumphalism," and the evils of enthusiasm were back in full force.

From now until 1985, I believe the following will happen to the charismatic renewal movement in Britain. (Similar forces—although not identical—are at work in America and Canada, so I expect the pattern to be repeated in those countries.) First, the renewal will continue to decline in numbers and in fervor. As it does so it will fractionize or split up around new emerging factions. There will be attempts (it has already started in the Church of England) to form new organizations to replace the Fountain Trust; their purpose will be to "gee-up" the flagging renewal. Many of the mainstream charismatics will support these ad hoc bodies and will remain loyal to a Pentecostalism that will be of a more muted and less revivalistic nature. (Many charismatic leaders are already admitting that tongues and prophecy have declined in the movement.)

Other charismatics will follow the itinerant evangelists who will look to new pastures in order to keep what it is for them both their life and their livelihood. What I call the "spiritual nomads" (those who always go "where the action is") will split up and follow their favorite leader into his self-appointed exile. At the moment, I believe that the evidence suggests that many mainstream Pentecostals will forsake their denominations and became involved with the house church movement. Some of its leaders have called to the charismatics to "Come Out . . . ," and already whole congregations have seceded from the Baptist Union.[13]

The house church movement, which sociologically speaking belongs to classical Pentecostalism, will have little appeal to Catholic charismatics. They will cohere around their own charismatic leaders more than any other mainstream Pentecostal grouping. Indeed, I think that alone of the new Pentecostals, the Catholics will resist fractionalism (so many of their leaders are priests that they will eventually weld the new charisma onto the old structure). Catholicism will survive revitalized. Its Pentecostalism will be tamed, or channeled, into other spiritual directions.

Part of the problem for the neo-Pentecostals is that they have to face the reality of all revivals (even with a "posh" name like renewal): church history shows that they always come to an end. Perpetual Pentecost was unknown in the early church. By the fifth century A.D., John Chrysostom knew nothing of Pentecostalism. When Pentecost goes, it leaves in its wake memory, nostalgia, and the faint stirrings of the nascent experience. Using Pentecostal terminology, I have referred to this, elsewhere, as a "time of blessing."[14] It is difficult to recapture the full excitement and feelings of a lost love: remembered glimpses, hints, and shallow sentimentality are usually the best we can muster. When Pentecost leaves (and I shall believe that sociologists would do well to understand it experientially and not organizationally) like the beloved, we can invoke the *Paraclete* with noise, clapping, choruses, or tongues, but too easily the machinations are ritualistic responses: outward forms to clothe the inner nakedness. Many classical Pentecostals have had to face this truth often with great honesty and dignity. Sometimes, they settle for "going through the motions" in what becomes a quite developed though restless liturgy. For those who do not become trapped in Pentecostal nostalgia, which is itself embedded in outworn yet cherished rituals, they must look forward to a new Pentecost, a new awakening, another revival.

The new charismatics will have to learn how closely they are related, after all, to their older cousins. Their immediate future is to undergo (with their movement) change, mutation, and perhaps even cessation.

13. This was the thrust of my report on the restoration churches: *The Dales Bible Week* (BBC; August 8, 1982).

14. Atherton, "An Easter Pentecostal Convention."

CHARISMATICS' VIEW OF CHRISTIAN LIFE, THEIR ATTITUDE TO SECULAR SOCIETY, AND THEIR FUTURE IN CHRISTENDOM

The new Pentecostals have underscored the essential component of experience in religious life. For them, belief and liturgy grow out of an encounter with a "God who is alive." While the "fire in the bones" burns deeply, not only for the individual Pentecostal, but also for groups who share together—and hence reinforce—a common life, the experiential takes precedence over theologizing and the establishment of the parameters of belief and conduct. In the anarchic first phase of neo-Pentecostalism, Christian life was reinterpreted as "living in the Spirit"; "entering into freedom" was understood to mean not only experiencing the power of God in the form of ecstatic experiences, but also release from formal (charismatics see this as synonymous with "dead") Christianity. Traditional liturgies were not forsaken, but they often became forms of worship that were less well attended than the newer freewheeling services.

At the same time, for many charismatics, their personal Pentecost went beyond the restrictions of classical Pentecostalism. They would talk about the gifts of helping, teaching, and administration, and they were concerned with psychological wholeness as well as the traditional sins.

During the second phase of the renewal movement, the emphasis on experience and individual piety (which shared the sentimentality, if not the narrow morality, of their charismatic cousins) gave way to more outward expressions. Evangelization, social concern, and the need for community were interests that dominated charismatic literature. An attempt was made to see the Christian life in terms of duties and responsibilities, as well as of experiencing joy and exercising spiritual gifts. In America, particularly by Catholic Pentecostals, there was talk of "liberating structures" as well as saving individuals from sin. To some extent, in the same sense that "hippies" gave way to "yippies" in the 1960s, so the 1970s saw a politicization of Pentecostals. On the whole, however, this did not lead to a major new development within the renewal. It certainly did not lead to political activism. There were greater political awareness, avowed stands against racialism and social injustice, and a marked interest in ecological problems. These primarily remained epiphenomenal to the charismatic renewal, and can really be seen as a passive liberalism that led to no radical change of direction.

By the end of the second stage many charismatics saw their Christian life in fairly traditional terms of piety, faithfulness, and discipleship. The Pentecostals had not radically altered denominational practices. In fact, it could be argued that even the freewheeling liturgies stem as much from secularization as charismatic fervor. They had certainly not threatened the hierarchal structures of the ecclesia. Little was contributed, by them, either to conservative and traditional theology, or to liberation and process theologies. Although, undoubtedly, hundreds of thousands of Christians had entered into new spiritual experiences, the institutional structure of the historical and mainstream churches remained unchanged. Pentecost may have changed lives, but it blew over the organizational structure leaving everything exactly as it was before.

This lack of innovation and change from within the renewal explains why the movement did not become significant, sociologically, in terms of social movements.[15] Why it did not become so can partially be understood by looking at the charismatics' view of the secular world. On the one hand, many Pentecostals engaged in secular activities just as they did when they were traditional Catholics, Presbyterians, or whatever. After 1979, however, with the switch from wholeness to holiness, from freedom to discipleship, there was a noticeable sectarian attitude to the secular world. There was increasing suspicion against the World Council of Churches, which some saw as entirely secular in orientation, if not demonic. Although no responsible observer of the renewal would go so far as to say that it was so "otherworld-affirming that it was this-world-denying," nevertheless, there are two ways in which neo-Pentecostalism has been closer to sectarianism than mainstream religion.

First, among many of the evangelical sections of the renewal, classical Pentecostalism's piety and eschatology has been adopted. Second, throughout all sections and factions of the movement, there has been a tendency to withdraw from secular life. This inward-looking posture certainly characterizes neo-Pentecostalism during its first phase; the new inner life and its outward expression (shared only with other charismatics) had little time for worldly pursuits. During phase two there was a greater concordat, both

15. See Banks, *The Sociology of Social Movements*. Banks improves greatly on earlier functionalist views of social movements. On the whole, however, his secular usage and insistence on innovation and social change shows that social movement is not a particularly useful tool to explain neo-Pentecostalism.

My use throughout this paper of such phrases as "social movement," "renewal," "charismatic movement," and "charismatic renewal movement," should not be seen as attempts at sociological definition. On the contrary, they are self-consciously applied folk-model terms. I prefer not to operationalize a term unless it clearly can be shown—empirically, if it is possible—to explain satisfactorily disparate data. Indeed, strictly speaking, as I hinted in my introduction, there is no such thing as a "charismatic renewal movement" that can be simply labeled "this" rather than "that": in reality, we are faced with multifaceted charismatic movements. That basically is why I feel that John Moore's adoption of "craze" to explain the disparate phenomena is not very useful. See his article: "The Catholic Pentecostal Movement."

with the secular world and ecumenism. By phase three, however, not only was "worldliness" increasingly rejected, but there was also decreasing emphasis on involvement in the secular theatres of government, and social and political protest. This trend will continue as the factional and fractionalized renewal retreats behind new borders. (If we were to drop the rather dubious use of sect, in sociology, as some form of religious organization, and see it in terms of ideological constructs adhered to by collectivities, then it would be the case that neo-Pentecostalism is, after all, sectarian.)

Pentecostal power has not, by itself, led either to the humanitarian and reformist activities of nineteenth-century Evangelicalism, or reproduced the deeds of Welsh Nonconformity at the beginning of the twentieth century. The revolutionary possibilities of a millenarian utopianism, such as the seventeenth-century Levellers espoused, find no echo in neo-Pentecostalism.[16]

Pentecostalism entered the twentieth century as a major new development of Protestant sectarianism. It appealed to—and presumably met the needs of—both the urban and rural masses. In its classical development, Pentecostalism remained imprisoned behind Fundamentalism. In Christian mythology, Noah, having failed with the raven, sends out the dove from the safety (yet enclosed world) of the ark. At first she returns because there is no land. She is sent out again and this time she brings back with her an olive leaf (itself, as the church fathers used to say, a symbol of anointing and power). The Dove is then sent forth again, and she never returns. The *Paraclete,* which Western iconography always depicts as the Dove, seems to have left the imprisonment of the sect. If I may follow my analogy strictly (though I am not speaking theologically), I think the immediate future of the liberated bird is to return to the Classical Ship with the new anointing.

In America the phenomenal rise of the new Fundamentalism is taking the steam out of the charismatic movement. The Church of God and Assemblies of God Pentecostal sects are not doing wonderfully well out of neo-Pentecostalism, but the new independent organizations look increasingly like a new form of classical Pentecostalism.[17] In Britain, the house church movement is benefiting greatly from the decline of mainstream Pentecostalism. Many of its members were in the renewal, and it has successfully integrated its worship from newer free styles of contemporary music with the old-style Pentecostal revivalism.

In short, the factionalism and fractionalism of neo-Pentecostalism is not only leading to the partial disintegration of the charismatic renewal, as

16. It has, of course, cropped up in classical mode both in North and South America.
17. Church Growth ministries are examples.

it has existed over the last fifteen years, but it is aiding and abetting the rise of a new classical Pentecostalism.

But to return to our analogy: will the Dove ever get away? In one sense, of course, she has already left. Having spread her wings, she will never be content simply to return to the ark. She has many new places to go: there are many areas of the Third World as well as Western Europe that have not yet received a visitation. The Eastern Orthodox Church and Catholic Poland may be high on the list for future arrivals. In another sense, however, there is no evidence that the Dove will be free from the ark forever; she will keep visiting from time to time. Thus, classical Pentecostalism will undoubtedly continue causing the same disruption and controversy that it has for most of this century. So too will neo-Pentecostalism flourish in new countries and old denominations (even though the present charismatic renewal is now slowly coming to a halt).

Certainly, it seems to me, sociologists have learned a great deal from neo-Pentecostalism: they have learned that they know very little about Pentecostalism. It has turned out to be a phenomenon capable of mutation and change, and against conventional wisdom it has taken root in the most unlikely of classes and denominations. Maybe we misrepresented it in its classical mode when we saw it as group response to societal disinheritance. We were too eager to adapt it to spurious doctrines of "false consciousness," and in our Procrustean manner insisted that it stay locked behind sectarian typologies of our own making. At the beginning of this paper I contended that Pentecostalism had "gotten out of hand." It has certainly gotten out of our hands: this is another sense in which the Dove is free. In its freedom although it has not yet demonstrated that it has the Pentecostal power to radically destroy societal or denominational structures, it clearly has had enough explosive force to shatter sociological shibboleths.

GLOSSARY

Baptism of the Holy Spirit

The phrase so often used to describe the Spirit-filling experience. It is still popular among many renewal devotees, but now rejected by many Catholics and sacramentalists as inconsistent with Catholic theology. Its usage gained popularity and sanctity in classical Pentecostal circles. Church history has seen this terminology before. In the Christian East, for example, Saint Simeon the New Theologian used it in a manner similar to modern charismatics. He did not see tongue-speaking as the legitimate Spirit seal; however; he did think tears were the correct sign of the Baptism.

Charismatic Renewal Movement

This is the usual terminology to index the present wave of Pentecostalism. Renewalists do not understand the term "movement" in sociological or organizational terms: it denotes a pneumatic, or Spirit-motivated, movement. Renewal is understood as renewing the churches in their traditional faiths and people in their personal commitment to God.

Classical Pentecostalism

Sectarian, fundamentalist, and evangelical; the elder denominational form of modern Pentecostalism.

Divine Healing

Catholics have resorted to traditional formulas and rites, but often they (and most Protestant groups) lean on methods derived from classical Pentecostalism. Often it is the direct method of the "laying on of hands" and shouting, "In the name of Jesus, come out." Usually, the demonology owes more to the "Bible Belt" than to traditional and patristic understanding of "principalities and powers."

Glossolalia

This is the Greek transliteration for "tongues of ecstasy." "Tongues" is the distinguishing feature of Pentecostal spirituality. It must not be confused with the phenomenon of *xenolalia*—or, speaking in foreign languages— which is rarely reported in charismatic circles. It was this phenomenon that was the feature of the day of Pentecost, not ecstatic utterance *per se*.

Neo-Pentecostalism

This is the "new wave" Pentecostalism belonging to groups within existing churches; it is neither necessarily sectarian nor necessarily evangelical in doctrine.

Prophecy

There is little use of either the biblical warnings to the nation, or foretelling. (David Wilkerson's *Vision* comes close.) Usually, prophecy is understood as "forth-telling." In practice this means offering homilies to the faithful.

Renewal

This is the shorthand version favored by most charismatics of the charismatic renewal.

Revival

This terminology belongs to classical Pentecostalism. It denotes an outpouring of God's Spirit resulting in mass conversions, healings, prophecies, tongues, and so forth.

Singing in the Spirit

This common phenomenon in charismatic circles—much seen at conventions—is where the congregation sings together in tongues. Need not be a group phenomenon; it is not clear if this practice is always endorsed in classical circles (though the house church movement practices it). After all, Paul rarely mentions, except in passing (1 Cor 14:15; Eph 5:19; Col 3:16), nor does it appear in the charismatic stories of the New Testament.

"Time of Blessing" or "Times of Refreshing"

It is typically a short period—meeting/convention—where God is felt to have been present in some special way. This often included Pentecostal phenomena, but may be simply a "good time had by all."

4

Thoroughly Modern

Sociological Reflections on the Charismatic Movement from the End of the Twentieth Century

(1997)

INTRODUCTION

When the "Marches for Jesus" began in cities in 1989 it was said by some of the organizers that marching on the streets was a way of "shifting the demonic atmosphere": they believed that cities and regions of the world could be controlled by "territorial spirits." Indeed, these days demonic infestations, which are legion, seem to be bound up with well-known and much sought after exorcists: Bill Subritzky from New Zealand, Derek Prince from the United States, Peter Horrobin from Lancashire, and the Reverend Arbuthnot from the London Healing Mission—are just some of the people who have a "special ministry" in the realm of unclean spirits.[1] Such beliefs and practices might seem evidence enough that the charismatic movement is a pre-modern throwback to a primitive or animistic religion—to an era, as Rudolf Bultmann would have put it, before the advent of wireless and electric light, when it was possible to believe in such things.[2]

---

1. See Hunt, "Giving the Devil More than His Due: Some Problems with the Deliverance Ministry."

2. Bultmann, "New Testament and Mythology," 5.

50

And it is not just a question of demons: oil miraculously appearing on hands at Kensington City Temple in London has been rumored (a feature of the American healing movement of the 1940s), roaring and laughing at the height of the "Toronto Blessing" of the 1990s, and that mainstay of classical Pentecostalism *glossolalia*—all these phenomena seem to inhabit a cultural universe beyond the ken of modernity. So we might be tempted to think that such religious supernaturalism in the modern world is culturally misplaced. To read the religious supernaturalism as primitive, however, is not only usually reductionist in intent, but it is also empirically indiscriminate: if charismatic religion is a throwback, then what are we to make of *The X Files*, alternative medicine, crystals and star gazing, the late-modern fascination with the weird and the unexplained, the replacement, we might say, of "Mere Christianity" with the merely strange? We might want to offer the rationalistic or aesthetic judgment that these things are bizarre or bewildering—even a form of pre-millennial tension or post-modern fragmentation—but we can hardly, I would have thought, be satisfied with the epithet "pre-modern."

Perhaps we would be on surer sociological ground if we were to reserve judgment on the pre-modern or primitive status of charismatic phenomena and note that they appear to be firmly fixed to those religious movements that we can see to be not so much pre-modern as anti-modern. Following Troeltsch and Weber's classic division of church and sect, there have been few sociologists[3] who have not viewed Pentecostalism and its many charismatic mutations as "culturally denying" in some sense and thus resistant to modernity. In Niebuhr's seminal *Christ and Culture,* for example, it is quite clear that all things Pentecostal would fit his rubric of "Christ against Culture." Admittedly, theologian John Howard Yoder and sociologist Bryan Wilson would prefer the notion of "conversionist" to describe the sectarian nature of charismatic groups, but like Neibuhr and Troeltsch before them, they too accept that such sects are still essentially movements resistant to the modern world; certainly not institutional and symbolic carriers of modernity.[4]

We might want to make a proper case that some expressions of charismatic religiosity cannot be classified by sectarian notions of conversionism,[5] but in this chapter I prefer not to become embroiled in typological issues, but rather to argue that charismatic Christianity is neither essentially pre-modern

---

3. Walker "Fundamentalism and Modernity: The Restoration Movement in Britain."

4. See Yoder, "A People in the World: Theological Interpretation," 252–83; and Wilson, *Sects and Society.*

5. The renewal movement, for example, resides in the historic churches and can hardly be said to have majored in "revival."

nor anti-modern. On the contrary, I shall argue, charismatic Christianity has embraced modernity either begrudgingly (making Pentecostalism reluctantly modern) or with enthusiasm (with the result that Pentecostal religion can be called thoroughly modern). Such a revisionist historiography seems apposite as we near the end of the twentieth century, for we can now look back on 100 years of Pentecostal and neo-Pentecostal religion. I do not wish to assert that there are no world-denying elements in charismatic Christianity, nor no anti-modern aspects to such movements—especially when second adventist hopes are high; but more plausibly I do want to argue that charismatic Christianity is more modern than not.

REVIVALISM IS ITSELF A MODERN PHENOMENON

Pentecostalism, and its charismatic outcrops, is the twentieth century's most successful embodiment of revivalism. Revivalism itself came into being at the dawn of the Enlightenment and thus can be properly classified as a modern phenomenon. I have argued elsewhere that the literary culture that developed with the invention of printing in the later fifteenth century facilitated not only critical rationality, but also individualism and pietism.[6] The Age of Reason was also the age of revivals. Both John Wesley and Jonathan Edwards, born in 1703, were admirers of science. Edwards may have been a high Puritan, but he was considerably influenced by John Locke and Isaac Newton.

The Methodist Revival in England and the First Great Awakening in New England also have to be seen, in my opinion, as part of the cultural shift from feudalism to capitalism. In the United States in particular, the revivals ensured the successful transmission of Protestant religion from feudalism into the modern era, but they also sounded the death knell for the already crumbling Puritan Covenant of 1620. To see the eighteenth-century revivals as the cultural carriers of modernity may seem a strange idea; after all, we tend to think of them in opposition to the Enlightenment preoccupation with rationality, Deism, and Unitarianism. Or again, we may be reminded that Gotthold Lessing characterized the Enlightenment as a "big ugly ditch" that halted historic Christianity in its path.

But the early revivals were not opposed to critical rationality, individualism, and progressivism in and of themselves. Jonathan Edwards, for example, may be remembered for his frightening sermons on God's wrath and eternal perdition, but he also provided a thoroughly modern psychological

---

6. Walker, *Telling the Story*, 61–74.

account of the revivals and his own wife's religious experiences.[7] Perhaps the most convincing evidence of the modernizing tendencies of early revivalism comes from Jon Butler's revisionist accounts of the American Awakenings (especially the Second Great Awakening at the advent of the nineteenth century) where he demonstrates that the passion and piety of the revivals also fuelled the progressivist vision of the American dream. The Puritan vision of the "city set upon the hill" settled down to a dream of a decent and respectable life in the new Republic. When revivalistic fervor cooled it left a strong residue of ascetic Protestantism, with its commitment to literacy and hard work and, in time, provided a ladder of social mobility.[8]

The early revivals had unintended consequences, not least because their emphasis on experience and the self was not only thoroughly modern in itself, but also conducive both to the religious freedom of the Republic and to the pietistic but theologically non-specific "civil religion" of Middle America.[9] More obviously, the revivals were themselves aided by both the technology and the principles of modernity. Not only is this the case with the appropriation of firstly the telegraph and later the phonograph for the more routinized revivals and urban missions of the nineteenth century, but it is also the case that revivalists came to see their campaigns in terms of pragmatic techniques. This assertion does not hold for the First Great Awakening in New England or the Cane Ridge Revival in Kentucky: the first revivals were too new, spontaneous, and unexpected to be honed into a technique. But the assertion does hold for Finney's great revivals of the early years of the nineteenth century. As Finney writes in his *Lectures on Revival*, "A revival is not a miracle, or dependent on a miracle, in any sense. It is purely philosophical results of the right use of constituted means as much as any other effect produced by the application of means."[10]

Henceforth, American Camp Meetings, holiness gatherings, and revival campaigns became formatted and routinized: nightly meetings, demotic preaching and singing, altar calls, and "anxious benches." To this was later added mass publicity, showmanship, and most important of all, business acumen. George Thomas goes so far as to say that nineteenth-century revivalism was isomorphic with the rise of early forms of modernity.[11]

---

7. Edwards, *Religious Affections*.

8. Butler, *Awash in a Sea of Faith*; see also Hatch, *The Democratization of American Christianity*.

9 See Bellah, "Civil Religion in America," 169.

10. Quoted in Seel, "Modernity and Evangelicals: American Evangelicalism as a Global Case Study," 293.

11. Ibid., 293.

The early revivals, then, contributed to the advancement of modernity because they provided a value matrix conducive to the ascetic Protestantism of early capitalism. The enthusiasm, freedom, individualism, and moral values of the revivals entered the mainstream of American society: revivals helped reinforce the work ethic and the expressivism so dear to the heart of nineteenth-century America. They also provided a legitimate context for public emotion, which, in time, became transferred to the secular contexts of athletics and politics. Vestiges of early revivalism remain in American religious life today, in the legacy of sacred songs, vernacular preaching, special conventions, and special visiting speakers. The long-term and lasting effects of the revivals, however, have not been the continuation of an evangelical Camp Meeting tradition, but the establishment of numerous denominations and established sects, the contribution to civic life through the building of hospitals and universities, and the provision through education and self-help of a ladder of social mobility from the working class to the middle class.

The thesis that classic revivalism was both a contributor to the modernizing process and in turn adapted to the modernizing process seems less contentious if we contrast these revivals with the millennialism of early charismatic religion. Pentecostals were convinced that the end of the world was imminent, whereas a proper modern confidence characterized the great revivals—of Wesley, Whitfield, Edwards, and Finney. Certainly these founding modern evangelists could see Lessing's ditch as an obstacle in their path, but they were convinced that they could jump across it and ride on into a hopeful future. For them there was hope in the future, for there was to be a future. In short, modernity was a challenge, but not a catastrophe that heralded the end of time, as it did for Pentecostals.

It is interesting to compare the optimism of the late eighteenth century-/early nineteenth-century American revivals with the outbreak of Irvingism in London in the 1820s. We can properly see Irving as the "morning star" of Pentecostalism,[12] and he is certainly the most interesting precursor of twentieth-century charismatic Christianity. For our purposes in this chapter what is interesting about Irving is not the outbreak of tongues in Regent Square in October 1830, nor even the establishment of Twelve Apostles in the wake of his ministry: what is striking is that Irving, the Albury Circle of which he was a part, and their prophetic journal, *The Morning Watch,* were all convinced that the French Revolution signaled not only the end of an age, but the end of time. Irving believed that modernity was essentially

12. See Allen, *The Unfailing Stream*, chap. 6.

evil and was to be resisted: the role of the saints was to endure the coming crisis until the eagerly awaited, and soon to be expected, rapture.

Irving, unlike Edwards and Wesley, was deeply romantic. Attached to Coleridge and an upholder of feudal traditions, Irving had no place in his worldview for the future. The only future for modern culture was its eventual destruction. The immediate future of the church was to be snatched from the world like a brand from the burning coals.[13]

The American counterpart to this eschatology of disaster began in New York State in the 1820s with the Church of the Latter Day Saints (they too were tongue-speakers in the early days) and it continued with William Miller in the 1830s, despite the failure of Miller's predictions; modern day millennialism entered the American bloodstream like a foreign body opposed to the health and progress of the cultural organism. We not only think of the Christadelphians, Seventh Day Adventists, and Jehovah's Witnesses, but also of an abiding fascination with the "final things" by the ever-growing evangelical movements of the 1860s onwards. Consequently, the optimism of the First and Second Great Awakenings, of early American revivalism, was dampened by pessimistic rumblings fuelled by the many holiness movements that emerged from the Camp Meetings and disaffected Methodism. In time, America was to become the homeland of modern millennialism under the enormous influence of Schofield's theories of dispensations outlined in the Bible that bears his name and which was first published in 1909.[14]

PENTECOSTALISM AS TWENTIETH-CENTURY REVIVALISM

There are a number of reasons why Pentecostalism can be seen as antimodern in contradistinction to the modernizing tendencies of the early revivals. First, from the early days of Charles Parham at Kansas in the 1890s and Pastor Seymour in Azusa Street in Los Angeles from the first decade of the twentieth century, the manifestations of tongues, prophecy, exorcisms, and so on, led to almost universal condemnation by what Irving used to mockingly call "the religious world." The jerks and barks of Cane Ridge

13. See Walker, *Restoring the Kingdom*, chap. 11.

14. It is not without irony that Schofield learned his millennial theories from the writings of John Nelson Darby, one of the founders of the Brethren Movement, which, through its own prophetic conferences at Powerscourt in Ireland, were feeding off the same adventist theories as Irving and the Morning Watch. Mark Patterson, a doctoral student at King's College, London, thinks that it might be established that Darby's dispensationalism actually led back to the Albury group and possibly Irving himself.

were outlandish enough for many mainline Christians, but claims that the charismata of the New Testament had been restored to the modern world of science and steam trains seemed preposterous.

Second, the fact that such "signs and wonders" was appearing among black and white "uneducated" people was considered to be evidence of their lack of plausibility. The fact that early Pentecostalism was a religion of the dispossessed has been exaggerated,[15] but it is true that the majority of the early Pentecostals were working class. For Marxists, as for Anderson years later, Pentecostal experience was an example of "false consciousness":[16] economically deprived, working men and women were turning their backs on the promise of progress through revolutionary struggle and were being hoodwinked by immediate emotional satisfaction on the one hand (the Baptism of the Spirit) and a false earthly utopia on the other hand (the literal thousand year reign of Christ and the saints).

This leads us to the third and, in the light of our earlier section on revivals, the most important reason why Pentecostalism has been understood to be against modernity: the new revivalism was "birthed," to use charismatic nomenclature, in adventist hope; Pentecostal revival was itself seen by its members as a sign of the end-times. Following Parham, many Pentecostals initially believed that the tongues were the evangelistic means whereby the whole world could receive the good news of the gospel.[17] So early Pentecostalism adopted a conversionist *modus operandi* because it thought that the time was short, the fields already "white unto harvest," and that revival—spearheaded by the miracle of tongues—would sweep millions into the kingdom of God as the precursor to the end of the world.

This is part of the reason why the "revival fervor" predicated upon charismatic experience and millennial excitation did not automatically in the beginning lead to civic responsibility and the lure of modern progress: Pentecostals were certainly not "right-wing" in the early days, but rather apolitical and culturally denying.

The antagonistic attitude of the other churches to Pentecostals also facilitated the Pentecostal rejection of both the established churches and

15. In Britain, for example, leadership initially came from the upper class of Reverend Alexander Boddy in Sunderland. The so-called "Cambridge Seven," which included Cecil Polhill, were from aristocratic backgrounds. Polhill, it could be argued, helped bankroll the Pentecostal movement and certainly kept Boddy's influential journal, *Confidence*, alive.

16. Robert M. Anderson, *Vision of the Disinherited.*

17. There as a confusion among Pentecostals between the *glossolalia* of Paul in Corinthians (1 Cor 12:13–14)—the normative experience of Pentecostal tongues—with the xenoglossy of Acts 2 when, according to Luke, people in Jerusalem could hear the disciples speak in their own natural languages.

the secular world. In this respect at least, when coupled with adventist fervor, classical Pentecostalism was, unlike the earlier revivals, initially antimodern. However, like those revivals, Pentecostalism, over time, became at the very least an unwitting symbolic carrier of modernity, as well as falling prey to the secularizing tendencies of the modern world. Its modernizing tendencies, however, vary between classical and neo-Pentecostalism on the one hand and between the First and Third Worlds on the other hand. Before we proceed to demonstrate this, there is one obvious, and much cited, objection to the claim that charismatic religion is thoroughly modern. This objection is to insist that Pentecostalism is, on the contrary, thoroughly fundamentalist and thus anti-modernist. I believe, at best, that this argument is a red herring; but because of its plausible appeal and widespread acceptance I will deal with it now in the form of an excursus.

PENTECOSTALISM AS FUNDAMENTALISM

Many of the early Pentecostals were pleased to boast of their fundamentalist allegiance. Official support was widespread for the *Fundamentals* published between 1912 and 1916 by leading conservatives from the Princeton School of Theology and their allies. Words like "inerrant" and "fundamentalist" appeared in many Pentecostal confessions of faith. In Great Britain, only a few years ago, the magazine of the Elim Church bore the legend on its front page that it was "Pentecostal, Evangelical, Fundamental."

There are, however, a number of problems in identifying Pentecostals with fundamentalists. The most obvious one is to show that the second generation of Pentecostals, both renewalists and independents, are not wedded to a fundamentalist epistemology. This is clearly so for many Anglican and Catholic renewalists, but we can also say it is the case for "new church" leaders like Roger Forster of Ichthus and Gerald Coates of Pioneer.[18] Furthermore, it is also not unreasonable to say that the recent and brief history of the Toronto Blessing demonstrates that biblical fidelity is not paramount for the new generation of charismatics; it is difficult to see how, for example, one could ground the Toronto Blessing in biblical narratives or scriptural proof texts.[19]

It might seem that this argument is sleight of hand, as neo-Pentecostals are only distant cousins to their brethren. This objection is epistemologically

18. See Coates, *Divided We Stand.*

19. In one of the most innovative and intelligent defenses of the Toronto experience, Patrick Dixon prefers science and history, rather than biblical exposition, to make his case; see his *Signs of Revival.*

quite strong—neo-Pentecostals are not typically wedded to holiness traditions as classical Pentecostals are—but it is phenomenologically weak: modern charismatics and Pentecostals are much the same. Admittedly, renewalists are gentrified Pentecostalists, but they are not a different genus, and the sociological distinctions we might have made, even ten years ago, between classical and neo-Pentecostal, are now difficult to sustain in the light of new charismatic alignments and the syncretistic tendencies of late Pentecostalism.[20] These days classical Pentecostals feed off the so-called independent or "new churches" that feed off renewalists, who in turn feed off classical Pentecostals. If we were to visit Kensington Temple in London, for example, we might discover that it is really Elim Pentecostal, but it is also awash in the methodologies of John Wimber and Rodney Howard Browne, Morris Cerullo, and the indomitable style of Colin Dye. Despite its virtually white leadership, Kensington Temple also reflects the earlier Camp Meeting style of its large Afro-Caribbean membership.

Alternatively, we can visit Saint Andrew's, Chorleywood, and be introduced to Anglican renewals, with its Wimber clinics, Toronto swooning, and whiffs of Pentecostal holiness prophecy via visits from some of the Kansas City Prophets (who themselves hark back to the healing revivals of North America in the 1940s under the controversial William Branham).

But if we were to accept the sleight of hand argument we would still have to contend with Don Dayton's revisionist history of American classical Pentecostalism in which he contends that Pentecostalism is certainly pietist and rooted in the holiness traditions, but it is only incidentally fundamentalist.[21] Fundamentalism was in the air before Pentecostalism came into being. To assert our evangelical legitimacy in the early part of the twentieth century we would have had to sport our fundamentalist credentials. And Pentecostals craved legitimacy among their evangelical peers, even if they were indifferent to everyone else. Fundamentalism, in other words, acted as a useful legitimation for a movement that wanted to demonstrate that it was faithful to New Testament Christianity.

Dayton's revisionism is particularly compelling if we look at the more extreme developments of Pentecostalism, for charismatic Christianity has not always been tied to orthodox belief, despite the fundamentalist label. Oneness Pentecostalism, for example, which developed soon after the revivals of Azusa Street in Los Angeles, was heretical in its understanding of God

20. Class distinctions still count. Renewalists are still primarily middle class, whereas Pentecostals are still primarily working class and lower-middle class.

21. Dayton, *Theological Roots of Pentecostalism*.

and refused to use the Trinitarian formula for baptism.[22] Again, if we turn to the Christology of William Branham in the 1940s, we find something more akin to Arianism than the orthodoxy of the Nicene-Constantinopolitan Creed.[23] And it is clear that if Charles Hodge of Princeton, or B. B. Warfield, the intellectual architects of fundamentalism, were to investigate the hermeneutics of say Kenneth Hagin and Kenneth Copeland of the Word of Faith movement, they would turn in their graves.[24] Indeed, in many ways the Pentecostal revivals by their very volatile nature have been a challenge to the scholastic rationalism of the fundamentalist movement. Pentecostals have certainly been Bible-lovers, but they have also been moved by the Spirit, spoken prophetic words, and received new revelations.[25]

Ironically, if we were to take issue with Dayton and see (to use a premodern analogy) Pentecostalism as essentially rather than accidentally fundamentalist, then this would actually strengthen our argument that Pentecostalism is modern. This is so because fundamentalism, despite its resistance to modern thought, is itself modernist. The Princeton theologians in the last quarter of the nineteenth century were convinced that the new higher criticism that was emerging from the liberal Protestant theology of Ritschl and Harnack, *et al.*, when coupled with the evolutionary theories of Charles Darwin, posed serious threats to the truth claims of historic Christianity. In particular, it was felt that redactive criticism and the like called into question the reliability of the biblical record.

In this respect, fundamentalism was part of the religious resistance movement to modernism at the end of the nineteenth century. Rome resisted through Vatican I and the papal dogmas, Protestantism through fundamentalism. Fundamentalism, however, unlike Vatican I, was thoroughly modern in method and intent. Nineteenth-century philosophers and scientists were looking for rational foundations of reality, so some conservative theologians felt it wise to do the same as part of an apologetically aimed strategy against modernism. The Princeton School alighted on a foundation

22. This was not, as is often thought, because they were anti-Trinitarian, but because they were Sabellian and hence denied the unique and distinct persons of the Godhead in favor of a threefold modalistic presentation of a monistic God.

23. Branham not only had trouble with defining Jesus as truly God, but he also was tainted, in the eyes of many Pentecostals, because of his association with Oneness theology.

24. See Smail, Walker and Wright, "Revelation Knowledge and Knowledge of Revelation: The Faith Movement and the Question of Heresy," 57–77.

25. Curiously, modernist Harvey Cox has come to see Pentecostalism in a more positive light precisely because of its experiential nature; see his *Fire from Heaven*. I think Cox is projecting twentieth-century self-expressionism into what I think will be an altogether different future. See my conclusion in this chapter.

that they believed would rationally shore-up the truth claims of Christianity.[26] To paraphrase a well-known fundamentalist book: Christianity is true because the Bible tells us so, and the Bible can be trusted, so the argument went, because God Who is Truth has revealed Himself as truth in the sacred text. The Bible by virtue of this fact is *ipso facto* both the vehicle and the locus of truth.

The sting-in-the-tail for what was an essentially rational epistemology raised to the status of religious dogma is that, as the Bible, as God's book, is true, it can never contradict itself: the Bible is no longer merely "infallible," to use a well-seasoned Reformation word, but it is also "inerrant." In practice, however, the notion of inerrancy is problematic because this new foundation of truth (unknown in dogmatic form by the early church fathers or the Reformers) had to deal with the tricky problem of textual contradictions, which appear to be legion. Furthermore, many, but not all, of the early fundamentalists recast the first two chapters of the book of Genesis as scientific accounts of the creation of the world so that the Bible was now set up in opposition to biological science, as well as to German Protestant theology.

The high tide of fundamentalist scholarship passed with the First World War where in many evangelical and Pentecostal circles it became ensnared with dispensationalist theories of prophecy. It also became increasingly sectarian and, in time, even anti-intellectual. After the debacle of the Scopes Monkey Trial in America in 1925, fundamentalism became an object of ridicule in most theological circles and, despite its resurgence in the 1980s through tele-evangelism, is now in retreat in many American evangelical seminaries.[27]

This does not alter the fact that early fundamentalism was a rational, not to say modern(ist), attempt to underpin the truth of the Bible by a tendentious theory of the inspiration of Scripture. Nevertheless, fundamentalism, by virtue of its biblicism, succeeded in constraining and controlling Pentecostal theology and practice: it kept the new enthusiasm within the evangelical fold and curbed its volatile excesses by an insistence on biblical fidelity.

THE MODERN TENDENCIES OF NORMATIVE CLASSICAL PENTECOSTALISM

If we grant that classical Pentecostalism was anti-modern in its revivalistic days, we do so simply because it was adventist and quite literally "other

26. Noll, *The Princeton Theology 1812–1921*.

27. Notably Fuller Theological Seminary in California.

worldly." Over time, however, as the routinization of charisma set in, Pentecostalism trod the well-worn path of American nineteenth-century urban
missions with all their pragmatic tendencies and replete with the latest
modern technologies. On the one hand, Pentecostals, unlike Methodists
and Anglicans, have not adopted a modern scriptural hermeneutic nor
acceded to Enlightenment doctrines of progress and critical rationality.
On the other hand, Pentecostals have been open to modern technologies,
advertising, and management techniques. Their commitment to demotic
hymnody—no doubt in order to subvert popular culture—has meant in
effect that they have been far more at home with mass media and consumer
culture than many of their mainline counterparts.

Furthermore, the fact that the Pentecostals of the twentieth century
have not been perceived to have joined the societal mainstream as obviously
as Methodists did in the nineteenth century is partially a question of their
anti-worldly ideology, but also partly a question of a slower assimilation of
modern values. Pentecostals, in the First World at least, have been reluctant
modernizers and have become thoroughly modern by a slow process of
cultural osmosis, rather than through ideological acceptance of the modern
world. In Great Britain, for example, before the First World War, Bible Colleges were originally eschewed as unnecessary for Spirit-filled Christians.
By the 1920s, however, the Elim Pentecostal Church has established a Bible
College, therefore ensuring the professionalization of its pastors and hence
contributing to the gradual modernization of the church. This process has
taken some forty years to come to fruition. Today, the Elim Bible College
has become Regent's Theological College complete with a director for studies with an earned Ph.D., an undergraduate BA, and a new MA course. The
Assemblies of God College at Mattersey Hall in the North East of England
has a similar story to tell.

It is David Martin's recent studies, however, that provide the most
convincing evidence of the modernizing tendencies of Pentecostalism,[28]
for if Pentecostals have been a little slow off the mark in diving into the
modern stream in Europe and North America, the opposite can be said of
South America: Pentecostalism is the fastest growing Christian religion in
the Third World, and in some Central and South American countries Pentecostals already number some forty million, which is approximately one in
ten of the population.

To be a Pentecostal in South America is to be modern in capitalist
guise. Pentecostal leaders are not only Spirit-led, but are also entrepreneurs
and small businessmen. "The Evangelical poor," on the other hand, says

28. Martin, *Tongues of Fire.*

Martin, "have adopted a discipline of life: no drinks or drugs, no fiesta, but only hard work, careful budgeting, honesty, family integrity, and discipline in the home. According to social workers, their children may well perform above average at school."[29] Despite the neo-Marxist rhetoric of Catholic Liberation Theology, Catholicism has not been a successful agency of modernity in South America. This is not just because Marxism is losing out all over the world to free enterprise, but because in South America Marxist Catholics are clearly outnumbered by the many traditional Catholics who support the feudal structures of the traditional landowners. Pentecostals, by contrast, are for free expression, free enterprise, democracy, hard work, individualism, and the Holy Spirit. They are thoroughly modern, but with "signs following."

At the very least, upholders of the view that Pentecostalism is anti-modern will have to revise, in the light of the empirical evidence, their thesis to say that Pentecostalism is reluctantly modern in the First World of advanced industrial societies, but in the Third World appears to be at least as significant a modernizing agency as Methodism was in Britain and North America in the eighteenth and nineteenth centuries.

Classical Pentecostalism since Azusa Street has always been an amalgam of ancient and modern—"a traditional service in the modern manner," as the advertising slogan goes. A feature of my own studies among the so-called "house churches" or "new churches," that are hybrids of classical and neo-Pentecostalism, is that rational and economic goals are often set and adhered to in a sensible manner, but these would often be buttressed by charismatic reinforcements. Bryn Jones of Covenant Ministries, for example, offered a perfectly rational argument as to why he had pioneered new churches along the West Coast of Scotland, England, and Wales, but also offered the insight that "we had a prophecy about that."[30] Gerald Coates of Pioneer is a very successful Christian leader in Britain, well organized, hi-tech, pragmatic, and modern, but he also takes notice of dreams, prophecies, and "promptings."[31]

(How many secular business agencies, we wonder, take advantage of New Age methodologies to improve their performance indicators?[32] Such

29. Martin, "Latin America Pentecost."

30. Interview at Church House, Bradford, with Bryn Jones on June 28, 1989.

31. In interview with Gerald Coates, at Church House, Esher, he told me of a woman's dream about a new direction in his life where he began to dress differently and change his hair style. While dashing off to the airport to meet an important contact he suddenly realized his blazer and new haircut were just as in her dream.

32. *The Sunday Times* reported on September 22, 1996 in its financial section that the European Bank had programmed astrological configurations as part of its financial

activities are surely typical of late- or post-modernity rather than indices of anti-modern sentiment.)

To suggest that classical Pentecostalism is at the least reluctantly modern and at the most thoroughly modern is not so much to point to its use of modern tunes, new technologies, and secular business techniques—though these are not without significance—but to register the fact that Pentecostalism has ministered to the poor and the disinherited in a culturally appropriate manner and in so doing has initiated them into the working processes and value systems of modernity. In short, Pentecostalism for the working classes has been a continuation of the ascetic Protestantism of Puritanism and the revivals of the Great Awakenings. It has provided modest but real social mobility for working class families in Europe and North America and a fast-track modernizing program for many in the Third World. Even if we want to apply a Marxist perspective to the phenomenon of Pentecostalism (which we mentioned earlier) and criticize it in terms of religious opium and "false consciousness," this is not to deny its modernizing tendencies, but rather to discredit its revolutionary potential.

FROM CLASSICAL PENTECOSTALISM TO CHARISMATIC CHRISTIANITY

It is surely no coincidence that when Pentecostalism was transformed from its working-class style to its middle-class one, we had moved from early to late-modernity: an era that with the advent of consumerism in the 1950s saw the demise of ascetic individualism and the rise of hedonistic individualism.[33] When in the 1960s middle class members of mainline churches claimed the "baptism in the Spirit" as their own, classical Pentecostalism found itself with what was initially perceived to be a rival in the revivalist stakes.[34] This new, or neo-Pentecostalism, was not only different in terms of social status and organization, but also in tone.

We noticed it first in the name used to tag the new enthusiasm. The specialist and non-threatening adjective "charismatic" replaced the proper noun Pentecostal. This was affixed to the altogether more restrained and non-evangelistic badge of belonging known as "renewal." To be in the charismatic renewal was to be a still committed Anglican or Catholic, Baptist or Presbyterian. A renewalist was for praise and sanctity, a devotee of religious experience, but he or she was not a revivalist. Those in the renewal found

forecasting.

33. See Bell, *The Cultural Contradictions of Capitalism.*

34. See Richards, *Pentecost is Dynamite.*

themselves in ever larger circles, and in increasingly successful ventures, but they moved together, with each other: they did not evangelize the un-churched in any systematic way as the Pentecostalists had done in the flush of the revivals.

Gradually, as the renewal grew tendentious, Pentecostal doctrines were dropped, such as the two-stage experience of conversion and Spirit baptism (which was inherited in part from the holiness days of belief in the "second blessing" of sanctification). Charismatics during the late 1960s underwent what I earlier called the "process of gentrification": they sported bishops and canons from the Church of England among their number, nuns and priests from Rome, and even a cardinal from Belgium. Theological literature of a scholarly fashion flowed from the pens of charismatic apologists.[35] They also attracted pop stars in their orbit, such as Sir Cliff Richard and even for a time captured Bob Dylan, who gravitated for a season to a Vineyard church in California.

To be a charismatic, then, was phenomenologically identical to being a Pentecostal, but culturally redefined by class, taste, and the late-modern preoccupation with therapy and self-fulfillment. Chorus singing, clapping, and dancing were incorporated into the new enthusiasm, but charismatics preferred their own tunes and songs—more middle of the road rock and modern anthem than Redemption Hymnal and Moody and Sankey.[36] They maintained interest in physical healings, but moved deeper into a realm of inner healings. People in the renewal were in touch with themselves as well as with God. As the Hobbesian and hedonistic individual replaced ascetic individualism in the larger culture, so the renewal reflected these changes in its style of worship and experientially driven theology. If Pentecostals in the First World were reluctantly modern in their early days, renewalists were thoroughly modern from the start.

The 1960s was a revolution of experience—sexual and chemical—and in some quarters this revolution was seen as counter-cultural. The char-ismatic movement in the churches reflected the idealism, the heightened

---

35. Most notably from Roman Catholics; see Gelpi, SJ, *Pentecostalism*.

36. In Martyn Percy's unpublished paper, "Sweet Rapture: Subliminal Eroticism in Contemporary Charismatic Worship," he demonstrates that by the time of Wimber (1980s) the jolly refrains of classical Pentecostalism, such as "In my heart there rings a melody," or "Since Jesus came into my heart" had been replaced by romantic and intimate songs. This theme continues to the present time. For example:

> I will be yours, you will be mine
> Together in eternity
> Our hearts of love will be entwined
> Together in eternity, forever in eternity.

Brian Doerkse, Song Book, *Isn't He/Eternity: Intimate Songs of Praise and Worship.*

experience, and the hedonism of this counter-culture, even though ideo-logically they were opposed to each other. Within a few years, the renewal also folded back into classical Pentecostalism. Songs, ministries, and styles began to cross over the classical/neo-Pentecostal divide. Oral Roberts, for example, during his successful reign as a televangelist from the late 1970s to the mid-1980s, became a Methodist. Like those other Pentecostalists, Jimmy and Tammy Bakker (unlike Jimmy Swaggert), he dropped the stri-dent fundamentalism and evangelist fervor of his earlier days in favor of a folksy, cozy approach.

Televangelism itself reflected the narcissistic streak of American hedonism. Christianity was repackaged so that increasingly there was little emphasis on asceticism—what you could do for God—towards self-gratification—what God could do for you. Steve Bruce superbly captures this mood change. The broad road is the pursuit of self-fulfillment, self-satisfaction, and self-esteem. The "power of positive thinking," roundly criticized by conservative Protestants for its "this worldly" orientation when it was presented by Norman Vincent Peale in the 1950s, now informs most religious television. This is less of a change for Robert Schuller (like Peale, a Reformed Church minister and a man who has never claimed to be a fun-damentalist) than it is for Oral Roberts, Jim Bakker, or Kenneth Copeland, "but the ghastly punning title of Schuller's *The Be Happy Attitudes* will stand as a sign of the orientation of most televangelism."[37]

It was not only televangelists who got in this groove. Writing in the 1980s, James Davidson Hunter demonstrated that evangelicals generally and charismatics in particular were borrowing heavily from secular thera-peutic models and looking for life-enhancing satisfaction. Here are some of the typical titles Hunter selected from the shelves of Christian bookstores:

- *Transformed Temperaments*
- *Defeating Despair and Depression*
- *God's Key to Health and Happiness*
- *Feeling Good about Feeling Bad*
- *How to Become a Happy Christian*
- *How to Become Your Own Best Self*[38]

The influence of the therapeutic must not go unnoticed.

37. Bruce, *Pray TV*, 237.
38. Hunter, *American Evangelicalism*.

NEO-PENTECOSTALS, INDEPENDENT, AND CHARISMATIC REALIGNMENTS IN LATE MODERNITY[39]

If by neo-Pentecostalism we mean specifically the charismatic renewal movement in the mainline denominations, then I think we have to say that it existed in a pure form for only a very short time—say, from 1965 to 1980. The 1970s was the decade of its greatest influence when barely a major denomination had not been flooded with the new songs, the excitement, and the renewal of religious commitment. Looking back, it was the Kansas City Conference of 1977 that stands out as the Woodstock of charismatic ecumenical experience. At Kansas City the renewal seemed at its most joyous and least strident. Final and formal worldwide recognition for the renewal came, however, in 1980 at Bossey, Switzerland, when the World Council of Churches held its one and only consultation on the movement.[40] By the time I wrote "A new light for the churches" on the Agenda page of *The Guardian* on November 24, 1980, the renewal was already waning.

Now, over fifteen years later, I think that although the renewal was analytically distinct from classical Pentecostalism—not least because it was middle class and non-denominational—I now believe that it was never a totally distinct phenomenon; it was never exclusively middle class or totally free from sectarianism.[41] Neither did it totally free itself from Pentecostal theology and practices. Father Peter Hocken has demonstrated that a number of independent movements, classical streams, and new renewal groups not only overlapped but intertwined in Great Britain at least from the 1960s.[42] Men from classical Pentecostal backgrounds, such as David Du Plessis from the Assemblies of God and Cecil Cousens from the Apostolic Church, had considerable influence on the theology and belief systems of the burgeoning renewal. Maverick groups, such as the North American healing movement of the 1940s and the "Latter Rain" movement of Canada in the 1950s, provided numerous personnel who found their way into the renewal in one way or another.

From the late 1970s until the present time, what we have seen since the heyday of the renewal is the emergence of numerous independent

---

39. By late-modernity I am signaling consumer capitalism, rather than affirming a Marxist theory of capitalist development.

40. I was at the consultation representing the British Council of Churches with Professor James Dunn and the Reverend Michael Harper.

41. See my concept of the "sectarian implant" in "Harmful Religion," *Leading Light*, 5–7.

42. Hocken, *Streams of Renewal.*

ministries, maverick organizations, new networks of churches, and para-church groups. These new movements did not destroy the renewal movement, but they did rival it, then penetrate it, and eventually alter its nature. In the 1980s, for example, by far the most significant charismatic growth in Great Britain came from the so-called restorationist house churches. These were certainly not renewalist for they taught a radical separationist doctrine and condemned the historical churches as moribund. With their commitment to apostolic and prophetic leadership, and their "shepherding" or discipleship doctrines, these independent churches were in effect a threat, both to the renewal and to classical Pentecostalism. Restorationism was not a new version of classical Pentecostalism as I had mistakenly thought in 1985: it was a syncretistic amalgam of classical, renewalist, and independent streams.[43]

Restorationists, therefore, were like renewalists in terms of their middle-class affiliation and their emphasis on experience and new songs. They were also similar to classical Pentecostalists in two respects: first, they were as enthusiastic as Pentecostalists, and second, they drifted into enclaves that were sociologically sectarian in character. That is, in many ways, they were a throwback to Irving and the Catholic Apostolic Church (CAC) of the 1830s.[44] Like the CAC, restorationists initially thought that their movement in itself heralded the end of time. In this sense, they were millennialist in orientation, as were both Irving and early Pentecostalists; however, restorationists were optimistic about the future and were committed to the establishment of a powerful church before the thousand year reign of Christ.[45] This "eschatology of victory" led them to be optimistic about the future, and by the early 1980s their business acumen and organizational flair lent them a thoroughly modern, if not progressive, air.

By the mid-1980s, however, strange things began to happen. As Bryan Wilson put it to me at All Souls, Oxford, during one of my regular visits there, religious changes were taking place at a bewildering pace in the late twentieth century.[46] This speeding-up process meant that Christian religious formations were coming and going, starting and stopping, with the speed we associate with new religious movements. Restorationism in a ten-year period underwent the kind of growth, changes, splits, and realignments that took Elim and the Assemblies of God sixty years to undergo.

43. See Walker, *Restoring the Kingdom*.

44. Not at least in their espousal of apostles and prophets.

45. It was envisaged that powerful Christian communities and businesses would flourish.

46. Walker, *Restoring the Kingdom*, 333.

With the advent of niche marketing, video and audio tape sales, rapid movement from country to country, and the beginning of information technology, charismatic Christianity went into overdrive in the late 1980s. The Evangelical Alliance persuaded most of the house churches, now being called "new churches," to join them. The family oriented Spring Harvest celebrations became a catch-all charismatic supermarket where classical Pentecostals, renewalists, independents, and non-charismatic evangelicals came together. In 1993 alone some 80,000 people attended Spring Harvest.

Meanwhile, a Californian charismatic by the name of John Wimber made considerable impact in Britain from 1994 onwards. Initially popular with Anglican renewalists through his connection with the late Canon David Watson, Wimber soon appealed to the new churches too. Terry Virgo, restorationist apostle of New Frontiers in Hove, became a close friend. Wimber majored in spectacular "slayings in the Spirit," and whenever he went there was, as Nigel Wright put it, the smell of cordite.[47] Wimber was controlling, but Californian in style, not strident in the Bible-belt tradition.[48] Wimber prefigured what was to come in the 1990s in the form of Benny Hinn's spectacular ministry and the mayhem of the Toronto Blessing.[49]

Following Wimber's success many of the restorationists "loosened up" and began to work with people that they had earlier eschewed. Gerald Coates, for example, apostolic leader of Pioneer in Cobham, Surrey, went on to become a national church leader working with the ecumenical Youth with a Mission (YWAM) and Roger Foster of Ichthus in South London to establish the "Marches for Jesus" as a worldwide phenomenon by 1994.

If this were not enough, the classical Pentecostals began to make a comeback. Elim and Assemblies of God recovered from the raiding parties made on their fellowships by restorationists. Kensington City Temple in London (Elim) probably has the largest church membership in Great Britain, and their leading pastor, Colin Dye, now has one of the highest profiles of any charismatic leader in England.

In the 1990s, however, British Pentecostals appear virtually indistinguishable from renewalists and independent charismatics in terms of hymnody and practices. All these groups, regardless of social class or denominational affiliation, crossover in terms of their songs, video ministries, paperback tales of the miraculous, favorite gurus, and so on. They are all

---

47. A phase he frequently used in a lecture series on the charismatic movement organized by the C. S. Lewis Centre in the early 1990s entitled "The Love of Power and the Power of Love."

48. See Percy, *Words, Wonders and Power.*

49. For a less than enthusiastic view see Porter and Richter, *The Toronto Blessing—Or is It?*; see also Roberts, *The Toronto Blessing.*

open to penetration from overseas ministries: Kenneth Copeland, John Wimber, Morris Cerullo, Derek Prince from America; Rodney Howard Browne and German evangelist Reinhart Bonnke from South Africa; and Bill Subritzky and John Smith from New Zealand. All have been blown over by the Toronto Blessing.[50]

The last two decades have seen charismatics riding a roller coaster of excitement that to the sober-minded outsider seems almost, at times, like frenzy. There seem to have been more demons, more outlandish experiences, a greater thirst for new things, than classical Pentecostalism ever knew. We cannot put this down to millennialism, even though a literal millennium approaches and may yet make its impact in terms of adventist excitation; but neither can we talk of revivalism as being the cause of such excitement in the sense of church growth resulting from evangelization. Instead, charismatic growth has resulted primarily through recycling Christians from one denomination to another or renewing pockets of established denominations and sects.

Perhaps we cannot altogether account for these directional changes (given their multi-casual nature), but we can usefully attempt to characterize them. The argument of this chapter, after all, has been that the charismatic movement has followed the same contours of secular modernity from its early to its late phase: it has in fact been for the spirit of the age, rather than against it. It has perhaps, in David Harvey's understanding of late-capitalism, capitulated to the consumer and experiential hedonism of late-modernity and become commodified and corrupted.[51] It has arrived, at the dawn of the new millennium, as no longer reluctantly or thoroughly modern but ultra- or hyper-modern.

The hyper-modern status of the charismatic movement is highlighted by the so-called "Toronto Blessing" from 1994 to the present time. Whether the laughing experience has come in Toronto fashion, complete with growls and jerks, or in the Rodney Howard Browne guise—no animal noises but gales of uncontrollable laughter—Toronto has become a watershed in charismatic experience. Toronto has not yet been shown to be the prelude to a kind of nineteenth-century style religious awakening like Finney in America or a twentieth-century style revival like Roberts in Wales. So what has it been? Sociologically, at least, it seems clear that it has been a "craze."[52]

---

50. This probably does not hold for the remnant of British Catholic renewalists. The rise of the Evangelical Alliance and the numerous independent Protestant groups has not been conducive to Catholic sentiments.

51. Harvey, *The Condition of Postmodernity*.

52. John Moore adopted this category from Smelser's typology of changing collective behavior to investigate Catholic renewal in the 1960s; see his "The Catholic Pentecostal

Toronto is phenomenologically similar to some of the lesser known aspects of Wesley's and Edwards' revivals and some of the excesses more usually associated with the New Age human potential movement. On the other hand, it has been typical of classical Pentecostalism: falling like nine-pins, guffawing and gasping, uncontrollable crying and laughing are not unknown in the older revivals, but they were untypical or epiphenomenal. Powerful preaching, the gifts of the Spirit, chorus singing, and conversions were their hallmarks. Therefore, we could certainly say that contemporary charismatics have been happy to engage with what we might call thauma-turgical and theanthropic therapy. This is reflected in the emphasis by Toronto enthusiasts on God visiting his people, blessing them, playing with them, releasing them, and refreshing them.

Indeed, for many touched by Toronto, it has been impossible to interpret it with the theological tools at hand. In a way, Toronto has been an abyss of primordial experience—a disintegration of liturgical and biblical norms. Many who looked into the abyss have abandoned charismatic affiliations altogether. Pete Fenwick, for example, respected elder statesman from the Sheffield House Church, sees Toronto as Pentecostalism gone mad. Others, such as Clifford Hill, sociologist and prophet, see the whole thing as an omen of disaster. Former enthusiasts for Toronto, such as Holy Trinity Brompton, are now concentrating on *Alpha* courses as God's direction for the future.[53] John Wimber has disowned Toronto and excommunicated John Arnott, pastor of the Toronto Vineyard Church. Some people, somewhere, are still falling over, giggling, and feeling blessed, but the momentum of the movement is passing. The craze, like modernity, seems to be fading with a final gasp.[54]

But in many ways we may want to see Toronto as the logical outcome of recent charismatic developments. Over the last ten years, charismatic Christianity has drunk deeply at the well of modern cultural forms: the "clinics" of John Wimber; the concern with inner healing; the endless in-house entertainment of conference, convention, and celebration—for all the world like a spiritual equivalent of the rave culture. No longer restrained by fundamentalist edicts, or the mainline theology of writers like Anglican

---

Movement," 6.

53. *Alpha* is a course of Christian initiation, not dissimilar to the early church cat-echumenate, but with the expectation that it will lead on to personal conversion and perhaps the baptism in the Spirit.

54. This seems to have led to two reactions; either waiting for the next big wave or revival, or realizing that Toronto is a bridge too far and retreating into a more "business as usual" (normative) Pentecostalism.

Tom Smail and Catholic Steve Clark,[55] charismatic Christianity increasingly appears fey and orphic.[56]

Therefore, when all is said and done, as we near the end of the twentieth century, the defining theologian of the charismatic movement will turn out not to be Jonathan Edwards, or Charles Hodge, or even Charles Parham: they were all too constrained within the bounds of historic orthodoxy. The theological father of the movement will turn out to be none other than the father of modern liberal theology, Friedrich Schleiermacher, who, in rebelling against German rationalism and classical theology, arrived at a religion of feeling and God-consciousness, which he managed to meld with the pietism of his Moravian background. Charismatic Christians have not formally followed Schleiermacher, for he is associated with liberal Protestantism, but they have unwittingly followed his direction because of their growing tendency to allow experience to become the touchstone of orthodoxy.[57] This touchstone is not a return to New Testament Christianity, as believed, but a thoroughly late-modern concern with the self and its satisfaction.

Pentecostalism rushed into the twentieth century like a hurricane at Azusa Street, Los Angeles, in 1906. Perhaps it finally blew itself out at Toronto Airport in 1994. Azusa Street acted as a beacon to enthusiasts from many countries: pastors and church leaders came to see the revival for themselves and through them the Pentecostal blessing was diffused and distributed throughout the world. Toronto has repeated history in this respect, but because of air travel and the internet the diffusion has been far quicker—perhaps too quick to have a lasting effect. Churches take time to build up and establish themselves, but Toronto may have been merely a new experience in a dying modern world that treasures novelty for its own sake and craves signs and wonders as its daily fare.[58]

---

55. See Smail, *The Giving Gift*; and also Clark, *Redeemer*.

56. This is one of the major themes of Harold Bloom's *The American Religion*.

57. Such a generalization probably does not hold across the board. I doubt if this is a fair assessment of Anglican Renewal Ministries, for example, nor the ecumenical movement associated with Father Michael Harper and The Sword and the Spirit communities. And although this trend can be seen in many new churches, it would be a distortion to say it is an accurate characterization of Ichthus communities and all those within the Pioneer network of churches.

58. Although Professor William Abraham of Southern Methodist University and Graham MacFarlane of London Bible College (both excellent scholars whose judgment I value) feel that Toronto, although a mixed blessing, has more to recommend it than I can see for the moment.

CONCLUSION

Neo-Pentecostalism has been more thoroughly modern than its classical counterpart, but also more open to the cultural obsessions of late-modernity. I believe that classical Pentecostalism has, on the whole, been modern in a positive sense, though more obviously so in South America and South Korea than in Europe and North America. At the very least, Pentecostalism throughout the world has not only provided meaning and succor to its adherents, but it has also equipped many of them with the values of ascetic Protestantism so useful to the modern enterprise and so essential for social mobility in a capitalist economy.

Conversely, with the possible exception of the early renewal movement, neo-Pentecostalism has overstressed self-experience and what Jung Ha Kim has called "supply-side spirituality."[59] But as modernity has waned and subsided, this concern with the self and commodity religion has run the risk of becoming an indulgence, if not a "sinking into decadence." Arguably, this decadence has infiltrated classical Pentecostalism, unleashing the narcissistic and irrational forces that were latently there but mostly kept under control.[60] But because of the pluralistic nature of late-modernity the inevitable syncretistic strands of the religion of experience have become increasingly volatile. Far from seeing Pentecostalism rushing into the new century with the force of the old, I believe that it will be buffeted by theological confusion and social fragmentation.

If we follow Zygmunt Bauman[61] instead of David Harvey and see the modern world, not as decaying, but as fading—in transition to postmodernity—we must ask whether charismatic Christianity is well equipped to survive in the future. Postmodernity not only eschews the metanarrative of rational discourse, but also distrusts the "lordship of the self" and inner experience. If the world emerges like Foucault's landscape, where reality is seen as a discursive achievement and the certainty of universal truths are denied, what will charismatic utterances mean? It mattered not in modernity if tongues were interpreted as babblings because they were seen to release or realize the self. But with the self "on hold" what will *glossolalia* come to signify? On the day of Pentecost, xenoglossy was seen as a

---

59. Supply-side spirituality like supply-side economics is a feature of an abundant or affluence ideology. "Demand-side spirituality" would be more concerned with the fight for justice and deliverance associated with the poor. See Kim, "Sources Outside of Europe," 63.

60. Nowhere is this more obvious, in my opinion, than in the recent fascination with demons. See my chapter "The Devil You Think You Know."

61. See, for example, his *Intimations of Postmodernity*.

reversal of Babel—a time when charismata as gifts from God indicated his presence. Real presence—any wager on transcendence—as George Steiner has shown,[62] is a problem in post-modern understanding. Given such a linguistic turn, therefore, will xenoglossy and *glossolalia*[63] be a return to a new Babel where tongues will be seen as meaningless noise—a sign of absence—of the *deus absconditus*?

We should, however, be careful not to confuse post-modernism as intellectual fashion with a genuine cultural shift to a postmodernity. "Perhaps," I wrote recently, "postmodernism is not the ideology of the future, of the Internet, mass culture, and cultural pluralism. Instead, it is the language of limbo; the go-between gossip of transition; the discourse of leave-taking, traveling from modernity to the as yet not yet."[64] If post-modernity turns out to be a new cultural era, we can expect that it will share as many continuities with the past as discontinuities; so there is no doubt that Pentecostalism will survive in the future. In the Third World, for some time to come, it will no doubt continue to be thoroughly modern. But in the post-industrial societies a different religiosity is likely to abound. It will be one that will not repudiate the past. Nor will future religion always want to see God do a "new thing," which late-modern charismatics have craved. A post-modern religion will certainly look for a "form of life" and a narrative of belonging, but it will not trust experience to be at the heart of things. It will be one that will open up to other living traditions. It will be one that will value story over feeling, narrative over experience, canon over text, and prophecy over tongues.

In fact, such a religion is happening right now under the nose of the charismatic movement. Like a phoenix from the ashes, the alternative liturgical movement is emerging from "Happy Clappy" Land, as the Reverend Nick Mercer calls it,[65] and merging with Celtic spirituality, Taize chants, Eastern Orthodoxy, Reformed theology, and other charismatic happenings. Such a syncretistic mix may or may not end up Christian, as the Nine O'Clock Service[66] forewarns, but then neither will it be modern anymore.

---

62. Steiner, *Real Presences*.

63. Notwithstanding my earlier distinction between tongues as natural languages and ecstatic utterances, they are both treated in the New Testament as post-Pentecostal experiences.

64. Walker, *Telling the Story*, 180.

65. Former vice-principal of London Bible College and now an Anglican priest in the liberal Catholic tradition.

66. Under the leadership of the Reverend Chris Brain, the Nine O'Clock Service moved from Wimber neo-Pentecostalism to Matthew Fox neo-Paganism. See Howard, *The Rise and Fall of the Nine O'Clock Service*.

5

The Theology of the Restoration of "House Churches"

(1984)

INTRODUCTION: THE HOUSE CHURCH MOVEMENT AS A CHARISMATIC PHENOMENON OUTSIDE THE MAINSTREAM CHURCHES

During the late 1970s, when the charismatic renewal was at its zenith in Great Britain, leading figures in the movement became increasingly aware of another strand of Pentecostalism, the house church movement. In 1979, the British Council of Churches, in association with the Fountain Trust, held a consultation with senior British churchmen to discuss the significance of the charismatic renewal.[1] The consultation included Michael Harper, David Watson and Tom Smail (who with Colin Urquhart were probably the best-known leaders of the renewal in Britain during the 1970s). It was Tom Smail who first introduced to many of the denominational leaders present the house church movement as a distinctive brand of neo-Pentecostalism.

---

1. The Fountain Trust was an independent organization that promoted renewal within the mainstream denominations; it was charismatic rather than revivalistic.

Since that time the Fountain Trust has collapsed, and the denominational version of charismatic renewal has entered decline. The house church movement, on the other hand, has become Britain's fastest rising religious phenomenon (as evidenced by BBC Radio 4's documentary on March 23, 1984). In 1979, even though Tom Smail made it quite clear that the new movement was sectarian in nature, a number of church leaders at the BCC consultation still tended to identify house churches with the charismatic renewal *per se*.

The belief that the house church movement seems to have risen to sudden prominence by clinging to the coat-tails of the renewal movement is an illusion. In reality, the so-called house churches have their roots outside mainstream Christianity; they are firmly planted in Protestant sectarianism. Although it is true that members of the new movement include disaffected renewal supporters, both the leadership and the theology are essentially sectarian. (This is not to belittle it in any way, or an attempt to downgrade its significance; it is merely an attempt to place it in its historical context.)

Almost nothing has been written about the new movement so far. The pioneer work is the MA dissertation of Joyce Thurman, which is now published under the title *New Wineskins*.

By drawing on her work augmented by my own research (over the past two years), we can safely draw the following conclusions concerning the nature and form of the house churches. First, it must emphatically be said that the phrase "house church movement" is a hopeless misnomer. While it is true that both the idea and reality of the church in the house plays an important part in the new movement, what has really emerged are not house churches, but simply churches. Secondly, the notion of the house church movement masks the fact that there are in reality different movements. Of these, the South Chard group and Pastor North's churches are perhaps the most important historically, but if they are not yet a spent force, they have certainly been overshadowed by two other groups. The first of these are the "restoration" churches, which are a group of churches linked together not only by common ideology, but by personal commitment under a rubric of "apostolic" teams. These churches do not have house groups, which are essential to the movement, but they are part of the overall structure. To demonstrate that it is churches which are the center of life we need only note that in Bradford, under the apostolic team of Bryn Jones, a congregation of 600 regularly meets, while in Hove, under the apostleship of Terry Virgo, 500 regularly meet. There are many other churches where attendance is much larger than the average Baptist and classical Pentecostal gatherings.

"Restoration" is not the official title of these churches (leaders still, on the whole, eschew the notion of denomination or sect), but restoration is the most commonly used word, and it is the name of their magazine. Terry Virgo dislikes labels, but feels that if there has to be one "restoration" is the best.

The second large group is a more disparate, less structured collection of churches (or fellowships) that are offshoots or splinter groups from restoration. Their theology is basically the same as restoration, but they tend to be less conservative than the parent body. Although they are organizationally separate, there tends to be a mutual recognition of ministry. As there is virtually no difference concerning the fundamentals of the faith between these two groups, I usually refer to both movements as Restoration 1 and Restoration 2, respectively (or R1 and R2 for short). In addition to these major groupings there are numerous independent fellowships, such as the large community as Basingstoke, and the Ewell fellowship (featured on BBC Everyman's "Unearthly Powers" in 1982). As the restoration churches (particularly R1) are the largest and fastest growing of the "house churches" (restoration leaders would not be unhappy if I suggested that we now bury that name once and for all), the rest of this paper will concentrate on some central theological beliefs of restorationism and, where possible, their sectarian origins.

THE THEOLOGY OF RESTORATIONISM

The true significance of the charismatic renewal is that it made inroads into Catholic and sacramental Christianity as well as traditional evangelicalism; members included theological liberals as well as conservatives. Restoration, on the other hand, is clearly a Protestant evangelical expression of Pentecostalism. In many ways its central theological tenets are those of the classical Pentecostal sects: a belief in the "born again" experience as the initiation into the church (an invisible body of Christ), a belief in believers' baptism, and a commitment to the baptism of the Holy Spirit as the means whereby God initiates believers in Pentecostal power. This power, as most Pentecostalist sects believe, opens up the possibility of the supernatural charismata, as demonstrated in the Acts of the Apostles and outlined by Paul in 1 Corinthians 12. As with other Pentecostalist and evangelical groups they understand sacramental worship as mere signs and symbols of the faith. They are strongly adventist and, like so many Pentecostalists, they believe their leaders do not like the term "fundamentalist" (because of its negative overtones). And yet, many of their attitudes are fundamentalist, such as, a commitment to creationism and a repudiation of the evolutionary theory. (I do not think this is a dogmatic ruling, but it is a tendency I have observed.)

Given the similarity with classical Pentecostalism it may seem surprising to some that they are forming yet one more strata of Pentecostalist life. Walter Hollenweger has sensibly pointed out that theological similarity does not, in itself, promote unity.[2]

Restorationists place a great deal of emphasis on healing, and the reality and dangers of demonic powers. In this, as with their lively liturgical style, they are very little different from the older classical Pentecostalists. They do have, however, a number of doctrines that are not typical of, say, Elim and Assemblies of God in Britain, or the Church of God and Assemblies of God in America. Their more unusual doctrines were sometimes in evidence in the earlier stages of some classical Pentecostal sects. Other doctrines, as we shall note, belonged to other sectarian theologies. (It is misleading to suggest that restoration leaders think that they are original, although I believe that many of them do not see their sectarian ancestry; they would rather say that they are involved in a new movement of the Holy Spirit.)

"Restoration," then, stands for a radical anti-denominationalism. Leaders proclaim that denominations are not in the plan of God. In the New Testament, they point out with some accuracy that there is simply "the church." They see the church universal as the congregation of "born-again" believers, and the local church as a fellowship that "breaks bread" and follows the apostles' teaching. How close this is to the vision of John Nelson Darby (1800–1882). This Northern Ireland clergyman, who became the leader of the Exclusive Brethren sect, originally envisaged a worldwide church where brethren would meet without clericalism, denominational structures, and ritualistic liturgies choking the simplicity (as he saw it) of New Testament apostolic doctrine. (Curiously, and only time will tell how significantly, I have heard a number of people from Restoration 2 jokingly refer to R1 and R2 as the "Exclusive" and "Open" Brethren.)

The question of what God intends the church to be, and how it should be ordered is the fundamental ecclesiological issue that makes restoration so distinctive. For them, the matter is clearly set out in Ephesians 4:8–12. In particular, verses 11 and 12 (NEB) are the key: "And there were his gifts: some to be apostles, some prophets, some evangelists, some pastors and teachers, to equip God's people for work in his service, to the building up of the body of Christ." What emerges from this is a clearly delineated hierarchical structure. At the top are the apostles. These men are not elected, but are believed to be divinely appointed. Apostleship is something that has to be demonstrated to members of restoration, so that leadership conforms to the pattern of Max Weber's charismatic leadership as well as a strictly

2. Hollenweger, "The House Church Movement in Great Britain."

theological view. Restoration teaching on this matter contrasts the democratic election of Saul to kingship (seen as against God's will) with the divine appointment of King David. This is then used, typologically, to explain the system of apostleship as outlined in Ephesians.

Chronologically, prophecy preceded apostleship. After apostleship became established the apostles then initiated and established prophets, pastors, and other leaders. In practice, an eldership system has emerged whereby an apostle heads a team of men (who may or may not be pastors; they are often house group leaders). Recently, restoration has started a greater evangelical "outreach" under the apostleship, but it is hoped that evangelists *per se* will emerge. Certainly there are prophets: Arthur Wallis as the elder statesman of restorationism is not an apostle, but his prophetic role is widely acknowledged.

Allied to this ecclesiology (which is also an organizational principal) is what has become known as discipleship, "relatedness," or more brutally— from outsiders—submission. Although many people within restorationism tend to downplay it, this doctrine is quite different from the usual practice of discipleship as understood in most Pentecostal churches. There, discipleship is usually seen as a personal response to God's prompting—no doubt under the watchful eye of the pastor, but with little organizational control over believers. Most classical Pentecostals simply do not have a mechanism within the local congregation—or the larger church—to operate such a system of control.

In the restoration movement, however, discipleship is a serious affair that covers every area of believers' lives: children submit to parents, wives to husbands, all to elders, who submit to apostles, who in turn (in collegiate fashion) submit to each other. Subjects for direction do not only include what are usually understood as spiritual matters; they include the financial, social, and sexual matters of life. The whole system is seen as one of personal relationships: things are worked out and talked out together. Apostles and elders do not give orders, and it is clear that elders take their responsibilities very seriously and conscientiously.

Strictly speaking, the discipleship issue (or "relatedness") is not derived from a theological position at all. Although the scriptural canon is replete with stories and homilies on what could be called "discipleship," there is no evidence that the early church operated a system such as that in operation in the restoration churches. Such a system is open to abuse, especially in lay communities where the strictness of, say, a monastic rule cannot apply. Such strictness has had its historical counterpart in Protestant history. One thinks of the Puritan Covenants of the seventeenth-century expansion and perhaps more so of the Shakers during the eighteenth-century expansion of the American frontier. As Joyce Thurman points out, the churches we have been examining offer alternative societies: God's kingdom is not of this world. In that sense, discipleship is understood by this charismatic movement as an eschatological imperative; a restored kingdom needs restored believers—soldiers of the church militant.

While discipleship and ecclesiology may seem marginal theological concerns, it is precisely these concerns that mark restoration off from its classical Pentecostal counterparts. If on the level of churchmanship and attitudes to women we can detect echoes of the Brethren movement (and a number of apostles and elders are ex-Brethren members), the ecclesiology is a modern version of older Pentecostalism.

The precursor of modern Pentecostalism is the Catholic Apostolic Church. This nineteenth-century charismatic movement, like the restoration churches, included many professional and middle-class adherents. Nicknamed the Irvingites (after Edward Irving), they organized their churches according to a novel interpretation of Ephesians 4: the hierarchy included not only apostles and prophets, but also angels! Irving, however, was not only a charismatic; he was a traditionalist. In this he was in marked contrast to the holiness sects that were to be the crucible of twentieth-century classical Pentecostalism. The modern successors of Irving, therefore, are not restoration, despite the similarities of interpretation of the Ephesians' epistle. (The Irvingites' successors are the so-called Orthodox Church of Great Britain; their chosen see is Glastonbury[3]).

The direct roots of restoration's ecclesiology are to be found in the Apostolic Church founded towards the end of the great revivals of Glamorgan in South Wales before the Great War. Bryn Jones, the most well-known of restoration's apostles (and an outstandingly gifted preacher) was born in Aberdare; this is the heart of revival country. For a time, in Wales, Bryn Jones was a member of the Assemblies of God Church. Almost certainly he would have come across the Apostolic Church. Not to be confused with the British Israelite United Apostolic Church of Faith, this sect is dominated by Wales. It lacked Bryn Jones' worldwide vision of the restored church, but it nevertheless set up churches organized according to the principles that restoration leaders find in Ephesians 4. The Apostolic Church may have been founded before the Great War, but it never really emerged as a powerful denomination, nor was it able to rival Elim and the Assemblies of God.[4]

---

3. This is a sociological observation. Theologically, I think the Irvingites are far superior.

4. Nevertheless, they have had great success in Africa and more recently South America.

Having attended a number of Welsh Apostolic meetings in the 1960s and restoration services in the 1980s, I would say that of the two the Apostolic Churches are the most insular: their hearts are still in the singing revivals of mining Wales, and their tongues and voices are more Welsh *hwyl* than glossolalia. However, the Apostolic Church is the natural precursor of restoration's ecclesiology, though without the discipleship structure interwoven with its apostleship network.

CONCLUSION: WILL RESTORATION RESTORE THE KINGDOM?

The fact that many of the theological tenets of restorationism are the same as mainstream evangelicalism should not blind us to the fact that this is true of all forms of classical Pentecostalism. I have attempted to show briefly that those aspects of restoration teaching that mark them off from other charismatic groups have their roots in Protestant sectarianism. There is one other distinctive feature of restoration theology (though, I believe, "religious teachings" is a more accurate term than the over-extended use of the term "theology") which is noteworthy, and this is "kingdom theology." In his highly entertaining book, *What on Earth is the Kingdom?* Gerald Coates points out that Jesus Christ did not come to set up a church, but to establish a kingdom. We have already noted the anti-denominationalism of this new movement, and the idea of establishing the kingdom, or restoring the purity of the early church, is a dominant theme.

The Lord Jesus is the king who has divinely appointed his apostles to establish the kingdom in enemy territory: the territory is the world, and its prince is Satan. As the Jewish zealots have taken Zionist communities into the Arab-held West Bank, restorationists are reclaiming territory for God in the form of fellowships, churches, and communities. Restoration does not wish to become merely another denomination: it wants to establish the kingdom! Although this is clearly reminiscent of millennial sects, such as the seventeenth-century Levellers, there is nothing political implied here: the kingdom of God is within and yet also where his people reside. Restoration begins with restoring the kingdom; therefore, when the kingdom is ready—when the church is charismatically restored—the Lord Jesus will return to earth in power and glory.

David Tomlinson, an apostle in Restoration 2, has a strong commitment to a social gospel as well as the evangelical good news.[5] He is afraid that restoration will delude itself into thinking that it is claiming territory

---

5 Tomlinson later joined the Church of England and was ordained as a priest.

for the king, when it is in reality standing on the sidelines as a Godless world slips inexorably into hell. It is difficult to believe that you are on the sidelines when, as Restoration 1 shows, they can organize 10,000 people at the Dales Bible Week, and experience excitement and revivalist fervor wherever they go. But as Os Guinness has pointed out in *The Gravedigger Files*, such groups fail to realize that the forces of secularization have removed them to the periphery of our modern culture: pietistic and revivalist Christianity has become a consumer option in a pluralistic society. To restore the kingdom is to reclaim that part of culture that has gone over to the adversary: the political, industrial, and scientific infrastructure of modern societies that even mainstream Christianity has retreated from without hope of recapture.

6

CROSSING THE
RESTORATIONIST RUBICON
From House Church to New Church
(2002)

INTRODUCTION

This chapter considers one main issue: has the restorationist movement (formerly, though never formally, known as the "house church movement") radically changed its spots and become a different animal? Or, put slightly differently, is the fact that the house churches are now typically called "new churches" only a change of label for what is essentially the same movement, or is the new label itself indicative of organizational and ideological change?

To talk of "house churches" or "new churches" is to recognize that we are using folk models (or "first order" constructs), for such terms were conjured out of common usage and the popular desire for identification; not for analytical precision. A "second order" approach (that of a sociological rubric) was followed in *Restoring the Kingdom*,[1] in which I identified a coalition, or core formation of the so-called house churches in terms of

---

1. All four editions contain different material, but the 1998 edition is the most altered; it not only includes substantial new chapters but also proposes a revision of the Restorationist ideal type. All quotations here are from the 1998 edition of *Restoring the Kingdom*.

a Weberian ideal type, which I called "restorationism."[2] Having identified the essential features of the ideal type, I distinguished two forms of restorationism which I called R1—the more conservative restorationist enclave the approximated closely to the ideal type; and R2—the more liberal restorationist faction that was more restorationist than not, but less like the ideal type than R1.

This comparison of folk models with sociological rubrics raises a secondary question related to the demise of the term "house church" and its replacement by the title "new church," namely, is the sociological rubric of R1 and R2 still operative now that there is a popular perception that house churches have mutated into new churches?

It is not known who first coined the phrase "house church movement," but it was in existence in the mid-1970s and widely used by the early 1980s. I first came across it in 1979, at a British Council of Churches consultation on the charismatic renewal. This meeting included the late Canon David Watson and the more recently deceased Bob Gordon—leading figures in the renewal at that time—as well as Michael Harper[3] and Tom Smail. In a talk given by Tom Smail,[4] he presented the house church movement, not merely as a phenomenon, but as a problem. He did so because he looked upon it as a growing independent sector outside the mainline churches that was beckoning charismatics to come and join what some were already seeing as a new sectarianism.

In 1982, after covering a house church Bible Week for Radio 4's *Sunday* program I decided that I would begin an academic investigation into these so-called house churches. By March 1984, when I was writing *Restoring the Kingdom* and researching the documentary "Front Room Gospel" for BBC radio, I was convinced that the house church label was a misnomer that obscured more than it illuminated.[5]

Take, for example the notion that this extra-denominational movement was made up of churches in houses. The title of the BBC radio documentary

---

2. The term "restorationism" denotes a qualitative understanding of (so members believe) the work of the Holy Spirit. Leaders of the new movements insist that denominations are not in the plan of God. The restoring of the church as is was in its pristine form is to restore a charismatically ordained church, and one in which Christians are seen as living in a kingdom run according to God's order and rules; cf. Walker, *Restoring the Kingdom*, 39–40.

3. Michael Harper was the first director of the (now defunct) Fountain Trust, an ecumenical charismatic movement that initially included house church independents like Arthur Wallis as well as Anglican and Catholic supporters. Fr. Michael Harper, is presently a priest in the Antiochene Orthodox Church.

4. Smail made this comment when he was the Director of the Fountains Trust.

5. "Front Room Gospel," BBC Radio 4 program.

gave the impression that churches had sprung up in front rooms as suddenly and as ubiquitously as "store-front" churches had grown in the early twentieth century in the urban United States. Now, it is true that some of these independent churches did begin in houses, but the popular idea that all of them started in this way is a legend. Two examples of those that did are Gerald Coates' church in Cobham, after he and his wife left the local Brethren assembly and gradually gathered round them an independent fellowship, and John Noble's, which started in his home at Romford. However, the popular misconception does not hold for "apostle" Bryn Jones, who began his mature ministry in an independent chapel in Bradford. Nor does it hold for scores of affiliated "house churches," because they were already independent assemblies before the house church label was applied to them.

Even if it could be said that the house church movement had an almost secretive, or at least separate, cottage existence in its early days, like nascent Quakerism in the seventeenth century, by the early 1980s the typical house church was housed not in homes, but in buildings outside family dwellings—ready-built churches, reinvigorated old ones, church halls, schools, cinemas, or public meeting places belonging to local authorities. Admittedly, most of these churches did incorporate house groups; however, this was hardly unique, as many mainline denominations encouraged house groups at that time, and still do.

The wide circulation and frequent use of the label "house churches," despite the absence of empirical examples, can be explained in part by its "sound bite" media appeal. Typical of evangelical reporting in the 1980s was *Buzz* magazine's article "Shepherds or Sheep Stealers," in its August 1984 edition. The phrase "house church movement" (or its acronym, HCM) liberally peppers the report, as indeed it does the letters written in response to the article. The editor of *Buzz* magazine at the time, Steve Goddard, recalls that there was no question of calling the HCM anything else as no denominational or self-identifiable title had emerged. "What I remember from those days," says Goddard, "is that the Charismatic Renewal suddenly found itself surrounded by churches that had seemed to come from nowhere. The response of the denominations was to close ranks and fight off the enemy as best they could. The house church label sounds bland enough now, but then it carried with it a sense of the unknown, with a hint of menace."[6]

Another problematic feature of some evangelical reporting at that time was the indiscriminate application of the house church label. The fact that there were independent churches mushrooming in the shadow of the charismatic renewal masked the reality that there were several different

6. See Goddard, *Buzz* magazine (August, 1984).

formations hiding under this rubric, and numerous independent churches that were not affiliated to any group whatsoever. True, these independent networks and non-affiliated fellowships shared generic features—they were, for example, virtually all charismatic and evangelical—but in other significant respects they were different.

The difference was partly a matter of organizational structure and partly a question of leadership. By 1985, for example, it could be said that the label "house church movement" covered the interrelated teams of "apostolic" churches led by Bryn Jones, Terry Virgo, Tony Morton, and fellow-travelers such as Barney Coomes. It also included a similar formation under the leadership of John Noble, Dave Tomlinson, and Gerald Coates. The latter group was also affiliated to the churches associated with Peter Fenwick of Sheffield House Church (that is its official title), which was nevertheless run on more Presbyterian that apostolic lines.

In addition to these networks, however, there was the Ichthus Fellowship of South London under the leadership of Roger Forster (although Forster has never considered himself to be an apostle). There were yet further examples of extra-denominational Christianity (e.g., the churches of Chard in Somerset and the fellowships of Pastor North).

By 1984 it was clear to me, through talking to church leaders and reading Christian newsprint, that virtually all the excitement, resistance to, and fear of the house church movement was really centered on what were referred to above as the apostolic churches. These churches were the most radical, the most controversial, and the fastest-growing Christian movement in the United Kingdom. Their belief that they were restoring the New Testament church, and the fact that they were run by a charismatic apostolate—as two earlier charismatic movements had been (the Catholic Apostolic Church in the nineteenth century and the Apostolic Church in the twentieth)—led me eventually to characterize them by the term "restorationist."[7]

While house church movement was a folk term particularly favored by the evangelical media and leaders of the charismatic renewal, it was one the new radicals themselves did not encourage. Without exception, everywhere I went in house church circles I met resistance to the phrase. In interviews with Arthur Wallis and Keri Jones at the Dales Bible Week in 1982 they both made it clear that it was not of their making, or to their liking. Furthermore, the former apostle Dave Tomlinson poured scorn on the misappropriation

---

7. I was greatly helped in this by Bryan Wilson's use of the phrase "restored churches" when talking about the Brethren and the Catholic Apostolic Church; cf. Wilson, *Religious Sects*, 207.

of the label in an in-house newsletter,[8] and "apostle" Terry Virgo would often say or write "so-called" house churches.

Such an aversion to the obstinately sticky label is not difficult to understand: when you believe that you are in the vanguard of God's kingdom, when you think that you are restoring the lost and forgotten charisms and offices of the New Testament church, when you are convinced that the kingdom of God is going to swell and fill the whole earth, you do not really want to rally behind the banner bearing the legend "house churches."

However, while restorationists did not want to muster behind such a limp standard, the sheer vacuousness of the house church ephemeron served a useful ideological purpose for them: namely, to deny that they were a new denomination in the making. Putting it pragmatically, it was better to admit to belonging to the "so-called" house church movement than to admit that you were members of a fringe church, or to admit to "giving birth to another sect," as former apostle George Tarleton put it.[9] In its early days, as was the case with the Brethren movement before it, the rhetoric of restorationism was to eschew denominational expressions of the church in favor of simply being a member of the church catholic and apostolic.

The resistance by the principal phalanxes of the HCM to the process of denominationalism also led members of the movement to avoid using the term "restoration" as a proper noun to describe themselves. They would often say that they were "in the Restoration," and Terry Virgo could say in 1989 that he had been "a member of the so-called Restoration movement I guess for a couple of decades . . . ."[10] But no one would say "we are a member of the restorationist church," for to do so would be to capitulate to denominational language. In other words, although the house church movement label was a misnomer that did not accurately portray or identify restorationists, it also by its very obfuscation helped protect them from unwelcome publicity and denominational visibility.

Nevertheless, although proper denominational nouns were denied, the various factions of restorationism *did* congregate around identifiable and concrete organizations. Byrn Jones' churches were initially identified by outsiders as "Harvestime" because of the name of its commercial operation. In time, Jones' churches became a network supporting what the leadership preferred to call Covenant Ministries. Tony Morton also organized his churches under the Pauline sounding Cornerstone Ministries. Terry Virgo,

8. Newsletter headed "House Churches. Never heard of them?"; and Walker, *Restoring the Kingdom*, 33.

9. Tarleton is one of the few former apostles to have written about his experiences in his *Birth of a Christian Anarchist* (1993); see also Walker, *Restoring the Kingdom*, 287.

10. Cf. Walker, *Restoring the Kingdom*, 339.

after a parochial seaside stab at Coastlands, transformed his churches into the altogether bolder New Frontiers International. Gerald Coates' Pioneer echoed this missionary agenda, while Dave Tomlinson and John Noble adopted more modest badge of camaraderie under the title of Team Work and Team Spirit respectively.

R1 AND R2

What all these different organizations could not hide in the mid-1980s was that they all lived in the restorationist orbit. There was a sharing of common ideological precepts ranging from restored apostles and prophets to a belief in "discipling" or "shepherding"—i.e., that all members of restorationist churches, from apostles to children, should be in a paternalistic relationship of mentoring and monitoring. To live in the restorationist orbit was not to co-exist in a common denominational structure, but as members of religious networks under apostolic direction. The apostles at the head of the several restorationist networks worked in concert, demonstrating that their distinctive religious life existed in an acknowledge affiliation. Tomlinson, Coates, and Noble, for example, came together at the Staffordshire Showground. The Dales Bible Week performed a similar function for Byrn Jones and his colleagues (though this was not so central to the ministries of Morton and Virgo, and ceased after 1983). Furthermore, *Restoration* magazine included Virgo, Morton, and Jones on the editorial board.

Highlighting the networks in this way throws into relief the fact that the restorationist movement had two basic shapes, or "streams," to use charismatic jargon. This is not so much to point to the historical fact that these streams once formed one river until they went their separate ways in 1976, but more to indicate that the divergent streams differed in style and restorationist purity. In breaking down mid-1980s restorationism into the algebraic R1 and R2, I wished to distinguish R1 as the more conservative restorationist formation and closer to the ideal type than the more liberal R2. The R1/R2 typology was in no sense an attempt to force a new label of identification on the house church movement, nor was it intended to suggest that restorationists should "come out" by openly declaring that they were restorationists all along. Rather, it was designed to facilitate an analytical understanding of the new radical churches, enabling one to give some theological and sociological shape to the amorphous movement still called house churches. Furthermore, the mapping of restorationism as a heuristic exercise was consonant with the new radicals' self-understanding of their movement (although not identical to it).[11]

Following the publication of the first edition of *Restoring the Kingdom* in 1985, the R1 and R2 rubric had some unintended, albeit short-lived consequences—not least because the evangelical media and some house church leaders adopted it. For example, after an extract from the book appeared in *Buzz* magazine—a mildly satirical chapter that suggested persons needed something like a "visa" to get into the restorationist kingdom[12]—Gerald Coates responded by sending in an R2 headed visa complete with a signed photograph. Certainly many rank-and-file house church people utilized the rubric for a while, as the hundreds of letters I received from Restorationists testified.[13]

I was invited to attend Festival 86, a restorationist celebration event, and defend myself in front of several hundred R2 critics. Most were friendly and seemed to like the R1/2 designation. R2 members were receptive to the rubric, I suspect, because they were anxious not to be lumped in with R1, whom they saw as too conservative, and in the process of becoming denominationalized. R1 members were more ambivalent towards the schema, for, on the one hand, the R1 variant of the ideal type suggested greater social control and stronger shepherding practices than R2, while, on the other, it also implied greater radicality.

The R1 and R2 rubric remained in the popular evangelical consciousness from approximately 1985 to 1988; its mnemonic quality no doubt aiding its utility as a device of identification.[14] From the late 1980s, however, R1 and R2 as badges of popular restorationist recognition begin to lose currency. A new folk model—the much-heralded "new church"—was emerging. This was to alter the tenor of the R2 variant of the restorationist ideal type.

FROM HOUSE CHURCH TO NEW CHURCH

One criticism of the move in sociology to replace the term cult (and sometimes sect) with the less emotive phrase "new religious movement" is that this is more an exercise in political correctness than advancement

---

11. Interestingly, the influential sociologist and phenomenologist Alfred Schutz believed that the harmony between folk and analytical constructs was a useful test of the sociological adequacy of ideal types; cf. Schutz, "The Problem of Rationality in the Social World."

12 Walker, *Restoring the Kingdom*, 197–211

13. Ibid.

14. The fact that it was intended as a heuristic device in the service of sociology of religion was no doubt overlooked.

in conceptual understanding. Despite the obvious growth of syncretistic structures (often born out of the creative tensions generated by East meeting West), new religious movements, on examination, look remarkably like cults and sects. Even the adoption of the epithet "new" has been less than helpful, as newness does not appear to be linked only to the last few decades, but in some writings reaches back to the Mormons, Theosophists, and the Jehovah's Witnesses of the nineteenth century.[15]

By contrast, the concept of "new church," although clearly a folk model, does refer to an identifiable time frame. New churches refer specifically to Christian formations that may reach back to the 1950s and 1960s, but that typically have come into being from the 1970s to the present time.

But what are new churches? For the evangelical media of the 1990s the phrase seemed to be simply a new portmanteau term replacing the old 1980s house churches tag. Yet in a way this media term is an improvement on the old one, if only because it no longer maintains the pretense that relatively new religious formations are springing up and coexisting in people's homes. The now popular new church tag also connotes the most important and widely acknowledged fact about house churches: they are charismatic fellowships that came into existence outside the established religious structure—both mainline denominations and the Pentecostal and evangelical sects.

However, we can learn a great deal more about new churches when it is recognized that the phrase is not essentially a media invention to provide a new sound bite to replace the outdated and jaded old one.[16] On the independent church sector, and the phrase initially gained circulation in the R2 churches. It is possible to be more specific still: although he may not have coined the phrase, Gerald Coates emerged as the champion of the new concept from 1988 onwards. The idea seems to have germinated in Coates' mind just before a conference of independent churches in Sheffield in September 1988.

As early as June 1987, leaders within R2 were rethinking many of the basic tenets of restorationism. A certain disenchantment had set in regarding paternalistic monitoring (known as shepherding), and attitudes to

15. Perhaps I did not read it as carefully as I should have done, but I was left with the impression after reading Eileen Barker's introductory text on new religious movements that the book was certainly helpful and practical, but not yielding much in the way of analytical precision. Certainly it has been the case that the cult-watching organization that Professor Barker helped found, INFORM (Information Network Focus on Religious Movements) receives enquiries from the older as well as the newer sects; see Barker, *New Religious Movements*.

16. Many secular journalists have picked up the new usage; cf. Cotton, *The Hallelujah Revolution*.

women's ministry were changing. In particular, the hierarchical structure of apostolic ministries was challenged and a more functional, pragmatic, and diaconal concept was beginning to emerge. Leaders were becoming more ecumenical and were beginning to co-operate with other churches under the auspices of the Evangelical Alliance and the Spring Harvest organizations. The feeling was prevalent at the time that what were still being called the house churches had lived through their heyday. As the R2 prophet David Matthews put it, "we never set out to be a permanent feature of the landscape and we have no vested interest in maintaining the house church movement; . . . if we need to give the house church thing a decent burial, let's do it. May it rest in peace!"[17] Matthews was not to know at that time that in 1988, a short while before the Sheffield conference organized by Gerald Coates, restorationism was to give a thoroughly decent burial to the theological architect of the restorationist movement in Britain, Arthur Wallis. Wallis' death, coming as it did on the eve of the conference, was a blow to the restorationist churches, but a spur to Sheffield's success.

What was significant about the 1988 conference is that Coates had called together churches from R1 and R2, as well as other independent leaders like Stuart Bell and Roger Forster. Clive Calver, then general secretary of the Evangelical Alliance, was an honorable participant. Even the controversial leader of the Jesus Army, Noel Stanton, was there. The Sheffield conference was the crucible of the transformation of house churches into new churches, because it was a sign of a newfound co-operation and mutual recognition of ministry among the burgeoning but often competing independent churches. It was the occasion, as Clive Calver saw it, for Coates to emerge as the statesman of the restorationist movement;[18] he was prepared to stress the common ground from other charismatic expressions of Christianity.[19]

As David Matthews was to put it to Gerald Coates at Sheffield, the funeral of Arthur Wallis and the conference itself was the end of an era and the beginning of a new one.[20] The new era would appear, in the minds of some of the Sheffield participants at least, to be in one in which the radi-

17. Cf. Walker, *Restoring the Kingdom,* 347.

18. Interview with the author at the Evangelical Alliance in Kennington on 8 September 1989.

19. It would be misleading to say that Coates abandoned restorationist ecclesiology at that time, or any time. What he did do was put on hold his personal theological predilections for the sake of charismatic unity. His work with Roger Forster of Ichthus and Lynn Green of Youth with a Mission (YWAM) on the city marches of the 1990s exemplifies this.

20. Cf. Walker, *Restoring the Kingdom,* 378.

cal churches would be more open handed, both with themselves and with older denominations. This characterization seems to have been more than pious wishful thinking, for from the autumn of 1988 the denominational charge levelled against old house churches that they "poached" from other evangelicals, became less vehement.[21]

While this new sense of restorationist cooperation was undoubtedly principled, it is not too reductionistic to say that it was also a sign that the radicals were losing their fire and settling down. Whatever the case, after 1988 the "new church" rubric quickly spread. All R2 churches adopted it. So too did Terry Virgo's churches along the South Coast. As recently as 1998 Hove elder John Hosier gave me the impression that the designation "new church" was adopted by many of the fellowships in New Frontiers. Today, new churches seem to be a catch-all phrase, adopted in virtually all restorationist churches and independent charismatic assemblies.

An exception would be Covenant Ministries, where the new church rubric is certainly acknowledged, but is not enthusiastically embraced. Yet as early as 1989 Bryn Jones was demonstrating his awareness of the term. In an interview in Bradford, before Covenant Ministries relocated to Nettle Hill, he explained that he did not go to Sheffield in 1988 because he wanted to meet fellow Christians on the basis of a spiritual commonality in Christ, not under the auspices of the house church movement, or what they call "new churches."[22]

For those of us outside the new church ambit, looking in at the phenomenon, a strange circularity appears to be in evidence. Despite the fact that house churches now sport a new label, it looks, just under the surface at least, as if nothing has changed: the old suit has been dry-cleaned, but it remains essentially the same garment. At the very least, the new umbrella term, like the old one, embraces disparate churches with clearly distinguishing features as well as some generic properties.

To a certain extent this view is confirmed by Gerald Coates. He accepts that new church "has become something of an umbrella for anything Anglican, Catholic, Baptist, Methodist, Salvation Army and classical Pentecostal, etc." He feels that such an umbrella also includes many of the new Black churches, which he considers not to be in the classical Pentecostal tradition.[23] He also thinks that 90 percent of new churches are charismatic and that 60 or 70 percent are linked to network apostolic teams. In other words,

21. See Terry Virgo's remarks in Walker, *Restoring the Kingdom*, 331.

22. Ibid., 371.

23. In this he is mistaken. Admittedly many of the African Caribbean churches are small, but they are more classical Pentecostal than not (though the same cannot always be said for African churches).

he means that the majority of the new churches are still restorationist fellowships of one kind of another—or at least second-generation adaptations of them.

However, Gerald Coates has said that he thought new church was more a question of ethos than of denominational exactitude,[24] giving Holy Trinity Brompton as an example of a historic church that merited the title new church, while stating he could think of new independent churches that had fallen into old patterns of thinking and ministry.[25]

It would be unfair to expect Gerald Coates to provide a tight definition of new church, for this is the sort of second-order exercise not typically engaged in by Christian activists. It is clear, however, that while recognizing that many new churches are restorationist in origin, Coates accepts that the new church umbrella is far bigger than the old HCM. As he put it in the closest to a definition of "new church" that he could attempt, "If new church is simply a title covering what is not picked up by Anglicanism, Catholicism, Methodism, Baptists, Pentecostalism, etc.—it follows that anything outside of these denominations which is orthodox in faith is New Church . . . ."

By looking again at the sociological rubric of R1/R2, it is possible to make some further progress in determining (a) whether new churches are just house churches in disguise and (b) in what ways, if at all, restorationism has itself changed. Such a review is worthwhile because the key to understanding the nature of change in independent charismatic sector lies in R2.

During the second half of the 1980s restorationists in both R1 and R2 ceased to grow at the rate they had in the first half. Indeed, growth was often static or negative. But whereas in 1985 the unheralded separation of the ministries of Virgo, Jones, and Morton did not radically alter the ideological character of R1, R2 as a restorationist cohort began to break down altogether from 1988 onwards as apostles Tomlinson, Coates, and Noble no longer cohered together as a recognizable partnership. As working relationships between them faltered, and as the previous levels of growth ceased, not only did they gradually break up, but as they drifted apart they began to be less fiercely wedded to a restorationist ideology.

In time, and after considerable disruption to his network, Tomlinson was to abandon restorationism, so that by 1990 his churches began, as the Americans say, to go "every which way" and ceased to operate as

---

24. This ethos includes "church planting," being open to the prophetic, and being receptive to successive waves of the Spirit—such as those stemming from Toronto and Pensacola. Although such an ethos can be found in many charismatic churches these days, it is doubtful whether it is in the distinctive hallmark of the "new church."

25. Interview with the author at Coates' house in Esher, February 5, 1997.

a recognizable restorationist network.[26] As for John Noble, although he remained in "covenant relationship" with Gerald Coates, his network had already considerable declined by the late 1980s, and by the early 1990s his organization was disbanded, some going into Pioneer, others to different networks or to independence.

In practice, therefor, by the beginning of the 1990s R2, as one of the two shapes of the restorationist churches, no longer really existed, either as a workable interlocking network or as an overtly restorationist movement. Certainly much of the shepherding structure had loosened to the point of collapse, and although an apostolic network survived in Pioneer, aided by Noble's input, this was far less doctrinaire than yesteryear, and far more open to other churches, both old and new, than in the past. In particular, the more open and liberalizing influence of Roger Forster (particularly over the issue of women's ministry), and the growing recognition of John Wimber's contribution to charismatic Christianity, radically altered the tenor of the shrunken R2, so that it cannot be said to have remained a distinct and unique restorationist movement, but was instead quite self-consciously reborn as the broader charismatic new church.[27]

So, to re-pose the secondary question once again, "does the R1/R2 typology still work as a meaningful sociological rubric?" the answer is no. It has virtually no application to the new churches of the 1990s. Logically, given that R2 no longer really exists, the algebraic adumbration of R1/R2 can be dispensed in favor of the sociological designation restorationism, thereby maintaining its status as a classical ideal type to help explain the rational and coherent features of a distinctive movement of late-twentieth-century revival.

To return to the main question, "did restorationists change their identities in the transmogrification from house church to new church?" the clear answer is that many, especially in what used to be called R1, did not, despite dallying with the new church concept. Restorationism continued in the form of Terry Vergo's New Frontiers and Bryn Jones' Covenant Ministries, and probably in Derek Brown and Barney Coomes' churches, and possibly even Tony Morton's. But many restorationists from the now defunct R2 did cross the Rubicon and have become more obviously charismatic evangelicals in independent guise and less obviously committed restorers of the New Testament church.[28]

26. Tomlinson was ordained deacon in the Church of England in 1997 and priest the following year.

27. Although to personify this birth process Gerald Coates can claim the role of midwife.

28. It is not so much that apostolic and prophetic ministries have been eschewed,

So within the new church catchment area we can identify restoration-ists, former restorationists, fellow travelers, and charismatic churches that are clearly not restorationist at all. It is difficult to predict which of these cohorts will win out in the long run. For the time being the restorationist movement seems to have faltered from the days when it ruled the roost in the house church farm. If it is not yet quite on the defensive, with the probable exception of New Frontiers it is hardly on the front foot pressing forward. It would seem, then, that for the moment at least, the energy and excitation rests with those who have enthusiastically embraced the "new church," not only in name, but ideologically as a drive towards greater catholicity and a move away from fundamentalist security.

In the long run, however, the very openness of those who have en-dorsed the new church ethos will also result in the dilution of their ideologi-cal purity, which in turn will militate against sectarian distinctiveness. The very appeal and *raison d'être* of restorationists in their house church days was that they were a radical alternative society run on theocratic lines. Such an idealistic yet casuistic structure was always going to be a hindrance to church growth,[29] but it strikes me as a surer—and longer-lasting—building than the jerry-built new church founded on ecumenical effervescence and revivalist verve.

---

but rather that the separatist and exclusivist doctrines that formed such a vital part of restorationist kingdom theology have been abandoned; cf. Walker, *Restoring the King-dom*, 339, 404.

29. So far no religious movement ever run by a charismatic apostolate and sport-ing restorationist credentials has ever succeeded in becoming a mass movement in the Western world (although the Welsh-based Apostolic Church has considerable success in Nigeria).

MERE CHRISTIANITY AND THE SEARCH FOR ORTHODOXY

7

Notes from a Wayward Son

(1995)

A s every boy from Eton knows: there is only one other school (even though Harrow has recently dropped like a stone down the tables of the top educational establishments). This sense of identifying oneself over and against the significant "other" is familiar to me, for I was born into the Elim Foursquare Gospel Church and for us there was no other church of equal standing save our great-rival-cousin—Assemblies of God.

It was not that we did not know of any other churches. We knew of the Christian Brethren (smart but suspect) and the Baptists and Method-ists (dead as dodos). Because I was brought up in Tonypandy and Neath in Glamorgan, Wales, until I was eight, I knew of Ebenezer Chapel as something quintessentially yet mysteriously Welsh. Of more significance was acquaintance with the Apostolic Church, a small Pentecostal denomi-nation with nearby headquarters, which, we were told, sported doubtful credentials.

As for Anglicans, we knew that they were religious, but we doubted if they could be "saved" because they believed in infant baptism and did not seem to understand, so we thought, the need for conversion. But even I knew they were better than Catholics, who were apostates and sinners. Cer-tain members of our congregation whispered that nuns killed babies and that the pope was the "whore of Babylon" (though I never did understand this exotic reference).

Years later, when I was in London in the early 1960s, I used to hear similar things said at Hyde Park Corner in the name of Protestant truth, and less rabid but equally condemning things from a certain separatist Calvinist chapel at Westminster.

Except for the Assemblies of God, where I knew of (but nothing about) Donald Gee and Nelson J. Parr, my life was surrounded by the great names of our church: Pastors W. G. Hathaway, W. Greenwood, P. Brewster, and what was already then a living but tarnished legend, Principal George Jeffreys. To be frank, we never talked of Jeffreys in the present tense: he was that great evangelist of the past.

It might be thought that it must have been strange living in such a small denomination so out of concert with the mainstream churches and so out of touch with the world. In fact, it was not strange at all. Son, as I was, of an Elim pastor, and with a mother who was also a preacher and singer, the Elim movement was the main focus of my life. It may have been small, but it did not seem so to me, for we were always mixing with other Elim members in special meetings and conventions.

Life was circumscribed by the church and my parents' commitments. I went to Elim three times on Sunday, often on Saturday, sometimes to the mid-week prayer meeting. Our entertainment was the church, which doubled as chapel and music hall. There was great talent within Elim (there probably still is), and we enjoyed and expected a good sing and dramatic presentations of the gospel. Long before it became normative in mainstream churches, we were playing guitars, singing in quartets, shaking tambourines, and sometimes clapping our hands and tapping our feet (though this was going too far for some pastors).

It meant, therefore, that although the world was officially banished from our doors—there was no drinking, smoking, going to the theatre, cinema, or dance hall—we would sway to our beloved choruses set to waltz, swing, or sanitized ragtime.

Our response to the arts was sectarian. Not only did we officially eschew popular music, there was also little investment in either classical or modern composers. Indeed, there was little investment in high culture. Good reading, for example, was not so much forbidden as ignored. Other children may have read *A Tale of Two Cities* and *Tess of the D'Urbervilles*, but I read *Edgar Nelthorpe* and *Eric: Or Little by Little*. Enid Blyton's books were encouraged when we were younger, along with Christian novels such as *Treasures of the Snow*, but there was no particular encouragement to read the standard children's classics such as *The Wind in the Willows* or *Winnie the Pooh*. When I went to grammar school at the age of seventeen, all of my middle-class Christian friends were weaned on C. S. Lewis' *The Lion, the Witch, and the Wardrobe*. I'd never heard of it.

We may never have gone to the plays of Noel Coward or Shakespeare, but we were not short of drama. The Holy Spirit moved among us with power, so we fervently believed, though our meetings were usually very jolly and unassuming. There would be prophecies and tongues, healings, and testimonies of wondrous happenings. At times the jolliness would become sheer excitement and it would seem as if the building would rock with the thrill of it all. And yet to me, as a small boy, it was just what we did in our church, and was no more bizarre than I imagine reciting the Office together would be for the staunch Anglican.

Sometimes we held "Great Divine Healing Crusades," though this was more a declaration of hope than a description of reality. God was with us and we felt him in our midst and heard him through prophecies and the interpretations of strange tongues (though for the life of me I cannot remember a single prophecy from those times).

We would swoon at the latest adventist teachings, which always seemed to predict that we were poised on the edge of disaster, the world about to be plunged into Armageddon, while we were whisked away to meet Jesus in the clouds.

This had a great effect on me as a small child. I remember one day getting out of bed and going into my parents' room, only to find them absent. They did not respond to my call, and I was suddenly overcome with dread at the thought that "the rapture" had taken place and I had been left behind.

The biblical prophecies also fueled my starved intellect. Fundamentalists as we were, prophetic interpretations were a legitimate source of imaginative, albeit fantastical, speculations. *The Mark of the Beast* was one particularly lurid book about the Antichrist I remember reading and enjoying. I liked stories about demons too (exorcisms were, in fact, part of the repertoire of Pentecostalism, but we rarely practiced them).

I was not considered to be a particularly bright child. School was a strain for me: it reinforced my belief in the wickedness of the world and the perfidiousness of lost souls. It was not a place to learn from; it was more a place in which to show off. I was not particularly popular with other children, partly because I was different, being Elim, but mainly because I was a "big-head." It was amazing, for one who knew so little about the world, how much I had to say about it.

Showing off was of course frowned upon in Elim, unless it was done in the interests of the church. So if you could sing a bit, which I could, and talk the proverbial hind leg off the donkey, then showing off was allowed under the guise of singing sacred solos, giving testimonies, or preaching. But at school I liked to show off through acting plays. It was the only time I remember being praised by the teachers.

Predictably, at the age of eleven I failed to gain a place at a grammar school, but my primary leaver's report promised that my acting ability would get me far; there was no mention of my brains. In fact, going to secondary school opened up the first fissure in my worldview. We had two teachers, "Basher Brooks" and "Toby Twirl," who thought that I was not a complete dunce. They introduced me to literature and a love of history, and helped me to move on to the grammar school when I was seventeen, in 1962.

But the crucial spiritual period of my young life was 1959-60. My father had been ill for a long time, having suffered a stroke in 1957. It changed his personality, and it was difficult for him to cope with my precocious presence. And then, when I was away at a camp in August 1959, with young people from churches other than Elim, my father died unexpectedly. I was not taken to his funeral, and my anger at this, and my guilt for upsetting him in his final years, lived with me well into adulthood.

There was no pension from the church, and nowhere to live when my father died, so my mother rented a small bungalow from a Strict Baptist. (This may seem a curious fact to remember, but the denominational tag for us in those days was a primary means of personal identification.) We had very little money, but living in our new home was a time of great comfort to my mother and me, for not only were we close, there was also a great deal of religious activity to keep us occupied (my sister kept her counsel about father's death, and soon moved on to university).

I was nominally Christian from the age of twelve, and intellectually a convinced Elimite, but religion did not really fire me in any way. By now I was a teenager, with an interest in bikes and cricket, the cinema—which I used to sneak into without telling mother—and girls.

It was April 1959 when I was still fourteen years of age that I finally found out for myself what Pentecost was all about. I was visiting Neath in South Wales, where I used to live as a small boy. On the Easter Monday I was sick and could not go hear the flown-in American speaker at the Elim "city temple." Later in the day I recovered, and although I knew they were supposed to be suspect, I wandered down to the local Apostolic Church, which was holding its own convention.

Much of the service was in Welsh, but I remember it as crackling with energy and rippling with congregational excitement. I noticed a girl who was showing an inch of petticoat below her knee. (She noticed me noticing her, and pulled her skirt a little higher.) During one of the intervals I approached her and tried what I hoped was casual but sophisticated chat (so necessary to me in those days, for I was barely five feet tall!). Her brother—who was on crutches, I remember—cornered me outside and threatened to do me harm if I tried any "funny stuff!" And then we went back inside.

It was now evening. The pastor invited all those who wanted to "tarry for the Spirit" to come to the front. I went, though I have no idea whether it was true longing for God or bravado—or both. The pretty young girl came out, too, but she was some distance away from me. We knelt in a prayer line against the mahogany nonconformist pew. I prayed for the Spirit with fervor, but little expectation. One of our church members, sometime previously, had told of waiting on the Spirit for nigh on twenty years, so I was not assuming that the "baptism" was an automatic right.

I was at the end of the line. When the pastor reached me he put his hands on my head. Something happened that was unexpectedly physical. I felt from his hands what these days a New Ager might call "waves of energy," and then my tongue locked solid, and the Walker of the chat was struck dumb. I tried to talk, but all I could manage was a stammer of disconnected sounds. Then the sounds connected and the tongues rushed out, and I felt good, but strange, and a little frightened.

So this was the baptism! I set off for home, which was no less than the manse of the Elim church. I staggered about the street like a drunk. This is what I thought at the time, not knowing firsthand the perils of alcohol. (Looking back, and with a more varied experience than I had then, I think "feeling drunk" was an excellent analogy.) The pastor at the manse, whose name I have forgotten, poured cold water on my baptism of fire (it was, remember, from the hands of the less than favored Apostolics!), and I went to bed dispirited, only to wake up in the night, merrily peeling away with a fresh triple of the tongues.

It has to be said, as a matter of fact, whatever spiritual or psychological interpretation we might want to put on it, the "baptism in the Holy Spirit" changed me radically. Whereas before I had been indifferent to Pentecost, I now was fervent about it. Zeal, rather than goodness, would probably be a fair description of me at that time, for I soon found that Pentecostal experience did not of itself bring the long-suffering fruits of the Spirit.

On the contrary! For although I now became an evangelist and boy-preacher, I also became more conceited than I had been before the "baptism"—if such a thing were possible!—and my increased swagger and cockiness meant that I made enemies at school. At church I became a gospel singer who played guitar (delusions of grandeur in this area were to accompany me long after I abandoned Pentecostalism). More significantly, I also became a soul-winner in the best Elim tradition. No boy was safe from me at school. I remember the time I confronted twins at the urinals, where I insisted they could not leave until they made a decision for Christ. One was saved and the other got away!

Soon I had organized a Christian Union. Several boys were converted (one still attends the Elim church in Worthing) and we had lively if idiosyncratic Bible studies. I became head boy, and after a shaky start, went on to grammar school. By now I was running an evangelistic youth team and was as committed a Pentecostal as I have ever been, but after 1961 I ceased to be a member of Elim.

It is difficult to say why this happened. I drifted away rather than choosing to leave on a point of principle. My reference group had changed. When I got to the grammar school my friends were mainly middle-class, and if they had any religious allegiance it was to the Church of England. I began to attend an Anglican evangelical church, but I never joined (or was invited to, for that matter). There were more and "posher" girls there, and one stunning girl, who attended the Sunday night "Squash," led me effortlessly away from the inner sanctum of evangelical piety.

She was glamorous and worldly-wise, smoked Gitanes, and was rich. More intoxicated with the girl than with God, I went to London Bible College in 1964—not wanting to do so, but feeling that I ought to for the sake of my mother because I had promised her that I would go.

I must have been the College's most inglorious son, for I only stayed a term, feigning a mental breakdown in order to get out. Quite suddenly I stopped believing in God. No doubt this had nothing to do with London Bible College, but when I left I dropped Pentecostalism—and all things religious—for, so I thought, wider shores.

By now my soul and senses were full of the sounds and enticements of the Sixties. For seven years I did without God and made do with sociology, pop music, and armchair socialism. I never took the Marxist bait, partly because I was not persuaded intellectually by its Hegelian dialectic, but mainly because the Marxists I met reminded me too much, in terms of psychological profile, of the Pentecostals I had left behind. I was still interested in religion from a sociological standpoint, but eschewed emotionalism and what I had come to believe was psychic mumbo-jumbo.

In fact, that is putting it in too cerebral a fashion. I had become allergic to all things evangelical and Pentecostal. If I had been asked to write of Elim at that time, I would have come up with something of the bile and squinted version of Jeanette Winterson's *Oranges Are Not the Only Fruit*. I was not so much ashamed of my background as contemptuous of it: like Ms. Winterson, I liked to think of myself as the butterfly who had escaped from the claustrophobic chrysalis.

And then in 1971—after the usual twists and turns of coping with adult life in the present age—I found God again as suddenly as I had lost him. Or to be exact, God found me—and in a way that was both typically Pentecostal and yet atypical: it happened in a dream.

I was on a modern dance floor, and I was a teenager again. The room was noisy and crowded, but then directly in front of me a man from the crowd came into focus, and it was Jesus. He asked me to dance. I protested, for we Pentecostals did not dance. The invitation not only took me by surprise, it also embarrassed me: how could I dance with *him?* How could Jesus ask *me* to do such a thing?

And then the Lord spoke to me (I say the Lord advisedly, for the Jesus of this dream was not a figure that in any way resembled a familiar friend). He said, "If you do not dance with me, I can have no part of you." I knew I had to do it or he would turn away, so I lifted my right hand to take his left and I extended my left arm to embrace his right, and like a young girl I was led away on a merry dance that had something of the character of a quickstep or a Gay Gordon. I was desperately happy.

Of course, such intense emotion recollected in waking tranquility would lead, one might imagine, to an instant debunking: a cold dose of psychological reductionism. And indeed there were no doubt many personal circumstances at the time that could be said to have brought on the dream. But the fact is that when I awoke I was a believer in a Christian God again, and it never occurred to me to interpret the story in terms of, say, repressed homo-eroticism, or spicy food, let alone unhappy circumstances.

Since that day in 1971 I have, from time to time, examined the dream-encounter in more or less objective fashion, but although the vividness of the dance has faded, my belief in the Lord of that dance has not. I also learned another dance lesson from the dream that has stayed with me ever since: experience does not always come with a ready-made theology. To believe in God again, as I did then, was one thing, but how was I to understand him? I was surprised to find that I did not want to go back to the church of my youth. This discovery was reinforced by my rediscovering the Bible, or rather my discovery of it: for it was so long since I had read it with evangelical eyes that the much-loved scriptural passages of my childhood seemed strange and enigmatic.

This led to a determination to begin from scratch, and for me that meant beginning with church history. It came as a bit of a shock to discover that there were fifteen hundred years of vibrant and exciting Christian witness before the Reformation. As a boy I had swallowed the usual sectarian interpretation of Christianity: that there was Jesus, the Bible, and me—church history was not high on the list of Pentecostal priorities. But in reading the history I became excited at the development of Christian doctrine down through the ages. I remember in particular reading for the first time J. N. D. Kelly's *Early Christian Doctrines* and being stunned by the brilliance of the early church fathers (and to think I had wasted all these years studying sociology!).

Indeed, so immersed did I become in the history of the early church that I changed the direction of my post-graduate studies so that I could relate the theology of the fathers to the issues of present-day social science. I recall that my supervisor received a curt note from the London University board of sociological studies enquiring whether my doctorate, "Two Versions of Sociological Discourse: The Apophatic and Cataphatic Grounds of Social Science," was on the level!

It was also in 1971 that I encountered for the first time the charismatic renewal movement. I soon discovered that a charismatic was a middle-class Pentecostal (a conviction that remains with me still). It was strange for me, as an ex-Elimite, to find the Pentecostal experience at large in the mainstream churches. I sought out some Catholic charismatics who were my neighbors in southwest London. They were graciously accepting of me—caught as I was in a denominational no-man's-land—and their friendship did much to lessen my prejudice against Roman Catholics. I was more amused than bemused to find them speaking in tongues and praying over each other, yet without any of the pious trappings of my childhood. They drank alcohol and smoked (and sometimes even swore) and refused to take themselves too seriously.

And yet, for them, Pentecost was serious business: it had lifted them out of nominal Catholicism into a committed Christianity. "The baptism" had something of a conversion experience about it: there was nothing more important to them than their newfound faith. Their Pentecost was anarchic and liberating, breaking them free from the boundaries of ritual and dogma. And yet, among some of them, it had also led to a fey spirituality: morality ran wild, and a number of people were seriously hurt and bewildered as they discovered, as I had as a young boy, that Pentecostal experience does not automatically lead to holiness, sound judgment, or moral sensibility.

Not that I was any less of a mess than they were—far from it. But for the first time since my days as a Pentecostal I began to sense some worth in my upbringing. We were narrow, but there was depth. Certainly we were puritanical, but there was something of the high Puritan idealism among us. There was not much scholarship in evidence, but we were not stupid. (How I have longed, as a professional watcher of the charismatic "stars" over the years, that some of the modern-day charismatics had an ounce of that working-class "nous" of the Pentecostals who could more often than not sniff out a "wrong-un" or spot the latest supernatural fashion as no more than a passing wind.)

Despite the mixed blessings of the Roman Catholic renewal, I already knew in 1971 that I was beginning to turn toward Catholicism, or at least sacramentalism. But I found Roman Catholic liturgy alien to me, and I felt that the papal claims were unconvincing in the light of my studies of early church history. I had already read Timothy Ware's *The Orthodox Church,* and was fascinated to have stumbled across a tradition that was curiously both mystical and yet down-to-earth. And then one night on television I saw Archbishop Anthony Bloom, as he was then, in conversation with Marghanita Laski.

I was deeply impressed by his graciousness and intellectual toughness, so I rang the Russian Orthodox Church and requested an interview, ostensibly to talk about the Russian revolution. It was disconcerting to have this perfectly relaxed archbishop smiling in agreement with me while I fidgeted away in a denunciation of the Orthodox Church and all its reactionary ways. (I was a sociologist, and a socialist of a kind, and thought this was one way to put him on the defensive.) When I paused for a breath, and because I did not really have anything else to say, there was a long silence; the archbishop looked straight at me, and after what seemed an unnaturally long wait, he said, "Now tell me, why have you really come to see me?"

And so it began—the journey to Orthodoxy which was to lead to my joining the Russian Church in 1973. The sheer sensuality of the Russian liturgy was at first an offense to my Pentecostal puritanism. I used to stand in the church with my eyes closed so that I would not have to see all the colors, icons, and the unregimented bobbings and crossings of the faithful at prayer. The music would overwhelm me with its richness and solemn emotion, and in the darkness, despite the pungent incense, it was almost like being back in the Welsh valleys with the male-voice choirs and the *hwyl* of the Apostolic Church.

Of course, in time I adjusted, and became a Pentecostal exile in a diaspora church whose own experience has been "singing the Lord's song in a strange land." I discovered that Orthodoxy had its own charismatic tradition, but that its cultural and spiritual roots lay in Eastern spirituality and contemplative prayer, rather than in Western enthusiasm and frenetic singing. To this day, I believe that the sobriety of silence in the Eastern Church is one of the lost chords in the charismatic melody.

Perhaps more significantly, I learned from Orthodoxy that God the Holy Spirit is a person, not a power, and that this same person who brooded over the waters of creation also overshadowed the maiden of Israel, raised Jesus from the dead, and continues to bring to the church all that God the Father has revealed through the Son. The Spirit can therefore never be raw power without sacrificial love, intuitive and psychic force without sober counsel, a strong advocate on our behalf without also convicting us of wrongdoing.

But Russian Orthodoxy was to do something else for me in terms of my Pentecostal past and my continuing involvement with the renewal in the present. Orthodoxy stressed the healing-and-restoration model of forgiveness perhaps more than the juridical one. To be forgiven also leads to reconciliation. For me, this reconciliation started when Metropolitan Anthony (as the archbishop had now become) was able to show me that I was not coming to the Orthodox Church to find Christ: I had already discovered him as a young man, and now he was leading me to the Church.

Furthermore, he insisted, for me to become Orthodox would be counterproductive if I thought that I could exchange one religious ghetto for the enclosedness of another. Because of my past, he told me, I should try to build bridges between the Orthodox tradition and the other Christian confessions who were out of communion, or not of sympathy, with the Eastern Church (or more to the point, as I discovered, just plain ignorant of it).

This pastoral advice was, in fact, to become the latent spring of the C. S. Lewis Centre, which was founded in 1987; but in the 1970s the immediate effect was for me to begin to shed my shame and bitterness for my sectarian past and to reappraise it without rancor.

I learned to appreciate—as did the Anglican C. F. Andrews, when looking back on his childhood in the Catholic Apostolic Church—that the Spirit is sovereign: He blows where He wills, and breathes life into the most unlikely and least promising of organisms.

Elim means "place of refreshing" in Hebrew, and if it also had its stagnant pools it was not without its vigorous spas. For it was in Elim that I first learned that,

> Jesus loves the little children,
> All the children of the world.
> Red and yellow, black and white,
> All are precious in his sight.
> Jesus loves the little children of the world.

There was incipient racism there, as in all churches, but I never doubted that humanity was by definition co-humanity under one God.

It was in Elim that I first learned of the centrality of repentance in the Christian life: "At the cross, at the cross where I first saw the light and the burden of my heart rolled away." It was in Orthodoxy that I was to find the fulfillment of that message, for I discovered that being "down at the cross" was not a psychological expurgation of guilt, but a continuous process of self-losing and spiritual renewal.

What we might call the ceaseless need for repentance is endemic in Orthodox spirituality. "Lord Jesus Christ, Son of God, have mercy on me, a sinner" runs the Jesus Prayer: there lies the antidote to charismatic triumphalism and the messianic pretension that bedevils Pentecostal movements.

But being reconciled with the Elim of my past was to bring to mind a rude good health that, notwithstanding a certain kind of crankiness, never entirely gave way to the mountebanks and mavericks of the charismatic fringes. There is a long tradition of making mistakes: they have been going about their Pentecostal business for eighty years and have learned from their errors and misdemeanors.

The charismatic renewal, being middle-class and new to the game, thinks it does not have much to learn from its older and less fashionable cousin. It is mistaken. Classical Pentecostals may still be Bible fundamentalists, yet at least they have fallen into the habit of "testing all things" by Scripture. Indeed, their holiness tradition shines through, for they have not entirely lost Wesley's commitment to the quadrilateral: faith, reason, Scripture, and experience. It is only when the experiential swamps Pentecostalism (whether classical or modern-day charismatic) that everything becomes unbalanced and those negative aspects of the tradition—sentimentality, fanaticism, the lust for power—come roaring through with the undiscriminating force of a tidal wave. What kind of religious revival will we see if these powers are loosed on the world?

Elim and the Assemblies of God have it within their resources to sound a restraining and correcting note to the present charismatic movement if they have the will to do so. It is hard to raise a voice, however, when you are made to feel second-class cousins, as classical Pentecostals so often are by both the historical denominations and the so-called "new churches." I remember that as a boy I could withstand opposition, but not belittlement. Few people can stand up and be true to themselves when they are being looked down upon; so often the result of being either shunned or patronized by fellow Christians is to embrace the less uncomfortable ally of exclusivism and to rattle blunted sabres behind the buckler of inverted snobbery.

Today, however, Elim and the Assemblies of God have gained in confidence: they now have available nearly four generations of experience to draw on. Would that the renewal movement, and the house churches, had harkened to the wise warnings of Pastor John Lancaster, when in an article in *Decision* magazine some years ago he wrote eirenically but incisively of "the cult of the self-conscious." I showed it to another wayward Pentecostalist, Professor Walter Hollenweger. He agreed with me that it was one of the most balanced and timely views of the charismatic movement he had seen, for this Elim pastor had put his finger on the dangers of leaders who had ceased to be God-centered and had become so self-conscious of their significance in the divine mission that they were not so much promoters of Pentecost as purveyors of their own (often profitable) wares.

I also showed the article to Metropolitan Anthony. "This is good," he said; "this is Orthodox." He meant, of course, that the criticisms of Pastor Lancaster were the sort of criticisms that would naturally flow from the Orthodox tradition: for Pentecostalism and Orthodoxy share a common view on the supernatural. They both fervently believe in miracles, and because of the seriousness with which they hold to that belief they both also insist that fraudulence, superstition, and shoddy spirituality should be exposed as an affront to the gospel. (At their worst, both Pentecostalism and Orthodoxy have a long history of "wonder-working" oddities, if it not outright chicanery.)

Arthur Wallis, the late senior statesman of restorationism, once referred to me, objectively enough, as an "ex-Pentecostal." Denominationally this is, of course, true. I would have never, however, reneged on my past experience, even though I would have to say unequivocally that my churchmanship, theology, and spirituality are Orthodox. Since I became Orthodox, I have not been ashamed of being a former Pentecostal—nor, on the whole, do Pentecostals seem to be ashamed of me. Indeed, it is surely one of the oddities of being an accredited lay preacher in the Orthodox Church that I have preached far more in charismatic churches than in Orthodox ones. Even stranger was my experience in 1988 when I was taken by an Orthodox priest in Tulsa, Oklahoma, to be introduced to the faculty of theology at Oral Roberts University. Later in the week I was to run a series of workshops at the St. Anne's Orthodox Institute attended by professors from Oral Roberts University! These encounters, which many might see as eccentric, are by no means atypical of my experience in North America and Europe over the last few years.

I well remember when I attended the World Council of Churches consultation on the renewal in Switzerland in 1980. Naturally, I spent most of my time with the Orthodox delegation. They were curious about, rather than censorious toward, the charismatic crowd. ("Why do they jump around like Chinese crackers?" asked one of the priests from Lebanon.) However, the senior member of the party, Metropolitan Irenaeus from Crete, was particularly taken with a West Indian gospel group from a Pentecostal church in London. He bought one of their music tapes, and as he was stuffing it deep in his cassock I asked him if he had enjoyed their music. "No," he said, "I did not much like their songs, for they were too sentimental, but I was deeply impressed with the singers, and I want always to remember them. I feel that they are really like us inside."

Inside my heart Pentecostalism and Orthodoxy abide like the subject and interpreter of an unfinished biography: they are not interlinked like some mysterious monophysite conjunction; they are separated by time and experience, by preference and commitment, by intellectual conviction and, yes, by estrangement. But they have both had to come to terms with the fact that there is only one Spirit of truth, one Comforter, and in Him they have learned to exchange not merely a greeting, but a kiss.

8

Under the Russian Cross

A Research Note on C. S. Lewis
and the Eastern Orthodox Church

(1990)

Lewis was a thoroughly Western man, steeped in the thought patterns of Augustine, Aquinas, and medievalism. If his philosophical idealism ultimately harked back to Plato, it was refracted not so much through the fathers as through later Thomism and the comfortable Englishness of T. H. Green.

And yet it is surely one of the greatest accolades that we can bestow on Lewis that this "Christian for all Christians" is avidly read and admired by thousands of people in the Eastern churches. In Great Britain, for example, in the bookshop of the Russian cathedral at Ennismore Gardens in London there are basically two types of books on sale: Orthodox books, and a huge array of the writings of C. S. Lewis. And Metropolitan Anthony is a great admirer of Lewis and of Lewis' friend Charles Williams (and is also, of course, the chairman of the trustees of the C. S. Lewis Centre).

My contact with the Orthodox in the United States, which ranges from the Antiochene Church, and the Greeks, to the more Russified flavor of the Orthodox Church of America, suggests that Lewis is probably the most widely read of all Protestant writers. And it is not only among the Orthodox diaspora in America and Europe that this is so. I remember being present at a dinner party in London some years ago at which a senior Greek bishop from Constantinople begged me to send him Lewis' *Out of the Silent Planet*, mentioning in passing that in his opinion Lewis was really an "anonymous" Orthodox![1]

The evidence that Lewis himself was well acquainted with Eastern Orthodox theology and practice is, however, scanty. Certainly in his earlier writings he shows little acquaintance with the Greek fathers, and his cast of mind, with its commitment to classicism and the moral law, was clearly of a more *cataphatic* caste than the *apophatic* die of the Eastern Church.

Nevertheless, it is unfair to suggest that Lewis knew nothing at all of the Eastern fathers. We have his own admiring comments concerning Athanasius and his theology in "On the Reading of Old Books."[2] Furthermore, as I have argued elsewhere,[3] the "deep magic" of Narnia invoked by the White Witch in *The Lion, the Witch, and the Wardrobe,* is a clear echo of the ransom theory, much loved by the early Greek fathers—especially by Gregory of Nyssa—in which the devil is seen as holding rights over the human world because of the fall. These rights God respects, and because of his innate justice he is prepared to pay the devil his dues. But Christ, like Aslan, knows of a deeper and more hidden "law" than the devil knows. In any event the devil is "tricked" by the cross,[4] for Jesus is no mere mortal in thrall to Satan: he is the God-Man—pure and without sin. In Gregory of Nyssa's words, Jesus "was the bait on the fish-hook."[5]

The fact that this theory of the atonement was abandoned by both East and West would not have worried Lewis (though in the West, but never the East, Christ's death on the cross was later seen as a ransom necessary to appease the anger of a wrathful God). We know, anyhow, that Lewis was not attached to one particular theory of the atonement; but it is so typical of him to have used the primitive ransom doctrine in that most famous of all

---

1. The word anonymous is a humorous, oblique reference to Karl Rahner's famous notion of the "anonymous Christian."

2. Lewis, "On the Reading of Old Books," 25–33.

3. Walker, *Enemy Territory,* 45.

4. Cf. Augustine's comment: "The devil jumped for joy when Christ dies; and by the very death of the Christ the devil was overcome: he took, as it were, the bait in the mousetrap. He rejoiced at the death, thinking himself death's commander. But that which caused his joy dangled the bait before him. The Lord's cross was the devil's mousetrap; the bait which caught him was the death of the Lord'; see Bettenson, ed., *The Later Christian Fathers,* 222.

5. Cf. Gregory's *oratio catechetical (magna)*—or Great Catechetical Oration: "In order that the exchange for us might be easily accepted by our human nature so that, as with a greedy fish, the hook of divinity might be swallowed along with the bait of flesh," Bettenson, ed., *The Later Christian Fathers,* 142.

the Narnian chronicles, simply because it was good myth and worked well in the context of what I have called the "divine drama" of salvation.[6]

All of this is in itself interesting—for Lewis buffs at least—but it is hardly proof of Lewis' interest in Eastern Orthodoxy.

Lewis' apologetics and his imaginative stories are not liberally peppered with references of allusions to the desert fathers of the *Philokalia*,[7] nor to the later treasury of Russian spiritual theology. Nevertheless, he did encounter Eastern Orthodoxy, though not primarily in books, nor in Greece or the Baltic states, but in Oxford through the Russian diaspora. In particular, he was a friend of Nicholas and Militza Zernov from the 1940s to his death in 1963. (He used to refer to Nicholas, who was one of the great characters of the diaspora as an "Oxford institution.")

Militza Zernov told me[8] "we have certainly talked with C. S. Lewis (we are calling him Jack) about the Orthodox Church. He was deeply interested in it." Nicholas Zernov, who had a reputation for being persistent and persuasive, managed to involve Lewis in a number of his activities. For example, Nicholas helped to found the Fellowship of Saint Alban and Saint Sergius, which still exists today. Its purpose was to bring Eastern and Western Christians (especially Anglicans) closer together. Militza Zernov recalls that Lewis went to one of the early summer conferences at Abingdon, where he was involved in all the discussions of the differences between the Eastern and Western churches. She cannot recall the year. We know, however, that Lewis read at least one paper to the Fellowship, on "Membership," for it was published in *Sobornost* on June 31, 1945; it is still available in various Lewis collections.[9]

Less well known is the fact that Lewis attended a meeting at Saint Gregory's House in Oxford (again, Militza Zernov is not sure of the date), which was another one of Nicholas Zernov's ecumenical ventures to bring Christians of the East and West closer together. There, Lewis read a paper entitle "A Toy, an Icon, and a Work of Art." To my knowledge this paper has never been written up and published. (Perhaps someone somewhere can recall the content of this pMaper of maybe has even recorded it?)

For many years it has been a common practice in Oxford for the Greek Orthodox and the Russian Orthodox to share a common church, while

6. Walker, *Enemy Territory*, especially chaps. 1 and 2; see also Taliaferro, "A Narnian Theory of the Atonement," 75–92.

7. Cf. *The Philokalia* (1981), 4.

8. This is from a recorded conversation in Oxford (August, 1987). All subsequent quotations from Mrs. Zernov are from this conversation. I wish to thank Mr. Jacob Osborn for his help with this recording.

9. Lewis, *Fern-seed and Elephants*, 11–25.

maintaining their distinctiveness. Whether or not it was this Oxford church that Lewis attended I do not know, but Lewis certainly attended at least one Orthodox liturgy and was clearly moved by it:

> What pleased me most about a Greek Orthodox mass I once attended was that there seemed to be no prescribed behavior for the congregation. Some stood, some knelt, some sat, some walked; one crawled about the floor like a caterpillar. And the beauty of it was that nobody took the slightest notice of what anyone else was doing. I wish we Anglicans would follow their example. One meets people who are perturbed because someone in the next pew does, or does not, cross himself. They ought not even to have seen, let alone censured. "Who are thou that judgest Another's servant?"[10]

Curiously, though surely it is of some symbolic importance, the Orthodox faith was to play some (albeit small) part in Lewis' funeral. As Militza Zernov recalls:

> When Lewis died, it was very little known in Oxford; but we knew about his death, and we wanted to come to his funeral. It was in the church near where his home was, and I prepared a cross with white flowers for his grave. When we arrived the church warden said that C. S. Lewis' brother, Major Lewis, had made an arrangement that there were to be no flowers in church. (He was very severe in his opinions.) So my cross was put outside the church. But we were early, before the beginning of the service, and then the news came that C. S. Lewis' brother was very unwell.[11] So the warden said, "Well, let's bring your cross in." And so the coffin was very high up in the middle of the church, and the white cross was put at the foot of this arrangement. And when his coffin was put in the cemetery, which was around the church, my cross was put on his coffin. So in that I was very happy that I could say farewell to him. And I am sure he would be pleased with it, because he appreciated beauty very much.

So there we have it. Who would have thought? Jack Lewis was buried under a Russian cross of white flowers, beneath an English November sky. And in their distinctive ways all of Christendom's divided church were

10. Lewis, *Prayer: Letters to Malcolm*, 12.

11. As Walter Hooper has told me, "It was no great secret that Major Lewis was in fact drunk." His absence is confirmed by J. R. R. Tolkien in one of his letters, dated November 26, 1963, which briefly describes Lewis' funeral, and the people who were present at it; see Carpenter, ed., *The Letters of J. R. R. Tolkien*, 341.

represented there when it must have seemed that for a moment there was a synergy of heaven and earth—a suspension of time, an instance of "big magic," when that "other country" was fleetingly transported to our own.

9

Young Jack

(2002)

Many people are not aware that the man who wrote over forty religious books is also the author of several major works in literary history and criticism. From *The Allegory of Love*, published in 1936, to *English Literature in the Sixteenth Century, Excluding Drama*, published in 1954, and on to his last major work, published in 1964, *The Discarded Image: An Introduction to Medieval and Renaissance Literature*, C. S. Lewis spanned forty years of English scholarship. He spent thirty of those years at Magdalene College, Oxford, and then ten years at Magdalene College, Cambridge, where he was also Professor of Medieval and Renaissance Literature.

I mention this not only to give Lewis due honor now we are well past the centenary of his birth, but also to remind us that his religious imagination was baptized in oceans of great literature. His university achievements also remind us that this Oxford don was exceptionally talented and very, very bright—a fact that the film *Shadowlands* totally fails to reflect. His examiner at Oxford when Lewis went up in 1918 remarked that he was better read than any undergraduate he ever met.

SNAPSHOTS OF A LIFE

All of this might lead us to conclude that while C. S. Lewis was undoubtedly brilliant, his personal life was really rather boring. Not for him a life of adventure like Robert Louis Stephenson, trekking into the wilderness of California or braving the Pacific storms on course for exotic islands in the South Seas. No, except for a brief spell in the trenches in 1918, and a rather late romantic marriage to feisty New Yorker Joy Davidman in 1956, Lewis remained virtually ensconced, like a latter day Rapunzel, in the ivory tower of university scholarship. He escaped the college quads only for the occasional walk and the more than occasional trip to the pub, where he liked nothing better than the company and conversation of other intellectual men. Lewis liked women, too, but he preferred them to be striking and clever, rather than beautiful and decorous. He seems, for example, to have had a hankering for, as well as a horror of, the witch Jadis in his book, *The Magician's Nephew*. "A dem fine woman," Digory's Uncle Andrew called her in the concluding words of that book.

Lewis' outer life was fixed from early manhood. This rather large, plain, red-faced, yellow-toothed, disheveled, and balding man, whom A. N. Wilson, Lewis' most acerbic biographer, described as looking rather like a "pork butcher," rose early, read and wrote all morning (he never typed), supped too much beer at lunch, walked it off in the afternoon, often with dog, dined in college rooms, went to pub, his favorite being the Eagle and Child, where he conversed late into the evening with friends—often with the so-called "Inklings," which included fellow writers Charles Williams, J. R. R. Tolkien, and occasionally Dorothy Sayers.

Lewis virtually chain-smoked throughout the day and night, both cigarettes and pipe, enjoyed bawdy humor with his beer, and was very loud and cheery—not at all retiring in manner or pious in outward behavior. Christopher Tolkien once wrote to his famous father that Lewis had said he was giving up beer for Lent, after downing three pints in quick succession.

Sometimes, Lewis would briefly leave Oxford to give invited lectures—always travelling by train, for he hated cars and could not drive—and in 1942 he famously broadcast on BBC Radio a series of talks that were repackaged and published in 1952 as *Mere Christianity*. Despite the fact that he hardly ever read newspapers, he wrote for the *Daily Mirror* during the Second World War, and even sallied forth from the closeted world of Oxford to talk religion to the troops.

When he was in his home, the Kilns at Oxford, which was most of the time, he enjoyed a correspondence with literally hundreds of ordinary people—many of whom lived in the United States. Perhaps nothing was more remarkable of Lewis than that this most academic and closeted of men had the common touch and a touching faith, like his hero G. K. Chesterton, in the moral good sense of ordinary people.

As a tutor Lewis was outstanding, but also demanding; he never backed down from an argument and he liked to win. His hectoring and sometimes bullying style was too much for some; the English poet John Betjeman, for example, came to loathe him. He certainly could go over the top, as on the occasion when he chased an unfortunate undergraduate down the stairs from his rooms at Magdalene with a sword and shouted at him not to come back until he had learned to read a text correctly.

But for most students Lewis was an inspiring and tireless tutor. One of the most extraordinary accolades he ever received came from the infamous literary critic, Kenneth Tynan, who staged the nude musical *Oh! Calcutta!* in Britain. In later life, he called Lewis the greatest man he had ever met and admitted: "If I were ever to stray into the Christian camp, it would be because of Lewis' arguments as expressed in books like *Miracles.*" And he asked for these words of C. S. Lewis to be read out at his funeral:

> These things—the beauty, the memory of our own past—are good images of what we really desire: but if they are mistaken for the thing itself they turn into dumb idols, breaking the hearts of their worshippers. For they are not the thing itself; they are only the scent of a flower we have not found, the echo of a tune we have not heard, news from a country we have never visited.

We could go on in this tantalizing way, taking snapshots of Lewis' life, but if we want some real insight into his work and life—his inner life which was never boring—then it is better if we turn to his childhood and early manhood, because it is there that the real Lewis, the champion of historic Christianity, the Christian apologist, the writer of children's classic tales, emerges.

JACK'S CHILDHOOD

Lewis was born on November 29, 1898 in Belfast. His father, Albert, of Welsh extraction, and his mother Flora, the daughter of an Irish clergyman, were both intellectually gifted and financially comfortable. The first thing to understand about Clive Staples Lewis was that he was an Ulster Irishman with all that that entails. When he was little and being toilet trained, his nanny used to call his stools "little popes."

The second thing to understand is that he had an elder brother, Warnie, whom he adored and remained loyal to all his life. Warnie was a lifelong alcoholic, and when Lewis was buried in Headington Quarry church, Warnie could not attend because he was drunk. It was Warnie who was the first to call Clive "Jack," the name Lewis was called all his life by his friends. At the age of eight, Jack could write in his diary, "Hoorah! Warnie comes home this morning. I am lying in bed waiting for him and thinking about him, and before I know where I am I hear his boots pounding on the stairs, he comes into the room, we shake hands and begin to talk."

And how they talked and played. In 1905 they moved to Little Lea, a large, rambling house in Belfast with attic rooms, creaking corridors and acres of space. There, young Jack and Warnie played and wrote stories together. Little Big of Boxen (a land of talking animals) was just one of the characters to emerge from Jack's pen and paintbrush. Little Lea was a haven for two rather lonely little boys whose parents preferred that they be neither seen nor heard.

The third thing to understand about Jack Lewis was that he loved his mother Flora more than anybody in the world. She was his rock, his security, his joy. In 1908, when he was just ten years old, Jack's mother died after a long fight against cancer. The young boy's life was shattered. He had to attend her wake where she lay in an open coffin, the marks of corruption probably visible. Jack never really got over his mother's passing, nor the decay of death.

It is not surprising that years later, in *The Magician's Nephew*, Digory's mother is lovingly described on her deathbed, as if she were Flora: "There she lay, as he had seen her like so many other times, propped up on the pillows, with a thin, pale face that would make you cry to look at." And can we blame the middle-aged Lewis for curing Digory's mother of the terminal illness with the magic apple from Narnia? Never was a childhood wish fulfillment more touching, more understandable, more lovingly displayed; it was an imaginative balm to heal the broken heart.

A few short years after writing the first Narnia tale, Jack Lewis was to see his dear wife Joy seemingly healed of bone cancer by prayer, only for the two year remission to be cruelly ended by Joy's premature death. Lewis' despair, anger, and the inklings of hope are starkly revealed in his scorchingly honest book, *A Grief Observed*. In my opinion, this short tract on grief, pain, and faith offers greater Christian vision and conviction than the rather clever but cold defense of God's dealings with the world of suffering in *The Problem of Pain*, written by Lewis in 1940.

ADOLESCENCE, MYTHS, AND LEGENDS

On the day that Flora died in 1908, the Shakespearean quotation on her calendar was from King Lear: "Men must endure their going hence." It seems that small boys must also endure such loss, because just two weeks later, young Jack, his grief still raw, was sent to boarding school in England. Not only was this cruel in itself, but Lewis found the school itself cruel. The matron was obsessed with spiritualism, and the headmaster was so unstable that sometime after Lewis left he was found to be clinically insane.

Five years later, at the age of fifteen, he entered one of England's most famous private schools, Malvern College. Lewis hated it. Far too clever for boys and teachers alike, and poor at games, he was mercilessly bullied. In his autobiography, *Surprised by Joy*, Lewis barely mentions that he was wounded in the Great War, but spends pages raging against the English boarding school system and his misery at Malvern. He later explained this by saying that he had expected war to be brutal, while he had believed that school would be a haven of security and the nursery of civilization.

Jack lost his childhood faith in God after the death of his mother and under the iron regime of school life. Throughout his adolescence he was without faith and convinced intellectually that reason alone was the answer to understanding reality. But his heart told him something else. Lewis was deeply romantic by temperament and remained so all his life. He loved the ancient romances of Arthur, the Norse Legends, the epic beauty of *Beowulf*, the allure and charm of fairy stories. He was more at home in the world of ancient literature than he was in the modern world—something that held true for his whole life. Years later he wrote of the joy of reading old books, and his mature conviction was that part of the cure for the maladies and follies of the present age was to step back imaginatively into older times where we can gain perspective on the "chronological snobbism" of our own.

Nowhere was Lewis' romanticism more apparent than in his love of pagan myths. He records in his autobiography that he knew they were lies, but believed them to be "lies breathed through silver." He recalls a strange experience that happened to him on hearing the line from *Beowulf*, "Balder the beautiful is dead." It created in him an emotional frisson, a thrill, a longing for the object of that emotion. He called this longing by the German word *Sehnsucht*, which suggests unrequited love, unbearable longing, mystic yearning.

Lewis came to believe that such longing was a desire inspired by true reality and not merely a psychological or subjective experience. Such a belief is both an echo of the old philosophical argument for God based on desire and a deeply romantic conviction that truth can be intuited through what the nineteenth-century Romantics called "the affections."

He later divided the acquiring of all knowledge into two modes of perception. Intuition or imagination he called by the French term *connaitre*. He believed that imagination was the organ of meaning, and that a "baptized imagination" was essential for successful Christian mission and nurture. Straight rational knowledge, the faculty of reason, he was to call *savoir*. For him, reason was the natural organ of truth. In his early days, although he was ideologically committed to the superiority of *savoir*, his heart was given to *connaitre*.

Lewis, then, was a romantic by disposition before he became a romantic by conviction. His commitment to romance and reason—to *connaitre* and *savoir*—can be seen by the subtitle to his first Christian book after his conversion. The book, published in 1933, was entitled *The Pilgrim's Regress*, and the subtitle is, *An Allegorical Apology for Christianity, Reason and Romanticism*. *The Pilgrim's Regress* is not one of Lewis' great books, but it points to much of his future work.

John, our pilgrim, is born in Puritania and dreams, or intuits, a beautiful island. He goes in search of this paradise along what Lewis calls the main road. This reminds us of Lewis' great viaduct of "mere Christianity" which towers over the uncertain terrain of marsh and tracks. In the *Regress*, the main road is bordered by the north lands of cold but strident reason leading to arrogance and atheism. To the south, the siren lands of emotional unreason beckon him.

The message is clear: reason and romance when both taken to excess can kill. Stay on the main road, adopt the golden mean, stick to the viaduct of "mere Christianity," don't let the letter of the law kill, or romantic longing overcome you. If you are an Anglican, like Lewis, you might of course see the main road in terms of the Anglican *via media*.

It's also worthy of note that in *The Pilgrim's Regress*, Lewis, who spent most of his adult life believing the doctrine of progress to be a poison stemming from the philosophical Enlightenment, asks us to see pilgrimage in terms not of civilization marching onwards, but a personal return to the garden, a regress to the world of childhood wonder, an inward turn where we find in the stillness of our heart the place to go "further up and further in." When pilgrim John eventually finds his paradise, it turns out to be adjacent to home. Home, after all, is where the heart is.

Between the time Lewis left Malvern School and took up his studies at Oxford University, he spent three years with a private tutor, W. T. Kirkpatrick, at Great Bookham in Surrey. A former teacher of his father, the private tutees called him "the Great Knock." Under his tutelage—for the Great Knock was as much a tartar as a tutor—Lewis became precociously proficient at ancient languages. Before his youth was out, he had become fluent not only in Latin and classical Greek, but also New Testament and Attic Greek.

The time with the Knock was an important period of Lewis' life, for the old man was a stickler for logic and a master of Socratic dialogue. A. N. Wilson tells the amusing story that when Jack arrived in Great Bookham, he remarked that Surrey was much more wild than expected. "Stop!" shouted the Knock. "What do you mean by wildness and what grounds had you for not expecting it?"

He then continued to show Lewis that what he had said was unreflective, if not meaningless. Lewis was later to say that the Knock would have been a Logical Positivist if born at a later date. As it was, he was also a humanist and an unbeliever.

COMING HOME TO MYTHOLOGY AND FAITH

When Jack Lewis arrived at Oxford in 1919 shortly after the Great War, he was intellectually on the side of progressive thinking in philosophy and set against the truth claims of Christianity. Interestingly, Lewis rejected Christianity not only because of siding with progressive thinking, but also because his great love and knowledge of pagan myths convinced him that it was not original. Rather like the German theologian, Rudolph Bultmann, Lewis felt the story of the Christ King was unhistorical, for it was so like the dying corn king of primitive fertility mythology, or echoed the death-resurrection motifs found in Osiris and Balder.

The problem was that Lewis found it harder to reject Christians. Men such as Owen Barfield, Hugo Dyson, and J. R. R. Tolkien were all Christians, and he preferred their company, as well as their aesthetics, to the progressive set he aspired to belong to. To make matters worse for an Ulster Irishman, Tolkien was a Roman Catholic!

Between 1920 and 1925, when Lewis was elected to a fellowship in English language at Magdalene College, Oxford, both his interests and his beliefs tilted away from progressive ideas and towards the *sapientia* (or eternal wisdom) of the ancients on the one hand, and to religious belief on the other hand. Lewis found, despite the Great Knock's predilection for positivism, that he had little sympathy for the new philosophy stemming from Moore, Whitehead, Russell, and Wittgenstein. He found instead that he preferred the idealism of Victorian idealist T. H. Green, and the Cambridge Platonism of the seventeenth-century philosopher Henry More.

Above all, he was convinced by the arguments of the eighteenth-century bishop and philosopher George Berkeley that spiritual reality is primary and material life is the appearance or perception of the spiritual world. He seems to have been at least half convinced by his friend Owen Barfield that the most primitive animism, which saw spirits, elves, and sprites in every brook and tree, was in some sense profoundly true.

This philosophical shift is no small matter in Lewis' development, for once he embraced idealism and strains of Platonism, he was never to abandon them, and as we shall shortly see, they helped him to embrace Christianity.

By 1929 Lewis had recaptured his childhood love of mythology to such an extent that he had come not merely to revel in them, but also to believe that they embodied truth greater than the truths of fact. Lewis later came to believe, as Samuel Taylor Coleridge had done before him, that the ancient myths were a gleam of divine light illuminating the human imagination. Myths were refractions of spiritual or divine reality.

Jack was not yet a Christian, but he had become a theist—he believed that a personal God of some kind existed. In his rooms at Oxford, he got down on his knees as a dejected convert, and assented that God was God. In 1929 also, Albert Lewis died at the age of sixty-six. Lewis was full of remorse and felt guilty at the way he had often ridiculed his father. He was not yet to know it, but he was close to conversion.

This happened in 1931 and there were two parts to it. The first part was intellectual conviction, and it was Tolkien, egged on by Hugo Dyson, who helped bring it about.[1] Tolkien convinced Lewis that what was original and unique about Jesus Christ is that he was myth become fact. To use a notion of Lewis' later writings which he gleaned from Bishop Berkeley, higher and spiritual things could be transposed into lower, material ones. In the incarnation, myth was grounded and yet still remained myth despite its particular historical embodiment. Divinity and materiality co-inhered, and Jesus Christ of Nazareth was not only revealed as Immanuel—God with us—but as one of us: the God-man (although this is expressing it in a more theological way than Lewis typically did).

The second phase of Lewis' conversion might be called the existentialist part. On 28th September 1931, Jack went on a trip with friends to Whipsnade Zoo. When the journey began, he was still not a convinced Christian, but by the time he arrived he was. In the language of Francis Thompson, the "hound of heaven" had at last caught his prey.

---

1. Since I wrote this account of "young Jack," my friend and colleague Alister Mc-Grath has convincingly demonstrated that Lewis' account of his conversion is incorrect, not in terms of the stages he went through—the process we might say—but the dates. In short, it was 1932, not 1931. Cf. Alister McGrath, C. S. Lewis: A Life.

CHAMPIONING THE FAITH

By 1931, when Jack Lewis was thirty-three, his intellectual habits and religious predilections were mostly formed. He never abandoned his love of mythology, his belief in an almost magical and certainly supernatural world. His commitment to reason and romanticism was unswerving. Existentially, however, Lewis had changed from the old man and had begun the long regress to the new one. Once he had turned to Christ he never let go, even though his faith was sorely tested when Joy died. He once said that you should stick to a great idea when it has commanded your attention and if he ever had considerable intellectual doubts about Christianity he never wrote of them—although in *A Grief Observed* he does question the goodness of God.

On the level of wish-fulfillment, I think Lewis would have followed Christ even if he had doubted whether the myth of the dying king had indeed been grounded as historical fact. In his Narnia book, *The Silver Chair*, Puddleglum defies the witch by saying: "That's why I'm going to stand by the play-world. I'm on Aslan's side even if there isn't any Aslan to lead it. I'm going to live as like a Narnian as I can even if there isn't any Narnia."

But of course I am just speculating here. What I think is of religious significance is that once Lewis turned to Christ, Christ commandeered his attention day and night. Lewis knew he was intellectually arrogant and intimidating, and so when he embraced the Christian faith he also embraced its disciplines. He attended Anglican liturgy weekly and faithfully took the Blessed Sacrament. Despite his Ulster Protestantism, his Anglicanism was more High Church than low. He attended confession weekly when he could, and took spiritual direction for his life from the local priest.

Not only did he give virtually all his free time to writing and defending the Christian faith, but he also gave his money to charities and people in need. If A. N. Wilson is correct in his unproven assertion that he had sexual relations when he was a young undergraduate with Mrs. Moore, the mother of his wartime friend Paddy who had died in the trenches, he more than atoned as he looked after her well into her old age, doing the most menial chores cheerfully and without stint.

Looking back now, we can see what a champion of the faith Lewis was—and remains today through his writings. When the theologians and Christian philosophers fell like a pack of cards before the advance of liberalism in between the two World Wars, it was Lewis who armed himself for the fight. While not a professional philosopher, he wrote of *The Problem of Pain*, upheld the classical moral virtues in *The Abolition of Man*, defended *Miracles*, and advanced the cause of historic Christianity with skill and bombastic aplomb. Speaking of the generation just before and after the Second World War, Professor Basil Mitchell, a professional philosopher formerly of Oriel College, Oxford, said of Lewis that "he both intellectually and imaginatively made Christianity seem credible again."

But it was not only the intellectuals who took heart. In 1942, the "apostle to the sceptics," as Lewis had become known, wrote a work of devastating wit and spiritual power, called *The Screwtape Letters*, ostensibly written by a senior devil (Screwtape) to his nephew Wormwood. So brilliant and imaginative was this book, and yet so accessible to the general public, that Lewis became a household name, and his (rather flattering) likeness appeared on the cover of *Time* magazine.

Jack wrote three science fiction novels, the second of which, *Perelandra*, is one of his great works; but he went on to pen the seven Narnia chronicles which have now become nothing less than children's classics. The chronicles are more episodic than epic, more impressionistic than pre-Raphaelite in detail. They are not careful "sub creations" in the Tolkien mold and in fact Tolkien did not like them.

The children are white, middle-class English boys and girls with somewhat stilted and "golly gosh" speech. Except for the spunky Lucy, the girls are not very interesting. What is interesting is that Lewis turned his hand to children's fairy tales after being defeated in a debate on naturalism at the Socratic Club at Oxford in 1948 by the formidable Elizabeth Anscombe. After this episode, Lewis never wrote Christian apologetics again.

Instead, he regressed to his childhood, fell back on his imagination and let his word pictures and baptized images tumble onto the page in almost reckless abandon. Everything from neo-Platonism, patristic theology, Norse legend—even Father Christmas—was thrown into the mix. On the one hand, the Narnia stories are careless, incomplete works (the chronology does not fit, for example). On the other hand, they are immediate, magical, and emotionally intense. They are "ripping yarns," because Lewis himself lets rip. Although they appear to be written for children, I think they were really written by Lewis for himself, and possibly for his brother Warnie.

Tolkien's *Lord of the Rings* is without doubt the more accomplished work, but Narnia grabs the attention with its power and numinous quality. Lewis, of course, wrote the Narnia stories, not as Christian allegories, but as myth. He would have been content, I am sure, if through them children learned of good and evil, the cardinal virtues, and perhaps even experienced *Sehnsucht* for themselves.

IO

SCRIPTURE, REVELATION, AND PLATONISM IN C. S. LEWIS

(2002)

INTRODUCTION

Lewis was, as he always admitted, an amateur theologian.[1] It would be unreasonable, therefore, to expect what Lewis believed about Scripture and revelation to be expressed in systematic form. Furthermore, there is only one substantial secondary source that I know of that has attempted to glean Lewis' scattered thoughts on these matters, and that is Michael Christensen's excellent little book *C. S. Lewis on Scripture*.

What we can say with some certainty about Lewis is that he did not subscribe to the view—still widely held in the American Bible-belt—that Scripture is itself God's revelation to humankind. I know of nowhere that Lewis denies that the Bible in some sense reveals something of God's intentions for the world, but neither do I know of anywhere where he talks of revelation in terms of propositional truth, or of isomorphic pairings between biblical words and God's utterances. Lewis without doubt believed the Scriptures to be inspired, but then, as he wrote to Clyde Kilby at Wheaton College in 1959, "If every good and perfect gift comes from the Father

---

1. For example, "I am a very ordinary layman" (Lewis, *Mere Christianity*, 6); "I write as one amateur to another" (Lewis, *Reflections on the Psalms*, 9).

of Lights, then all true and edifying writings, whether in Scripture or not, must be in some sense inspired."[2]

Now the reason that this is interesting, if not curious, is that in the 1960s Lewis was hailed by, if not hijacked by, American evangelicals as one of their own, and Wheaton College, which extols a theology much like Billy Graham's, continues to this day to house the greatest collection of Lewis manuscripts and memorabilia on the American continent. In particular, Wheaton still subscribes to the Scripture-as-revelation school as first propounded by Benjamin Warfield and colleagues at the Princeton School of Theology at the turn of the century.[3] The popular shorthand for this view of Scripture, as we know, is "inerrancy," and Lewis would have none of it, seeing it as part of the baggage of fundamentalism.

And so, what I intend to do here is first of all to outline Lewis' objection to what he believed to be fundamentalism;[4] secondly, briefly, to show what approach he *did* take to Scripture; and third, to outline his rather expansive view of just how God does reveal himself to the world. When looking at Lewis' account of Jesus Christ as particular and perfect revelation, I will argue that his excessive idealism—his tendency to Platonize reality—leads him to unfortunate and unsatisfactory theological expressions.

LEWIS AND FUNDAMENTALISM

The fierce controversies in the United States of America concerning the authority of Scripture in the latter half of the nineteenth century passed by Lewis. It is clear, however, that insofar as he encountered them at second hand, and while he was more unhappy with the whole tenor of modernist

---

2. *Letters of C. S. Lewis*, 480.

3. For Princetonian theology and its view of Scripture, see Noll, ed., *The Princeton Theology;* Balmer, "The Princetonians and Scripture: A Reconsideration"; and for the historical background of fundamentalism see Marsden, *Fundamentalism and American Culture.*

4. He explicitly disavows of fundamentalism in the essay "Fern-seed and Elephants," where he writes that "we must not, however, paint the picture too black. We are not fundamentalists. We think that different elements in this sort of theology have different degrees of strength" (108–9). Yet he does not disparage it, as he makes clear in the chapter on "Scripture" in *Reflections on the Psalms*: "One can respect, and at moments envy, both the Fundamentalist's view of the Bible and the Roman Catholic's view of the Church. But there is one argument which we should beware of using for either position: God must have done what is best, this is best, therefore God has done this. For we are mortals and do not know what is best for us, and it is dangerous to prescribe what God must have done—especially when we cannot, for the life of us, see that He has after all done it" (94).

thought—of which we will say more later—he was almost as unhappy with the kind of defense of the Bible that insisted that it was true because (a) God has spoken in it through the divine inspiration of the biblical writers; and (b) God being God can be trusted to guarantee the truth of his words. A consequence of this view of Scripture, as being underpinned by God's guarantee, is that the Bible contains no errors or contradictions. That is to say, to use the jargon again, it is inerrant. For some fundamentalists—even today—this means that the Bible contains not only infallible knowledge of God and our salvation, but also right knowledge of science, mathematics, and historical data.

Lewis found this approach mistaken, not because he thought that it smacked of foundationalism, nor even that it made the truth of the Bible dependent on a theory of knowledge. He disliked it because he felt that it failed to take into account the intentions of the biblical writers. He assumed, for example, that the writers of the creation story were engaged in myth-making, not descriptive science.

Lewis also felt that the inerrantist view failed to take the human fallibility of the Scriptures seriously. The fact that Lewis could see obvious contradictions and loose ends in Scripture convinced him that the Bible was not "fixed": if it was a seamless robe, men would call it a fake.

In his 1959 letter to Clyde Kilby, Lewis pointed out a number of obvious contradictions in the New Testament, which included the inconsistencies of the genealogies of Jesus as recorded in Matthew 1 and Luke 3, and the differing account of the death of Judas in Matthew 27:5 and Acts 1:18–19.[5] Lewis thought that harmonizing these accounts was illegitimate: it was, he believed, fallible men divinely inspired who wrote the pages of the Bible, not infallible men divinely inspired, nor even fallible men who dictated directly from God's speech without human imagination or interpretation playing its part.

Speaking of interpretation, I assume that we can apply Lewis' view of reading literature in *An Experiment in Criticism*, published in 1961,[6] to his view of understanding the Bible. In *An Experiment*, Lewis rejects the approach of identifying great literature in terms of an aesthetic canon, such as the modernist critic F. R. Leavis wanted to impose upon Western texts, in favor of one identifying it in terms of texts that produced good readers. "In reading great literature," he says, "I become a thousand men and yet remain myself. Like the night sky in the Greek poem, I see with myriad eyes, but it is still I who see. Here, as in worship, in love, in moral action, and in knowing,

5. Lewis to Clyde Kilby, *Letters of C. S. Lewis,* 480.
6. Lewis, *An Experiment in Criticism,* 141.

I transcend myself; and I am never more myself than when I do."[7] Perhaps this reminds us of George Steiner's wager on transcendence when reading a text against Derrida's slippage of meaning![8] More appositely, we seem to have here Lewis offering *reading itself* as revelatory.

Certainly the key to understanding Lewis' approach to Scripture is to recognize that he writes, not as a theologian, but as a literary critic who spent his life immersed in literature, ranging from romance to myth and from realistic narrative to fairy story. To talk of the Bible as containing only historical fact, or propositions, was nonsense to Lewis, for such an idea fell down on the parables of Jesus and the majestic poetry of the Psalms.

But Lewis went further and wondered if God did not intend to give us sacred fiction as well as fact in the Bible. Writing to Corbin Carnell in 1953, he suggested that "the whole *Book of Jonah* has to me the air of being a moral romance, a quite different kind of thing from, say, the account of King David or the New Testament narratives, not pegged, like them, into any historical situation."[9]

He later suggested, in 1959, to theological students at Westcott House in Cambridge, that Jonah was a fictional story flavored with Jewish humor.[10] At other times, Lewis suggested that the books of both Esther and Job, like Jonah, had the air of sacred fiction, not only because of their once-upon-a-time literary construction, but also because none of these books fit into a known geography or historical time-frame—unlike Jesus, who was born in the time of Caesar Augustus and suffered under Pontius Pilate.[11]

LEWIS AND MODERNISM

The above evidence, while scanty, is strong enough to see that Lewis was no biblical conservative in the fundamentalist sense; but as I will now go on to show, neither was he a modernist or a theological liberal in the accepted sense.

7. Ibid., 141.

8. George Steiner, *Real Presences*. For helpful discussions of this aspect of Steiner's thought, see especially Anthony C. Yu, "A Meaningful Wager," 241–44; and the following three essays: Ronald A. Sharp, "Steiner's Fiction and the Hermeneutics of Transcendence,"; Gerhard Neumann, "The 'Masters of Emptiness' and the Myth of Creativity: George Steiner's *Real Presences*"; and Robert P. Carroll, "Toward a Grammar of Creation: On Steiner the Theologian," in Nathan A. Scott, Jr and Ronald A. Sharp, eds., *Reading George Steiner*, 205–29, 247–61, and 262–74, respectively.

9. Lewis to Carnell, quoted in Christensen, *C. S. Lewis on Scripture*, 104–5.

10. Lewis, "Fern-seed and Elephants," 108.

11. Lewis to Janet Wise, cited in Christensen, *C. S. Lewis on Scripture*, 106–7.

The first thing to say is that although Lewis may not have had any kind of worked-out doctrine of biblical inspiration, he undoubtedly believed that the Scriptures were a sacred text that did not need defending, simply because they were acknowledged by all the mainline churches as their authoritative teaching. I know of nowhere in his writings, however, where Lewis advocates the *sola scriptura* of the Reformers.

If I have understood Lewis correctly, the issue of historicity in the Bible matters only in matters of dogma, such as the great salvation events of the incarnation, death, resurrection, and ascension of Christ. These he believed to be narratives of fact. He thought it childish to say that a mathematical miscalculation—say, how many people are recorded as having died in battle in the books of Judges or Kings—had any bearing on the truth of the Gospel narratives, or somehow called God's veracity into question.

But let us turn to his attack upon the modernists, starting with Rudolf Bultmann. Lewis felt that Bultmann's demythologizing program suffered from one fundamental flaw: Bultmann did not know enough about mythology to recognize a myth when he saw one. Lewis granted Bultmann superior knowledge in anthropology and hermeneutical sophistication, but doubted if he had read enough mythical material to know a myth from a fact, or a historical narrative from epic poetry.[12] In his essay "Modern Theology and Biblical Criticism"—more widely known these days as "Fern-seed and Elephants"[13]—Lewis readily and happily concedes that there is myth in the Bible, but he insists that the Gospel of Mark, and even much of the Gospel of John, is historical narrative and not the mythologizing of historical events for didactic or dogmatic purposes, as Bultmann supposed.[14]

To understand Lewis' critique of Bultmann is to recognize that this is not so much the literary critic talking as the thoroughgoing supernaturalist. Lewis was a lifelong opponent of naturalism.[15] That is to say, he not only believed in miracles but logically expected them as a normal expression of God's dealing with the world. Frankly, I think Lewis' account of miracles in the book of that name is more a defense of supernaturalism than an explication of the miraculous in terms of a doctrine of God and divine agency. Following his friend Owen Barfield, Lewis believed in an almost magical

12. Lewis, "Fern-seed and Elephants," 106–7.

13. The original title was used in the earlier, larger collection of Lewis' essays entitled *Christian Reflections*; the more popular title was conferred on it by Walter Hooper when compiling a later, shorter collection, as he explains in the Preface to *Fern-seed and Elephants*, 9.

14. Lewis, "Fern-seed and Elephants," 107–11.

15. For Lewis' analysis of the deficiencies of naturalism see Lewis, *Miracles*, chap. 3; see also Lewis, *The Abolition of Man*.

cosmos populated by creatures and forms more in keeping with Pseudo-Dionysius's *Celestial Hierarchies* than the supernatural agencies of the Bible.[16] Be that as it may, Lewis accused liberals like Strauss and Ritschl of the nineteenth century, or Harnack and Bultmann of the twentieth, of unquestionably believing in the canon "if miraculous, unhistorical."[17] In short, Lewis claimed, modernists did not believe in miracles because that was part of the skeptical tradition of the modern age. He insisted that this skepticism was a philosophical prejudice and not a scientific datum.[18]

Lewis had other critical comments to make against biblical scholars, but I have only space to mention here his conviction that he felt it was unlikely that modern critics could understand the ancient texts better than the early church fathers who were far closer in time, temperament, and culture to the New Testament than we are.[19] In his 1954 Cambridge inaugural lecture "De Descriptione Temporum,"[20] he insisted that if an ancient Athenian, even a stupid one, could speak to us now of Greek tragedy, it would unseat much of modern scholarship.[21]

Extending this insight, in his talk to the Cambridge undergraduates at Westcott House in 1959, Lewis asserted that the judgments of modern scholars are less to be trusted than those of the old ones. He cited some interesting anecdotal evidence, namely, that in numerous literary reviews of his own works he had read what the authors supposed he was doing when he wrote them. In every single case, he said, the critics were wrong. For him, it followed that if contemporary critics could not gauge accurately the originations and intentions of modern writers, why should we trust their judgments on the old ones? How convenient it was, he said, that the ancient writers—being long since dead—could never contradict the modern critics, however preposterous or outrageous their views might be![22]

---

16. Lewis discusses Pseudo-Dionysius in *The Discarded Image*, 70–75.

17. Lewis, "Fern-seed and Elephants," 113.

18. Ibid., 113.

19. Ibid., 118–19.

20. Lewis, "De Descriptione Temporum," *Selected Literary Essays*, 1–14.

21. Ibid., 13: "One thing I know: I would give a great deal to hear any ancient Athenian, even a stupid one, talking about Greek tragedy. He would know in his bones so much that we seek in vain."

22. Lewis, "Fern-seed and Elephants," 114–17.

LEWIS ON REVELATION

What did Lewis believe about revelation? Christensen identifies six modes or types of revelation, which he takes from Lewis' various writings.[23] Four are identified in *Mere Christianity*—universal conscience, pagan good dreams, Jewish election, and the incarnation.[24] Two more, *Sehnsucht* and the numinous, are highlighted in *The Problem of Pain*,[25] though *Sehnsucht* is also identified in *Mere Christianity*[26] and *The Pilgrim's Regress*,[27] and is perhaps Lewis' favorite Romantic motif.

These different modes of God's self-revealing demonstrate that Lewis saw the Bible neither as the locus nor exclusively as the focus of revelation. Lewis certainly did not take Barth's position that Jesus Christ alone is God's revelation—though, like Barth, Lewis saw the Scriptures as pointing to revelation, rather than embodying it. Neither can it be said that Lewis conceived of God's revelation primarily in terms of the events of salvation history. Indeed, I wonder whether Lewis really understood revelation in theological categories at all, or adequately distinguished mediated revelation from unmediated experience or spiritual illumination. Certainly, as we shall see, at least two of his modes of revelation are more like inklings of spiritual reality than the unveiling of God.

I have decided to divide Lewis' six modes of revelation into two parts—general or incomplete revelation and particular or perfect revelation. In doing this, I don't think it is accurate to say that Lewis had any worked-out or systematic view of revelation, but he did, with certain inconsistencies, have a general orientation towards it. This is informed by his philosophical idealism, which often emerges in classical Platonic or neo-Platonic terms, but sometimes in the form of the Cambridge Platonism of the seventeenth century and, in its more rational guise, through the idealism of Bishop Berkeley in the eighteenth century.[28]

When Lewis tells us in the preface to *The Pilgrim's Regress* that his intellectual progression was from "popular realism to Philosophical Idealism; from Idealism to Pantheism; from Pantheism to Theism; and from Theism

---

23. Christensen, *C. S. Lewis on Scripture*, 74–83.

24. Lewis, *Mere Christianity*, 51.

25. Cf. Lewis, *The Problem of Pain*.

26. Lewis, *Mere Christianity*, 118–19.

27. Lewis, *The Pilgrim's Regress*, 12–16.

28. For a more detailed treatment of Lewis' idealism than can be given here, see James Patrick's essay "C. S. Lewis and Idealism"; see also James Patrick, *The Magdalen Metaphysics*.

to Christianity,"[29] he neglects to tell us that his philosophical idealism continued to inform his Christianity; indeed, as we now know, it did so for the rest of his life. On the one hand, Lewis was a rationalist and defended reason as an organ of truth (which he called *savoir*); he tended to see reason as the ability to determine the truth or falsity of particulars. On the other hand, Lewis was a Romantic who believed that to grasp universals you needed the organ of imagination (which he called *connaître*).[30] Imagination provided humankind not with truth statements—that is a function of reason—but with meaning. Meaning is possible only through intuiting reality imaginatively. As Lewis puts it in "Myth Became Fact," "truth is always *about* something, but reality is that *about which* truth is."[31]

For Lewis revelation is either about the translation of absolute or spiritual reality into the natural world, or the intuiting, in some sense, of absolute reality which is idealistically conceived. More dynamically and personally, we might say that revelation is about God breaking into the world in order that we may break out. For Lewis, however, as we can see in the Appendix to *Miracles,* the natural and supernatural worlds can coinhere, so there is not a radical spiritual/natural dualism in his thought.[32]

Strictly speaking, Lewis follows Berkeley in a denial of materiality, not in the sense that he doubts its existence, but in the sense that he doubts realism's account of it. Always allergic to naturalistic explanations, Lewis prefers Berkeley's defense of common sense to that of the eighteenth-century Scottish "common sense" philosopher Thomas Reid—seeing material things not as sense objects, but as perceptions of objects, perceptions themselves being conceived as collections of ideas in the mind; what causes these ideas, however, is not a correspondence with the empirical reality, but the will of God. Indeed, for Berkeley the universe is conceived not only theo-centrically, but as something whose *esse* was *percipi* (i.e., one which existed because it was perceived).[33] When Lewis in *Prayer: Letters to Malcolm* says "Matter enters our experience only by becoming sensation (when we perceive it) or conception (when we understand it),"[34] this could have been lifted out of Berkeley's *A Treatise Concerning the Principles of Human Knowledge.*

---

29. Lewis, *The Pilgrim's Regress,* 9.

30. Lewis, *The Four Loves,* 115.

31. Lewis, "Myth Became Fact," *God in the Dock,* 43.

32. Cf. Appendix A: "On the Words 'Spirit' and 'Spiritual,'" *Miracles,* 173–77.

33. For a detailed discussion of Berkeley's philosophy see Papas, *Berkeley's Thought,* especially chap. 5, 'The Esse is Percipi Principle.'

34. Lewis, *Prayer,* 123.

In Berkeley's philosophy humankind could perceive reality directly from the mind of God, and indeed was sustained by it. The Catholic writer Christopher Derrick tells of the occasion when he asked Lewis what philosophy God would espouse—without hesitation Lewis replied, "Berkeleyan idealism."[35] I think that Lewis championed Berkeley all his life against naturalism, but he was unerringly Platonic when it suited him. Like the Cambridge Platonist Henry More (1614–87), he thought of reality not in terms of a radical spiritual and material dualism, but of one is which spiritual emanations, or extensions, to use More's language, penetrate deep into the phenomenal world (in the Kantian sense of phenomenal).[36]

We might think, then, in the light of this, that in his understanding of revelation the problem for Lewis was how to account for the ways in which God does get through to us, and, conversely, to account for how we receive revelation and get through to God. The answers Lewis tends to give are not typically couched in the language of the absolute sovereignty and freedom of God. His is not so much a crisis theology, where God bursts into time and history *á la* Barth, but more a stumbling *supra*natural theology where humankind follows the clues left by God in the human heart and imagination. When Lewis does talk of God's one decisive or perfect breakthrough in the incarnation, he employs the language of myth becoming fact, wherein Jesus Christ touched down on the earth like he was a being from another world disguised as one of us, but in reality being a phantom.

Before we look more closely at the six modes of Lewis' understanding of revelation, I think that we need to understand Lewis' view of God's self-revealing in terms of what we might call a mode or model of operation. This model Lewis calls "transposition,"[37] and is itself Platonically conceived.

Transposition is a philosophical theory from above. On one level, it is a radical theory of meaning; Lewis, like his mentor Berkeley, assumes that you cannot make sense of the natural world without recourse to a higher spiritual reality. The naturalist, Lewis explains by way of example, would be likely to think of *glossolalia* as gibberish because he would explain it in terms of sensation, hysteria, etc., whereas the phenomenon is transformed in meaning if you understand speaking in tongues as an outflow of spiritual reality—in this case, literally the *Holy Spirit's* activity.[38] More generally,

---

35. Cf. Derrick, *C. S. Lewis and the Church of Rome*, 213.

36. On More's significance for Lewis see Patrick, "C. S. Lewis and Idealism," 160–61.

37. "Transposition," in Lewis, *Screwtape Proposes a Toast and Other Pieces*, 75–93.

38. Ibid., 75–76.

however, Lewis is interested in the transposition, or what he calls "transvaluation," of spiritual life into the natural world and vice versa.[39]

Lewis assumes that the spiritual realm is the primary reality, in a hierarchical sense, over the natural world, though not against it, for, as we have already seen, he thinks they can coinhere. He also assumes that the spiritual is the richer medium. The problem of transposition, therefore, is how to transpose higher into lower, richer into thinner mediums without losing some of their height and richness. Lewis explicates the problem of transposition by using examples of musical notation to score the complexities of a composition, and he also cites the difficulty of translating using only lines. Clearly, in some way these two levels of reality are connected. Lewis insists, however, that there is no isomorphic relationship between signs and the things they signify,[40] but he does think that spiritual reality—the higher realm—can be grasped imaginatively, not so much through symbolism or allegory—though they help—but by what he calls sacrament: the participation or coinherence of the natural with the spiritual.[41]

That this can happen, Lewis is convinced, is because primary spiritual reality can seep into the natural world and in various ways draws us "further up and further in."[42] The best men and women can hope for in temporal existence, therefore, is to partake of spirituality not analogically, but experimentally and experientially: even Holy Communion, Lewis believed, is a spiritual reality that comes through a physical act of eating. This literal transformation of matter into spiritual value is at the heart of Lewis' doctrine of the incarnation and the ascension.

Material life, then, for Lewis, is not so much a copy of the real—absolutely not what in postmodern terminology we would call the mutation of the real into hyperreal[43]—but a diminution of spiritual reality, the symbol of it, an etiolated world. This sense of a pale imitation, a "shadowland," clearly echoes classical Platonism. Materiality, however, is a barrier to spiritual reality, not because it is gross and heavy, but because it is too flimsy, too docetic.[44] Transposition of nature into higher reality works not by bringing the higher down to earth, as it were, but by allowing spiritual life to draw nature unto itself, hence purifying and illuminating it, and almost, in a sense, sub-

---

39. Ibid., 93.

40. Ibid., 80–81.

41. Ibid., 83.

42. As Aslan says towards the end of chap. 14 of *The Last Battle*: "Come further in! Come further up!"—the implications of which become apparent in chap. 15.

43. On the notion of the hyperreal, see Eco, *Travels in Hyperreality*.

44. Lewis, "Transposition," 90.

stantializing it. Lewis, as we shall see, thinks that the incarnation itself can be understood as transposition because, as the so-called Athanasian Creed says, the incarnation is achieved "not by conversion of the Godhead into flesh, but by taking of the Manhood into God."[45]

(Incidentally, before we move on we can see from this idealist reading of reality where Lewis gets his concept of the "weight of glory" in the sermon of that name,[46] or again the idea of the solidity of heaven in *The Great Divorce*.)[47]

GENERAL OR INCOMPLETE REVELATION

Numinous

The numinous is the weakest and most underdeveloped notion of revelation deployed by Lewis. In *The Problem of Pain* he talks about the numinous in terms of experiencing it.[48] Influenced by Rudolf Otto's *The Idea of the Holy*, Lewis wants to say about experiencing the numinous that it is more than the human capacity for awe or wonder—say, as we get in the nature mysticism of William Wordsworth—and something closer to dread in the presence of holiness. "He's wild, you know. Not like a *tame* lion," say the beavers of Aslan, in *The Lion, the Witch and the Wardrobe*.[49] Or, as Lewis puts it in *Perelandra* (aka, *Voyage to Venus*), "suppose you struggle through to the good and find that it also is dreadful?"[50] Echoing this theme, Lewis reminds the fictional Malcolm that the "erotic analogies" of spiritual union need to be supplemented by "I fell at his feet as one dead."[51]

On the one hand, Lewis takes it that all humankind can brush up against God in this way. Such an encounter is more an inkling of God, an experiential imprint of ultimate reality, an illumination, rather than a revelation; but it *is* God nudging us. On the other hand, there appears to be nothing specifically Christian in Lewis' understanding of the numinous. It is certainly not the beatific vision of mystical theology couched in terms of apophatic wonder. It is more like a flash of inspiration—devoid of

---

45. Ibid., 91.

46. Lewis, "The Weight of Glory," in *Screwtape Proposes a Toast and Other Pieces*, 94–110.

47. Cf. Lewis, *The Great Divorce*.

48. Lewis, *The Problem of Pain*, 4–13.

49. Lewis, *The Lion, the Witch and the Wardrobe*, 166.

50. Lewis, *Voyage to Venus (Perelandra)*, 14.

51. Lewis, *Prayer: Letters to Malcolm*, 15.

revelational content, but which enflames the imagination as the organ of meeting.

Sehnsucht

Sehnsucht is related to the idea of the numinous, but it is a far more significant concept in Lewis' religious lexicon than the *numen*. Lewis was convinced that the deep longing many of us have for that certain "something"—that unnamed desire—is the longing for heaven; the desire for God, as he says in *Mere Christianity,* which only God can satisfy.[52]

Of course, *Sehnsucht* reminds us of the medieval argument for the existence of God from desire. But Lewis does not really use it in this formal way. For him, *Sehnsucht* is a God-given revelation of longing, a restlessness for God in Augustine's sense, but intense. Yet it is unfulfilled longing, unrequited love, deeply Romantic in it non-rational yearning for ultimate reality. Lewis admits that *Sehnsucht* can be mistaken by naturalists merely as emotional *frisson*—as when he shuddered at the line from Longfellow which announced that "Balder the beautiful is dead."[53] Lewis throughout his life believed that *Sehnsucht* was a trumpet-blast from the far country: a real penetration of notes from Gabriel's horn, if you will, into natural reality.

Sehnsucht is the longing for Paradise, first tasted in a dream that drives John on his pilgrimage in *The Pilgrim's Regress.*[54] It is the intimation of spiritual satisfaction presaged in Charles William's romantic theology.[55] It is an echo of joy from Joy itself. For Lewis, the satisfaction of this longing was possible only at the final *apocalypsis,* as we can see by the Unicorn's joy when he comes to the inner Narnia in *The Last Battle:* "I have come home at last! This is my real county! I belong here. This is the land I have been looking for all my life, though I never knew it till now. The reason why we loved the old Narnia is that it sometimes looked a little like this."[56] And, we might add, picking up from "Transposition," as lines drawn on paper look

---

52. Lewis, *Mere Christianity,* 118–19; Lewis writes that "If I find in myself a desire which no experience in this world can satisfy, the more probable explanation is that I was made for another world" (ibid., 118).

53. Cf. Lewis, *Surprised by Joy,* 20.

54. Cf. Lewis, *The Pilgrim's Regress,* chaps. 1–6.

55. For more information about Charles William's theology, see Horne, "A Peculiar Debt: The Influence of Charles Williams on C. S. Lewis," in *A Christian for all Christians,* 83–97.

56. Lewis, *The Last Battle,* 161.

three-dimensional;[57] or, as Lord Digory says of the real Narnia[58] (and note how Digory ends the speech with Lewis' famous giveaway: "It's all in Plato, all in Plato: bless me, what *do* they teach them at these schools?!").[59]

Conscience and the Moral Law

Following Aquinas, and really Aristotle before him, Lewis is convinced that "conscience" is universally given—shall we say a "medium of revelation" or a "natural capacity" to intuit the moral law. Interestingly, Lewis is more Thomistic than Platonic here. Although he disliked Aristotelianism because he always felt that dealing with particulars tended towards naturalistic explanations, much of his thinking on morality can best be described as generically intuitionist, rather than specifically Platonic. In his best apologetic work, *The Abolition of Man,* Lewis defends what we usually call classicism and what he called the *Tao*—that is, the belief that there are universal moral goods to be known from within our own minds and hearts. Lewis makes the interesting assertion that although different cultures have different values, it is remarkable how close to each other they are. But an absolutely universal feature of all cultures, he argues, is that they all have a moral sense that we *ought* to do some things rather than others. For Lewis, the sense of numinous and the adoption of morality are linked: "When," he said, "the Numinous Power to which [people] feel awe is made the guardian of the morality to which they feel obligation, religion is the result."[60]

Israel and Election

In *Mere Christianity* Lewis seems, for once, to come close to the traditional theological language about God and covenant when he admits that God "selected one particular people and spent several centuries hammering into their heads the sort of God He was."[61] The key to this understanding was the giving of the law, the Torah of the rabbis, and in particular the Ten Commandments. However, Lewis makes very little of this covenant, and I cannot really find anything in his work that suggests a doctrine of election; this is why I have not included the choosing of Israel under the rubric of particular

57. Lewis, "Transposition," 81.
58. Lewis, *The Last Battle,* 159.
59. Ibid., 160.
60. Lewis, *The Problem of Pain,* 10.
61. Lewis, *Mere Christianity,* 51.

revelation. Indeed, despite a nod to what we might call the Jewish chapter in the grand narrative of the gospel, I suspect that Lewis sees the giving of the law as somewhat akin to the giving of dreams to pagans. That is to say, law is a different form of spiritual reality than the iconic dream world of pagan myths, but both extend from the same divine source.

Good Dreams: Pagan Intimations of Christ

My reason for the assertion that election is not a key concept in Lewis' religious thought is to be found in *The Pilgrim's Regress*.[62] For, while Lewis does not deny that God chose a people, he does insist that God did not leave the rest of the world without help when he gave the Jews the law. Therefore, not only was there conscience, the numinous, and *Sehnsucht,* God also sent to the pagans good dreams. The Shepherd People, as he alludes to the Jews in *The Pilgrim's Regress,* were a people of rules, but people who can't read need pictures to help them see aright, so God sent to them myths as divine but refracted light upon their imaginations. Pagan myths, then, are nothing less than the shadowlands of revelation—flickering images of reality like the shapes seen by Plato's unenlightened people who lived in the cave, but could not directly see the sun. Pagan myths, therefore, which Lewis loved so much, and which had enthralled him since childhood, were not for him false religions, but *incomplete* ones, not false lights, but *dimmed* ones. In *The Pilgrim's Regress* he insists that neither the rules of the Shepherd People, nor the pictures of the pagans, were full revelation for they both lacked something. In a remarkable passage, he says, "The truth is that a Shepherd is only half a man and a Pagan is only half a man, so that neither people was well without the other, nor could either be healed until the Landlord's Son came into the country."[63]

We cannot pass over Lewis' view of myth too quickly, because without it his doctrine that Jesus is "myth become fact" makes no sense. Lewis always loved pagan myths, even in his progressivist realist days. He tells us in *Surprised by Joy* that he knew as an adolescent that they were lies,[64] but he believed them to be "lies breathed through silver."[65] At Oxford, part of his argument against the veracity of Christianity was that it was too unoriginal to be true: it smacked of the dying Corn King[66] or the myths of Balder, Osiris,

---

62. Lewis, *The Pilgrim's Regress*, 191–97.

63. Ibid., 196.

64. Lewis, *Surprised by Joy,* 62–65.

65. Cf. Carpenter, *J. R. R. Tolkien: A Biography,* 151.

66. Cf. Lewis, *Miracles,* 117–20.

and Apollo. Then, on that fateful night of September 19, 1931, Hugo Dyson and J. R. R. Tolkien convinced him that Christianity was a myth, but the only true one, because Jesus alone was myth-become-fact while remaining myth—that is to say, God as *mythos* remained the ultimate reality beyond mere facticity.[67]

Lewis never lost his faith in or support of this argument for the incarnation; though he never demonized other world religions, or denied that all great myths were divine in origin. Full mythical transposition from spiritual reality into particular religious truths was not possible for pagan myths because these myths were themselves forms (I mean this Platonically) or spiritual emanations from the divine or spiritual emanations from the divine *mythos,* and could not be successfully transposed without a diminution of mythical power and meaning. But perhaps God himself, as the author of myth, indeed as myth *par excellence,* the prototype of all mythology, could become particularized without loss of essence.

PARTICULAR OR PERFECT REVELATION?

Jesus Christ: Myth Become Fact[68]

Jesus of Nazareth is the fullest, final, and fulfilled revelation of the rules of the Shepherd People and the pictures of the pagans. Jesus as the dying King steps out of the dreams of mythology and becomes historical fact while yet remaining true myth—that is, to repeat, ultimate reality beyond what we might call mere facticity. Or, if you wish, the veil of myth is parted and God steps into the full glare of historical reality, and yet, being God, remains forever veiled and mysterious—always unknown, even in his revealedness.

But it is precisely at this point, as we move from Lewis' account of general but incomplete revelation to the Christ event, that the whole Platonic machinery of supernaturalism and transposition from spiritual to natural realms begins to jar. Lewis is certainly orthodox in asserting that God in Christ came down from heaven, but it is doubtful if he grasps the mystery

---

67. See Lewis' letter to Arthur Greeves of October 18, 1931: "What Dyson and Tolkien showed me was this: that if I met the idea of sacrifice in a Pagan story I didn't mind it at all; again, that if I met the idea of a god sacrificing himself to himself . . . I liked it very much and was mysteriously moved by it: again, that the idea of a dying and reviving god (Balder, Adonis, Bacchus) similarly moved me provided I met it anywhere *except* in the Gospels. . . . Now the story of Christ is simply a true myth: a myth working on us in the same way as the others, but with this tremendous difference that it *really happened.*" Cf. Lewis, *They Stand Together,* 427.

68. See Fiddes, "C. S. Lewis the Myth-Maker," 132–55.

of the incarnation in terms of the hypostatic union, and the assumption of human flesh, the stuff of material creation, into the Godhead. Of course, in "Transposition" he claims that human nature is swallowed up into the Godhead and divinized.[69] God has not so much come down, as taken up creation into pure spirit in perfect transposition. God becomes man, if you will, not by becoming one of us, but by taking into himself materiality and transposing it into higher reality.

The same transposing motif is used in describing the general resurrection in *Prayer: Letters to Malcolm*.[70] Lewis says of the physical resurrection that it will not be material, as we understand it, because the "sensuous life as it is raised from its death . . . will be inside the soul."[71] My initial reaction when I first read these lines was that it somehow reminded me of putting the forms back into the minds of God, or of the visionary alchemy of a Paracelsus.

In the sermon "Myth Became Fact," I believed that Lewis keeps his Platonic canopy intact when describing the incarnation, for while he admits that myth is now perfect fact, it remains perfect myth and still needs to be grasped by the imagination as myth.[72] I know that Lewis asserts the historicity of the virgin birth, and accepts the reality of the cross (though he does duck theories of the atonement), but I am not sure that his account of the incarnation is theologically adequate. As I wrote in the *Church Times* on the 100th anniversary of Lewis' birth, "Eternal reality outside of time that becomes concretized in a particular body in time is not an incarnation—the assumption of human nature—but a particularization of eternal being. Jesus the myth become fact reminds us more than it should of the archetypal lion touching down in the English countryside in Charles Williams' novel *The Place of the Lion*."[73]

I remain unconvinced that in Lewis' account of the incarnation God becomes sufficiently earthed as the particular human being Jesus of Nazareth. He is not so much the God-man, who is flesh of our flesh, as the temporarily earth-visiting God. In fact, we know that Lewis believed that God might also have other bodies in other worlds. In one of his letters to a child, for example, he said, "Of course, there is one thing Aslan has that Jesus has not—I mean the body of a lion. (But remember, if there are other worlds

---

69. Lewis, "Transposition," 91.

70. Lewis, *Prayers*, 120–24.

71. Ibid., 121.

72. Lewis, "Myth Become Fact," 44.

73. Walker, "A Little Too Much Plato," 11.

and they need to be saved and Christ were to save them as he would—he may really have taken all sorts of bodies of which we don't know about.)."[74]

This vision of God, out of the silent heaven, visiting and saving worlds, one by one, through a multiplicity of incarnations, raises interesting questions about the uniqueness and efficacy of the atoning death of Christ, and its role in releasing the groaning cosmos from its time-bound necessity. We might think that Paul's sense of the unfreedom of the universe (Rom 8:19–21) is also a legitimate extrapolation of earthly fallenness. We know, however, that Lewis did not hold to this view, as his novel *Perelandra* and his essay "Religion and Rocketry" make clear.[75]

CONCLUSION

I have not in the second part of this paper been trying to argue that Lewis is unorthodox in his Christian beliefs, but rather to suggest that he does have a habit of idealizing concepts beyond their theological usefulness. We remember his strange ecclesiology in *Mere Christianity,* where instead of the church being imaged as a body, or even as a building, it is seen as an idealized hall of principled beliefs which somehow are incarnated, or particularized, by the anterooms leading off the hall, such as Congregationalism or the Anglican Communion.[76]

Idealization can also lead to a wrong view of matter though, as we have already seen. Lewis turns Gnosticism on its head by turning gross matter into phantasmagoria (but nevertheless, in a gnostic manner, he still demeans it). Or again, the divine condescension is classically seen as an event in which God divested himself of his glory, and in entering the created world declared it holy in his person. In *Mere Christianity,* however, Lewis asks us to imagine that becoming human for God is something like us becoming a slug or a crab.[77] This is an unfortunate and ugly metaphor which it seems is intended to convey something of the horror for God of becoming human. But the general tenor of Lewis' thought, as we have seen, is that God does not sink down to our level as we would descend to the lower forms, but rather sucks up humanity into the Godhead, hence transposing its material limitations into infinite spiritual horizons.

---

74. Lewis, *Letters to Children,* 52.
75. Lewis, "Religion and Rocketry," 86–95.
76. Lewis, *Mere Christianity,* 11–12.
77. Ibid., 152.

Reflections on C. S. Lewis, Apologetics, and the Moral Tradition
Interview with Basil Mitchell
(1990)

Andrew Walker: Professor Mitchell, you knew C. S. Lewis and were involved with him in the Oxford University Socratic Club. Can you tell me about the Socratic Club before you became its President when Lewis left for Cambridge in 1954?

Professor Basil Mitchell: Well, before he moved to Cambridge Lewis had been President of the Socratic Club, and a formidable lady called Stella Aldwinckle had been Chairman. I started to go there regularly when I came back from the Navy in 1946.

When Lewis left I became President and Stella Aldwinckle continued as Chairman. And during that period, I think it is fair to say, it was really the liveliest philosophical society in Oxford.

Walker: What influence did Lewis have on your generation of Christians? I mean, was he a *major* influence on you?

Mitchell: Undoubtedly. I think he was a major influence on large numbers of people who had been brought up as Christians, who had somewhat drifted away, and who hoped it might be true but had come to think it probably wasn't; and he, both intellectually and imaginatively, made it seem credible again.

Walker: Lewis has sometimes been referred to as "the apostle to the skeptics." That might have been true for the decade 1940 to 1950, in which he did a great deal of his apologetical work, but there was a watershed in his output, wasn't there?

In his autobiography *Surprised by Joy* he makes a distinction—and I suppose this is true of the whole of his epistemology—between two ways of knowing. He talks, if I remember rightly, about *savoir* and *connaitre*—and I suppose the imaginative side, the intuitive side of Lewis, became even more apparent in the 1950s when he wrote the children's stories *The Chronicles of Narnia*. And it is the intuitive side, "Lewis the storyteller," that most people think of today. In 1988, for example, half a million copies were sold of *The Lion, the Witch and the Wardrobe*[1] alone. The apologetical side of him is not so well known, and not so much thought of, but in the 1940s it was Lewis the apologist who was making the play, wasn't it?

Mitchell: Yes, it was.

Walker: I suppose that anyone who is an *aficionado* of Lewis, or who is particularly interested in Lewis' apologetical work, remembers the dreaded event of 1948.

In 1948, the Socratic Club held a debate on the subject of naturalism between Lewis and the young Catholic philosopher G. E. M. Anscombe as she is normally known. Now this debate is significant because a number of people thought that Lewis lost it. Whatever is the case, he ceased to engage in much apologetical work from that time until he died in 1963.

You were at that particular meeting. Perhaps the chances are you won't remember very much of the actual debate, but what can you remember of the atmosphere and the tension of that time?

Mitchell: I can't remember the debate at all clearly. I don't have the sense that anything decisive happened at that moment, although it is the case, as you say, that from that point onwards Lewis obviously concluded that he wasn't equipped to cope with the professional philosophers.

---

1. Lewis, *The Lion, the Witch and the Wardrobe*, chap. 6, note 1.

Perhaps it would be of interest to you if I told you about a sequel to that encounter. John Lucas (a philosopher colleague of mine in Oxford) conceived the idea of having a rerun of the Anscombe-Lewis debate—except that he would undertake to uphold Lewis' side of the argument, and Elizabeth agreed to this. This debate took place (I can't remember when—sometime in the 1960s), and on that occasion, I think it would generally be agreed, Lucas succeeded in sustaining Lewis' side of the argument. If one were to think in terms of winners or losers, I think maybe that Lucas was the winner on points, but there wasn't on *that* occasion any kind of tension.

Walker: What was Lewis' argument against naturalism?

Mitchell: Well, the point in Lewis' book on *Miracles*[2] that Elizabeth Anscombe particularly fastened upon was his claim that a naturalistic philosophy is logically incoherent. By which he meant that if you try to explain everything that happens in the world, including human decisions and human beliefs, in terms of scientific laws (e.g., that at such and such a point, such and such an individual would be persuaded by certain arguments)—it follows that that person's acceptance of that argument cannot be the result of his being influenced by rational considerations, but is simply the result of whatever the antecedent scientific conditions were.

However the thesis is worked out in detail, the essence of the claim is that, if on the basis of scientific laws, whether physical or biological, someone's beliefs can be predicted, then it follows that those same beliefs cannot be arrived at by a process of reason.

Elizabeth attacked this argument of Lewis', maintaining that he had failed to distinguish between various senses of causation, and that, if you made the required distinctions, you could see that it is quite possible for a belief to be caused by some scientifically explicable process and yet at the same time to be a rational belief.

Now in the debate—I mean the rerun debate—Elizabeth and John agreed as to what the original Lewis-Anscombe dispute had been about, and Lucas simply maintained that on the substantial issue Lewis was right and that, for the sort of reasons Lewis had put forward, a thoroughly naturalistic philosophy was logically incoherent. And the outcome of that debate was to make it perfectly clear that, at the very least, Lewis' original thesis was an entirely arguable philosophical thesis and as defensible as most philosophical theses are.

So there was no warrant for supposing that in the original debate Lewis had been shown to be just hopelessly wrong. It was rather that he was

2. Lewis, *Miracles*.

not equipped with the kind of philosophical techniques which were needed at that stage to cope with a highly professional performer like Elizabeth Anscombe. And so Lewis probably drew the correct inference and decided that he couldn't take on the professional philosophers at their own game.

Walker: I think we've established something very important here, because what you have suggested is not that Lewis had no inkling of how to do philosophy, but that his methodology was deficient, and particularly, I suppose, in terms of the post-Russellian, Moore, and Wittgensteinian revolution in philosophy just after the First World War.

Lewis never, so far as we know, really read modern philosophers, did he? And in that sense one doesn't see him as being able to wield the techniques necessary in order to confront the philosophers of his day. Do you think this was really just a deficiency of method?

Mitchell: I think it was a lack of familiarity with the way that philosophy was done at that particular time. Lewis and most of the educated people of his generation had been brought up on an essentially Platonist philosophy, whose methods were literary rather than scientifically analytical. When they were confronted with the so-called "revolution in philosophy" pioneered by Russell and later, of course, sharpened by Logical Positivism as represented by Sir A. J. Ayer and others, they were simply baffled.

They were not only baffled, they were convinced that it couldn't be true: they knew in their heart of hearts that this was too narrow and arid a conception of what philosophy ought to be. On the other hand, they saw no particular point in spending a great deal of time in trying to master this sort of philosophy in order to come to grips with its exponents. Not being professional philosophers themselves, they had other things to do.

And I suppose that Lewis, after the encounter at the Socratic Club, realized that if he was going to take on people like Elizabeth Anscombe, he would have to do a lot of homework. He had no particular aptitude for—and no particular interest in—the dominant philosophy of his day, and he could better spend his time doing the other things that he was supremely good at.

Walker: Which, of course, he went on to do in the 1950s.

Mitchell: Yes.

Walker: I think there are one or two things we could pick up here. Let me start, if I may, with an analogy.

In the 1970s, when I was doing my doctoral studies on the philosophy of science, one of the big disputes in those days was between Sir Karl

Popper's conception of what philosophy should be about and what he felt a certain kind of Oxford philosopher thought philosophy should be about.

I wonder if that isn't really very far removed from what you've just said about Lewis. The issue is not just a question of method, but also a question of purpose: What is philosophy *for*? As you said earlier, there was certainly aridity about that new philosophical climate that Lewis noticed. It was almost as if he said, "If this is what the new philosophy is, do we need to bother?" I am not saying that he just dismissed it out of hand, but that, to use your phrase, "in his heart of hearts" he felt it wasn't right.

We, however, have come a long way since the 1940s and the 1950s, when Logical Positivism and conceptual analysis held sway. Are we now in an atmosphere in which a more traditional metaphysics is likely to make a comeback? Because, although Logical Positivism is dead, conceptual analysis isn't quite, is it?

Mitchell: Going back beyond that question a bit—if I ask myself why it never occurred to me to go into this sort of question with Lewis, I think the answer is that at the time I met Lewis I was a young philosophy don, and I realized, firstly, that I was going to have to spend my professional career in an intellectual atmosphere where philosophical analysis was dominant and, secondly, that if I intended to continue to take religion seriously, I was going to have to meet this challenge head-on. Now, for the reasons that we've already discussed, Lewis wasn't the man to help in that endeavor, so it was clear to me that although I'd been very greatly influenced by Lewis, and was enormously indebted to him, so far as this particular matter was concerned, my vocation was different from his.

As a result of that realization I found myself getting together with a number of people like Austin Farrer, Eric Mascall, Ian Crombie, Michael Foster—and at an earlier stage Iris Murdoch and Richard Hard, and at a later stage John Lucas—all of whom were more or less uncomfortable with what seemed to us to be the unduly circumscribed nature of the task of the philosophical as understood by the analytical school at the time. And we tried to master the techniques of logical analysis in such a way as to open up once again the possibility of genuine metaphysical discussion.

In fact, this particular group went on meeting for virtually forty years. It ended only three or four years ago. What its influence may have been I simply don't know, but it is true to say that in the last fifteen years or so that narrow philosophical orthodoxy which prevailed, in this country at any rate, since the War has loosened up quite remarkably, and the need to vindicate metaphysics as a respectable enterprise has been widely recognized, with the result that, for example, philosophy of religion is now quite widely practiced and accepted as an entirely respectable discipline.

Interestingly, this development has been even more marked in the United States than in this country. The Society of Christian Philosophers in the States numbers, I'm told, something like nine hundred teachers of philosophy, and it is the largest single section in the American Philosophical Association. It is a quite remarkably flourishing institution.

Walker: I think it's worth pointing out, I'm sure you'll agree, that this is really quite remarkable if we look back to the 1940s, and even that early 1950s, when metaphysical philosophy really was ruled out of court.

Mitchell: Yes.

Walker: I suppose we could specifically relate your intention to continue this sort of work to the fact that you took over the presidency of the Socratic Club. How long were you involved with the Socratic Club—to its close in the 1960s?

Mitchell: Well, as you know, I became President of the Socratic Club in 1954 when Lewis went to Cambridge. I remained as President until the Socratic Club finally came to an end round about 1970. So that was quite a long period.

And when the Socratic Club came to an end it wasn't, I think, anything specifically to do with a general lack of interest in the philosophy of religion, but rather to do with a lack of interest in University societies of that kind. The effect of the late 1960s was to cause a massive reduction in the number of undergraduate societies at Oxford. People just didn't any longer want to meet and discuss in this rather formal way.

Walker: I'd like to turn to something else now, if I may. We've seen how Lewis had an influence on you in your early professional life, and how to a certain extent you continued the sort of work he was doing, specifically of course with professional philosophers. I'd like to pursue two topics with you now.

Firstly, I'd like to ask you about Lewis' weaknesses as a philosopher—if you can think of anything specific. Can you, for example, identify any particular kind of argument that he used that you yourself would not use?

And, secondly, when we've considered those weaknesses, I'd like to turn the whole thing on its head—because I think it would be really rather misleading to suggest that Lewis couldn't do any philosophy at all—and I would like then to consider his strengths. After all, what was it about Lewis' work that influenced you? Which particular books that he wrote did you find the most profound?

So those are two questions really. Let's start with the weak side of Lewis. As an apologist, speaking now in the philosophical sense, not just in the broader rhetorical sense, where do you think Lewis' weaknesses really showed? Particularly in those books such as *Miracles* and *The Problem of Pain,* and perhaps even *Mere Christianity.*

Mitchell: I don't think that I want to think of it in those terms, because to think in those terms of Lewis' weaknesses as a philosopher would imply that one *regarded* him as a philosopher, whereas it is much more true to say that one didn't at that time regard him as a philosopher *at all,* because a philosopher, as one understood the term, was someone working within certainty fairly precise limits, and arguing in certain fairly clearly delimited ways, and Lewis just didn't fit into his pattern. One regarded him as a lively independent thinker, but not specifically as a philosopher. He'd read the Greats, he'd taught philosophy for a while, he was well acquainted with the philosophical classics, he had the sort of mind which, had he addressed himself to the questions that engrossed philosophers of the time, would have made him into a good philosopher by professional standards—but he simply wasn't "one of the club," so to speak, and if you were asked to give a list of the leading philosophers in Oxford—or even of *the* philosophers in Oxford—Lewis wouldn't have been mentioned among them. So it wasn't a question of specific weaknesses; I mean, he produced some good searching arguments and clearly had a feeling for what was philosophically interesting and what wasn't, but he didn't go into questions with the kind of meticulous care for detail that was particularly characteristic of the philosophers of that period.

Walker: Can I just take you up on that? I think this is a very good point you've made, because one of my criticisms of John Beversluis' really rather devastating critique on Lewis' work, *C. S. Lewis and the Search for Rational Religion,* is that he tends to treat him as if he were a professional philosopher who didn't do very well. But you're really suggesting that to treat Lewis by the criterion is unfair, that he never really claimed to be a philosopher, he was just a chap who felt he ought to take on, as it were, the fashionable theories of the day.

Mitchell: Yes. You see, I think that with hindsight one can see that even the best philosophy of Lewis' day, done in this particular analytical tradition, was subject to a number of pretty severe limitations.

The whole idea of philosophical analysis assumed that it was possible to isolate certain questions and deal with them very, very rigorously, in such detail that almost inevitably you couldn't attempt large and subjectively important questions—they were simply unmanageable. So perhaps it wasn't entirely accidental that the philosophers of that period thought that you couldn't *in principle* handle philosophically very large questions.

Now I think that you can see in retrospect that if you're going to do that, and handle somewhat limited questions very minutely, you can only do it at the expense of making some very large assumptions that never enter into the argument at all, that are just not questioned.

Walker: You mean the hidden presuppositions by which one allows oneself to continue to do this kind of micro-philosophical work?

Mitchell: Yes, that's right. And I think that among Lewis' strengths as a thinker was his ability to see that there were very large assumptions being made, and to attack those assumptions.

A work that provides a very good example of this approach is *The Abolition of Man*. A great deal of what passed for moral philosophy at that time did assume a subjectivist (or what, in his book *After Virtue*, Alasdair MacIntyre calls an emotivist) position. In *The Abolition of Man* Lewis attacked this head-on—and I think in retrospect one can see that he was entirely right to do so.

It took people like MacIntyre, who had gone through the mill of logical analysis, to show by precise philosophical reasoning what was wrong with the subjectivist approach to ethics. However, as we have seen, this was not the sort of task Lewis himself was equipped to undertake, but he had the larger vision to see intuitively that there was something profoundly wrong with it, and he marshalled arguments against it which are of considerable philosophical weight, although they are not technical philosophical arguments.

Walker: I think that is an extremely helpful way of highlighting the value of *The Abolition of Man*. It demonstrates something you said earlier, that to a certain generation of Christians who thought that one couldn't any longer consider Christianity intellectually respectable, Lewis showed that you really could put up some quite reasonable arguments in its defense—that one didn't have to assume that the enemy has all the good arguments. So, regardless of whether judged by the philosophy of his day they were sufficiently philosophically technical, Lewis' arguments persuaded many people of good intelligence that Christian apologetics was still possible.

Furthermore, *The Abolition of Man* is important not simply because in it Lewis uncharacteristically (in comparison with his method in his other works) builds up very good critical arguments against certain kinds of fashions, particularly against "subjectiveness" (as he calls it) and relativism, but also because he spells out almost disarmingly the position of classicism, or what he calls the *Tao*, which he doesn't so much defend philosophically as present as an accumulative argument. Do you feel that *The Abolition of Man* is an apologetical book that has lasted?

Mitchell: Oh yes. I think remarkably well. And I think it is very interesting, the convergence between Alasdair MacIntyre's argument—both in *After Virtue* and in his most recent book *Whose Justice? Which Rationality?*—and the line that Lewis was taking in *The Abolition of Man*. You could say that in *The Abolition of Man* Lewis had sort of intuitive vision of the kind of argument that in a more philosophically sophisticated way MacIntyre has marshalled in these books.

And of course another very interesting thing is the extremely circuitous route by which MacIntyre has arrived at his present position.

For a short period he tried to hold together the philosophy of Logical Positivism and the theology of Karl Barth. (And you can see how they would fit together, in that the Positivists assert that theological statements are nonsense and Barth says "Yes, of course, you're absolutely right; looked at from the standpoint of human reason they're nonsense—that's why it has to be a matter of divine revelation!") Well, Alasdair was holding these two things together and arguing that, for this reason, there couldn't be a rational debate between theism and atheism. And I wrote an article entitled "The Justification of Religious Belief" which was concerned with querying this and suggesting an alternative, which I later developed in the book *The Justification of Religious Belief.*

Walker: I would have thought that the argument of *The Justification of Religious Belief* is something of a bridge between Lewis and the more recent MacIntyre—in fact, it's MacIntyre before MacIntyre—in that it thinks through the presuppositions on which a great deal of modern thought has been based.

Mitchell: Yes.

Walker: I particularly remember the way in which you deal in that book with the idea that only the belief in theism has these intellectual problems. In fact, all philosophies of life have these same sorts of problems. And in that respect, would it offend you to say that one can see you in the Lewis tradition?

Mitchell: Oh no, not in the least. I'd be very pleased to be told that. But the interesting thing I was suggesting about MacIntyre is that I had rather hoped that my article might, among other influences, persuade him into a more central tradition of rational Christianity. In the end, though, he gave up Christianity altogether and only came back to it comparatively late in his career, and came back to it by way of actually passing through the states of mind which he subsequently criticized—so he was criticizing, so to speak, his past self. And it's particularly noteworthy that some of the criticisms that he eventually made of the positions that he used to occupy do very much reflect the general line that Lewis was taking in *The Abolition of Man*.

Walker: I absolutely agree with you. *After Virtue* is a book that many people have recognized as a major work. And yet it constantly reminds me of Lewis' approach.

Perhaps, though, it has one or two advantages over Lewis. The first is that is has, I think, a sociological grasp Lewis simply didn't have. And secondly it is more professionally marshalled.

Mitchell: The point of convergence between MacIntyre and Lewis is that, like Lewis, MacIntyre argues that there is a central moral tradition which one can't dispense with—which can be developed, but which can't be altogether rejected. And that this tradition is a shared tradition. It can't be thought up, as it were, by a single individual—it has to be something that is widely accepted in the society. And that is not far from saying what Lewis says in *The Abolition of Man,* that the acceptance of the *Tao* is a function of being human, and that those people who, post-Nietzsche (or maybe even post-Hume), have been trying to regard ethics as essentially the creation of individual preferences are eventually depriving themselves of what makes them human. Now I think that this is very much the central theme, both in MacIntyre's book and in Lewis' essay.

MacIntyre is—and always has been—someone who is extremely sensitive to the cultural currents of the age. He has had, as it were, to be carried along by all these currents before coming to a point at which he can make a true evaluation of them.

I'm intrigued that quite often people remark on the resemblance between the book I wrote about morality, *Morality: Religious and Secular,* and the book written by MacIntyre, and ask did I get it from MacIntyre or did MacIntyre get it from me? And the answer must be "Neither," because I certainly did not get it from MacIntyre. When *After Virtue* appeared, I was intrigued because it was so different from the things I last heard MacIntyre saying. And I'm perfectly sure that MacIntyre wouldn't have read anything that I wrote—it's very unlikely, because he was moving in really rather different intellectual circles. But there is quite a considerable convergence there.

What has happened now—and not only in the case of Alasdair MacIntyre—is that there's a great sense of the wheel having come full circle, and the issues that were supposed to have been disposed of twenty or thirty years ago are now all being hotly debated again. And that means that some of the people who were writing then, and whose works have been neglected, have been revived and are being studied once more.

Walker: Yes, I agree. John Macmurray's personalist philosophy, which is exemplified perhaps most clearly in his *Persons in Relation*, and which went through a period of almost total neglect, is now being taken up—rediscovered—by various theologians concerned with theological anthropology. What do you think has caused "the wheel to come full circle?"

Mitchell: I think that the chief influence was the development of the philosophy of science. If you remember, the Logical Positivist movement started as an attempt to make a clear demarcation between science and common sense on the one hand and metaphysics and theology on the other. But work in the philosophy of science convinced people that what the Logical Positivists had said about science was not true, and, by the time the philosophers of science had developed and amplified their accounts of how rationality works in science, people discovered that similar accounts applied equally well to the areas which they had previously sought to exclude, namely theology and metaphysics.

I think the work of Thomas S. Kuhn was crucial here—particularly the thesis developed in his book *The Structure of Scientific Revolutions.* Although subsequent criticism has shown that Kuhn exaggerated the incommensurability of these "paradigms," as he calls them, nevertheless the essential truth of his discoveries remains—namely, that when it comes to making a choice between large-scale scientific theories, there isn't any system of rules that will enable you to do it. It's got to be done by a careful comparison of the two systems, each of which claims to provide a complete overall explanation of the phenomena. You have to say either that there's no way of choosing, or you have to say that there is a way of choosing, but that it's a matter of which explanation offers the best overall account—and this will eventually be a matter of judgment. But then, if that's true in comparing large-scale scientific theories, it's equally true in comparing metaphysical systems—whether theistic or materialistic—or indeed in comparing different moral theories. So you find yourself, simply as a result of taking seriously developments in the philosophy of science, embracing a concept of rationality that is broad enough to include all the things that Lewis and his contemporaries took for granted were worth arguing about. And that's why a lot of the stuff Lewis wrote doesn't seem anything like as out of date as one would have expected.

Walker: I have to agree with you about that. In 1988 I did a tour of American and British cities during which I gave lectures on Lewis to mixed audiences, ranging from a thousand people at Greenbelt to eighty people in the chapel at King's College London. The extraordinary thing was that not only were people obviously extremely well read in Lewis' works, but they were fascinated by his arguments and felt that people were still benefiting from them.

I'd like to change the subject now and, in drawing to a conclusion, raise something I'd like your views on. It's something I know you've been working on.

On the one hand, it strikes me as almost a truism—not from a philosophical point of view, but from a historical and cultural point of view—that if you have a daily face-to-face social interaction with people, of the kind that you get in a village (or that you used to get in any pre-industrialized society), where there is a certain amount of shared views about how the universe works (at least in ethical terms if not necessarily in physical terms), then to a certain extent it means that moral discourse can proceed—that at least we've got in common a basic idea of what's right and what's wrong.

But, on the other hand, I frequently find in modern industrial society, particularly with undergraduates—regardless of whether I'm doing theology or I'm doing sociology—that many of them share the view that everything is "just a matter of opinion," and that to suggest that there may be some objectivity that exists almost irrespective of one's subjective opinion is a terrible cheek, or at the least a very strange idea.

Is this second feature, do you think, just a fashion that we're going through—one that Lewis almost prophetically saw forty years ago—or is it a result of features of our contemporary world such as vastly increased social mobility, mass immigration, and the mass media, where there are so many views on sale that people are very confused about what truth might look like? Do you think, for example, that we are witnessing a vast change in the way that our culture works, or do you see this as a philosophical problem?

Mitchell: Well, first of all, I meet you with an example from my own teaching experience. I remember particularly—this was over ten years ago now—I was taking an undergraduate class of about fifteen students with someone else in the philosophy of religion at a "prestigious liberal arts college" in the United States, and I became very rapidly aware that they reacted strongly against any attempt to provide a rational criticism of, or to look for a rational defense of, their religious views. And this is what I found—it was an interesting cross-cultural thing—that one would just get them to read essays, and I would start, habitually, in the way I would an Oxford tutorial, and I would say "Yes, well that was an extremely interesting presentation. I'm not quite sure, however, that I understood what you were getting at in that first paragraph. I wonder whether you could explain it a bit more." And then the chap would go on, usually saying a whole lot of further things. And I would say, "No, I didn't want you to tell me some other things that you think. I just wanted you to explain to me what you actually meant by the things that you said in that particular paragraph." And then with difficulty I'd get them to elucidate a bit, and then I'd say "Yes, I think I see that . . . but in that case, is that really consistent with what I took you to be saying in your summing up? In your first paragraph you were saying such and such, in your final paragraph you were saying so and so. On the face of it these two aren't consistent." And they *very* much disliked this. And I came to the conclusion that it wasn't just that they weren't used to this sort of Socratic method, but it was also that they were discussing the nature of their religious beliefs, and they thought that religion wasn't susceptible to this sort of treatment. What had been expressed were their opinions, and their attitude was "If I contradict myself, then I contradict myself."

So from my own experience I'm sure that you are right, and that it's very, very difficult to get students today even to conceive of the possibility that there might be some truth of the matter, independently of what they happen to think about it.

And, of course, in argument one has to proceed by putting them into a situation where actually they are not prepared to leave it simply as a matter of opinion. For example, nowadays if you say "Well, some people think that it is a good state of society in which all the arrangements are made for the convenience of men, but some people, on the other hand, think that such a patriarchal society unjustly exploits women," you'll find that they're not prepared to sit on the fence as far as *that* is concerned—they're against the patriarchal society, and they are against the exploitation of women, and you can then go on to say, "Well, in that case, what is it about the exploitation of women that is wrong? After all there are many societies—historically, probably more societies than not—which have grossly exploited women. It can't be just a matter of what is acceptable in society, and if it's a matter of individual opinion, well it wouldn't be a very difficult matter to go into the streets and find someone who would agree with the exploitation of women, though perhaps he would not use that language."

Walker: I've had that experience. For ten years I taught social-workers social ethics—not because I was qualified to do so, but because no one else would do it. They were being taught sociology, psychology, and "social work practice." But since nobody was sitting down and saying "Well, considering you are making decisions every day, such as whether you're going to take an old lady into care, or are going to take a child away from its parents, let's consider the ethical implications of your job"—and being as they also had very strong views about such phrases as "social justice"—I thought it would be a very good idea if we actually looked at those ethical ramifications and at phrases like social justice.

And what I found time and time again was this scenario: We would get a lot of people in a large room, all of whom claimed—or most of them anyway—that they didn't have any interest in morality in the traditional sense—certainly not in sexual morality—and then as time would go on we would find that the room would be divided into people who felt very, very strongly about one or two specific issues. Abortion would be one (they were against it because it was some kind of murder; or they were for it because it had nothing to do with killing, it had instead to do with the right of a woman to control her body; or whatever). So words like "rights" would crop up. That was alright. But then, when I asked them to clarify why they held these views, they were lost, totally lost—and in fact most offended that I should ask them these questions. And that, it seems to me, is a demonstration of the fact we considered earlier, that we live in a culturally pluralistic world where there can't, as it were, be a common conversation.

Mitchell: This of course is one of the points that MacIntyre makes very strongly, doesn't he?

Walker: I think that is probably why his perspective has an enormous appeal for me. But—given that we've agreed that the kinds of questions Lewis was talking about in the 1940s are now at least more respectable, and that we can once again ask the bigger questions—I suppose the question we must then ask is "How do we get people to take traditional moral questions seriously if (a) they have no philosophical or moral training and (b) they tend to see morality very much as a matter of personal opinion?" I mean, what's the way forward?

Maybe we could end on that question, because we've gone a long way down a fairly drunken road, and because it seems to me a very practical and yet existential problem, which people have to face: "What do I believe in, and why?"

Given the fact that we've stated that there are these problems that we've both encountered, what do we do?

Mitchell: Who is "we?"

Walker: I think, if you like, teachers, or anybody who confronts a group of people who are concerned about morality.

Mitchell: I think that part of the answer is implicit in what you've been saying, namely that one does need education in ethical questions. And this is becoming increasingly apparent in various spheres.

I would have thought that what you were trying to do with your social workers was entirely the right way of proceeding because in the intellectual situation which you have described—in which when you ask people if they have any moral principles, they say "No"—it's no good just starting off with a discussion of moral principles which, *ex hypothesi,* they say they haven't got. But if you start off with the sort of situation in which they find themselves, and *then* try to get them to take seriously how they would or should proceed in those situations, well the moral problems and the moral principles come out of it,

For example, we've got something called The Ian Ramsey Centre in Oxford, and we've been having a seminar on the rights of elderly people. (Here too social workers are involved.) What are you to do if you have an elderly person who wants to go back home, but there are serious doubts about how competent she is (it's nearly always a she, because women last so much longer)? Well, usually the social workers feel that they ought to do what the patient or the client wants, so far as that is possible. But then what's going to happen if the old girl falls down the stairs? What about the responsibilities of the family and of the neighbors? Very often the family and the neighbors say, "Look, even with the best will in the world, we can't be looking after her twenty-four hours of the day—and if we do less than that she's not going to be safe." So, well, what matters? Take, for example, the autonomy of the individual. How much weight does one give to autonomy in the case of someone of doubtful competence? How does one measure competence? Should we ask what's best for the individual? But we may ask, "best" in what terms? In purely physical terms? In social terms? And so forth?

One can't help feeling that your social workers, when presented with actual cases, would see that inherent in the situation is usually not one, but a number of moral principles that they have to identify and then somehow or other weigh in order to resolve the question. What they certainly won't be prepared to say, when faced by the actual situation is that they should do just what they feel like.

Walker: No, they wouldn't. It seems to me that an axiom of Lewis' approach to morality—probably following G. K. Chesterton—was that he tended to take it for granted that there was something called common sense.

Now I'm not sure that he ever articulated that in terms of a theory, but he felt that when he was appealing to people, he could appeal to their sense—not only a logical sense, but a moral sense.

But I've found that when dealing with today's students it's no longer possible to make this assumption. I don't mean to say that I don't appeal to some "innate sense of morality"—whatever that means—actually I do, but I have to make it conscious for them to believe that there are absolutes. Because, as you say, if you face them with a concrete, real-life situation all sorts of moral issues will emerge. To try and then relate those issues to general moral principles is, it seems to me, an enormous undertaking.

Mitchell: I think it's understandable that you should feel that way, because I think there are two things—maybe even three things—about Lewis' situation that would remove him quite a bit from the situation of your social workers.

The first is that he was aware of belonging to a common culture. I mean, the people that Lewis associated with at that period did represent, in this country, very largely a homogeneous group of people of a certain cultural background which could be taken for granted.

A second thing is that Lewis had a very strong sense of history. I mean, he was a good classical scholar, and a medievalist, and he was familiar with the whole sweep of English history and literature.

Walker: But he saw himself in a living tradition.

Mitchell: Yes, in a living tradition. And the third thing is, of course, that, apart from the Great War, his experience was very much a one-class experience, wasn't it?

In these three respects his life-situation would be very different from your social workers. And of course, as we see in his "De Descriptione Temporum," that splendid inaugural lecture at Cambridge, Lewis saw himself as really at the end of an age.

Walker: "A specimen," as he says, a dinosaur of the past.

Mitchell: Yes, what I've just been saying about him he would have recognized.

Walker: Yes. I think he would. He saw himself as one of the last of a dying species.

ORTHODOX PERSPECTIVES

12

THE PROPHETIC ROLE
OF ORTHODOXY IN
CONTEMPORARY CULTURE
(1996)

Since the Middle Ages until recently, prophecies in the West have ranged from portentous prediction (for example, the fifteenth-century Girolamo Savonarola) to pretentious presumption (the nineteenth-century Mormon founder Joseph Smith). Today that prophetic role tends to be interpreted in three ways.

In liberal churches, it is usually interpreted politically. The prophets in this line need to be supporting one party against another party, or one cause against another cause. The legitimate biblical concern for the poor and oppressed becomes a legitimation for a social or liberation gospel, which all too often ends up being a different gospel. Prophets of such a religion take on the characteristics of an *agent provocateur,* or a romantic activist—more a follower of Marcuse than Moses.

In fundamentalist and conservative Protestant circles, prophecy is prey to religious enthusiasm, seen either in millenarian or ecstatic terms. Millenarians, such as the American televangelist Jack Van Impe, interpret eschatology, not as the final judgment, but as a second advent. Adventist prophets search the Scriptures, notably the apocalyptic passages, in order to help them look for and recognize the signs of the "end time." Charismatic churches tend to stress divine inspiration over and against tradition and sacred text—as if one could somehow distinguish *rhema* from *logos*—or, they insist on the legitimacy of immediate and unmediated revelations alongside revealed tradition. The prophets of such a religion are more in the line of Montanus than Mark the Ascetic.

THE PROPHETIC FUNCTION

As a matter of fact, both of these conservative Protestant traditions reflect—though refract—strands of Orthodox teaching. Irenaeus, for example, included a millenarian section in his apologia *Against the Gnostic Heretics*, and Saint Simeon the New Theologian stressed that the inspirational side of spiritual life should be normative for the Christian.[1] But these lesser known prophetic traditions are not the core prophetic concept in the Orthodox Church. In order to discover what that might be, we can do no better than begin with the Russian catechism, where we read the following:

> "Anointed" was in old times a title of kinds, high priests and prophets. Why then is Jesus the Son of God, called "the anointed?" Because to His Manhood were imparted without measure all the gifts of the Holy Ghost, and so He possessed in the highest degree the knowledge of a prophet, the holiness of a high priest and the power of a king.

In the patristic era, the interconnection between Christ as king, priest, and prophet was continually held in creative tension. However, all these titles shared in common the generic feature that they are charisms of Christ's humanity, conferred by the anointing of the Holy Spirit.

Father Schmemann, drawing on earlier literature, reminds us in *The Water and the Spirit* that when Jesus came out of the waters of Jordan at his baptism, there was the first public demonstration of the true nature of the Son of God. The Trinity was revealed, and Jesus coming up out of the water was a way of showing, as it were, the divine stature of who he really was. The full stature of Jesus as a human being, however, was that in receiving the Holy Spirit from the Father, he was anointed to be the greatest of the prophets, our one true high priest and supreme mediator between God and humankind, and our everlasting king—one who rules with intrinsic authority and absolute justice.

---

1. Cf. Saint Simeon the New Theologian, *The Practical and Theological Chapters & The Three Theological Discourses*.

Schmemann makes the claim—as daunting as it may be for us to accept this—that, when we too are baptized, and immediately afterwards chrismated with oil, this is also a Trinitarian action and a threefold calling, that we may be like Christ in our anointed humanity. So we are grafted into the body of Christ through the waters of baptism in the power of the Holy Spirit, and affirmed by the Father to be joint-heirs with Christ. We too are called to be a prophet, a priest, and a king.

This is why Irenaeus is so foundational for Orthodox theology. He stressed the incarnation as the event that enabled men and women truly to become what they are called to be: not merely restored to the innocence of paradise and the (forever lost) unfallen flesh of Adam, but recapitulated in Christ's new humanity as coheirs with him of God's future kingdom. We are permitted to be coheirs in this kingdom only because we have become members of this new race through adoption into Christ's divine life.

The New Testament calls our Lord the second or final Adam (1 Cor 15:45) because he is both the origin and fount of this new race, but also its apotheosis or fulfillment. To "put on Christ," therefore, is to acquire through grace what allows us also to acquire the charisms of Christ's anointing.

We might say that the incarnation initiates the future kingdom because it marks the beginning of eschatological time: the end-time when God from the future (the *eschaton*) enters the space-time continuum of created existence. Through that decisive moment of history—when eschatological time entered ontologically into the human situation—the future of the created cosmos, and of all men and women who have put on Christ, is destined to be greater than anything Eden knew.

Eden, however, was a world in which human beings knew something of prophecy, priesthood, and kingship. Before the fall, man and woman were in communion with God. They were stamped with God's character or image, and made in his likeness. Adam and Eve, in Schmemann's memorable phrase, were "matter made articulate": God's prophets or "spokespersons" to the world. They were priests too because it was a unique function of human beings as bearers of God's image that they could mediate between the created earth and God Himself. They offered God to the world and the world back to God: "Thine of Thine Own" in the words of the Eucharistic prayer. Human beings were kings also, not as overlords, but as regents or royal stewards of the Lord's good creation.

The prophetic role is the one I want to dwell on in the rest of this chapter even though, as we have seen, it rightly belongs in concert with our priestly and kingly functions, given to us at the birth of the world and now restored to us in Christ.

The prophetic function is very simple, and I would like to spell it out if I may in a simple sentence: to be a prophet is to know and speak the mind and will of God. It was the fall that hid this knowledge from us, just as it perverted our God-given kingly power, and weakened our natural propensity for mediation between the created order and God.

Throughout the Old Testament, we read from time to time of men and women who had flashes of insight—people who seemed to be able to reconnect with the original created human being who kneMw God's mind, and who could speak the will of God. We think specifically of Moses and Elijah, or of Jeremiah, Amos, and the other prophets. But in the New Testament, it is the Lord Jesus who is supremely our prophet, and we are called as baptized disciples to follow in his footsteps. The words of Paul make this quite clear: "Therefore, if anyone is in Christ, he is a new creation. Old things have passed away, behold, all things have become new" (2 Cor 5:17).

Strangely enough, many people find it difficult to associate prophecy with our Lord simply because we think of him as our Savior, or as divine, or as the God-man. While the epistle to the Hebrews draws our attention to Christ as our High Priest, and Orthodox Tradition has long associated Jesus with the Judge-King (*Pantokrator),* whose kingdom shall have no end, the word "prophet" is not automatically a word that comes to our lips. I suspect that this is due also to the fact that we tend to distinguish our Lord from the last of the great Old Testament prophets, John the Baptist, the forerunner to the expected Messiah. But clearly it is right and proper to see Christ in his humanity as being a prophet, a new creation, and a new creature, one who knew and spoke the mind and will of God. Therefore, Luke is the most important of the four Gospels when it comes to the prophetic role of our Lord, for in his gospel we read that Jesus identified himself as a prophet (Luke 4:24). Speaking in the synagogue at his home town of Nazareth, Jesus said: "The Spirit of the Lord is upon me because he has anointed me to preach the gospel to the poor; he has sent me to heal the brokenhearted, to preach deliverance to the captives, and recovering of sight to the blind, to set at liberty them that are bruised, and to preach the acceptance year of the Lord" (Luke 4:18–19).

In the Old Testament, taken as a whole, it is more accurate to say that the prophets were not so much *foretellers,* as *forthtellers* of God's mind and will, the ones who proclaimed God's word. Jesus begins his ministry forthrightly in Mark's Gospel with the words: "Repent and believe the gospel" (1:15). Jesus, the Son of God made Son of Man, is therefore revealing to us the mind of God. God's will for us, which is nothing less than the gospel, is that like the prodigal son we must turn from our failure and degradation and return to the Father who is always ready to re-affirm and cherish us (Luke 15). It is the Son who reveals this to us, who alone speaks the truth from the mind of God, who is the way home, life itself (John 14:6).

THE PROPHETIC ROLE OF THE DIASPORA

I am mindful, following the example of John Chrysostom, that Holy Tradition needs to be applied to our contemporary condition. So having grounded the role of prophecy in the life of Christ himself, I would like to turn to the role of the prophet today, writing as a Western member of the Orthodox diaspora.

But first there is something that we must make clear, and it is something that I believe we Orthodox already know in our hearts. It is that we must try to avoid individualistic notions of the "prophet": *he* is a prophet, *she* is a prophet, or *I* am a prophet. There may be individuals whose utterances are more prophetic than others; we know also from the writings of Irenaeus that there were still institutional prophets in the late second century. However, what makes the prophet significant is not the novelty of individual insight, but the faithful recollection of Tradition. Tradition is the divinely inspired—though human, and hence fallible—mediation of the mind and will of God.

A better way of understanding this is to recognize that Orthodoxy distinguishes individualism from personhood. Individuals are disconnected persons, separate islands of consciousness, solipsistic beings, lost selves; whereas persons are ontologically constituted by their relation to others in community, and supremely through the Holy Spirit. The Holy Trinity may be the only true, perfect communion, where relationships are unbroken between the distinct, though never separate, divine persons, but members of the church are by definition joined one to another. We are what we are as persons because, as Paul puts it, we are "joined together" (Eph 4:16).

We are prophets precisely, and only, because together with our Lord we are the *totus Christus*. We are prophets because we are "little Christs." We are prophets because we are adopted by the Spirit into a new personal creation—this newly constituted humanity of which Christ is the firstborn through the incarnation and resurrection (see Col 1:18). In one sense, therefore, the church cannot help but be prophetic. I think it was Father.

Justin Popovic who said that the past is always present in the church, and therefore the church is always contemporaneous.[2] That is to say, it is not really possible for the church not to be prophetic today, or at any time. But what does it mean to be prophetic? To reiterate: it is to know and speak the mind and will of God.

I would like now, as I promised I would, to point to something rather more concrete and specific that affects us all. I would like to talk about the prophetic significance of the Orthodox diaspora in the modern world. We could be reductionist and say: "Well, of course, we can understand the diaspora entirely in terms of war, civil strife, sociology, and economics," and that is perfectly true on the political and cultural level. But prophets are called by God, and I think it is also true, on the spiritual level that God called the Orthodox Church into the West. With all its faults and weaknesses—and hopefully not blind to its faults and weaknesses—the Orthodox Church finds herself in a world both secular and religious that is becoming increasingly fragmented and polarized. In such a world, all that the Orthodox Church is called to be is to be herself. To be herself *is* to be prophetic.

I would like to give you an example of what I mean. A colleague of mine at one of the American universities where I teach says that, increasingly, Protestant Christians are beginning to understand that the history of this fragmentation within Christendom goes back at least to the Reformation—and we would want to say much sooner. While the Reformers genuinely desired to return to the catholicity of the creeds and councils, they instead gave us reformation *ad nauseam*. What my colleagues and some of his friends see when they look at the Orthodox Church is a body of Christians who have maintained the apostolic faith, because the canonical structures have been maintained and kept secure.[3]

My friend claims that one of the greatest failures of the Reformation was precisely that it did not recover or recapture the foundational canonical structures of Christianity that were laid down, not only in the New Testament, but also by the fathers of the church. In that sense, what the church does by being itself is pointing to unity and showing something of the mind of God. That is what Khomiakov's remarkable booklet, *The Church is One*, contends. It is certainly audacious, but it is also auspicious and prophetic in an age of disunity. It is not so much that unity is a question, as Roman Catholics might put it, of an unbroken apostolic succession, as if this were an entitlement to legitimate churchmanship—like a deed of property or a

---

2. Cf., Popovic, *Notes on Ecumenism*.

3. Thanks to William J. Abraham of Southern Methodist University; cf. Abraham, *Canon and Criterion* for a fuller discussion of these arguments.

right to dominion. And it is certainly not a question of untrammeled holiness in the Wesleyan sense of perfectionism—God knows that we have sinned immeasurably.

To be cataphatic, unity for us is an ontological fact. In the language of Metropolitan John of Pergamon, we *are* the church instituted by Christ and constituted by the Spirit, and yet apophatically, our unity is the mystery of our calling.[4] For lest we should boast, we are reminded, paradoxically, that to be Orthodox is to be willing, if it is possible, as Paul says, to be castaways that all may be saved (1 Cor 9:20). Our unity, then, is not an expression of smugness, but of *mission*. The Lord Jesus himself makes this clear in his prayer for the church: "That they all may be one: as thou, Father, art in me, and I in thee, that they also may be one in us: that the world may believe that thou hast sent me" (John 17:21, KJV).

The diaspora's role in mission, however, has been mixed and not always prophetic. Orthodox missionary shortcomings in the West have been elegantly articulated by Metropolitan Philip of the Antiochene Church in America.[5] He says that the diaspora has arrived bodily in the West, but remains absent psychologically. He says that there are Orthodox Christians in North America who are still living elsewhere "in their hearts." The "old country" naturally exercises a strong pull on the imagination and memory, but it can also lead to a perpetual daydream where Christian responsibility is neglected by nostalgic longing for the past.[6]

Metropolitan Philip argues that one of the problems with this is that members of some churches have not spoken to the West with a prophetic voice because they have not seen themselves as missionaries or prophets, but merely as a ghetto, holding together that which they had lost in the past. His argument over the last ten years or so has been that the Orthodox Church must cease to be a diaspora church in the sense of a museum or an ethnic enclave and become a missionary church.[7] For Orthodoxy to be institutionally present in the West is not enough. It is not here merely to survive or even to wax strong. It is here to mediate the presence of God the Holy Spirit, or to put it in the language of this chapter: its prophetic role is to speak the mind and will of God.

What Metropolitan Philip says may not be popular with all Orthodox Christians, but I believe it is a rather more positive way to look at the role of

4. Cf. Zizioulas, *Being as Communion*.

5. Cf. "The Thoughts of Metropolitan Philip on Missiology," Father Joseph Allen, ed., at http://www.antiochian.org; and Peter E. Gilquist's biography, *Metropolitan Philip*.

6. Ibid.

7. See in particular Metropolian Philip's "Address to the Episcopal Church" at http://www.antiochian.org.

the diaspora over the last decades. First, let me look at this quite sociologically. I have been a member of the Russian Patriarchal Church in Great Britain for twenty-three years. When I joined in 1973, I saw myself as a guest in the Russian Church; being a guest, albeit a welcome one, did not distress me. I realized that when a new group arrives from one land to another, if it is going to maintain the structures and traditions of the church, sometimes it has to be, as a I think Metropolitan Anthony of Sourozh once said, "sniffy." It wants to put its roots down and create something firm and deep before it grows; otherwise, we know what can happen: the plant will be force-fed and soon wither and die.

My own view is that the diaspora has needed to be in the West for a while and bide its time before it reaches out in mission—although, like Metropolitan Philip, I think that the time is ripe. The diaspora needs to realize its "inbuilt strength" that can feed its prophetic role in the world: people who are refugees, who come from one land to another, are, if you like, resident aliens. They are resident in the country, but they do not really quite belong. Strictly speaking, that is what all Christians are, regardless of whether they are actually in an historical diaspora or not, for we are citizens, not of earth, but of heaven.

Therefore, to a certain extent, to be a "resident alien" means that you are open to the prophetic. That is why C. S. Lewis, always out of sorts with modernity—like the anti-hero of Dostoyevsky's *Letters from the Underworld*—was the outstanding European Christian apologist in the twentieth century. We notice in literature and in the secular world that the outsider often has an interesting way of seeing things. He or she has a unique perspicacity that insiders do not possess, because things happen underneath the noses of insiders, but they cannot see the obvious staring them in the face. So I think there is a very positive sense in which the diaspora, because of its marginality, its status as the outsider, is well positioned to be prophetic—as long as it remains attentive to the mind of God.

To be on the edge, or on the boundaries, as Paul Tillich liked to talk of it,[8] is a curious experience demanding great discernment as well as faithfulness to the Tradition. Orthodox Christians who settle in the West discover a mystery. On the one hand, by being what we are, Orthodox, with all our weaknesses, witness to the "one holy catholic and apostolic church." On the other hand, we discover, to our amazement, that there is more of a family resemblance with the heterodox than we had imagined. We find brothers and sisters in Christ in many countries. Even if they are estranged family members, the family resemblance is unmistakable.

---

8. Cf. Taylor, *Paul Tillich: Theologian of the Boundaries.*

This was one of the great shocks for Nicolas Zernov when he arrived in Europe from Russia some years after the Bolshevik Revolution. He discovered that there were Christians everywhere and many of them were asking for Orthodox help and illumination for Western theological problems. He found (as do many Orthodox today) that there were heretics too, but he became convinced that the adage of Metropolitan Sergius Stragovodsky of Moscow is true: "we know where the Church is, but we do not say where the Church is not."[9]

For many years in Great Britain, Metropolitan Anthony has supported what little trickles of Orthodoxy he has been able to find bubbling up in other Christians, even if they never fully flow into the Orthodox Church. He has been encouraged by the many Christian people who have been committed to the sort of historic Christianity that allows real debate to take place between East and West.

The diaspora still has a long way to go before it turns from a siege to a missionary mentality, but I believe that the Orthodox Church is turning outwards as Nicholas Berdyaev wanted it to and is beginning to share some of its treasures with others. I think, for example, that the ecological dispute is one major area where the majority of Western theology really has little to say about the relationship between humankind and the material universe, because it does not seem to have a full, organic understanding of the relationship between priesthood, prophecy, kingship, and the world. This is one major debate where we have something to offer, something prophetic to say.[10]

I know there are some Orthodox who feel that it is not our job to help Western Christians solve their problems. I believe that we cannot take that view: this is not only exclusivist, it is Pharisaical. I believe the right attitude is much more than we are here, and that if we can offer help, then we will. One of the ways we can do this is by displaying for people what our theology is, what our spirituality is, not in a proselytizing, declamatory way that always makes people feel uncomfortable, but simply by spelling out some of the problems we are all facing together as Christians in the modern world.

The World Council of Churches' Faith and Order Commission, incidentally, with all its faults, is better than it might have been precisely because of the contribution that the Orthodox Church has made to it. If anyone ever wants evidence that some good has come out of ecumenical dialogue, just

---

9. See Zernov, *The Russians and Their Church.*

10. See in particular Berdyaev, *The Fate of the Modern World.*

look back over the last ten years and see how the Trinity, baptism, and a high Christology are back on the agenda of the World Council of Churches.[11]

And we could go further. A number of leading Reformed theologians, of which Bishop Lesslie Newbigin is one, were of the opinion that the Orthodox delegation at the WCC Conference at Canberra in 1991 saved the council from disaster, when they were urged by Chung Hyun-Kyung, the controversial Chinese feminist theologian, to embrace a syncretistic understanding of faith far beyond the boundaries of revealed religion. It is ironic that a number of radical thinkers, particularly those interested in women's and interfaith issues support the Orthodox on the *filioque* clause, so that they can free the Spirit from the Son and let him loose on the world.[12]

The Orthodox response to Professor Chung and by implication to all those who would turn the Holy Spirit into *Sophia,* or a deistic immanence, was to say in effect: "Our Tradition is rich in respect for local and national cultures, but we find it impossible to evoke the spirits of 'earth, air, water, and sea creatures.' Pneumatology is inseparable from Christology, or from the doctrine of the Holy Spirit confessed by the church on the basis of divine revelation."[13]

Here the Orthodox Church—heartlands and diaspora as one—faced with a theological crisis as deep as the paganism of early centuries was unequivocal. Without a hint of the Erastian and pragmatic spirit that has sometimes bedeviled our witness, we spoke the mind of God.

Not all Orthodox prophecy has been so dramatic. Sometimes it has been a case of a gradual opening up of the Orthodox Church's Tradition to the outside world. Metropolitan John's book, for example, *Being as Communion,* is now standard reading in many evangelical colleges in Great Britain as well as in Reformed seminaries. And the Orthodox adherence to the Cappadocian understanding of the Trinity has had great influence in recent years, moving people away from a sterile modalism or impersonalism to a dynamic model of personal communion. Not enough has been made of it, but the accord between the Reformed tradition and the Orthodox Church on the *filioque* and the doctrine of the Trinity has been a major breakthrough in ecumenical dialogue.

Those Orthodox who say that Protestants and Catholics can never understand the Eastern Church are sometimes guilty of failing to learn the theological jargon of the West, or of seeing how far Orthodox concepts can

---

11. Cf. the Would Council of Churches, *Baptism, Eucharist and Ministry.*

12. Cf. *Signs of the Spirit: Official Report, Seventh Assembly, Canberra, Australia, 7–20, February 1991.*

13. Ibid.

translate into Western forms. Tell a Pentecostal that icons are images of the holy and he will turn away in disgust. But talk to him of the synergy of God and man and tell him that icons are paintings inspired by the Holy Spirit and he will prick up his ears. Or try telling a radical feminist, without due care and attention, that the Orthodox Church will not reconstruct Father, Son, and Holy Ghost into a functional triunity of Creator, Redeemer, and Sustainer, and she may lose interest or take offense. But make the effort to explain to her that there is no gender in the Holy Trinity and that the Father is not male (nor the Spirit female) and she will listen with respect. Sarah Coakley of Harvard University, an Anglican, will even argue that it is the Holy Trinity, properly understood, that is the best antidote to patriarchy— in the oppressive sense in which feminists use the term.[14]

These examples remind us of the most neglected dimension to being prophetic: it is not enough to know the mind of God; one also has to speak it in the language and cultural contexts in which we find ourselves. This should also remind us that prophecy is not the obverse of *ascesis*: that is, just as the charism of discernment operates through the spiritual fruit of sobriety, so too does prophecy speak from the familiarity of ascetic attention to the mind of God, on the one hand, and the culture in which we live, on the other. Prophecy, in short, is hard work, both in listening to and speaking from the mind of God.

SELF-CRITICAL ORTHODOXY

But now, if I may, I want to be less self-congratulatory about what Orthodoxy may be able to do for the West. This is because I think Orthodox Christians face what we might call in colloquial language an "attitude problem" in their dealings with those outside their community. To be prophetic is to speak the truth from the mind of God to the church and the world, but Paul reminds us that we should speak the truth in love (Eph 4:15). Love can be stern or severe as well as gentle, but it is never a big stick with which to beat other people, who see things differently from us, over the head.

It is not necessary, and it is sometimes inaccurate, in talking about the West, always to insist on using the language of heterodoxy or heresy to describe its religious beliefs and practices. To believe that there has been no richness of Christian Tradition outside Eastern Orthodoxy since the Great Schism is either ignorance or myopia—as if Calvin never once rang true, or as if Charles Wesley never wrote magnificent Trinitarian hymns! What allies of the Orthodox would find if they scoured the West is fellow travelers,

14. Cf. Coakley, "Creaturehood before God."

whether it be Edward Irving on the Holy Spirit, Ives Congar on the church, or Jürgen Moltmann on creation.[15]

The question I am raising here is not to doubt the richness of Orthodox heritage (for to do so would be to abandon the church), but to ask whether the Orthodox are willing in their critical judgment of Western traditions also to look at themselves a little more closely.

I am not talking about importing Enlightenment rationalism into Christian Tradition, with its concomitant cynicism and superior intellectual airs, nor am I suggesting a diminution of respect for the patristic tradition. I am talking about ensuring that the Orthodox Church speaks with a prophetic voice.

This needs nothing less than spiritual discernment: remembering to distinguish Tradition from customs; noting the gradations between dogmas, theological opinions, and pious opinions; knowing when either *eirenic* or "polemical" theology is called for; having the discipline not to quote canon law or the fathers as indiscriminately as fundamentalists quote texts of Holy Scripture; not falling into the trap of liturgical legalism while (quite properly) distancing Orthodox Tradition from moral legalism.

It may be true, as my friend said, that Orthodoxy has preserved the form of the church in its canons and in its theology, but in practice Orthodox Christians have often failed normatively to *be* the church. That is to say, the outward form of religion has been sustained in terms of rites and practices, but sometimes there has been very little inner reality of knowing the mind of God. Let me show you, if I may, what led to this critical train of thought, this self-examination. It begins in the passage from Luke that I quoted earlier when Jesus said: "The Spirit of the Lord is upon me because he has anointed me to preach the gospel to the poor . . . ."

We later read in Luke 4:24 that Jesus makes it quite clear that prophets usually have no honor in their own country. It is John Chrysostom who points out, in his homily on this passage, that Jesus is talking about his own brethren here. That is to say, it is we ourselves who often fail to hear the prophetic voice, and not other people. A similar point was made some years ago by the late Father Lev Gillet in a sermon in the Russian Cathedral in London. He was speaking on the passage in the Gospel where Jesus, struck by the fact that as a prophet he had no honor in his own country, among his own kin, or in his own house, could only marvel at the unbelief of his brethren (Mark 6:1–6). Father Lev wondered why it was that the Orthodox

---

15. Cf. Moltmann, *God in Creation*; Congar, *I Believe in the Holy Spirit*; Irving, *The Day of Pentecost, or the Baptism with the Holy Ghost.*

of today, who know so much and have had so much given them—were so steeped in unbelief and sin.[16]

Self-important and self-serving prophecy is prophecy without cost, without pain, without repentance. For to point the finger outside—at the West, at the heterodox—prevents us from having to look inside ourselves. When we do that, when we berate others for their shortcomings and neglect our own, we cease to be prophetic altogether and become stiff-necked Pharisees unable to bend our heads in supplication and prayer, and hence unable to know the mind and will of God. It was not for nothing that the church fathers rightly saw that the repentant publican was the true model of Orthodox spirituality.

There is not spirituality in Orthodoxy without repentance. It is repentance that gives to spirituality its route to the mind and will of God, not some vague cultural essence that we have somehow picked up and kept going over the years. Spirituality is something that we have to rediscover in every generation in order that we remain prophets in fact and not merely in principle; that we are renewers of Tradition, and renewed by it, and not merely rehearsers of it.

I would like to give if I can some concrete example of this. I do not wish to speak out of turn, but I think it is important that we understand that prophecy is bound to be uncomfortable for us if we are outside the will of God. The Orthodox Church has to weigh the wisdom of casting stones at other confessions when it has the horror of the Balkans in its midst.

A journalist once rang me and asked, "As Orthodox, are you embarrassed at what is happening in Bosnia?" I remember what struck me most about his question was this: what a terrible word to use—"embarrassed." The word that comes to mind when we think of the Lutheran Church and the Third Reich is "ashamed." Bosnia is not a question of embarrassment. It is a question of having to admit that sometimes even in the heartlands of Orthodoxy, as well as the hinterlands, sin abounds. There is no other word for it. We cannot dress it up.

Orthodox scholars and apologists might properly object that the Bosnian Serbs are not in fact from the traditional heartlands of those successfully socialized into the Orthodox faith. This is a matter of historical fact. If Catholic Croatia was deeply influenced by fascism in between the two World Wars, Orthodox Serbs in Bosnia were subject to a surfeit of secularization under Marxist Socialism during and immediately after the Second World War. We could also properly object that the mass media are not objective in

16. See in particular the fine bibliography by Elizabeth Behr-Sigel, *Lev Gillet: A Monk of the Eastern Church.*

their reporting of the Bosnian War. Serbs, too, have been on the receiving end of "ethnic cleansing," and they suffered as a people in the Second World War in the tens of thousands at the hands of Croatian fascists. Many of us know this, and it does help us to understand the present situation a little better, but it still does not make the Serbian conduct acceptable.

Of course, the Church is not institutionally responsible for atrocities, which have been rightly and courageously condemned by some of the hierarchs. But the fact remains that ordinary men from Orthodox churches have been involved in crimes against humanity. Sometimes the genuine light of Christian community throws shadows of ethnic exclusivity and tribal allegiance which can overcome that light, unless it burns brightly in the hearts and minds of ordinary men and women.

Russia provides us with perhaps a more pressing scenario for self-examination. When Russia was in the grip of Soviet rule, many Orthodox around the world were not slow to criticize the Church there at that time. But now, as Communism loosens its grip, will we also feel able to stand up to the present dangers: for there is a threat of a Slavophile neo-fascism within the Church itself, with its concomitant hatred of Jews and Freemasons. There is a national fanaticism hatching in some seminaries and parishes and a hatred of all things Western.

This danger is all the greater because much of what has been imported to Russia from the West is indeed evil: consumer hedonism, pornography, greed, and pragmatic triumphalism. All the more reason that the Church should remain true to herself! When, however, a leading hierarch of the Russian Church can encourage the publication of a right-wing daily newspaper of a virulent kind, saturate church bookstalls with thousands of unacceptable pamphlets and watch while that old forgery much loved by the Nazis—*The Protocols of the Learned Elders of Zion*—rears its head again, it is time for the Church to speak out with clarion certainty.

Here the prophetic voice is unambiguous. There is Orthodoxy, the Church, and there is a counterfeit religion looking much the same. It has identical symbols and liturgical practices to the true Orthodox Church, but its spirit is not the Spirit of adoption whereby we cry "Abba Father" in repentance and reconciliation, but the spirit of discord. This is not to attack the Church, but it is to recognize that within the *ecclesia,* within the fold of God, we can and do find wolves in sheep's clothing.

Orthodox problems in the diaspora are mundane compared to those in Eastern Europe, but they are nonetheless serious for all that. Cardinal Suenens once told me that Catholics in Belgium and France could no longer survive in the Western world without true Christian commitment, because there was no longer a benign Christian culture to encourage their faith.

Nominal Christianity is a particular temptation for Orthodox living in Europe or North America, cut off from their Orthodox homelands, with their tacit cultural support for the Church.[17]

How many Orthodox people, for example, have become like those Anglicans who put down "Church of England" on the form when they are admitted into hospital, but who rarely attend a church? Does "Orthodox" mean any more than "I belong to a particular denomination"? In Great Britain, perhaps our missionary work needs to begin with our own people. For many thousands of Cypriots who have been secularized by the forces of modernity, or who have married outside the Church, Orthodoxy has been diluted almost to the point of sterility. Even traditional rites of passage are becoming a thing of the past.

The purpose of such severe remarks is this: for Orthodoxy to be prophetic, it constantly has to remind itself that this is impossible without knowing the mind and will of God. To know and speak the mind and will of God is beyond human reasoning unless we are grafted by the Holy Spirit into the living Christ and his church. In order to ensure that the graft is not rejected, we have to be daily renewed through repentance in the very life of the risen Christ.

Orthodoxy does not mean "right belief" if by that we mean no more than antiquarian exactitude, learning dogmas by rote, or talking and preening ourselves like a parrot. Orthodoxy is better understood as *true worship*, which is the overflowing of God's personal love into the church. This overflowing is like abundant wine brimming in the cup from which we must drink deeply if we want new life, and drinking is both a physical act of opening our mouths and a spiritual act of surrender, of opening our hearts.

Let me end in this way. By the grace of God, the Orthodox Church came to the West. I believe it really is the true church, spotless and holy in the mystery of its sanctuary, but also teeming in its empirical life with Judases and Pharisees as well as publicans and sinners. Orthodox prophecy is the voice of the mind of God to the world, but also to the Church. That same voice warns us that when Jesus says, "I am the vine and you are the branches," it is quite clear that branches can wither and die if they are not grafted firmly onto the vine. There is no life in a dead branch, no Spirit-bearing sap; the prophetic voice is silenced.

17. Cf. Walker, "Interview with Cardinal Leon-Joseph Suenens," 73–80.

13

INTERVIEW WITH METROPOLITAN ANTHONY OF SOUROZH

(1988)

Andrew Walker: Metropolitan Anthony, you have been in England now since 1948 when you first came here as the Chaplain to the Fellowship of Saint Albans and Saint Sergius. That means that for forty years you have been in Britain and have obviously seen an extraordinary number of changes in Christianity since you have been here. On the whole, do you feel that these changes have been for the better or for the worse?

Metropolitan Anthony: My general impression is that these changes are for the worse. On the one hand, society at large has become a great deal more secular. Not that it has acquired a secular ideology (yet), but it could be defined a little in the way in which Paul defined people by saying, "Their god is their belly." It is not a new theology, but it is simply a lack of ideal, lack of ideology, or lack of faith.

But what I feel is much worse is that the church, in order to try to keep within its boundaries as many people as possible—whether they are believers or half-believers or no believers at all—has watered down the message to the point of no longer expressing the message of the gospel. And this, I feel, is a betrayal of Christ and a betrayal of the gospel, and also a failure to fulfill our mission, because it is not by a watered down Christianity that one can save the world, but rather it is by presenting all the message of Christ in all its majestic and awesome greatness, and also in its extraordinary *human* quality.

Walker: I know that C. S. Lewis would often use the expression "Christianity and water" as a means of saying that, for many years now, Christianity has been presented in a form that modern Christians seem to think secular people need. There is this idea, isn't there, that we need to "make the gospel relevant." Of course, Lewis' argument is that in trying to make it relevant we water it down. What sorts of examples of "watered-down" Christianity do have you in mind?

Anthony: One could give many examples. What strikes me most, because it is a more accessible example, is the attitude of so many theologians and preachers to the person of Christ. Problems of Trinitarian theology are far from remote from people's concrete perceptions, but the question about Christ is absolutely crucial. Is Christ "God become man"—true God and true man—or is he a remarkable man who in an allegorical sense was the Son of God more than anyone else is a son of God?

This question leads us a long way. On the one hand, if Christ is *not* the Son of God become the Son of Man, all the gospel falls, and the door is open to identifying the Christian message with all religious messages of the world—Christ becomes one of the many preachers or wise men. While on the other hand, the crux of Christianity is our proclamation, our passionate conviction, that in Christ the fullness of the Godhead has abided in the flesh; that it is a historical event; that God has entered the world and is now in the world; that in a way, one may say, the end has already come with the incarnation, and we are expecting the end as a glorious advent of Christ at the end of time. However, the end is not to be understood as a point in time, but as a fulfillment, and it is already there for us to see. In Jesus we have got before us the only real true man, because to be real and true as a human being means to be at one with God; short of this we are sub-human.

Walker: Do you feel, then, that many of the modern gospels—the watered down gospels—simply do not have a gospel for modern man?

Anthony: No. I don't think they do have a gospel for modern man, because gospel means "good news." And what is the good news that one can find in a watered-down Christianity?

When I discovered the gospel as a teenager what struck me was that it is a message about God being so close, so deeply concerned with *us*, and also—simultaneously and inevitably—that man is so great. I am reminded of the phrase of Angelus Silesius, who says that "I am as great as God. God is as small as I"—and this is the vision of *man* as well as being a vision of God. And I feel that unless we have got an ideal that is vast enough, great enough, challenging enough, there is no point in having Christianity as one possible world outlook.

Walker: But, of course, what happens so often today is that you hear this sort of critique: "Well, this is all very interesting, but it is extremely primitive. It is the sort of thing you could have talked about before the philosophical Enlightenment, but now that we live in a 'scientific' age, when we know miracles don't occur, how can we possibly talk in this outdated, metaphysical language?" When you hear those sorts of things, which I hear all the time, what sort of replies do you give?

Anthony: I don't know anything about metaphysical language. What we say about Christ is experiential. We could say in the same terms as Paul said that we know the risen Christ. I know that God exists because I have *met* him. It is not a fairy tale or something I have inherited—or we have inherited— from our grandmothers; it is a personal experience about *knowing* him. And so it is as certain to those of us who believe, as so many other things which are not rational but which are both reasonable and real. We do not speak of beauty or love in other terms than we speak of God. It, too, is a direct experience. It *cannot* be proved; it is known only from within.

Walker: Is there perhaps, as some people may say, a danger that if we over- stress the experiential side of our faith, which is so important to us person- ally, we may make our experience the test of the authority of Scripture?

Anthony: Of course there is a danger. The two must coincide. The test of our experience is in the Scriptures, not the other way around. But if the Scrip- tures remain an ancient document that we examine (as one can examine old parchments and try to date them) without any way of relating to the event described, it remains a dead letter. While in the early Christian age, what is striking is that a message reached people indeed. Believing comes from hearing . . . but at the same time this hearing opened up the mind and the heart to an understanding.

I think that what is essential in the hearing—in the gospel, in the mes- sage of the apostles, in the message of the saints—is that it speaks truth that reaches us, and to which we can respond by saying, "Yes, that *is* the truth; that *is* beauty; that *is* something which has disclosed to me a depth which I vaguely perceived within me, but which I could not comprehend; and there it is—opening up, light shining, something blossoming out—a victory of life and truth within me, which convinces me of the gospel.

There is a passage in one of the ascetics of the early years of the church that says, "If God himself stood before you and said to you to do this or that, yet if your heart could not say, "Amen" to it, don't do it, because God does not need your doing, but the harmony that can be established between you and him." I am not quoting exactly, but that is the thought. And the message of the gospel, if it doesn't awake in us a sense of being the truth, is vain.

Walker: All right, let's move on to something else. If it is the case, as you have put it, that we are not really hearing the gospel today, but we are listening to watered down gospels—gospels that are not really a gospel for the modern man—what do you think is the way forward, given the fact that, of course, God has ways that we know not of? What do you think Christians should be doing in the face of these watered down gospels?

Anthony: I believe there are two things. The one is to go back to the gospel as it stands, and proclaim the gospel that was lived and manifested by Christ, seen and proclaimed by the apostles, and then by their disciples.

But there is also another side to it. The apostle Paul already said that "the name of Christ is reviled because of us," and when we look at the history of Christianity we can say that the Christian world has proclaimed and spoken the gospel, at times with great eloquence and truth, but that at large the Christian world has not *lived* the gospel, and certainly not built a world that is worthy of the faith which we proclaim. And when we think that we are coming ever nearer to the two thousandth anniversary of Christianity, we can say that we have betrayed the gospel by the kind of world we have built in *all* its parts.

Walker: It is certainly true, I believe, that we have perhaps stressed "orthodoxia," and not "orthopraxia," to such an extent that people are not very impressed these days by our beliefs unless they can see something in our lives. In this respect, do you think it is perhaps the case that a great deal more emphasis needs to be given in the Christian life to holiness and prayer?

Anthony: I am quite certain of that. I remember a saying, an old saying, of Christianity to the effect that no one can turn away from the secular world towards eternity if he has not seen in the eyes or in the face of at least one person the shining of eternal life. Also, I remember that in a broadcast made during the war C. S. Lewis said that when people see a believer, what they *should* say is, "Look, statues are coming to life!" Well, we *are* statues—and not always the most beautiful ones—and yet people meeting us cannot say that here are beings of another world, possessed of another dimension than anyone else, which is a significant thing.

I am not talking of trying to build a city of men that is more palatable or less monstrous than the one we have already built. The city of men which we are called to build should be coextensive to a city of God in which the first citizen should be Jesus of Nazareth, both God and man, vast enough to contain the whole divine mystery. And this is what we are not doing.

Walker: Do you think that there has been too much emphasis on church unity on the basis of togetherness, and not enough on the emphasis on repentance? I say this because we hear a great deal about ecumenism in terms of trying to arrive at common statements of agreement, but do you think that what is needed more in a divided Christendom is for people to repent?

Anthony: I think that if you take the word "repentance" in the way in which most people understand it, as bewailing one's past, instead of doing anything about one's present and future, it is not the kind of thing we need. But if by repentance you mean turning away from the twilight toward the light, turning Godwards and *moving* Godwards, then indeed we need repentance in that sense. And this can be done, as you said before, in terms of prayer, in terms of a deeper spiritual life, because it will direct us Godwards and it will be born of our communion with God

To attempt unity on terms that are *less* than the gospel is a betrayal of Christ. There is nothing else to be said from my point of view about it, because it is totally indifferent whether the Christians of the world are at one or not if they are not truly Christian. And there is no other way of being a Christian than to be Christian according to the gospel in the image of Christ—singly and, in the image of the total Christ, collectively.

Walker: A few years ago, at an ecumenical gathering I attended, a senior churchman said that he didn't know that we could even say what it means to be a Christian. You have talked a great deal about the gospel, the primitive gospel. What does it mean, according to the primitive gospel, to be a Christian?

Anthony: Ultimately, to be Christian means to be such a person that anyone meeting us should have met Christ himself. This is a very radical claim. Of course, we are not full light, but twilight. People meeting us should say, "I have seen the light." That *is* being a Christian.

Walker: I wonder if I could ask one question to add to that: I suppose people might say, "Well, if that's what being a Christian is, how do I become one?"

Anthony: You don't try to become one. One does not try to become a saint; one doesn't try to become a ray of light. One simply tries, from the twilight in which we are, to enter into God's light in adoration, in worship, in prayer, in obedience. And it just happens. Because anyone who would set his mind towards becoming a saint would end in nothing but pride and silliness! Humility is part of it, and humility means being capable of listening to God and doing and being what God expects us to be, without asking more. What happens next is God's!

Walker: Thank you very much, Metropolitan Anthony.

14

HOMILETICS AND
BIBLICAL FIDELITY
An Ecclesial Approach to Orthodox Preaching[1]
(2014)

I
t is difficult to know how best to characterize Orthodox preaching: to
call it public discourse is to tell us nothing of its content, and to add the
prefix "theological" suggests some kind of specialized academic treatment, which is neither helpful nor accurate and misses the essential biblical nature of Orthodox preaching. As the New Testament was written in
everyday Greek perhaps it would be helpful to look at some of the common
usages that emerged in the mainly Greek-speaking Eastern Church.

The word "preach" does not exist in Greek, but there are several terms
that we can translate into English as preaching. Preaching can be the announcement of good news, "good tidings of great joy" (Luke 2:10 NKJV),
though we usually think of announcing good news as the gospel (*euangelion*). The most common Greek term translated in English as preaching in
the New Testament is *kerusso* (used sixty-one times); this word is associated with *kerygma* because the kerygma centres on the message of salvation
(though it only appears in the Greek text nine times). *Kerusso* is stronger
than announce and even more so than *diangello* (widely announce) and
katangello (publicly announce). *Kerusso* is stronger because it is a proclamation, or the sort of important message associated with a herald. It has

---

1. I shall use transliterations throughout this text.

a town crier, "Hear ye, Hear ye," feel about it. Another example would be a Royal proclamation of pardon; perhaps even something more intimate, like the annunciation to Mary by the Angel Gabriel[2] that, although she is a virgin, she will become the bearer of God (*theotokos*). In the words of Saint Athanasius of Alexandria:

> Today is the beginning of our salvation
>> And the revelation of the eternal mystery!
>> The Son of God becomes the Son of the Virgin
>> As Gabriel announces the coming of Grace.
> Together with him let us cry to the Theotokos:
> Rejoice, O Full of Grace, the Lord is with you'!

There are two more NT Greek words that I want to include in this chapter (though there are others) to highlight an Orthodox understanding of preaching; they are *dialegomai*, which means discuss or converse, and *didache,* which means teaching (pedagogy) Although, like Catholics and Protestants, Orthodox have a history of missions and evangelization, there is not usually a special mode or style that characterizes preaching for such special tasks; modern theological writers like Alexander Schmemann have stressed that missiology needs to be rooted in ecclesiology,[3] and my aim in this chapter, with deep indebtedness to Schmemann, is to look at preaching "in the round" as an expression of the life and teachings of the Orthodox Church.

Therefore, a perennial temptation for all Orthodox is to confuse the empirical church with the eschatological church, to idealize it, and then to historicize it. This amounts to hagiography more often than not—as if every word of the desert fathers were worth re-iterating; or we conveniently forget that the downside to having your village priest as one of your own class (nineteenth-century Russian rural priests, for example, were usually from the peasantry) is that they were often ignorant of their own tradition and illiterate. The approach I am going to take is not to rubbish this idealization, for this chapter is neither historiography nor an exercise in chest-beating or confession of empirical in-exactitude (though we could do with a more balanced appraisal of our past). What I plan to do is to identify the key components of Orthodox preaching by taking an historical approach I believe identifies what is best about the practice.

Having said that there is in fact no identifiable unique way of preaching in the Orthodox Church,[4] I do think there are three historical factors that

---

2. Angels are usually heralds from God in the New Testament.

3. Schmemann, *Church, World, Mission.*

4. There are, however, different ways of looking at things. John 20, for example,

have shaped its development. The first is that Orthodoxy sees itself as a biblical church, or to be more precise, an *apostolic* one. In order to explain this
I will endeavor to show that to drive a wedge between Bible and Tradition
is alien to Orthodox sensibilities. The second historical factor is to highlight
that the ancient Sees of Alexandria and Antioch developed distinct styles
of hermeneutics that polarized the ancient church to a limited degree, although eventually both methods became absorbed in the Orthodox Tradition. Alexandria with its strong Platonic and Stoic influences on both Jewish
and Gentile populations favored allegorical approaches to the Bible (as did
the Alexandrian Jewish philosopher Philo [20 BC–30 AD], who adopted
the method from the church). In simple terms the Bible was read on three
levels—the literal meaning, the moral meaning, and the spiritual meaning.
Origen stressed both the need for divine guidance and intellectual rigor.

By contrast Antiochean hermeneutics did not go beyond the literal
meaning of the text and paid great attention to historical context. Antiochean Christians thought allegorical interpretations were fanciful and rejected any notion of hidden meanings in the text. Conversely, Alexandrian
Christians thought Antiochean hermeneutics were pedestrian and lacked
spiritual insight.[5] I am going to concentrate on the ministry of Saint John
Chrysostom, an Antiochean,[6] as my third key historical factor in the devel-

---

is most famous in the Western churches for the story of "Doubting Thomas," but in
the Orthodox Church he is hailed as a hero of the faith, a Confessor, for he is the only
person in the New Testament to call Jesus God, *ho kyrios mou kai ho theos mou,* literally
translated as "the Lord and the God of me."

5. These hermeneutical differences have been influential on the Christian church
from the patristic era to the present day (though like the Orthodox, Roman Catholics,
and Protestants have freely borrowed from both schools). C. S. Lewis, I would say, was
more Alexandrian in his interpretation of the Bible than a follower of the Antiochean
school (see the chapter in this book, "Scripture, Revelation, and Platonism"), and I
would say the preacher who exhibited the purest example of Antiochean hermeneutics
I ever heard was Dr. Martin Lloyd Jones of Westminster Chapel. His expository style
is seen at its best in six published expositions of the epistle to the Romans by Banner
of Truth.

6. I am aware that Chrysostom is deeply offensive to many Jews and Christians alike
and rather than excuse his anti-Semitism by pointing to his Arab parenting and culture
I prefer to take the view that even saints are sinners under grace; they are advanced
spiritually in many areas of their lives, but they are also retarded in others. Chrysostom
uses a particular rhetorical form known as *psogos* when he attacks Judaism and Jews.
This rhetorical style is designed to attach blame to a person or group and also pour op-
probrium on them. The quote that follows demonstrates why Chrysostom attracted so
much criticism: "Are you Jews still disputing the question? Do you not see that you are
condemned by the testimony of what Christ and the prophets predicted and which the
facts have proved? But why should this surprise me? That is the kind of people you are.
From the beginning you have been shameless and obstinate, ready to fight at all times
against obvious facts." *Adversus Judaeos,* Homily V, XII.

opment of Orthodox homiletics because he was a rhetorician, a charismatic preacher without peer in the early church, and the originator of the most widely used Eucharistic liturgy in Orthodox worship. My belief is that it is this liturgy—which bears his name—that is the repository and vehicle of Orthodox preaching.[7]

Preaching, therefore, is essentially ecclesial and expository rather than rhetorical or rhapsodic. Ironically, Chrysostom's preaching style is replete with historical flourishes, but his approach has been so influential that we will give him pride of place in this chapter. Typically, Chrysostom favored the sort of homily that BBC Radio 4 used to call "Lift up your hearts" before they gave us the anodyne "Thought for the Day." There is no better way in showing what he brings to the Orthodox table than to end this chapter with his Easter homily, used universally in the Orthodox Church today (and placed at the end of this chapter, by way of reference). When it is read everybody stands. This demonstrates his extraordinary influence on the Orthodox Church, as it is an honor usually restricted to the reading of the Gospel.

SCRIPTURE AND TRADITION

Before we pay due homage to the role of Chrysostom in the development of preaching in the Orthodox Church, it will be helpful to say something about how the Eastern half of Christendom believe that the Bible and Tradition cohere rather than live in dialectical tension, as seems to be the case in many Western churches.[8] I wrote at some length about this several years ago,[9] but there are a number of points I wish to reprise here. Perhaps the most important is to recognize that Orthodox believers think of themselves as people of "the Book." Preaching, therefore, is essentially *biblical* and fidelity to the gospel is its hallmark. In order to understand this primordial fact it would be helpful if Protestants did not read the history of biblical canonicity through the eyes of the Reformation and Counter Reformation. Events such as Luther's nailing his Ninety-Five Theses to the Wittenburg door in 1517 and the Council of Trent (AD 1545–63) are historically contingent on the fact that the West had already divided from the Eastern Churches in the Great Schism of the eleventh century. Strictly speaking, the early church was

---

7. I will not go into details here, but preaching in Orthodox churches is not only a function of the word; architecture and icons also tell the story. See Trubetskoi, *Icons: Church in Color.*

8. Though things are improving, see Williams, *Evangelicals and Tradition.*

9. Walker, "Deep Church as *Paradosis:* Relating Scripture to Tradition," 59–80.

not Roman Catholic or Orthodox, and Protestants did not exist (though heretics were legion). There was the *one undivided church.*

There were, of course, local customs, which we could think of as traditions if we wish, but to assume that these customs had anything in common with the theology of papal infallibility, indulgences, "works righteousness," etc., against which the Reformation doctrines of *sola fidei* and *sola scriptura* were opposed is to miss the mark. When the Orthodox use the word Tradition spelled with a capital T (and sometimes there is a prefix attached such as "Holy" or "Sacred") they mean the apostolic deposit of faith of the New Testament, as handed down from generation to generation and accumulating dogmatic and universal canonical form along the way (Scripture, creeds, conciliar councils, for example) and the authoritative, but not binding, sayings and writings of saints and savants of the church.

From at least the time of Irenaeus (c. AD 130–200) the issue of doctrinal authority in the church was never exclusively thought to be confined to written biblical texts. This was a pragmatic decision based on commonsense, not an ideological platform to launch polemical assaults on enemies of the church. In what was essentially an oral culture, Christian faith was handed on by word of mouth and religious practices sanctioned by time as well as texts enshrined in canonical certainty. Basil of Caesarea writing in approximately AD 380 said,

> Of the beliefs and practices preserved in the church . . . we have some derived from written teaching; others delivered to us "in a mystery" from the tradition of the Apostles; and both classes have the same force for true piety. No one will dispute these; no one, at any rate, who has the slightest experience of the institutions of the church . . . .[10]

Culturally, we need to remind ourselves, the early church belongs in Antiquity where in contradistinction to modernity it was *de rigueur* to look to the past for legitimating new arguments.

The honor given to ancient authorities was both appealing to the early church and compelling. It was appealing because until late in the second century there were still people alive who could remember people who "knew the Lord." Irenaeus was himself one such person; he was a disciple of the martyr Polycarp, who in turn was a disciple of the apostle John, "the disciple whom Jesus loved" (John 21:20, NRV). But honoring the past was compelling, for the great problem heretics had to overcome in order to overturn orthodoxy in the early church—however philosophically sophisticated their arguments were—was that of demonstrating that the apostles

---

10. Quoted in Bettenson, *Later Christian Fathers,* 59.

and their acknowledged successors also favored the same arguments, and this they could not do. So, for example, Marcion (expelled from the church in AD 144) failed in his project to exclude the Old Testament from Christianity because he could find no apostolic witness to support him; there was also the embarrassing fact that Jesus quoted copiously from the Torah.

In the modern era, the German Protestant theologian Adolf Harnack did much to promulgate the idea that the Orthodox Church was a Hellenistic hijacking of the primitive Jewish church.[11] It is certainly the case that the "way of negation," which is often thought to mirror Greek mysticism (*apophasis*, to give it its patristic form), lends itself to a contemplative spirituality in which silence is valued more than words. Such mysticism, however, is not a function of the *apophatic* logic of the Greek Athenaeum. As Jaraslov Pelikan has shown, such logic was a feature of Greek language itself,[12] and in classical culture trying to know who God is by telling us who and what he is not was thought to be a superior way of coming to know God while admitting there was an unknowingness in this method (*agnosia*), and that meant that all positive statements about God (the *cataphatic*) were provisional and subject to re-formulation. If the strong *apophatic* side to Orthodox Tradition—which affords it some modesty and leaves room for wonder and surprise—is put into abeyance, the Orthodox are capable of slipping into self-righteous fundamentalism and becoming unbearably smug.

It has been necessary to demonstrate Orthodox commitment to the Bible and creed as an antidote to the erroneous view that Orthodoxy is some sort of traditionalism in which biblical faith is fragile and tangential. When the Bible is carried into the nave of the church, it is carried aloft in such a way that it would warm the heart of a Scottish Presbyterian. Before the Gospel is read by the priest, the deacon intones "Wisdom: let us attend" and during the reading of the passage it is the only time you can be certain that all chattering will cease, for the faithful know that in a very special way God is speaking to them directly.[13]

But as I said at the beginning of this section, the Orthodox do not believe that true faith comes in unwrapped biblical form; there is a great deal of Tradition that comes from being a member of the body of Christ living in the commonwealth of the ecclesia and learning from received religious practices handed down. Jesus, of course, left no written gospel of his own. (The only writing attributed to him in the New Testament was writing with

---

11. Nowak, *Adolf Von Harnack.*

12. Pelikan, *Christianity and Classical Culture,* chap. 3.

13. During Holy Week at the end of Great Lent all four Gospels are read consecutively in one sitting—or more appropriately one standing.

his finger on the ground in the temple when the Pharisees brought to him a woman "caught in adultery" [John 8:6].)[14] And while we clearly have written accounts of his life and those of his disciples, they are by no means exhaustive. The final verse in John's Gospel reads, "But there are also many other things that Jesus did; if every one of them were written down, I suppose that the world itself could not contain the books that would be written" (John 21:25).

It is time to draw this preliminary discussion of Scripture and Tradition to a close. William Abraham—Professor of Wesleyan Studies at Southern Methodist University, Texas, and author of *Canon and Criterion in Christian Theology*—reminded an audience at a recent conference at King's College London that the Bible is the book of the church, and that the church is not a product of the Bible. This really is the bullet Protestants have to bite on if they are going to be loyal to the apostolic tradition and follow the main road as Lewis called it.[15] It took several centuries before a canon of Scripture was established,[16] but it is not really possible in the patristic era to isolate Scripture from canons of creeds, liturgical norms, and the writings of

---

14. John's Gospel neither tells us what language he wrote in or what he wrote—it might have been a doodle in his native Aramaic for all we know.

15. Cf. Lewis' "Preface" in *The Pilgrim's Regress*.

16. This is because there were several disputed books of apostolic origin (*antilegomena*). Jude, for example, was suspect because he quotes from the pseudepigrapha; and 2 Peter is suspect because it appears so late in the tradition; church authorities were not certain whether it was written by the apostle Peter or not. There were others, but by far the most contentious was John's Revelation. Indeed, although the Roman Catholic Church seemed happy with it from the Council of Ephesus (AD 431), probably because it was on Athanasius' (the hero of Nicaea) list of New Testament books, the Orthodox Church kept it at arms-length. In the fourth century John Chrysostom argued fiercely against its inclusion (mainly on grounds of contentious interpretations), and the Syrian Church did not include it until the fifth century. Remarkably, it was not accepted as canonical by Constantinople until the ninth century. Possibly because an ecumenical council never ratified Revelation, it is the only canonical book of the New Testament never to be read in the Orthodox services and is absent from the lectionary. Protestants also have their own *antilegomena* which calls into serious question the reliance on *sola scriptura*. To be fair, Calvin never denied the authenticity of John's Apocalypse (though it was the only book of the Bible for which he never wrote a commentary). Luther, on the other hand, initially excluded it, as he did Hebrews, James, and Jude. When he published his version of the New Testament in 1522, he placed them at the end of the main text with a preface, which declared mischievously that these books were not as authentic as the rest of Scripture, as they were disputed in the early church. A more plausible explanation is that Luther could find nothing of worth in them concerning his primary conviction of "justification by faith." The suspicion that Luther operated "a canon within the canon"—as if he were the sole arbiter of truth—is supported by his famous comment on James that it was an "epistle of straw," and on his unwarranted translation of Romans 1:17 as "justification by faith *alone*."

the fathers (though this is not to say that there is no hierarchy in canonical criteria). The late Father Lev Gillette, who always signed his writings as "a monk of the Eastern Church," put Scripture first, followed by the definitions of the Ecumenical Councils, next are the liturgical texts, and bringing up the rear the writings of the fathers.[17]

JOHN CHRYSOSTOM: FROM PAGAN RHETORICIAN TO CHRISTIAN PREACHER

Unless you are a person who has been influenced by the cult book *Zen and the Art of Motor Cycle Maintenance*,[18] there is a strong chance that you have never come under the spell of rhetoric and certainly not as it was conjured-up by Greek Antiquity. And yet, while rhetoric has a checkered career in Greek philosophy,[19] it was one of the most prestigious courses to study at the Athenaeum during the classical period of Greek philosophy. But rhetoric lost its glitter in Greece by the beginning of the Common Era. (It was more popular with the *polis* anyway than the philosophers partly because it had an egalitarian appeal to the baker and barber, etc.—for all citizens could become rhetoricians—and its role in early forms of democracy in Athens was significant.)

Rhetoric, however, had a second coming, not in Greece, but in Rome[20] and pagan cultures outside the Greek mainland. And it played a major role in Christianity, both in the West under Augustine[21] and in the East with Origen and Chrysostom. It was in Egyptian Alexandria where the most brilliant theologian of the first two centuries, Origen, put rhetoric firmly on the Christian map. But even then, with its association with pagan thought, dissimulation and potential for evil, it was considered suspect by many Christians. Consider this extract from an oration of thanks to Origen from one of his greatest disciples:

17. Cf. Behr-Sigel, *Lev Gillet: A Monk of the Eastern Church*

18. Pirsig, *Zen and the Art of Motor Cycle Maintenance*.

19. Not every philosopher was a fan. Plato had no time for it, but Aristotle believed that rhetoric was an art of persuasion and should be studied in its own right. Even Aristotle, however, realized that rhetoric could be used for evil purposes so that in itself rhetoric was neutral; see the very good entry on Aristotle's Rhetoric in the revised *Stanford University Encyclopedia*.

20. Cicero is probably the most influential Roman thinker on rhetoric and makes his mark before the Common Era begins (d. BS 43).

21. His defense of Christian rhetoric is masterly. See Augustine, *De doctrina christiana*.

For a mighty and energetic thing is the discourse of man, and
subtle with its sophisms and quick to find its way in to the ears
and mould the mind and impress us with what it conveys; and
when once it has taken possession of us, it can win us over to
love it as truth though it be false and deceitful, overmastering us
like some enchanter and retaining as its champion the very man
it has persuaded (deluded).[22]

150 years later, however, it was John Chrysostom of Antioch who
emerged in the Orthodox tradition as the pre-eminent Christian orator.
Renowned in his lifetime as the greatest living preacher, some 150 years
after his death he received the accolade of "golden mouthed"—Chrysostom
in Greek—which is more of a fond nickname than a formal title of honor.
In fact, we do not know his family name, only that his father was Greek
and his mother Syrian. There is not space to go into the details of his life
here, but there are aspects of his training and personality that explain why,
like his friend Basil of Caesarea, he is a hierarch of the church.[23] Unlike
Basil, however, he plays no serious role in Conciliar Councils or doctrinal
disputes; indeed, as an original thinker, he cannot hold a candle to any of
the three Cappadocians.[24]

To keep it simple, if we translate these theologians into modern categories we would call the Cappadocians dogmatic theologians and Chrysostom a pastoral/practical theologian. What is fascinating is that he and Basil
become friends before they became committed Christians, and both studied philosophy under the brilliant pagan rhetorician, Libanius, who was in
Antioch. Coincidentally, Antioch was the city in which Chrysostom lived

22. Saint Gregory the Wonderworker, as quoted by the Dean of Saint Vladimir's
Theological Seminary, Father John Behr, on the 1600 anniversary of John Chrysostom's
death. Orthodox Church of America, Parish of John Chrysostom, Home Springs, Mis-
souri, September 29th 2007. Original source, *Origen the Teacher; Being the Address of
Gregory the Wonderworker* (but no direct reference given).

23. Basil, *De Spiritus Sancta, 66.* Quoted in Bateson, *Later Christian Fathers,* 59.
One of the fathers from Cappadocia (which is in present-day Turkey), Saint Basil is
one of only three authorities in the Orthodox Church to be given the title hierarch.
The other two are his friend Gregory of Nazianzus, who we have already seen was also
honored with the title of theologian. The third hierarch is John Chrysostom, who is the
main subject of this section.

24. Personally, I would name four Cappadocians, not three, for the older sister of
Basil of Caesarea and his brother Gregory of Nyssa, Macrina, was both saintly and intellectually their equal. Whereas the brothers' friend, Gregory of Nazianzus, is considered
not only a hierarch of the church, but a theologian (there are only three men with that
title in the Orthodox Church, the other two being Saint John of the Gospel and Saint
Simeon the New Theologian). Macrina has been sidelined into an "influence" or "pious
mentor."

and where he was "home schooled," as the Americans say, by his widowed, young Christian mother. Chrysostom became a monk, but at his mother's request did not enter a monastery for some years. After being ordained "Reader," he became a monk at Mount Silipios under the spiritual direction of Diodore of Tarsus. John never did anything half-heartedly, and after a thorough grounding in church history and doctrine he went into seclusion. His ascetic feats were as legendary as his preaching.[25] He fasted so severely that his health never really recovered, and he slept only occasionally and even then standing up![26] In AD 378 his ill health forced him back to Antioch, where he was ordained deacon in AD 381 and priest in 386. Only priests were allowed to preach in the Syrian Church. From the time of his ordination, to the end of his life in AD 407, John's reputation as the greatest preacher in the Byzantine Empire was unquestioned.[27]

His reputation was already established by AD 387 before he left Antioch. Statues of the Emperor Theodosius were attacked by mobs in the streets of the ancient city when they heard that they had to pay more taxes. When word reached Constantinople that the emperor had been insulted the imperial troops were dispatched with orders to destroy the city. The local bishop and senior clergy were thrown into a panic, but Chrysostom—fearless and displaying his astonishing grasp of Scripture and rhetorical technique—delivered a series of brave, defiant, yet optimistic sermons to mixed crowds of pagans and Christians. The erudition of Chrysostom's *Homilies of the Statues* may have persuaded the emperor to spare Antioch; whether this is true or not, does not fully matter; the news of the local boy's oratory and personal holiness spread rapidly throughout the whole Byzantine Empire.

Chrysostom, in addition to being a trained rhetorician, who could adapt his style to any audience regardless of high rank or lowly status, was also a master of *dialegomai* (conversational or *ad lib* preaching). He could break off from his homily and address his congregation with exhortations or admonitions:[28] "Please, listen to me; you are not paying attention. I am talk-

25. He apparently knew the whole of the Bible by heart.

26. A feat of endurance popularized by the desert father Symeon the Stylite, a Syrian contemporary of Chrysostom.

27. The middle part of his life was spent in Constantinople where he became Archbishop in AD 398. His life as a bishop was steeped in controversy mainly because of his uncompromising attack on the wealthy, but also because he had a difficult relationship with the empress Eudoxia, who was a Christian, but capricious; she seemed to spend an inordinate amount of her time either playing a major hand in banishing John or bringing him back to Constantinople.

28. The English word for sermon is taken from the Latin *sermo,* which literally means talk or conversation.

ing to you about the Holy Scriptures and you are looking at the lamps and the people who are lighting them. It is very frivolous to be more interested in what the lamplighters are doing than in what the preacher is saying. After all I, too, am lighting a lamp, the lamp of God's Word."[29]

To use a modern term usually noted by followers of the Social Gospel in America, John clearly had a bias towards the poor. The rich and powerful constantly plotted against him because he was so overtly against wealth and privilege. He did not pull his punches. He would not absolve the wealthy of their sins unless they gave alms to the poor.

When he became the Archbishop of Constantinople, Chrysostom was the recipient of bad feeling by a number of senior bishops within Eastern Christendom, because unlike Rome, Antioch, Alexandria, and Jerusalem, Constantinople had no traditional ties with the era of the New Testament and the first hundred years of the apostolic fathers. Rather, it derived its status exclusively from being the seat of the Roman Empire since the Barbarian tribes had rent the Rome of the early Caesars from its empire, leaving the city subject to siege and periodic assaults.

John Chrysostom also made bitter enemies, notably with Bishop Theophilos of Alexandria. They were totally opposed over biblical interpretation: Theopholis followed Origen's metaphorical tradition, while Chrysostom believed that the Antiochan approach of letting the text speak for itself was the better way; he personally favored a more demotic delivery and was a pioneer in what we might call the triangulation method of preaching: a sound exegesis of the biblical text, the charisma of the preacher, and the specificity of the congregation/audience. Chrysostom remained formally opposed to the Origenistic method of interpretation until the day he died (though his own extreme and sometimes disingenuous rhetoric strays unbidden into Alexandrian linguistic territory).

John's Christianized pagan rhetoric, however, led to a homiletic standardization several centuries after his death, so that, along with fellow hierarch, Gregory of Nazianzus, their sermons were collected (and printed in later centuries) and used either as a model for preaching or were read out aloud in church. But it is not John's rhetorical influence on homiletics that is his major contribution to preaching; it is his liturgy. By this statement I do not mean to play down John's panegyric skills. His commentaries on Acts and Paul are masterly and not florid or over-embellished. We can tell what the nineteenth-century Caledonian preacher Edward Irving's preaching style is like from his writings, for all his sermons were written out in long hand in high Puritan style: to read Irving is to hear him. The same cannot

---

29. Kerr, "Seeing and Hearing the Gospel," *Preaching in the Early Church*, 19–29.

be said of John because he writes for the church in an exemplary expository manner. There are givens: Acts and the four Gospels are treated like history, and the apostle Paul as a divinely inspired fount of knowledge and wisdom. Therefore, it is with some confidence that we can say that reading John is like reading the Tradition handed down from the apostles.

Since John Williams Bugeon's research on the ancient Greek texts, it is well established that in the Byzantine texts (as Bugeon calls them),[30] a lectionary was in use from at least from the second century AD. The main Christian service of worship, the synaxis, was based on the Synagogue tradition, which included two readings from the Bible (the difference being, unlike in the rabbinical tradition, the Torah would be complemented by readings from the growing corpus of New Testament material). The synaxis in short was Bible readings plus prayers and the Eucharist.

The genius of Chrysostom's liturgy is that it contained not only the early synaxis and complete biblical lectionary (remembering that Revelation was excluded), but also a Christian calendar with feasts and fasts, saints days and themed hymns (the *kontakion*). 70 percent of the liturgy was directly taken from Scripture or paraphrases from the Bible. In addition to oral traditions, other texts known in Greek as *Anagignoskomena* were used; these are not biblical, but are considered venerable (they would be from the Pseudepigrapha, for example,[31] but also from the fathers).

Therefore, sermons in Orthodox churches since the sixteenth century have mainly been exhortations and homilies. There is no place for personal aggrandizement, hobbyhorses, or joy rides. The sermon itself is a moveable feast: it is sometimes available before the Eucharist, or sometimes at the end of the liturgy. Or there may be no sermon at all! I once heard Metropolitan Anthony of Sourozh say to an ecumenical gathering, "A sermon is an important part of the liturgy, but it is not essential, for the liturgy itself is the breath of the Holy Spirit bringing the words (*logoi*) of God to life." To be an inspired preacher (as he was) is a charism, not a result of professional training; gifted teachers like Bishop Kalistos Ware also stand out as preachers/ teachers, but what determines the minimum standard—the lowest common denominator in Orthodox preaching—is fidelity to the biblical text. A priest follows the lectionary not the dictates of his personal predilections.

30. Bugeon, *Byzantine Texts, Revision Revised.*

31. The New Testament is not without direct apocryphal sources, notably the quotation from 1 Enoch in the Epistle of Jude.

CONCLUSION

John Chrysostom's personal ascetic life, his dedication to pastoral theology, and above all his liturgical instincts, has left the Orthodox Church with an extraordinary legacy: in homiletics he is an exemplar *par excellence*, but his liturgy has provided an environment in which from cradle to grave Christians who are initiated into the body of Christ through baptism learn to become committed Christians primarily by attending the Divine Liturgy of Saint John Chrysostom. At Easter, the author of the liturgy we celebrate all year speaks to us directly. We can note something of the rhetorician here, for his homily has certainly been handed down orally. More importantly, we should notice John's generosity:

> If any man be devout and loveth God,
> Let him enjoy this fair and radiant triumphal feast!
> If any man be a wise servant,
> Let him rejoicing enter into the joy of his Lord.
>
> If any have laboured long in fasting,
> Let him how receive his recompense.
> If any have wrought from the first hour,
> Let him today receive his just reward.
> If any have come at the third hour,
> Let him with thankfulness keep the feast.
> If any have arrived at the sixth hour,
> Let him have no misgivings;
> Because he shall in nowise be deprived therefore.
> If any have delayed until the ninth hour,
> Let him draw near, fearing nothing.
> And if any have tarried even until the eleventh hour,
> Let him, also, be not alarmed at his tardiness.
>
> For the Lord, who is jealous of his honour,
> Will accept the last even as the first.
> He giveth rest unto him who cometh at the eleventh hour,
> Even as unto him who hath wrought from the first hour.
> And He showeth mercy upon the last,
> And careth for the first;
>
> And He both accepteth the deeds
> And welcometh the intention . . . .

15

OPEN OR SHUT CASE?

An Orthodox View on Inter-communion

(2003)

This paper was inspired by last year's Saint Andrew's tide Constantinople lecture given by Father Hugh Wybrew. Reflecting on the dogmatic tradition of the Church, Father Hugh argued cogently and passionately that somewhere along the line in early Christian tradition we began to move away from the New Testament understanding of faith as trust in and commitment to the Lord Jesus, towards an ever-increasing emphasis on faith as a complex system of doctrinal truth claims. In time—even perhaps as early as the conciliar creeds—such claims came to be seen as the facts of revelation woven into the rubric of a rule of faith.[1]

The long-term consequence of the paradigmatic shift within Christianity from existential faith *in* Christ to essentialist faith statements *about* him has arguably been a betrayal of the gospel, for churches have become married to their truth claims as if they, rather than the person of Christ, were the *sine qua non* of faith. These claims over the centuries have hardened into rubicons, which today Christians in the fragmented denominations of Christendom find it hard to cross, embedded as they are in their ecclesiastical enclosures and theological fiduciary frameworks. Exclusivists, of course, will make no attempt to break free from such enclosures, either on principle, or from fear of contamination from other confessions (a neurosis

---

1. Cf. Wybrew, *The Orthodox Liturgy*, where he outlines this development and argument.

that the anthropologist Mary Douglas calls the fear of ritual pollution).[2] Inclusivists, on the other hand, may break away, if they are bold, disillusioned, or unprincipled. They are more likely, however, to stay where they are for fear of being anathematized as spiritual pariahs and theological "scabs."

Father Hugh's mature reflection, after the frustrating experience of some twenty-six years of unresolved Anglican/Orthodox dialogue, is that we have become victims of our own propaganda: we are still bound to the long-standing ecumenical shibboleth that doctrinal agreement is the necessary precondition for inter-communion. Father Hugh wonders what God makes of it all. What Father Hugh makes of it is this: it is time for Christians to break out of their enclaves, come together with all their unresolved differences and to share the common cup "til the Lord comes." Father Hugh does not think we should do this because doctrinal agreement is unimportant—he is not advocating that we share the holy gifts with Arians or Unitarians—but because he believes that Christ-like mutual love should prevail (or take priority) over love of doctrine.

Therefore, in this address I want to respond positively to Father Hugh's proposals in the certain knowledge—lest we build castles in the air—that the majority of Orthodox Christians will reject them outright. I can hear the voices of their objections now, certainly the more strident ones, as pressing and demotic as journalese or televised "vox pop."

> "*Inter-communion is impossible with the heterodox because we are the One True Church, and their denominations are manmade institutions.*"
>
> "*It's all very well for an Anglican mawkishly to talk of coming together for love's sake; this is but a thinly disguised and recycled rendition of that tired old favorite of theirs, the branch theory: as we failed to succumb to the heavy guns of Hooker, Lancelot Andrews, and Pusey on this issue, we are unlikely to capitulate to light artillery.*"
>
> "*Inter-communion presupposes we are all legitimate expressions of the Body of Christ; well, we're not, for as a result of the Great Schism the apostate Latin West, and its Protestant progeny, are ontologically severed from the Church.*"
>
> "*Inter-communion, what inter-communion? How can we commune with others outside the visible Orthodox Church where there exists no sacramental grace at all?*"
>
> "*Inter-communion is unthinkable, because praying with heretics is uncanonical. Read for ourselves the 45th Apostolic Canon and the 23rd Canon of the Local Council of Laodicea. When*

2. Cf. Mary Douglas, *Purity and Danger*.

you've done this you'll realize that the only possible course for an Orthodox Christian is to withdraw from the ecumenical movement. Take heed of the words of the Apostle Paul: 'Come out from them, and be separate from them, says the Lord, and touch nothing unclean'" (2 Cor 6:17).

Finally, and this time moderately and soberly, the collective voice may be added of the Orthodox delegation at the North American Faith and Order Conference at Oberlin, Ohio in 1957. "Inter-communion," they said, "is not just a matter of common doctrinal agreement: it is a question of sharing a common faith, order, and worship."[3]

Against the backdrop of the Oberlin Conference, Bishop Kallistos Ware has outlined the Eastern position on inter-church affairs with great clarity in his book *The Orthodox Church*. It is a position that has not really changed in forty years. "Orthodoxy," writes Bishop Ware,

> . . . insists upon unity in matters of the faith. Before there can be reunion among Christians, there must first be full agreement in faith: this is a basic principle for Orthodox in all their ecumenical relations. It is unity in the faith that matters, not organizational unity; and to secure unity of organization at the price of a compromise in dogma is like throwing away the kernel of a nut and keeping the shell. . . . There can be only one basis for union—the fullness of the faith . . . .[4]

The question that I think still remains to be settled is whether the Orthodox criterion for *re-union*—that "there must first be full agreement in faith"—also holds for *inter-communion*? Or, to put it another way, is the case against a shared Eucharist an open and shut case, or a case of open or shut? The majority Orthodox view, as I have already indicated, clearly believes it is shut. Bishop Kallistos Ware has stated this conviction succinctly (although he does not tell us if it is his own view): "no unity in the Faith, no communion in the sacraments."[5]

I disagree with this verdict and in so doing I admit that I am siding with the group whom the bishop has called "a small but significant minority" who wish to pursue a more open policy.

The rest of this address is an exploration of this pursuit. I have chosen to present an autobiographical account as a way in to this controversial issue.

---

3. Statement of the Representatives of the Greek Orthodox Church in USA at the North American Faith and Order Study Conference, Oberlin, Ohio, September 3–10, 1957

4. Ware, *The Orthodox Church*, 318–19.

5. Ibid., 318.

Before doing so I would like to preface my investigation with two caveats. First, what follows is no more than a prolegomenon from a layman of the Orthodox Church. It comes with no official approval or collegial authority, and I consider it to be provisional and tentative, inquisitive and heuristic. Second, I shall only be looking at half the equation of Orthodox participation in inter-communion: namely, the grounds on which Christians outside the Orthodox Church might be admitted to the Eucharist within it.

AUTOBIOGRAPHICAL NOTES ON THE ACQUISITION OF AN OPEN STANCE TO INTER-COMMUNION

Like many a seeker looking for a spiritual home, it was Bishop Kallistos' book, *The Orthodox Church*, that captured my attention along the way and filled me with a longing to know more and inspired me to begin a search for a living Orthodox community. In 1971, I arranged to see Metropolitan Anthony, and after a series of meetings with him and regular attendance at the Liturgy I was received into the Church in 1973.[6]

During this period of discussion and instruction I had to overcome a certain inner resistance to the Eastern Tradition. This was partly a matter of coming to terms with the sort of issues Protestants are naturally averse to—prayers for the dead, relics, the role of the mother of God, the meaning of Holy Tradition, etc. But my other concern was personal: for although I found some cradle Orthodox and English converts who were conducive to my way of thinking, I also discovered that the Orthodox Church boasted armies of supporters who seemed to me to be exclusivist in their faith and inhospitable to other Christians.

Metropolitan Anthony, however, turned the tables on me, enabling me to see that I self-righteously assumed that I was morally superior to what I took to be the "hardline Orthodox," and that what I really wanted was for them to be removed so that the empirical life of the Church would be perfect. He said, trading on the old adage, "Don't look for the perfect church, for if you join you will spoil it." Chastened for thinking of the Church as a club of the like-minded, I eventually overcame my inner resistance to Orthodoxy and joined the Church for what it is: holy, catholic, and apostolic, but empirically a mixed community of faithful believers, publicans and sinners, Judases and Pharisees.

During my first few years in the Church I learned to sing two Orthodox refrains that enabled me both to engage with the religious culture that I had left behind and with those members of my new family who seemed

6. Cf. Walker, "Notes From a Wayward Son" in this volume.

hostile or indifferent to that culture. The two ritornellos were apophatic theology and the doctrine of economy.

Apophasis, it seemed to me, changed everything. On the one hand, Orthodox Christians, like Roman Catholics and Reformed Protestants, are committed to cataphatic theology: the East, for example, adheres to the Nicene-Constantinopolitan Creed of 381 AD; if that is not cataphatic theology, then I do not know what is. On the other hand, it seemed, Orthodoxy was reluctant to allow cataphasis the final word. This was not only because the apophatic method of the Greek Schools preferred the way of negation over the way of affirmation as a surer route to truth, but also because Orthodox apophasis does not believe that the ineffable can be satisfactorily rendered in any linguistic form—whether this be philosophical syllogisms, analogical thinking, or even mythopeism; theological language, therefore, even creedal statements, needed to remain both provisional and incomplete. God is always greater than any description we give of Him; God's transcendence, or otherness, can never be encapsulated by language. Even in the incarnation of the Eternal Son as Jesus of Nazareth, while he reveals through his actions something of his Divine nature, he remains as person veiled, hidden, and unknown.

This kind of thinking greatly impressed me, whether I found it in modern commentators like Vladimir Lossky or the later fathers, such as Gregory of Palamas, for I interpreted it to mean that ultimately Christian faith was a kind of enduring hope in the face of things unseen; it meant there was an unknowingness even in our experience of God—this *agnosia* I took to be ontologically crucial in sharing communion with God, but epistemologically weak in knowing and saying things about him.[7] I found apophatic theology liberating because it militated against conceptual certainty and arrogant truth claims: we as Orthodox needed to remain humble in the face of the future, for in the words of the Epistle "What we will be has not yet been revealed" (1 John 3:2). By the same token, I thought there was a need for a certain reserve in our mission to other religions and in our dialogue with fellow Christians. It was a reserve that the Nestorians displayed in their expansion into the Far East, which was predicated on a kind of "openness" to the possibility that God was already present there, albeit *sotto voce*.

This notion of reserve, I came to see, was not due to lack of confidence in the gospel (not timidity born of disbelief), but an apophatic reticence not to have the final say in God's relation to other religious communities. This view was later reinforced, when I encountered Metropolitan Khodr's article

---

7. Cf. Lossky, *The Mystical Theology of the Eastern Church*, and *Gregory Palamas: The Triads*.

on the economy of the Holy Spirit in a pluralistic world, and when I read Father Michael Oleska's dissertation on the holistic approach of the Russian Orthodox to the indigenous and vulnerable cultures of the Aleut Indians of Alaska.[8]

It is evident, however, that thinking in this way meant that I was now, in so many words, not thinking apophatically, but economically—though when I first encountered the idea of economy in the Orthodox Church I did not comprehend its full significance. It seemed to me initially to be a sort of portmanteau affair which allowed you to waive any rules that were a nuisance or got in the way of pragmatic or pastoral concerns: so, for example, if you did not have any water for baptism you did without, and it would still be spiritually efficacious; or if no priest was available to perform the rite, a lay person—male or female—could officiate and it would still be valid.

Divorce and remarriage appeared to be made possible by economy too: it seemed better to remarry than to encourage moral drift, preferable to call a marriage dead when it had died, rather than insist, in the manner of a legal contract, that it was indissoluble. Inter-communion, so I also discovered, was formally discouraged, but *in practice* could actually take place—a Catholic or an Anglican, for example, might be able to participate in an Orthodox Eucharist if she was unable to worship at her own religious services due to exile or temporary separation from her own country.

When I began to think beyond economy as practical and pastoral reasons for rule bending, and started thinking theologically of economy as God's action in the world, including His church, I soon realized that it was hard to fence in God: how do you put boundaries around a God of unconditional and limitless love? "God did not send the Son into the world to condemn the world," says John, "but in order that the world might be saved through Him" (John 3:17).

In my first few years as an Orthodox Christian, although I did, somewhat haphazardly, blend apophatic theology and the doctrine of economy together, I subsequently, after separating them analytically, begin to think they could be seen as complementary doctrines. Apophatic theology, in evoking reverential wonder before the mystery of God, broke the iron law of what postmodernist philosopher Jacques Derrida understands as the totalizing power of language. Economy, in recognizing the freedom of God's action in the world, discouraged the restriction and localization of God to an institution, time, or place. Taken together both doctrines undercut unwarranted certainty and intellectual conceit: God as immanent Trinity is

---

8. Cf. Khodr, "Christianity in a Pluralist World: The Economy of the Holy Spirit"; Oleska, *Another Culture/Another World*.

beyond our conceptual grasp, and God as economic Trinity, though present and active in the world, remains beyond our ken and outside of our control.

From the late 1970s onwards I used to apply the apophatic balm to soften the carapace of cataphatic theology. This, in combination with my desire to adopt a doctrine of economy as the antidote to Orthodox exclusivism, meant that it never crossed my mind that God was totally absent from other religions, let alone sister-Christian churches. Indeed, the Orthodox claim that interested me the least in those early days was that *it alone* was the one true, undivided church. Now I realize this public admission all these years later may be shocking to many of my Orthodox brethren; no doubt it suggests a certain naïveté or romanticism on my part. Moreover, from the exclusivist standpoint, the whole thing, I realize, could be put down to sloppy thinking, wish fulfillment, or just plain misunderstanding of the Tradition.

It was not that I was unaware of the universalistic claims of the Church by some Orthodox writers (in particular I was impressed by the logic of Khomiakov that the church, as the body of Christ, could not be divided),[9] but they did not sit easily with my experience. My own history is illustrative of this. When Metropolitan Anthony received me into the Church, he told me that God had met me as a young man and that it was Christ himself who had rescued me and led me to the Russian Church. I thought at the time that if God had been active in my youth outside the visible ecclesia of Orthodoxy, this was because the "Holy Spirit blew where he will," and the Church, while it could claim to be alive to his presence, could not circumnavigate him or claim exclusive rights to his Lordship.

I conceived then the idea of the Orthodox Church as an "ark of disclosure" where the Spirit dwelled, yet did not have permanent residence there. Like the dove in the story of Noah, the Spirit leaves the ark and spreads his wings over the troubled sea; returning when he chooses, the Spirit then brings the anointing chrism of the olive branch from the fertile land, which I interpreted typologically as heaven.

It struck me, by contrast, that if the Orthodox Church thought of itself as the ark of enclosure, as the ship which alone housed the remnant of God's people, and which alone contained the Spirit of God, it could not countenance the possibility—if I may extend the metaphor, that if any other ships were perchance upon the sea then they too might be visited by the dove with unction from the *paradisial pleroma*. By extrapolation, I thought in those early days, as I think still, that it is not possible to say with confidence that the sacraments in the scattered churches of Christendom are worthless, or

9. Cf. Khomiakov, *The Church Is One.*

that the Spirit of God does not operate in Christian confessions other than our own.

I felt that this viewpoint was reinforced by the fact that the Orthodox Church, on the whole, did not teach that the sacraments were validated by the legitimacy of apostolic succession (although the forensic language of validation and legitimacy, I learned, was not really intrinsic to Orthodox discourse). A better way of putting it would be to say that God's guarantee that "the mysteries" would be "holy and life-giving" was not dependent on the status of the magisterium—as if the laying on of hands in apostolic succession conferred a legal entitlement to office and a deed of sacramental efficacy. No, God's promise was a sovereign gift of the Holy Spirit.

But if this were true, so it seemed to me, that should a small Pentecostal group, worshipping in a corrugated roofed hut somewhere in Africa or South America, call upon the Holy Spirit to hallow the bread and wine, who dare say *a priori*, that their epiclesis is no more than hot air? Alternatively, to put it Christologically, where two or three are gathered in Jesus' name (Matt 18:20), who are we to say that he is not in their midst? The Lord Jesus himself admonished his disciples when they complained to him that someone outside of their band of fellowship was casting out demons in his name. "Do not stop him," he said, "Whoever is not against us is for us" (Mark 9:39–40).

From my earliest days as an Orthodox convert, therefore, while I believed Orthodoxy to be the most primitive (which in my lectionary is a positive word) and most authentic expression of the apostolic faith, I never thought we were the *only* expression of it. On economic grounds I took my stand with Metropolitan Sergius Stragarodsky of Moscow in proclaiming "we know where the Church is, but we do not say where the Church is not." I think this view, while not formally adhered to by vast numbers of Orthodox Christians, is more widespread in the practice of the Orthodox Church than is generally recognized. It is reflected in the reluctance to rebaptize converts who have already been baptized in the name of the Trinity, either as children or adults; it is that deep reserve I referred to earlier, a reticent sobriety that does not seek to gainsay the free action of God among other Christian Confessions. After reading Saint Basil's Treatise on the Holy Spirit, I came to understand that the Lord and Giver of Life, as the perfecting cause of God's reconciling plan for the world, is also, in Paul's words, "the Lord of freedom" (2 Cor 3:17). If He saw fit to fill the Gentiles with His divine presence at the house of Cornelius He may very well choose to dwell in the tents of the Old Believers, the Peculiar Baptists, and possibly even the Anglicans (Acts 10:1–32).[10]

FELLOWSHIP AND UNITY

It follows from this brief autobiographical sketch and these selective theological vignettes that I warm to Father Hugh's proposals for putting love before doctrinal exactitude in the cause of Christian fellowship.[11] I say *fellowship* rather than *unity* because I think one of the barriers to inter-communion for many Orthodox Christians has been a conviction that if divided Christians stand together at the Lord's Table as a sign of unity then it is nothing less than a lie. But perhaps we should think of standing together before the holy gifts as a prophetic act of solidarity and hope in the face of the very fact that we Christians are not yet united.

If Orthodox Christians substituted fellowship for unity in their thinking, then perhaps we could begin to see that being loyal to the Orthodox Tradition does not preempt sharing its treasures with others outside the Church, as both Nicolas Berdyaev and Nicolas Zernov longed for in their lifetime. Indeed, taking his cue from the thinking of Sergius Bulgakov in the 1930s, Zernov would remind Orthodox Christians that they were the guardians, not the owners, of the spiritual treasures of the Church, and that the more these treasures, including the Eucharist, were shared with others, the greater would be their efficacy in Orthodox Church life.[12]

Those few of us who favor a more open table than the Orthodox majority need, however, to be aware that we can get carried away by our enthusiasm. This is sometimes reflected in a cavalier approach to the Tradition, including a not altogether careful reading of Holy Scripture. For example, we are likely to hear Paul's exhortation to the church in Ephesus on "speaking the truth in love" (Eph 4:15) as a text that prioritizes love over truth claims to such an extent that truth is swallowed up in our eisegesis. Conversely, those who are bitterly opposed to inter-communion can also fail to interpret Scripture in a spirit of sobriety: they may very well hear the words of Paul to "speak the truth in love" as prioritizing truth claims over love and fidelity to doctrine over fellowship.

It seems to me imperative, therefore, that those of us who are seeking to lobby for a more open Eucharist must not think of our fellow Orthodox

10. Saint Basil, *Treatise on the Holy Spirit.*

11. Wybrew, *The Orthodox Liturgy.*

12. Cf. Zernov, *Eastern Christendom*; Bugakov, *The Bride of the Lamb*; and Berdyaev, *Truth and Revelation.*

Christians who are set against us on this issue to be, by definition, the enemy: we need discernment to distinguish between opposition born of bigotry and disagreement predicated on principled belief. There is all the difference in the world between people who reject a shared Eucharist in a spirit of holiness, deep regret, sadness, and even anguish, and the sectarian attitude, captured in the Gospel of Luke, which says of the Pharisees that there were "some who trusted in themselves that they were righteous and regarded others with contempt" (Luke 18:9). Saint John Cassias, and Evagrios the Solitary had a name for such a self-regarding attitude: they called it conceit, or "self-esteem." They considered it to be one of the most deadly of the passions, for it wasted the charity of the heart like a ravaging sickness leaving the gateway of the soul too weak to withstand the combined onslaught of the eight deadly sins.

TWO RUSSIAN APPROACHES TO ECUMENICAL RELATIONS

I would like now to turn to two great nineteenth-century Russian theologians—Alexy Khomiakov and Metropolitan Philaret of Moscow—to shed some variegated light on this issue of a closed or open Orthodox-stance to inter-communion. Khomiakov, a retired cavalry officer and leading light in the early Slavophil movement, was innovative and daring in his recasting of the traditional view of authority in the Church into the altogether more dynamic, pneumatological, and collegial concept of *sobornost*. But he restricted this wonderful insight to Orthodoxy alone. That he did so was due to the inherent logic of his argument that was born out of the belief that because the church was instituted by Jesus himself, and sustained by the Spirit of God, it cannot be subject to sin nor torn asunder. For Khomiakov there is but "one God, and one Church, and within her there is neither dissension nor disagreement."[13]

Khomiakov accepted as a matter of historical record that the Roman Schism of the eleventh century peeled away from the church, but left the fruit behind intact, which was ripened by the Holy Spirit. The Latin West, in contrast, was left dry, discarded, and lifeless. However, Khomiakov's tactic was not really to argue from history, but to assert a theory of divine providence: the Orthodox Church is the true church because after "the falling away of many schisms" she is "preserved by the will of God." Khomiakov's view of Western Christendom, especially Rome, was so stark and uncompromising that it can be presented in the form of an Aristotelian syllogism.

13. Cf. Khomiakov, *The Church Is One*.

Premise 1: Roman Catholics and Protestants cannot be Christians unless they are baptized into the Body of Christ.

Premise 2: There is no sacramental efficacy outside the visible Orthodox Church.

Conclusion: Catholics and Protestants are not Christians.

As far as I can see, Khomiakov's ecclesiology rejected any notion of existing in this world an invisible ecclesia that reached beyond the visible Orthodox Church and incorporated other denominations.

Yet there is a genuine economy in the Russian theologian's thought that we cannot in natural justice overlook. This should not really surprise us, for in many ways he was tender-hearted and progressive in his thinking—liberating his serfs, for example, before such an action was enshrined in Russian law. Khomiakov thought that it might be possible that God had established invisible ties between humankind and the church, though he believed that Orthodox Christians could not talk about them with any confidence, for such ties had not been revealed; the world would have to wait for the day of judgment before these unseen connections, if they existed, could be disclosed.

There is no doubt, however, that Khomiakov so trusted in God's goodness that he would not have hesitated to say, in the words of the author of Genesis, "Shall not the Judge of all the earth do what is just?" (Gen 18:25). But as brilliant and as humane in its own way as it is, I think Khomiakov's ecclesiology lacked what Saint Simeon the New Theologian called *diakrisis* (or discerning judgment), for the Russian theologian did not foresee how his exclusivist ecclesiology would fuel a closed and inward-looking second generation of Slavophils, who adopted a xenophobic nationalism that led Russian Orthodoxy by the nose down the wrong path (a trail from which it has not altogether escaped). Furthermore, as Nicolas Zernov has highlighted in his Introduction to Khomiakov's essay *The Church Is One,* he was not able to embrace his Anglican friend William Palmer as a fellow Christian, even though by all accounts he loved him and treated him as if he were a brother in Christ.[14]

In contrast to Khomiakov, Metropolitan Philaret of Moscow took a quite different approach to Christendom: he believed the way to determine the authenticity of Christian communities was to apply the Christological test of orthodoxy: if a religious community calling themselves Christian believed, in the words of the Philippian hymn, that "Jesus Christ is Lord" (Phil 2:11), then he could not bring himself to call them false. The Metropolitan

---

14. Khomiakov, *The Church Is One.*

was also of the opinion that Jesus alone, as head of the church, knew who were its true members; therefore, in contradiction to Khomiakov's thought, there was no isomorphic relationship in his ecclesiology between the invisible church and its visible manifestation.[15]

It was not that Metropolitan Philaret did not believe Orthodoxy to be the truest church—the only one in fact that had kept the apostolic faith in its fullness—but that it was perfectly permissible for Christianity to be kept alive in non-Orthodox churches, even if it was mixed with impure doctrines and practices. The general thrust of his thought was idealist; he understood other Christian confessions not to be so much true ones or false ones as *etiolations* of the one true church. His prayer for these confessions that still bore—albeit dimly—the divine imprimatur was that God would restore them to fullness of spiritual life.

Nowhere, to my knowledge, does Metropolitan Philaret actively encourage (or discourage) inter-communion; but as he does not deny the reality of spiritual life and sacramental grace in the Christian denominations outside the Orthodox Church, it would seem to be a legitimate extrapolation from his ecclesiology to suggest such an action is permissible if not desirable.

However, Metropolitan Philaret's open ecumenical stance, in contrast to Khomiakov's relatively closed-one, should not be understood as liberal in the modernist sense or as simply due to the Protestant pietism that, it has been said, influenced his thinking. Rather, his openness to the other Christians rested solely on an economic doctrine, not on a watering down of the apostolic faith.

CONCLUSION

In conclusion, we must ask what we can do in our own day. The Orthodox Church, I would suggest, still does not have a more helpful and realistic approach to inter-church relations than Metropolitan Philaret's. The theological resources that might allow us to re-characterize other confessions more positively—say as ontologically equivalent to our own while remaining different in many areas of faith and order—simply do not exist.

Granted that this is so I would like to suggest that the way forward in pursuing inter-communion is to stick to what we know, but not to be afraid to augment and extend the doctrine of economy to reflect the changing historical situation. The Orthodox Church has been engaged in intense

---

15. Cf. *Catechism of the Orthodox Church of Saint Philaret*; the *Catechism* is the best place to begin to see the basic contours of Philaret's ecclesiology.

ecumenical encounter now for over half a century. It has found, as did Nicolas Zernov when he first left Russia, that while the West is indeed bristling
with heretics, it is also brimming over with Christians.

In the light of this experience, we have to take action on the basis of
what we have found: we should shake ourselves free from the unholy torpor
that is the shadow side of Holy Tradition, and work towards providing an
open table for baptized Trinitarian Christians who have a personal faith in
the Lord Jesus Christ. I believe this would not only be an act of generous
hospitality, but also a recognition that despite a millennium of internal
quarrels, long-term separation, and even divorce there remain cords of love
that bind us Christians together as members of one family.

Substantially, there will be serious difficulties to overcome. There is
still the preliminary educational work to be done, even in the diaspora, of
challenging Orthodox isolationism, both in terms of the realities of cultural
pluralism and the desirability of ecumenical cooperation. For Orthodox
Christians ever to support inter-communion in any numbers, they will need
enthusiastic backing from a bishop who is both committed to the cause and
of sufficient resolve to withstand the inevitable opposition.

We must also heed Nicolas Zernov's caution: an open table does not
mean, he used to counsel, that we can open up to all and sundry. What this
means, and I would not be responding to Father Hugh in good faith unless
I mention this, is that we will not be able to avoid some agreed statement of
faith as a precondition to inter-communion, however minimalist we might
be prepared to make it.

Despite the rocky road of prevarication and procrastination that lies
ahead, I think Father Hugh's proposal for an open table should not be
rejected out of hand by Orthodox Christians. His fundamental assertion
holds true: we have put theological agreement, church order, and patterns
of worship before fellowship in Christ and with each other. In so doing we
have highlighted our differences at the expense of giving due recognition
to the common tradition we share, which C. S. Lewis has variously called
"Deep Church" or "Mere Christianity."[16]

Therefore, Orthodox Christians are going to have to learn the following: right believing is not *prolepsis* but *epilogos*. Correct doctrine neither
anticipates, promises, nor causes love. On the contrary, it is love, as the
apostle Paul says, that "believes all things"—that is the anticipatory promise
of doctrinal agreement (1 Cor 13:7). Affirmation of true faith as the envoi
or epilogue of love's story is a reality we fail to see, for it is right under our

16. Cf. Walker and Parry, *Deep Church Rising*; and see, of course, Lewis, *Mere
Christianity*.

noses: it is there in the deep structure of the Liturgy where we find that the dramaturgical movement of the Eucharistic rite flows from love to faith— not the other way round as we have insisted on making it: or, as the deacon sings, "Let us so love one another that with one mind we may confess." To which the people reply in joyful affirmation of the true faith: "Father, Son and Holy Spirit, Trinity one in essence and inseparable. Amen."

16

The Concept of the Person
in Social Science

Possibilities for Theological Anthropology

(1991)

INTRODUCTION: THE VIABILITY OF AN
INTERDISCIPLINARY APPROACH TO CONSTRUCTING
AN ADEQUATE THEOLOGICAL ANTHROPOLOGY

In "The Doctrine of God the Trinity Today,"[1] his introductory paper to
the British Council of Churches Study Commission, John Ziziouslas,
Bishop of Pergamon, makes a plea that theology should open itself to
the insights of other academic disciplines in order to see how an interdisciplinary understanding of "person" would both enlighten Trinitarian theology and enrich human discourse. He believes that the person is a current
notion in sociology and humanistic studies,[2] and he also points out that to
date little has been done to relate Trinitarian models of the person to notions of persons current in the social sciences.[3]

---

1. See Ziziouslas, "The Doctrine of God the Trinity Today," 19–32.

2. There is, in fact, no coherent or widely agreed on concept of the person in
humanistic studies.

3. Cf. Ray S. Anderson, *On Being Human*; Anderson's book is a good place to start
the discussion on theological anthropology, but it lacks a fully developed Trinitarian

It is undoubtedly the case that a theological anthropology derived from Trinitarian thinking would have significant implications for contemporary social science. Furthermore, Alasdair Macintyre in his brilliant defense of classicism in *After Virtue*[4] has already demonstrated how useful sociology can be in bringing to life and concretizing issues of moral philosophy that are so often left in the air in the form of abstract individualism. In principle, therefore, I see no reason why we should not find sociology in particular and social science in general useful to the theological enterprise.

However, Bishop Ziziouslas is being somewhat overly optimistic if he believes (as he seems to believe) that there is at present in the social sciences a single, widely accepted notion of "the person." Furthermore, until recently, such a notion has not even been a pressing concern in sociological theory or practice.[5] Thus, in the history of sociological thought not a single *major* social theorist has a developed a consistent philosophical anthropology, and most modem sociologists hardly ever use the word "person" at all.

For example, a brief look through the fourteen volumes of the *International Encyclopedia of Social Science*[6] reveals that "person" is not in the index (though "personality" as a purely psychological model is), and the closest synonym one can find is "self," as defined and developed by C. H. Cooley,[7] G. H. Mead (1863–1931),[8] and Erving Goffman (1922–88).[9]

Implicitly, however, notions of the person abound in the social sciences (as one would expect), and furthermore, they reflect (as one would also expect) the dominant strands of Western philosophy since the eighteenth century.

In this essay, I want to identify in a critical way some of these ideas of "the person" as they are now and have in the past been used in sociology. Ultimately, I hope to show that sociology *qua* social science cannot provide sufficiently strong grounds for constructing an adequate theological anthropology; but I hope also to demonstrate that sociology does provide some useful clues about personhood that theologians ignore at their peril.

theology.

4. MacIntyre, *After Virtue*.

5. Cf., Carrithers, Collins, and Lukes, eds., *The Category of the Person*; Lukes, *Individualism*. For a Christian perspective, see Evans, *Preserving the Person*. Other books that have bearing on this concept of the person in the social sciences are Rorty, *The Identities of Persons*, Peacocke and Gillett, eds., *Persons and Personality*, and Swinburne and Shoemaker, *Personal Identity*.

6. Sills, ed., *International Encyclopedia of the Social Sciences*.

7. Cf., Charles H. Cooley, *Human Nature and the Social Order*.

8. Cf., Mead, *Mind, Self and Society*.

9. Goffman, *The Presentation of Self in Everyday Life*.

These clues, taken together with other clues provided by patristic Trinitarian theology, suggest that a genuine theological anthropology *is* possible.

NOTIONS OF "THE PERSON" IN SOCIAL SCIENCE

Sociology was born in the nineteenth century, a child of two parents: an optimistic humanism that sought to improve the world and a positivistic empiricism that sought to understand, predict, and control human behavior. C. H. Saint-Simon (1760–1825) personifies the first parent, while August Comte (1798–1857) the second. Karl Marx (1818–83), if we take his work as a whole from the *Grundrisse* to *Kapital,* reflects the contradictions of this parentage.

It would be a mistake, however, to see Saint-Simon as an advocate of collectivism. He sees the state as a necessary evil, and his pre-Marxist socialism is essentially a collectivity for the good of individuals understood in Immanuel Kant's (1724–1804) moral sense. For Saint-Simon, therefore, as for Kant, rational beings

> are called *persons* because their nature already marks them out as ends in themselves—that is, as something which ought not to be used merely as a means—and consequently imposes to that extent a limit on all arbitrary treatment of them (and is an object of reverence). Persons, therefore, are not merely subjective ends whose existence as an effect of our actions has value for us: they are objective ends—that is, things whose existence is in itself an end, and indeed an end such that in its place we can put no other end to which they should serve simply as means; for unless this is so, nothing at all of absolute value would be found anywhere.[10]

The French sociologist Emile Durkheim (1858–1917), for all his "functionalist empiricism," inherits this strong, albeit abstract, moral individualism from German idealism,[11] and it can be found in more concrete forms in the work of Max Weber (1864–1920)—and can still be found in the writings of Ralf Dahrendorf.[12]

The dominant notion of persons in early British sociology, on the other hand, was gleaned from the hedonism of Hobbes and the later emendations of utilitarianism. As A. D. Lindsay correctly points out, much of modern

10. Kant, *The Moral Law: Groundwork of the Metaphysic of Morals,* 95–96.

11. Although it does not fully emerge until his last major work, *The Elementary Forms of the Religious Life.*

12. Dahrendorf, *Homo Sociologus.*

individualism (as I shall argue later, this is what much of sociological personhood turns out to be) is essentially Epicurean:

> The view is that society is nothing more than an aggregate of
> individuals; the doctrine of the state, law and justice are at best
> necessary evils; a scientific attitude of mind which leads to the
> acceptance of psychological atomism and hedonism; and a high
> valuation set on the voluntary association and the relation of
> contract.[13]

A characteristic of the philosophical individualism of the Enlightenment, whether in German idealistic form or in British utilitarian guise, is
its tendency to a-historicism and abstraction: essentially, human beings are
viewed as moral and/or methodological constructs; the person is a heuristic
device with "no guts or history," and, in its non-Kantian forms, no "self-
consciousness" either.

The "a-historical man," therefore, has had many lives since the nineteenth century. As an economic commercial cipher *a la* classical economics,
this "man" is a sort of *ratio* without *nous;* as conceived by behavioral psychology, he has no interiority, being depicted as a sort of "ping pong with a
memory" (but no intents); and as the functional man of Durkheimian sociology, he is so reified that he is synonymous with his role (and in this model,
groups are simply aggregates of persons perceived as interchangeable units).

When consciousness finds its way into both sociology and philosophy,
with it comes the perennial problem of solipsism in all its guises. Wilhelm
Dilthey (1833-1911) and Max Weber, despite their *verstehende* approach
(which at least admitted that there was more to behavior than meets the
eye), never found an adequate intersubjective approach to knowledge and
communication; nor did Edmund Husserl (1859-1938) and his student Alfred Schutz (1899-1959), despite the invention of *Lebenswelt*.[14]

Much of early existentialism, trapped humankind on a private island
of self-authentication, cut off from the mainland of history and tradition.
And in twentieth-century British philosophy in the analytical tradition,
we find how consciousness was for G. E. Moore (1873-1958) the key to
understanding the person, and that linguistic philosophy from Gilbert Ryle
(1900-1976) to A. J. Ayer (1910-90) was similarly obsessed with considering the person almost entirely in terms of the mind-body problem. So, for
example, Ayer notes that Peter Strawson, following Ludwig Wittgenstein

---

13. Cf., A. D. Lindsay, "Individualism," *Encyclopedia of the Social Sciences,* as quoted
in Steven Lukes, *Individualism.*

14. Schutz, *The Phenomenology of the Social World.*

(1889–1951), rejects the notion of a private language and self, but is left with the idea of a world inhabited by other private selves, like himself![15]

This gloss on either "empty" or "asocial" persons in Western intellectual life is not much improved by the contribution of psychoanalysis. Sigmund Freud (1856–1939) opens up the mind to the unconscious, but in expanding inner space at the expense of culture, his model leaves the ego and the libido causing havoc while the superego tries to act as an ineffectual referee. What Freud, like so many post-Enlightenment psychologists and philosophers, failed to do was adequately to see the person as, in Martin Heidegger's words, "man-in-the-world."[16]

And it was in this regard at least that the early sociologists made a significant contribution to notions of personhood. It was Marx who, scorning the abstractness of Enlightenment "man," observed that "man is not an abstract being, squatting outside the world. Man is the human world, the state, and society."

Even Comte—who in his very desire to understand social order denied Kant as a precursor, but accepted Hobbes—insisted that most philosophical speculation was metaphysical and meaningless, for it was not grounded in an observable social matrix.

The negative aspect of Comte's empirical persons is that, as with behavioral psychology, they have no inner space at all. (His denial of "minds" led him to a crude understanding of consciousness that was based on the neo-phrenology of Gall's cerebral theory!) But if Comte's persons were empty (and at the very least philosophical individualism had equated body and consciousness with self-consciousness), they were at least seen *in relation* to other people. For both Comte and Marx, the philosophical fiction of a social contract was nonsense: human beings were born into a culture, and a culture was a shared domain; the group, *not* the individual, is primordial.

Comte, however, was so committed to a "mindless" empiricism—as was John Stuart Mill (1806–73) in his early days[17]—that he refused the possibility that persons could be understood inter-subjectively or empathetically. They could, however, be understood as co-ordinates in a social matrix that could be measured mathematically. For Comte, group behavior was not the social action of Weber, based on rational means/ends intentionality;[18] rather, it was dictated by the invariant laws of natural science.

15. Cf., Ayer, *The Concept of a Person and Other Essays*, chap. 4; and Ayer, *Philosophy in the Twentieth Century*, 178–80.

16. Heidegger, *Being and Time*, chap. 4.

17. Mill, *August Comte and Positivism*.

18. Weber, *Basic Concepts in Sociology*.

FUNCTIONALISTS AND INTERACTIONISTS

Before returning to Marx, however, let us also trace what happened to Comte's successors in sociology, as the empiricist-functionalist school dominated early anthropology and provided the undisputed paradigm in American and British (but never German) sociology until the 1960s.

The structural-functionalists, as they are usually called, really began in earnest with Durkheim, and developed through the anthropologists Alfred R. Radcliffe-Brown (1881–1955), Bronislaw Malinowski (1884–1942), and the American sociologists Robert K. Merton (1910–2003) and Talcott Parsons (1902–79).

Wishing to eschew psychological reductionism, the subjectivism of Dilthey, and the idealism of Weber, the structural-functionalists opted for reification. On this perspective, persons as self-conscious individuals disappear entirely into normative social roles. The person is admittedly related to other persons in groups, tribes, and kinship, but it is these "social wholes"— and their structural segments—that are investigated, not the people in them. The "wholes" are the social reality, the social facts to be investigated. The proper study of sociological man is not "man," then, but social structures, in which men and women are empty, interchangeable atoms, mere things. Put another way, groups are made up of individuals, but individuals are simply the atomistic stuff of cultural matrices. If Freud virtually excludes culture from the ego, structural functionalists exclude ego from culture.

Durkheim, most interestingly, attempts to explain the rise of the modern individual not in terms of an abstract philosophy of individualism, but by means of sociological and historical changes. The individual, he claims in *The Division of Labor,* did not exist in the rural past, which he sees as a form of primitive collectivism. Rather, the individual self-consciously emerges, not because of Enlightenment philosophy and the language of individual rights (construed individualistically), but because of the move from what Durkheim calls the mechanical to organic society.

In his most complex work, *The Elementary Forms of Religious Life,* which demonstrates most clearly his debt to Kantian moralism, as well as his mechanical empiricism, Durkheim does begin to struggle towards notions of individuals finding their true personality. This was a moral problem for Durkheim because he saw modern individuals becoming either narcissistic or living in modernity in a state of *anomie,* or of confused normlessness;

how was the collective good to be achieved without the norms of a moral tradition, or moral traditions?[19]

Since Durkheim, however, structural-functionalists have continued down the reification path. The person is either an empty nobody (shall we say *personare*—in the literal sense of "sounding through"?) or a *persona* (or actor). Indeed, while it is true that the symbolic-interactionist school of Mead, Cooley, and later Goffman, utilizes talk of masks, actors, stages, games, plays, etc., to create a kind of dramaturgical face-to-face sociology, functionalists had already opted to designate persons by their social roles; or, to be more accurate, functionalists increasingly conceived societies in terms of normative patterns of behavior where the majority of citizens were socialized into a clear-cut "role-set" where the normative expectations were successfully internalized. (According to this schema, most deviant behavior occurs as a result of poor socialization.)

Therefore, not only does functionalist sociology operate with a cozy, consensual notion of social order that finds it difficult to account for violent change and rarely talks of power and conflicts of interest, it is also a sociology that has divorced the relational aspect of interaction from thinking, feeling, and intending subjects. Functionalism not only has no time for persons as people whose very identity is bound up with others; it also leaves little room for the moral individualism of Enlightenment "man." Functionalism is amoral; it admits of no significant interior life; and it does not conceive of meaningful "I-Thou" relationships. Functionalist language tries to circumnavigate ontology, or, in Martin Buber's words, the "essential relation" has been replaced by the "technical relation."[20]

Symbolic-interactionism and so-called sociological-phenomenology ("so-called" because it is a bastardized version of Husserl, with neither a transcendental ego nor phenomenological reduction) came into sociological fashion in the 1960s partly because there was a feeling that the functionalists had created the stage, and everybody knew their lines and said them perfectly; the problem was that there was no significant interiority; people were usually given bit-parts, but no one really complained. The new interactional sociology was designed to put the actor back on the stage with a vengeance (actually it had been around since the 1920s).

On the surface, things looked better from the point of view that "persons" were now, at least, subjects as opposed to robotic objects. Better to be an actor who can choose his own parts, fellow players, and stage, than a

19. Durkheim came to believe that sociology could itself provide the basis for morality; see Lukes, *Emile Durkheim, His Life and Work.*

20. Buber, *I and Thou.*

cipher, or unit, or actor who is assigned a "fixed" mask in order to fulfill a "scripted" social role.[21] Furthermore, this new actor was admitted to have not only consciousness, but also subjectivity; this actor could only be understood sympathetically (at least initially).[22]

But this surface change in sociological method did not really change the deeper structure. In the first place, there had been the tendency on the part of phenomenologists and symbolic-interactionists alike, to see men and women as actors orchestrating the world about them as if there were no constraints or objective obstacles to freedom. Secondly, these actors still had no history. The switch from macro-sociology to micro-sociology—from a sociology of the larger society to face-to-face interaction—merely repressed serious issues of power, hierarchy, and oppression.

But thirdly, and for us most crucially, we find that the person remains as the *individual* role player. Admittedly, this person now has an inner life and (as with Weber's sociology) is concerned with actions and goals. But he is still individualistically conceived, albeit now as a conscious "self" and no longer as a mere social atom. So, for example, Goffman in his *The Presentation of the Self in Everyday Life* clearly identifies "self" with "person."

In the 1930s, Mead had already made the distinction between the asocial "I" and the socialized "me."[23] We learn who we are, says Mead, by learning what other people expect of us. Cooley then developed the idea of others being a looking-glass for ourselves. Goffman, following this tradition, clearly understands the self as a social construct put together through interaction. But the thrust of Goffman's sociology is to see how this social construction of reality leads to the creation of selfhood and its fragile but determined push for survival and happiness.

In order to develop this idea Goffman develops a "dramaturgical metaphor" to explain the interaction. Like the functionalists, Goffman thinks of persons as actors in a play; only in this play they have a dazzling array of masks. But unlike the functionalist actor who is always word-perfect and neatly fits his "official role," Goffman's actor also plays what he calls "performance roles": the fool, the clown, the usurper, etc.; the actor will put on these performances in different settings and for different occasions and purposes. This interactional sociology allows Goffman to observe how persons (social actors) perform in jazz clubs, mental hospitals, bars, and other public places. What emerges in Goffman's work is an extremely elegant description

21. For an excellent example of this approach, see Jack D. Douglas, *Understanding Everyday Life*.

22. Cf., Schutz, "The Problem of Rationality in the Social World"; and Schultz, "Common-Sense and Scientific Understanding in the Social World."

23. Mead, *Mind, Self and Society*.

of actors performing multiple roles. He has, in short, taken a magnifying-glass to examine the minutiae of (sometimes ritualistic) "self-displays" in everyday life; but he too has little to say about societal structures, power, and human oppression.

But the question remains: Just who is this person, this self? In Goffman's early work the answer is simple: the person is the sum of his chosen social roles. Personhood is not something inner or private (or transcendental): it is a bundle of masks. Strip away the masks (like layers of an onion), and there is nothing inside![24] We can see, therefore, that Goffman's reaching back to *persona* and *prosopon* is perhaps not so metaphorical after all!

A number of scholars have insisted that Goffman is influenced by existentialism.[25] In his later works[26] Goffman does seem to be concerned with a moral dimension. It is almost as if he sees something (or somebody) behind the masks, encouraging the actor to rebel against both his formal and performance role playing; there seem to be elements of the search for freedom or authenticity that go beyond the self as an infinite collection of masks. Clearly, too, in *Asylums*[27] and *Stigma*[28] Goffman is concerned with problems of freewill, autonomy, and self-determination; but we do not find in his work the moral depth of a Sartre (for Goffman there is no "bad faith," only bad performances).

Goffman's "masked persons" are Mead's "socialized selves" without the asocial "I." But what happens to Goffman's persons when they go off duty? Do they stop performing altogether? What is the private *persona* like? This is difficult to say because Goffman's actors are all action and no reflection. When this particular "self" stops acting (and acting, by definition, is a social performance) we must assume that it ceases to exist.

So, using language that is quaint in Anglo-Saxon sociology, persons in both functionalist and symbolic-interactionist theories cannot be said to possess a basic "ontology." Functionalism only recognizes people as individuals who are interchangeable with anyone else, with persons as not unique or irreducible beings as they are in Kant. In addition, we may also ask: can Goffman's "self" be said to exist ontologically? I doubt it, and I certainly doubt—if I may say so without irreverence—that we would gain anything by re-construing the Holy Trinity on Goffmanesque lines: a kind

24. Cf. Laing, *The Divided Self*, where we see that Laing has some concept of an "ontological self" existing within the socialized self.

25. Ditton, ed., *The View from Goffman*; see also Drew, *Erving Goffman: Exploring the Interaction Order*.

26. Cf., Goffman, *Interaction Ritual* to Goffman, *Frame Analysis*.

27. Goffman, *Asylums*.

28. Goffman, *Stigma*.

of "peek-a-boo" Jesus, a look-alike Father, and a (now popular in some circles) "go-between" Holy Ghost, a perception of God as a collection of personas without true being or unity—a sort of Sabellianism turned on its head! Whatever else the Trinity is, it is certainly about communion constituting the very *being* of God, not dazzling displays of role-playing.

MARX AND PERSONHOOD

Let us return now to the sociological "founding fathers," especially to Marx, and pursue a different route—one that I hope will lead to a more adequate notion of personhood.

To recapitulate: Durkheim, Weber, and Goffman had their own versions of individualist philosophy, but they all saw the elemental fact of individual existence as being existence in a social order and culture. Comte wanted to control individuals by scientific standards and make them happy.[29] Durkheim, more modestly, wanted to discover scientific laws of society; Weber wanted to understand people; and Goffman wanted to capture the elegant display of selves in interaction with other selves; but Marx wanted to set men and women free.

Marx's moral concerns were dominated by a strong sense that there is unfreedom in the world, and that people are alienated from each other and from their work. Despite his German philosophical background, Marx turned his back on reflective philosophy and attempted to pluck Hegelian dialectic from the skies and ground it in history and matter. Marx's materialism, though alien to G. W. F. Hegel (1770–1831), and shared by neither Comte nor Durkheim nor Weber, was not the blind empiricism of positivistic science: it was the crucible of his moral outrage at the exploitation of human misery by the rich.

The influence of Feuerbach—and through him of Christianity—was not inconsiderable on the young Marx,[30] and a number of Russian Orthodox writers have seen much of positive value in the Marxist perspective,[31] that is, there is something almost incarnate and gutsy in Marx that is lacking in the other sociological fathers.

---

29. In this respect, Comte bears an uncanny resemblance to the Grand Inquisitor of Fyodor Dostoevsky's *The Brothers Karamazov*, as I have argued in "Two Versions of Sociological Discourse," 86.

30. Cf., MacIntyre, *Marxism and Christianity*.

31. E.g., Berdyaev, *Freedom and the Spirit*; and also Lampert, *The Divine Realm*, who is also clearly influenced by the Marxist tradition.

And yet, for our purposes Marx is ultimately a great disappointment. Recent Marxist scholarship has concentrated on Marx's earlier writings before 1848, when he published *The Communist Manifesto.* These writings show Marx still to be deeply under the influence of German idealism, and to be possessed of a deep concern, like his mentor Hegel, with authentic existence and freedom (notably in the *Grundrisse*).[32] The young Marx's writings appeal to the idealistic New Left of Western society far more than the "scientific socialism" of the later works. And yet, even here, it is impossible to find any elaborate theory of personhood.

What Marx does attempt is a rejection of the methodological individualism of most post-Enlightenment philosophy and science. (As this is essentially a technical issue in the philosophy of science, I shall not dwell on it here.) More importantly, he eschews moral individualism (goodbye to Kant) and attempts to ground personhood in terms of human community, an attempt that in the later works eventually gives way to collectivist materialism.

Persons do not exist as minds, or as non-empirical entities; they belong to a history (and not merely history in the abstract, but particular historical epochs). History is itself determined by the struggle of opposing groups to control the material forces of production. The whole of what we call culture is a superstructure predicated upon an economic infrastructure. This infrastructure (which includes the relationships that people have to the means of production) directly influences consciousness itself.

Whether he realizes it or not, a person exists objectively in a class. In a capitalist society, classes are simply the relationships that groups have to the means of production; for example, the bourgeoisie own the means of production, but the proletariat owns only their labor, which they sell for a wage.

And class-consciousness by the time of *Kapital* is itself determined by a material infrastructure. Oppressed persons (those in the largest and disinherited class—the proletariat) must become conscious of their class in order that the class "by itself" becomes a class "for itself." This self-awareness—of alienation and oppression—has its fulfillment in the revolutionary struggle to overthrow class and overcome the material grounds of opposition between men and women.

The utopian freedom of Marxism, therefore, is the freedom of one class over another, but on behalf of humankind as a whole. Consequently, ideas of individual freedom and authentic existence seen as other than class freedom are rejected as "false consciousness" and bourgeois individualism.

32. On Hegel as an apostle of freedom, see Colin Gunton's provocative essay "The Spirit as Lord: Christianity, Modernity and Freedom" and Gunton, *Enlightenment and Alienation.*

And by the time of Engels' *Anti Duhring* we have in early socialism a vision of morality and consciousness that is seen purely in class terms. The moral individual of Kant—the universal "man"—has been replaced by the class man. In the absence of a (not yet) true humanity, persons can be themselves only by supporting their class interests.

What actually happened in Marx's own lifetime was that the person as Marx originally understood him in the *Grundrisse* (with all his latent potential for freedom) was lost, and eventually became reified into a new abstract man: the socialist "man" of the future in whose abstract name crimes of the present are committed (the notion of the end justifying the means became endemic in Soviet Marxism).[33]

Rebelling in the 1840s against the individualistic concept of Enlightenment man—whom he saw as an object and a theoretical-construct—Marx longed for persons to be viewed as the subjects and not the objects of history. A person is a creator, with mastery over self and over the environment, but not over others. The man/woman for Marx is a "self" in relation to others, a *Gattungswesen* (species-being).

In his *The Essence of Christianity*, Ludwig Feuerbach (1804–72) had already in 1841 claimed that an individual is not complete as a human being without another. Feuerbach's essay, in particular its expression of belief in love, prefigures Martin Buber's (1878–1965) *I and Thou*, and its belief that humanity is always "fellow humanity," that is, looking towards personhood as a relational reality beyond mere individualism.

Marx took this up in historical and social form. Men are nothing, and can do nothing, except in contact and co-operation with others. For the early Marx the history of the world was a system of un-freedom in which people confronted each other as alienated and abstracted objects; the experience of human interaction was one of hostility, not fellowship. Conversely, individual persons would be free (would become subjects and not objects) only when they would recognize each other as members of a universal social being. To be a true *Gattungswesen*, in fact and not in theory, would be possible only when the basis of class inequalities (in the economic infrastructure) was overcome:

> Communism . . . [is] the real appropriation of the essentially human by and for man[,] . . . the complete and conscious return of man to himself as social, i.e., human man. This Communism . . . is the genuine resolution of the conflict between man and nature and between man and man—the true resolution of the conflict between existence and freedom and necessity, between

33. Cf., Kamenka, *Marxism and Ethics*.

the individual and the species. Communism is the riddle of history solved, and it knows itself to be the solution.[34]

Marx's belief that he had found the riddle's answer, or had cracked the hidden code of history, is the foundation of his historicism (which Karl Popper so brilliantly attacks in *The Open Society and Its Enemies*) and it fueled his scientific and positivistic socialism.

There is no doubt, therefore, that a careful reading of *Kapital* shows that Marx in his later life had subsumed his earlier interest in persons under his overriding concern to demonstrate the objectivity and scientific warrant of socialism. Thus, Hegel's inexorable laws of history (after all, Marx may have turned Hegel on his head, but he remained a Hegelian) and his own view of human freedom as emerging at the end of history, swamp much of his earlier idealism. Strictly speaking, Marxism is an evolutionary theory in which the alienated (and not yet really human) individual or the person is in a state of becoming. Class "man" (or Proletariat "man") possesses authentic consciousness, but true personhood arrives only when socialism as the apotheosis of human history arrives. Marxism in its many forms holds to this idea, and too often Marxist ideology has in practice been so Hegelian in its sense of demiurgy that the Marxist person is no longer real at all (i.e., man cannot know himself until he becomes something other than his empirical self).

Thus, in the later Marx's thought, Kant's "moral man" outside of time and history was transformed into "socialist man" and projected into future history (people in the here and now, "empirical men," do not matter and are not even real, for it is "man-as-he-will-and-must-be" that counts). Ironically, then, Marx, who before 1848 wished to eschew Kantian individualism in the name of human community, ended his career as a social theorist rejecting both individualism and community in the cause of collectivism. With collectivism, socialists arrive at a model of the human person that is little different from that of the functionalists: a person is interchangeable with others, and without distinctness or intrinsic worth.

And so, although Marxist sociology has maintained a powerful critique of capitalist society it has failed to provide a satisfactory interactional sociology, social psychology, ethical theory, and linguistic theory (though it has influenced semiotics). Marx did indeed open up personhood to relationalism, but only to deny altogether the distinctiveness of individuals as they become lost in the collectivism of class. In fact, we might put it as follows: that while we may say persons are more than individuals, we cannot say they are not individuals.

34. Karl Marx, *Early Writings*.

This is important, as many other Western Marxist intellectuals have attempted a more "dialectical" and a less "scientific" approach to freedom and personhood than Marx. In this regard we must also make mention of the Frankfurt School.

Here, Theodor Adorno (1903–69), Herbert Marcuse (1898–1979), and Jürgen Habermas (b 1929) attempted to meld the Marxist critique of capitalism with depth-psychology and anarchic insights. Freedom was a major theme of these so-called critical theorists, and in 1956, the Frankfurt Institute published a sort of manifesto program which said:

> Human life is essentially, and not merely accidentally, social life. But once this is recognized, the concept of the individual as the ultimate social entity becomes questionable. If fundamentally man exists in terms and because of others who stand in recip-rocal relation to him, then he is not ultimately determined by his primary indivisibility and singularity, *but by the necessity of partaking of and communing with these others* [my italics]. This finds its expression in the concept of a person, no matter how vitiated by personalist ethics and psychology this concept may be.[35]

This insight, which develops the earlier personalism of Marx, dem-onstrates that aspects of neo-Marxism (along with the thought of that ne-glected Scottish philosopher John Macmurray[36]) can provide clues for an understanding of personhood that runs counter to the mainstream West-ern tradition of construing the person in individualistic and/or modalis-tic terms. Needless to say, however, the work of the Frankfurt School has largely been rejected by those in the Anglo-Saxon empiricist tradition that still dominates sociology.

SOME THEOLOGICAL AND SOCIOLOGICAL REFLECTIONS

It is true to say that the founding "fathers" of sociology—Comte, Durkheim, Marx and Weber—all construed human reality in a thoroughly social way: by definition, they saw sociology as a study of societies, groups, and social collectives of various kinds. The "given" of sociology—the axiom on which the discipline depended—was the social nature of reality.

---

35. Quoted in Fletcher, *The Person in the Light of Sociology*.
36. Macmurray, *Persons in Relation*.

Although in the subsequent development of sociology it would be hard to find practitioners of the subject who disagree with that fundamental presupposition of social science (though it is not one that all psychologists share), curiously it has failed to provide a satisfactory matrix for understanding personhood.

In some versions of sociology (as we saw with the functionalists) the group swallows up persons so that people are little more than atoms or units. This is explained in part by the fact that both Comte and Durkheim were positivists in the scientific sense. We can see, for example, how Comte was the precursor of that aspect of Logical Positivism which ultimately hoped to reduce social interaction to the laws of physics.[37] And in his *The Rules of Sociological Method* we can understand quite clearly how, for Durkheim, the social facts to be investigated are not people, but the relations between them and the functions these play in maintaining the health of society (conceived as a social organism).

Thus, human beings in functionalist sociology are certainly seen as related together, but there is nothing distinctive, unique, or irreducible about them; they have barely any interior life at all, and their social actions in terms of their plans, purposes, and rationality are given short-shrift. We are therefore not going too far if we say that persons are conceptualized as separate entities bound together by the rules and mores of social collectivities—e.g., nation-states, economies, classes, families, etc. Furthermore, the atomistic individuals of the early functionalists are not philosophically equivalent to the moral individuals of Kant. No heed is given to Kant's commitment to autonomy. Persons, and more importantly the relations between persons, are real enough, but with no deep subjectivity.

We could suggest, then, that functionalist language echoes the modalism of Western theological thought from Tertullian to the Scholastics. But this would be unfair because, while such Augustinian language—for example, of *vinculum caritatis* and *relatio subsistens*—can be said to be modalistic and impersonal when talking of the Persons in the Trinity (cf., *De Trinitate*)—persons did at least, in Augustine's schema, have being and content.

Sociological functionalists, on the other hand, conceive of persons who are empty in the literal sense of "sounding through" (*personare*); and if we look also to the symbolic-interactionists, this emptiness remains (at least for Goffman); for reality can now be read off from the external role-playing of actors which constitutes their very personas. In short, what we find with much sociology is a depersonalization process whereby even the individual

---

37. Neurath, "Sociology and Physicalism."

as a thinking, moral, feeling subject is bracketed away in the quest for a "science of the social."

From Boethius' *individua substantia rationalis* to Kant's autonomous man of practical reasoning, therefore, we can see the emergence of the modern concept of a person as individualistic, rational, and moral (or hedonistic in not a few cases). At its worst, sociology took the husk of that individuality and made of it a "thing," "co-ordinate," or "unit," or "atom." In this respect sociology denied Enlightenment individualism at the very moment of giving lip-service to it.

On the other hand, when sociology has not reified the individual to the status of a social construct or employed a biological reductionism,[38] it has reoriented itself to something that bears an "elective affinity" to Kantian individualism. Thus, we can justly praise Weber's sociology for resisting the reification of functionalism and the impersonal collectivism of Marx. Indeed, stemming from Weber, and what John Rex has called the "action frame of reference,"[39] there has been a long development of sociological enquiry that has attempted to give back to human beings the dignity of interiority—and hence of rationality—while insisting on the interrelatedness of individuals to each other.

Within this tradition, and excepting of course the best elements of the Frankfurt School, it is difficult to think of any other branch of sociology than the neo-phenomenological school of Alfred Schutz[40] and Peter Berger[41] that has come closer to seeing personhood as neither individualism nor empty sociality. Perhaps the neo-phenomenologists never quite escape Kant's moral individualism, and perhaps they are over-impressed with the logical primacy of consciousness over the objective material world, but at least they try to hold in tension both the communality and distinctiveness of people in interaction.

On the other hand, despite both their understanding that human beings *qua* individuals are always social beings, and their dialectical attempt to see the culture *in* the ego and the ego *in* the culture, the neo-phenomenologists fail to relate persons to community, nor indeed do they have any strong sense of fellowship as constitutive of personhood. Their perspective ultimately fails to provide an adequate notion of the person, for what is needed is not a "dialectic of social and individual," which will achieve—or

---

38. A classic example of this is Malinowski, *A Scientific Theory of Culture*; a contemporary example would be E. O. Wilson, *Sociobiology*.

39. Rex, *Problems of Sociological Theory*.

40. Schutz, *The Phenomenology of the Social World*.

41. Berger and Luckmann, *The Social Construction of Reality*; and Berger, *Facing Up to Modernity*.

become—personhood; what is needed is coinherence between a socialized human species and discrete, self-conscious and acting members of that species.

But those of us who are looking for new directions in theological anthropology should be grateful, however, to the neo-phenomenologists for two things.

First, Berger recaptures the notion, articulated by the early Marx, that humanity is not an abstraction (nor is it the social organism of Comte); rather, it is "fellow-humanity": without the social there is no individual, and without the individual there is no society.

Second, the neo-phenomenologists have restored the centrality of language to human existence. Considering that it is difficult even to imagine culture without recognizing the primacy of language, it is surely extraordinary that sociologists have paid so very little attention to it. True, the so-called ethnomethodological school of Harold Garfinkel did attempt a radical analysis of speech-acts in terms of the rules of conversation and other forms of discourse.[42] But, like some sociolinguists, they tended to divorce the speech-act from the speaking actor (as the invention of writing was able to divorce the text from the interactional contact of the speakers/hearers in oral culture). This separation of the utterer from the utterance led at its most extreme to an understanding of the person as the artful producer of the rules of language. (Therefore, if we can usefully say that Goffman's person is a collection of masks, we can with equal utility pronounce the ethnomethodologists' person a "bundle of speech practices.") An even more radical linguistic turn can be found in the French post-modernist writers.[43] Nevertheless, the realization by the neo-phenomenologists that there must be a cognitive sociology[44] that takes account of language is an essential missing ingredient in the quest for understanding personhood.

CONCLUSION

Despite all its deficiencies, and its basic inability adequately to account for persons as other than individuals or empty social units, there are scattered

42. Garfinkel, *Studies in Ethnomethodology*; Sacks, Schegloff, and Jefferson, "A Simplest Systematics for the Organization of Turn-Taking for Conservation."

43. Indeed, these writers have attacked the whole notion not only of a developed personhood, but of Enlightenment individualism. See Jürgen Habermas' analysis of Foucault, Derrida, and Lyotard in his *The Philosophical Discourse of Modernity*. For a critique of similar influences in cognitive sociology, see my "Between Scylla and Charybdis: 'Analysis' and Its Heroic Quest for That Which is No-Thing," 73–85.

44. Cf., Cicourel, *A Cognitive Sociology*.

throughout sociology enough clues about personhood to help construct a theological anthropology. Taken at random, these clues include the following:

1. Persons have a culture: a person is always a person for someone or in relation to someone.

2. Persons cannot be said to be an asocial "I."

3. Persons cannot be said to be a socialized "me" without reference to other socialized "selves."

4. Persons have a language: communion is related to communication.

As we stated earlier, the members of the Frankfurt School gathered these clues together more succinctly than most sociologists. It is therefore not strange that Jürgen Moltmann, influenced as he is by Horkheimer, Habermas, and Adorno, should have used their insights to "socialize" the Holy Trinity in his later work. We can see, for example, how his *The Crucified God*[45] is an attempt to construct a theodicy of the Trinity; however, we can also see how the "patri-compassion" of the Father in the suffering of the Son dominates the cross-event in such a way that the Holy Spirit is virtually a *deus absconditus*. The Frankfurt School's approach to the person helped Moltmann to change this position and the *perichoresis* of John of Damascus also played a key role, so that by the time of *The Trinity and the Kingdom of God*[46] he arrives at a Trinity of communion: a coinherence of persons in which the Spirit plays a full part. (Does the more satisfactory treatment of the Trinity in this book mean, we wonder, if Moltmann has also reconsidered his unsatisfactory account of the suffering of the Father in the atoning work of the Son in *The Crucified God*? It might be we could conjecture, if he were to abandon his attachment to the idea that "the immanent Trinity is the economic Trinity.")

But if sociology has proved itself useful in constructing an adequate theological anthropology, a view 'from below' as it were it needs clues from patristic trinitarian theology, a view 'from above' in order to arrive at an anthropology consonate with a true notion of personhood.

Here, any fertile suggestions of such a theology will have to be mediated through the concept of the *imago dei*. But here also, of course, lies the problem: arguably, the triplicity of memory, will, and mind of Augustine's *vestigial trinitatis* has led both to the reinforcement of modalistic approaches to the Trinity (which characterizes so much of Western Trinitarian

---

45. Moltmann, *The Crucified God*.
46. Moltmann, *The Trinity and the Kingdom of God*.

thinking) and was the beginning of the long anthropological trek towards the person as individual that had so dominated our philosophy and jurisprudence since the eighteenth century.

The Cappadocian approach "from above," coupled with a sociology "from below," seems, at the very least, to point to an *imago dei* that is not individualistic. The *imago dei* is, of course, an iconic metaphor: the creatures are *like* the Creator; they bear His *image* and stamp (character); they do not share the nature of the prototype (certainly there is no partaking of the divine nature without the divine adoption by the Spirit). Nevertheless, even though we can say that the likeness has been virtually lost and the image made opaque through the fall, this is no reason to go as far as to say that we therefore have *no* clue as to the nature of God's being in Himself, and there is therefore no excuse for saying that we cannot construe the character of the *imago dei.*

If, however, we want to apply the *koinonia* of God's communion to persons created in His image, then we also have to begin to work with an understanding of personhood as constituted by membership and fellowship, combining the distinctiveness of being with a communality of nature. We may be reluctant heirs of the fathers' Platonic dualism of universals and particulars, but we are not yet sufficiently advanced in our understanding of personhood simply to abandon all talk of *ousia, physis, hypostasis,* and *perichoresis* as hopelessly outmoded and quaint. Indeed, to translate the tenets of classic Trinitarian thought into modern personalist language may very well be one of the major tasks of modern theology.[47] This task necessarily includes the *construction* of such a personalist language, for which we have yet to find.

But we would also need to consider other vital topics in Trinitarian theology in order to adequately ground theological anthropology (e.g., God's *aseity,* freedom, creativeness, and love). Further, we would need to consider more fully the following questions: How does the *imago dei* in human society correspond to God's Trinitarian community? In what sense is the church, as the *ecclesia,* the icon of divine love? Is human personhood only realizable eschatologically?

47. In order to create a new personalist language from the language of Greek ontology, it would seem to me necessary that (a) patristic thought should be translated into a superior language form (not merely contemporary), and (b) that this translation would occur without loss of information. This, I would suggest, is analogous to Bertrand Russell's attempt to translate ordinary language into the physical terms of logical atomism. While we could argue that physicalism, or "the thing" language, was a superior, more logical form to ordinary language, Russell eventually found that he could not make the transition without loss of information; see Yehoshua Bar-Hillel's seminal paper "Indexical Expressions."

These are the problems we need to explore, but the starting-point for our theological anthropology is the same starting-point as for our understanding of the economic Trinity: the person of Christ himself. It is out of the internal logic of the incarnation that God reveals to us his divine being and his response to fallen human nature. It is only in the Christ-event that the Kantian division between the noumenal and the phenomenal can be bridged: where matter and spirit coinhere, where human and divine natures partake in undivided personhood.

Therefore, it may very well also be the case that if it is true, in Barth's memorable phrase, that there is "no going behind the back of Jesus to God," it is equally true that there is no going back behind the back of Jesus to human persons.[48]

48. I would like to thank David Mackinder for his help in preparing this essay for publication.

ECUMENICAL THOUGHTS
ON CHURCH AND CULTURE

17

SECTARIAN REACTIONS

Pluralism and the Privatization of Religion

(1992)

There is something deliciously decadent about futurology. It is delicious because it enables us to indulge our fantasies, ride our hobbyhorses, and say virtually anything we choose. It is decadent because such deliciousness encourages self-indulgence at the expense of truth. This is not only true for what passes as prophetic punditry: it is true also for predictive social science. Social science has not found a sufficiently rigorous methodology to control the manifold variables of social behavior, nor has it been able to demonstrate that social prediction is even possible.

It is now old hat, but still true, that predictions made in public run the risk that the public will either falsify them or fulfill them. Marxist forecasts of the collapse of capitalism fall into this category: after all, both the bourgeoisie and the proletariat have a vested interest in the outcome of this prediction.

These preliminary remarks are a necessary caveat for an essay of this kind because I want to make no claims that anyone, least of all me, can make accurate guesses about the future of British Christianity. Most social science works with *ex post facto* analyses: with the benefit of (a) an adequate explanatory theory, and (b) fairly clear data, we can with some perspicacity and rigor discern the patterns of religious life in the past. Max Weber's work on the Protestant work ethic and capitalism would be paradigmatic of this approach.[1] We might want to say that the work on the development of sectarianism, such as early Methodism or classical Pentecostal movements, under certain conditions, is likely to develop in the future.

We might even, when we are being religionists, change gears and move from descriptive social science to the prescriptive mode, and say that we can learn from the lessons of history. It is a feature, for example, of the so-called house-church movement that its members are aware of the mistakes of past sectarian history and are determined to avoid the fate of their precursors. (On the whole, it has to be said, they look like they are failing.[2])

But even this sort of talk, while legitimate, is not without its problems. I agree with C. S. Lewis, who believed that the only lesson of history is that there are no lessons of history.[3] Certainly we should avoid the often untested belief that the past is the known crucible for the knowable future. And the idea that we can at least talk of linear projections of present trends is comforting as long as one is convinced that history is linear.

I have my doubts whether such a conviction is founded on a solid basis. It belongs more to the ideological baggage of philosophical determinism, and its more congenial cousin probability theory, than to reality. Many future events have the strange habit of contradicting trends and projected forecasts. For example, who would have predicted that the Arabs would take over their own oil and change the face of Western capitalism? Who could have foreseen that Communist Eastern Europe would collapse like a pack of cards? How many political commentators would have ever believed that Michael Foot would become the leader of the Labor Party or that Margaret Thatcher would become the longest serving Prime Minister of this century? And how many of us who are participant observers of contemporary religion would had marked George Carey down on our cards as the man most likely to succeed Runcie as the Archbishop of Canterbury?

When it comes to pinpointing the accuracy of particular social, religious, and political events, most pundits are as sophisticated and as reliable as the carpet bombing of American B-52s.

The future is an open texture of possibilities, both in terms of empirical history and what used to be called (until the poststructuralists deconstructed it) meta-history. Even those of us who still take eschatology seriously would be wiser in my opinion to see it as the fulfillment of creation rather than as the end of time. To take the latter view is to run the risk that we can plot the course, start the countdown, or, at least, read the timetable.

1. Weber, *The Protestant Ethic and the Spirit of Capitalism.*
2. Walker, *Restoring the Kingdom.*
3. Lewis, "De Descriptione Temporum," 3.

On examination, searching for the keys to the future becomes not an exercise in history or theology, but a retreat into historicism and teleology. In this respect, many Christian futurologists are little different from Marxist sociologists.

Such a long prolegomenon is not intended to put a dampener on the proceedings so I can say that life is chaos and all we can offer in terms of forecasting is spitting in the wind. On the contrary, we can still offer educated guesses rather than silly ones, informed opinions rather than ignorant ones, rationally considered options rather than random skips of fantasy. This is less exacting than science and less compelling than oracles, but it is also less pretentious and more recognizably human. Indeed, in this book we have been asked to share our hopes as well as cast the runes.[4] This, it seems to me, is still delicious, but not decadent: for without hope there is no future worth predicting.

SECULARIZATION AND PLURALISM

Out of the many possible changes over the next thirty years, I have chosen to concentrate on what I would like to call the potential shape of Christian organization. In abstract, my thesis is that sectarianism will increase at the expense of traditional Christianity, though I believe that there will be a minority opinion, mainly of theologians and intellectuals, who will want to embrace religious pluralism, not merely as a fact, but as good in itself. My hope for the future is that British Christianity will avoid both options.

What kind of future Christianity will have in Britain is one thing, but it is important to begin with the prerequisite argument that religion itself will have a future. When sociology began in the nineteenth century with the positivism of Auguste Comte and the socialism of Karl Marx, evolutionary models were all the rage. For Comte, history passed through three stages, the theological or fictitious, the metaphysical or abstract, and the scientific or positive. The last stage, which Comte understood to be not so much the modern age, but rather the final destination of human history, would witness the disappearance of religion as rational and scientific certainties dissolved metaphysical speculations into inalienable facts.

If Comte's positivism was unambiguously determinist, we find a more typical sociological response to religion in the work of Max Weber and Ernst Troeltsch. They were keenly aware of the disintegration of Christendom and the structural decline of Christianity in Europe. For them, the very processes of modernity—industrialization, bureaucratization, social

---

4. "This book" is Willmer, ed., *20/20 Visions: The Futures of Christianity in Britain*.

mobility—undercut traditional authority, which was the hallmark of pre-capitalist culture. Religious authority, they believed, declined as it became urbanized and modernized, for modernization, in dissolving rural communities, also dissolved the sacred *Weltanschauung* that traditional communities upheld.

For many of the classical sociologists, it was not so much philosophical rationality or scientific thinking that they saw as the direct threat to religious authority (this was more the line that the logical positivists, following Comte and Mach, were to take). They saw the decline of religious authority as bound up with the functional rationality of modern living, where the eternal verities and numinous qualities of Judaic Christianity were repressed by the materiality and facticity of the scientific and technical culture.

Following Weber, Troeltsch, and to a lesser extent Durkheim and Marx, many religionists as well as some sociologists have tended, until recently, to buy into a "secularization thesis" that insisted that religion was in inexorable decline. Such a thesis has been particularly compelling in Britain. Church attendance has been continually dropping from the beginning of industrialization to the present time, so that today approximately 10–12 percent of the population regularly attends church or worship.

As we enter the 1990s, however, we can see that such a frankly unsophisticated view—but still the popular one—of secularization is problematic. If, for example, it is the rational processes of capitalism, or industrialization, that has caused this decline in religion, why is it that in North America nearly half the population regularly attends church? Furthermore, there is recent empirical evidence that British church attendance is on the increase. Even the Church of England has shown a slight upturn on what had seemed to be its slippery spiral to extinction.[5] More noticeably, the Baptist Union and the evangelical and charismatic movements are experiencing substantial growth. As we shall see later, this is a more significant indicator of future change than the unexpected blip on the downward graph of Anglican church attendance.

But in Britain, since the Second World War, we have seen home-grown religion augmented by the steady immigration of cultural groups that adhere to other world faiths. More recently, we have seen the import of numerous, albeit small, new religious movements. This has fuelled the phenomenon we usually call "cultural pluralism," and, in so doing, has led to an increase of religious life in Britain.

---

5. There is a 1.5 percent increase according to the *Church of England Yearbook*. The statistics do not make it clear, but it would seem likely that the major growth is at the charismatic/evangelical end of the church. This is undoubtedly true of the growth within the Baptist Union.

Perhaps the most glaring weakness of the popular version of secularization, however, has been its over-concentration on institutional decline as measured by church membership. We need to remind ourselves that every survey on religious belief in Britain since the *New Society Report* in 1964 has shown that while 10 percent or so of the population attend church, 75–90 percent of the population insists that they believe in God.

Since the 1960s, sociologists of religion have shown an increasing interest in what has variously been called "invisible," "latent," or "incipient" religion. Canon Bailey's work, for example, demonstrates that while institutional Christianity is under threat, religiosity everywhere abounds.[6] People are incurably superstitious, and there is not only a fierce remnant of folk religion but also an increasing interest in the paranormal, the preternatural, and alternative belief systems.

On an impressionistic level, I have noticed over the last few years how students of religion are often indifferent to denominational Christianity and yet remain fascinated with religion; spirituality is popular with many of them, but this is often divorced from the rigors of theology. They are interested in aesthetics and mysticism, but openly hostile to dogmatic beliefs. There seems to be little embarrassment when talking of wholeness or holistic approaches, but an acute unease when talking of holiness. Religiosity, then, is welcomed by them, but it is diffuse and freewheeling. It is perhaps closer to that pluralistic phenomenon some are calling the "New Age."

The New Age is not yet a religious movement, in my opinion, but rather a mood of resistance to modernity; it is a mutational reincarnation of the counter-culture of the 1960s—part of the Greening of the Age where spells, smells, and bells mingle in jolly confusion. Just as people are increasingly trying aromatherapy to complement their chiropractors, so crystals and mantras are augmenting traditional religious artifacts and prayers.

I think we can say categorically that it is mistaken and misleading to suggest religiosity will disappear or decline in the future: it may very well flourish. The question is not, therefore, will there be religion, but what *sort* of religion will there be? And of course an obvious short answer is that it will be diverse, syncretistic, and volatile, as one would expect in a culturally diverse society. Britain is part of the global village and can no longer be understood in isolation from or without reference to cultural trends worldwide.

But it is at this point that I want to interpolate that there have been aspects of secularization that will affect all future religion in Britain and particularly Christianity. This has been called by Dobbelaere, among others,

6. Bailey, "Religion of a Secular Society."

"laicization," and it is bound up with a structural understanding of plural-ism and the privatization of religious life.[7]

Laicization, an untranslatable French neologism, denotes the fact that Christianity as the institutional church of Europe has been swung by the processes of modernity away from the center of social and cultural life and into its own privatized and peripheral sphere. Today in Britain, Christian religion survives, like all other religions, as a leisure activity or as an ideo-logical preference, but it has virtually no legitimate voice in the public mar-ket place. It has either been forced out, or it has voluntarily left, the public arenas of government, education, welfare, and the scientific and technical bureaucracies.

Modernity is in fact typified by the fracture between its public and private life. This is one of the ways it is differentiated from earlier cultures, such as feudalism, where the split between public and private, especially at the face-to-face level of village life, was virtually non-existent. Laicization has helped to facilitate the dichotomy of public and private in most Western cultures, leading to what is in effect a "structural pluralism."

We tend to think of pluralism these days either as a plurality of cultures and religions, or if we are theologians, we might be more familiar with, say, the theological plurality of a John Hick.[8] But it is structural pluralism that creates the institutional matrix in which cultural and theological pluralism flourishes.

That is to say, cultural and theological pluralism reside firmly in the private half of modernity's structural bifurcation. The private hemisphere is the world of family, leisure, sexuality, voluntary associations (including religion), and the personal search for meaning. The public hemisphere, to restate and expand what I said earlier, is the setting for the institutions of the modern state, professions, the shop-floor, and technological rationality, or what Martin Buber would have called the "I-It" relation, characterizes life in the public arena. It is often experienced by modern citizens as objective, but impersonal and alienating, so that the private world becomes a sanctuary where relationship—the "I-Thou" relations of Buber—can be sought.[9] The privatized world of meaning, where religion has now made its home, tends to become more subjective and have more expressivist modes of discourse than the public world.

Because of the privatizing effects of structural pluralism, it is no lon-ger accurate to call Britain a Christian nation if by that we mean a total

---

7. Dobbelaere, "Secularization: A Multi-Dimensional Concept'"
8. Cf. Hick, *The Myth of Christian Uniqueness.*
9. Buber, *I and Thou.*

culture—both public and private—that is nurtured and schooled by a Christian worldview. This is not to say that there was ever a time when Britain was deeply Christian. Rather, it is to say that British society was permeated by Christian values and supported by Christian institutions that brooked no serious rivals.

Turning to cultural pluralism we can say that institutionally it is facilitated in the private world by modern urbanization, where social groups and individuals of all kinds live in proximity together but without the common rural ties of family, kinship, territory, and traditional religion.

Different social classes, interest groups, and ethnic minorities jostle for attention and recognition in a world marked no longer by homogeneity, but heterogeneity; not cultural solidarity, but cultural diversity. Whether there is any longer an identifiable British culture is a moot point, but there are certainly many British subcultures. Mass media not only reflects this diversity, but helps foster it, so that even those still living in rural communities have access to and feel part of this cultural mélange. Indeed, the electronic media has the unique role in society of belonging to the public world, while promoting the cultural diversity of its private citizens.

It remains to be seen whether Christianity will ultimately embrace pluralism or seek to reject it, but it is important to realize that plurality, both structural and cultural, is the great social fact with which Christianity has to contend in the future. Indeed, it is pluralism, in its richness, confusion, and diversity that is shaping the future of Christianity in Britain.

WHAT WILL BE THE FUTURE SHAPE OF CHRISTIANITY IN BRITAIN?

In the light of this pluralism, I believe that sectarianism is the most likely development of Christian organization in the future. This, I concede, does not sound like good news; but wishful thinking is the parent of self-fulfilling prophecy and should play no part in forecasting, however inexact, our efforts may be.

Sects have proliferated in the nineteenth and twentieth centuries as a response to the very processes of modernity that undermine institutional religion. Secularization does not cause modern sects, but its oppositional force to Christianity helps facilitate them as agents of religious resistance. Of course, as sects develop against the spirit of the age—or in order to rescue an apostate or lukewarm Christian tradition—they habitually splinter into new movements. This fragmentation then itself facilitates cultural pluralism, which continues to undermine the legitimacy and plausibility of Christianity in British society.

Nevertheless, although modern sects are initially unintended consequences of secularization that in turn become part of the problem of cultural pluralism they do have admirable survival features. As resistance movements against the larger society, they seek to conserve their original vision against the encroachments of apostates and secularizers. Sects do not typically conform to the world: rather, they seek to conform the world to themselves. In practice, this means the creation of a bulwark against plurality. This can either lead to an inward-looking preservation society in which others are excluded, or it can lead to an aggressive recruitment agency in which the sect competes with other cultural agencies for personnel. Christians usually call this evangelism.

Broadly, churchmen and women are usually resistant to the idea of the sect, thinking of it as odd, theologically deviant, or bigoted. But Weber's definition of a sect as the "believer's church . . . solely as a community of personal believers of the reborn and only these," fits nascent Christianity very well.[10] The great Puritan Congregationalist John Owen, in coining the phrase "the gathered church," was enunciating the very voluntary principle that Weber and Troeltsch also understood to be the essence of sectarianism.[11]

It is true that sects have a bias towards triumphalism and exclusivism, but they are a successful recipe for survival in a situation of either persecution or adversity. The sect (unlike the broader church, which Weber saw as "a sort of trust foundation for supernatural ends, an institution necessarily including the just and the unjust"[12]) does not rely on natural community for its continued growth, nor does it overtly compromise with the secular forces of society: it creates community by association and, as I have already mentioned, forms an enclave of believers against the assault of alternative beliefs.

Structural and cultural pluralism will erode traditional Christianity at a faster rate than it will erode sectarianism, for pluralism undermines the cultural embeddedness of natural communities, such as the parish; but it is less successful against voluntary associations. Furthermore, the very openness of churches has already led them not only to embrace the secular world with increasing eagerness, but also to internalize its beliefs and

---

10. Quoted in Hill, *A Sociology of Religion*. 47.

11. Cf. John Owen, *Eshcol, or Rules of Direction for the Walking of the Saints in Fellowship.*

12. Weber, *A Sociology of Religion*, 47.

methodologies. It is in Anglicanism, Methodism, and the United Reform Church, and increasingly in Catholicism, that we have seen such succession of (usually liberal) philosophical and political fashions. This can be applauded or condemned on ideological grounds, but it is not unreasonable to assume that broadening out and embracing plurality will dissipate the distinctiveness of Christianity as a subculture and render it vulnerable to infiltration, take-over, or annihilation by its competitors. (In this respect, Islam would seem to have more nous than most of its rivals.)

Inward-looking sects, like diaspora churches, may be guilty of a siege mentality, but their very watchfulness and paranoia keeps them alive in a world hostile to absolute claims. But is this to be the future of Christianity? A head-down retreatist sort of religion where the gospel is divided into a thousand sectarian scraps, each snatch dimly echoing a distorted recording of the original but unfinished story?

Well, we must hope not, though *in extremis* such a situation would be better than no scraps at all, as we are reminded in Ray Bradbury's futuristic novel *Fahrenheit 451*, where, in a world denied access to books, men and women literally become the chapters of classical and sacred texts by committing fragments of the literary tradition to memory. We should not be too sanguine about the unlikely possibility of this, for the thrust of MacIntyre's *After Virtue* and Bloom's *The Closing of the American Mind* is that the survival of objective truth in a pluralistic society is already in question.

But over the next three decades we are not going to witness Christianity in a state of inertia or sectarian retreat: on the contrary, we are going to see sectarian expansion at the expense of the historic institutions. Or, to be more exact, historic institutions will also grow in so far as they choose to behave in a manner usually associated with evangelistic sects.

As we enter what Pope John Paul first called "the Decade of Evangelization," despite the fact that many historical churches have not the first idea of how to evangelize or whether they should in fact evangelize, there seems to be evidence of the beginnings of a British pragmatic "have a go" mentality. It is not so much that there is a deep commitment to the *euangelion*, but the logic of evangelism, to borrow a phrase of William Abraham,[13] means for many church leaders that most blessed of results: church growth (or, in the nomenclature of one member of the Church of England Board of Mission and Unity, "bums on seats!")

Therefore, while Catholics and Anglicans either dither or genuinely doubt as to whether and how to expand, charismatic Christians have already stolen a march on them.

---

13. Abraham, *The Logic of Evangelism*

Charismatics, and increasingly these days this tends to be the majority of evangelicals, have remained faithful to a version of Christian orthodoxy while enthusiastically adopting the trappings of modernity. This has all the hallmarks of a winner, like the advert that proclaims "a traditional service in the modern manner." While in the last thirty years many intellectuals have moved from the death of God, through New Testament demythologizing and existentialist angst, on to either liberationist/feminist theology, theological pluralism, or post-modernist playfulness, charismatics have been attempting to drag alive and kicking what they think is the New Testament worldview—complete with miracles and demons—across the uncrossable ditch of the Enlightenment and re-present it in the streets of Leeds and London, where last year 250,000 of them waved their fist at the devil and shouted "Make Way for King Jesus!"

Postmodernity may cut a dash at Clare College, Cambridge, but it does not cut much ice in the suburbs and inner cities of Britain where the Christian fellowships of both yuppies and the underclass seem to prefer jollification to playfulness, supernatural power to *différence*, and gospel narrative to nihilism.[14] This is not intended as a cynical aside: it is my conviction that intellectual fashions—however profound—have little immediate effect on popular culture. And whatever else we may think about it, charismatic Christianity has chosen to do its evangelism in the streets and the market place rather than the rarefied atmosphere of the senior common room.

This, it seems to me, offers not only a lesson to liberal intellectuals, but also to more conservative ones. The movement cloaked around Bishop Lesslie Newbigin known as "Gospel and Culture," of which I am proud to be a part, is mistaken if it believes that it will significantly alter the culture's receptivity to historic Christianity by persuading more intellectuals to join its gang.

Charismatic Christianity is the fastest growing measurable phenomenon on the British religious scene, and I can see no evidence that it is about to slow down. It is also the most self-publicizing, and in many ways the most innovative.

Until the 1960s, this charismatic Christianity—which is the gentrified title of Pentecostalism—was thought by most sociologists to be a religion of the working classes. Pentecostalism, however, has shown itself capable of extraordinary mutation. Remaining phenomenologically much the same as it was when it began at the turn of the century—with its emphasis on speaking in tongues, prophecies, healings, and miracles—it has been grafted into the middle classes, becoming what might be called a sectarian implant in

14. Cf. Cupitt, *Creation Out of Nothing*; and Taylor, *Erring: A Postmodern A-Theology.*

the heart of the historic churches and forming a "church within a church." This neo-Pentecostalism usually advertises itself in the mainline denominations as the "renewal."[15]

Given this development we must not assume that we now have the measure of Pentecostalism, for charismatic religion is essentially adaptive. It takes root in alien soils and yet continues to plant out under its own banner, and not only with the fecundity of the older sects, but also as a new breed that has the hybrid characteristics of both sect and new religious movement. (The so-called "faith movement," known colloquially as "health and wealth," would be a successful example of this hybrid.)

But modern Pentecostalists have also adopted and adapted from Anglican evangelicalism the methods of commerce and business in order to promote their message. While British charismatics do not yet have satellite TV, nor are they as wealthy as their American counterparts, they already major on high technology, build audio and video ministries around their many charismatic stars, create massive jamborees such as the Spring Harvest Festivals, and promote populism, as we have already seen, by calling out thousands of people to march on the streets. In 1991 and 1992 it is planned to extend the British marches into the cities of Europe.

Already there are signs that some of the self-styled "new churches," such as the group known as the restorationists, are following the American trend to create mega-churches similar to the Church on the Rock in Dallas, Texas, or the Crystal Cathedral near Anaheim, California. While there is nothing yet to compare in size with these churches, which can boast some 5,000 members, the Abundant Life Church in Bradford and Bracknell Baptist Church, are examples of purpose-built buildings that cater to one thousand regular worshippers. Under the direction of "apostle" Terry Virgo, Clarendon Villas in Hove is a refurbished older church with a congregation in excess of one thousand members.

When Pentecostalism began in the early 1900s it was a minority religion for the dispossessed. It has now come into its inheritance and, as it leaves the twentieth century, it is arguably the major religious force in Christianity, for it has broken the boundaries of class, race, and nation in a way that few branches of Christianity have been able to achieve. As David Martin's acclaimed study of South American Pentecostalism has shown, it looks as if charismatic religion will be as significant in that continent as Methodism has been in ours.[16]

---

15. See the chapter in this book "The Theology of the Restoration House Churches" to learn more about the renewal.

16. Martin, *Tongues of Fire*.

Religious revivals, as the Great Awakenings of America and early Methodism demonstrate, do not drop out of the sky: they are socially organized and all the signs are that British charismatics are organizing. They have come to dominate the burgeoning Evangelical Alliance and can put 80,000 people into the Spring Harvest residential holiday camps and call up 8,000 people to attend prayer meetings. At an international conference at Brighton in 1991 they were able to persuade the Archbishop of Canterbury to attend and the distinguished German theologian Jürgen Moltmann to address them.

Ideologically, charismatic Christianity does not overtly capitulate either to secularism or to pluralism. It stands for the certainties of "that old-time religion," and treats other religionists, not as equals, but as fair game in an open season of "hunting, shooting, and fishing." Some of the new churches consider the historic denominations moribund and invite people to leave and join them, or stay and renew their old churches according to the pattern of the new ones. And so the "church within the church" takes root again and the sectarian spores float across the formal boundaries of both church and sect.

Ironically, the charismatic sense of excitement, its preference for experience over doctrine, the tendency to value novelty against tradition, and its restless liturgy, leave it open to the secular society it wishes to foreclose. More tellingly, its almost "show-biz" obsession with the big-name charismatic stars, and its reliance on management and commercial techniques, renders it guilty of the old sectarian charge of worldliness. It preaches against the spirit of the age out of the spirit of the age. It stands up for orthodoxy, but in the rags of modernism.

CONCLUSION

I believe that Cardinal Suenens was right when he recently stated that Christianity can no longer rely on benign culture to see it through.[17] It will make no significant contribution in the hurly burly of cultural pluralism without a distinctive voice and a dedicated discipleship. In this respect, I think that sectarianism in the voluntaristic sense in which Weber understood it is not to be violently condemned.[18]

17. Walker, "Interview with Cardinal Leon-Joseph Suenens," 73.

18. In the case of many black Pentecostalist churches, it is their sectarian structures that have enabled them to resist the encroachments of the white society, both religious and secular. See also Mohabir, *Building Bridges*.

I believe, though, for the religious pluralist such a view is itself sectarian, that Christianity is not merely a good religion (actually, it is often not that): it is the truest one. Not merely for me, or for my set, but for the whole world. This also means that it is public truth, not my private opinion or some kind of permissible "form of life"; it is not to be seen as an option, or a preference, or a part of the colorful tapestry of pluralistic Britain, or a playful pastiche of post-Enlightenment possibilities. It is the gospel of hope for a fallen culture.

But while I believe that there is nothing wrong with being tough-minded, Christianity is not only about "right belief": it is also about good practice. We need, therefore, to be tender-hearted. As Christians we are called to love our neighbors—indeed, our enemies—and not to shoulder them aside.

Charismatic Christianity has a habit of being impatient with other expressions of Christianity. The new churches in particular seem to want to be part of the larger Christian body as long as they can lead that body by the nose. When one of the leaders of these churches can tell us that the new charismatic phalange will have to evangelize heathen Britain because no one else is doing it, this seems to be not so much a question of myopia, but a bid for power.

Indeed, my greatest fear for the future of British Christianity is that aggressive sectarianism of this kind will result not in evangelizing secular society, but in inhibiting the ecumenical drive for the unity of the church. Most of the spectacular growth of the new charismatic churches in the last ten years, for example, has been at the expense of other churches. Transfer growth is not what the Pope John Paul had in mind when he called for a "Decade of Evangelism."

If Christianity cannot harness her impatient but powerful sectarian spirit for the good of the whole church, then the unbridled sectarian spirit will do what unbridled sectarianism always does: break away from the common herd and run wild, taking fierce pride in having refused, unlike the other tame creatures, to be broken by the forces of apostasy and establishment. And with the certainty that it is conserving or restoring the truth, the sect becomes the harbinger of schism and discerption.

There is an extreme irony here. Sectarian Christianity rejects cultural pluralism, in contradistinction to much liberal Protestantism that embraces it either with joy or resignation. But the net result is the same: they both become swallowed up in the privatized world of structural pluralism where they participate in the babble of consumer religion and where everyone shouts their wares but no one knows how to conduct a common conversation.

It is this societal fracture, communal disorganization, and personal disintegration that are the very negative effects of the modernity which Christianity is called to redeem and heal. There can be no greater indictment of us if we remain simply part of the problem. It would seem as if linear history, as we suspected, was wrong and circularity may be right, for with this scenario we are, existentially if not literally, back to the linguistic turpitude of the Tower of Babel.

If my analysis of British society in terms of structural and cultural pluralism is correct, the great challenge Christians face in the coming decades is to break down the Tower of Babel and reconcile the public and private split in society. If the gospel is true and its light is not to be hidden, or apologized for, then it has to be not only proclaimed, but incarnated, in the structures of the culture. What sort of gospel is it if it is prophetically irrelevant in economics, government, or welfare?

Modern Christianity is still reeling from the mistakes of Erastianism and neo-Constantinianism. But the alternative to Constantine—and my hope for the future—is that British Christians will neither follow the liberal impulse and embrace pluralism as God's latest good gift, nor will they settle for aggressive and expansionist sectarianism at the expense of traditional churches. We are going to need the commitment and voluntarism of sects in order to survive, but we must reject the smugness, impatience, and exclusivity that are sects' usual corollaries.

What this will mean in practice is that we have to become missionaries to our own culture.[19] This is not an overnight affair. Like the apologists of the second century, we will need to take on the conventional wisdom of the Christian faith. Missioners accept as axiomatic that their job will be a long haul. It takes times to change thought patterns, untested traditions, and comfortable plausibility structures.

Christendom may be dead, but we who are its survivors dare not retreat behind the barricades of cultural isolation where we become merely one island of meaning in a vast but private sea where other islands float in splendid isolation. We are called to take the gospel to the whole culture, and that includes not only sailing to the other islands in the sea, but back to the mainland that we have left behind. We must return under the old banner of the cross, but this time we will not come to conquer but to sojourn.

---

19. This, it seems to me, is the unique contribution of Bishop Leslie Newbigin to the debate on gospel and culture. See Newbigin, *The Gospel in a Pluralist Society.*

18

Harmful Religion

(1995)

For many years I have thought that one of the silliest things I have ever heard was President Eisenhower's insistence that America should be driven by religion, although he did not care which religion it was! And yet, for a Christian, such a view is no laughing matter, for religion in itself is not necessarily good for us. Religion can mean human sacrifice to Moloch as well as self-sacrifice. It can legitimate war and genocide as well as sanction the moral values of a civilized society.

The history of Christianity in particular is one of murder as well as martyrdom. If historically it stood for the truth against what Christopher Fitzsimons Allison has called "the cruelty of heresy," it has often done so by being wickedly cruel to heretics. The modern world is arguably less blighted by such witch-hunting; and yet, we are no freer from Christian religious wars and terrorist activity than we were in the Middle Ages.

In the former Yugoslavia we see Catholic Croatians and Serbian Orthodox engaging in the "ethnic cleansing" of each other. Northern Ireland still bears the seeping scars of Protestant and Catholic tribal hatred, while in the United States millennial militias seem to be prepared to bomb Middle America into Armageddon.

When we turn our attention away from the international front to the home front, we find so often that in the apparent coziness of our local churches sin abounds. Of course, we know about and sometimes despair of the backbiting in the choir, the jealousy of the new pastor, the hypocrisy, "filthy rags" of self-righteousness. We are more reluctant, however, to explore the darker issues of how our churches relate to the power structures of the secular world, or how our religious leaders sometimes harm their flocks rather than feed them.

Recent revelations in Catholic Ireland demonstrate that harmfulness may extend to sexually molesting young children by priests. Some would say that harm has also been caused through a cover-up, or at least an unacceptable complacency, by the authorities.

The story which broke in the summer of 1992, of Anglican curate Chris Brain and the Nine O'clock Service in Sheffield, is not only one of sexual abuse and religious harm, but also appears to be one of myopia by the diocese. Of course, the authorities cannot be blamed for not knowing of the sexual misdemeanors, but leading evangelicals have suggested that they did seem curiously unconcerned about the theological deviancy of a "creation spirituality" that admittedly has its supporters, but would seem out of place in a diocese under a conservative bishop.

Such a criticism, however, needs to be balanced by other considerations. Charismatic evangelicals—rightly, in my opinion—may consider the influence of Matthew Fox to be unhelpful, but things were already going wrong in the Nine O'clock Service (NOS) when they were still under the influence of charismatic John Wimber. There was secrecy about NOS that many on the outside found odd, even though it was clearly very innovative and was subject in its earlier days to the positive influences of Robert Warren and Graham Cray.

It could also be argued in defense of the diocese that the Sheffield authorities did not wish to interfere with religious freedom. They had tolerated the Wimber "clinics"; watched with guarded interest the new directions in experimental liturgy; and when Mr. Fox appeared on the scene, they may have found his approach unorthodox, but he was, by the time of his second visit, ordained as an Episcopalian priest. It is easy to point the finger at the Sheffield diocese with hindsight, but myopia is not the same as culpability, or synonymous with a cover-up.

However, the Sheffield story reminds us that mainline Protestantism remains fiercely moralistic about sexual abuse (seen as harmful), while appearing to remain unconcerned with theological pluralism (seen as harmless). It clings to the vestiges of moralism, while appearing to abandon the revealed truth on which Christian morality depends. The idea that theological deviancy might be harmful makes no sense, of course, unless we are still committed to the idea that Christian truth sets us free, but untruth leaves us "bound up in chains."

The Study Guide of the *Forgotten Trinity* (the British Council of Churches report in 1990) argues that a misshapen theology can itself cause harm. It claims that a lopsided doctrine of the Trinity may produce a repressive patriarchy (too much Father), or a charismatic triumphalism (too much Spirit), or even a sloppy sentimentalism that trivializes the sacred (too much Son).

While there is much to recommend this approach, there is sadly no automatic link between orthodoxy and orthopraxis, between right believing and right living. An academically correct theology without a living spirituality can easily degenerate into legalism, and, in C. S. Lewis' words, "reverence itself did harm." In other words, just as antinomianism will probably lead to moral turpitude, so the imposition of sound theology, when it interferes with human dignity and freedom will probably lead to religious abuse. And we cannot argue from the empirical evidence that people of orthodox theology are more moral than those without it.

But what do we mean when we talk of religion itself being harmful or abusive? In recent years, two models of "religious harm" have begun to emerge in the United States. The first is what we might call the addiction model. After the fall-out from the televangelist scandals of the late 1980s, it was observed by many medical and psychosocial support groups that people were exhibiting all the traits of dependent personalities more usually associated with gambling and alcoholic addiction. A number of self-help groups, including Fundamentalists Anonymous, were set up to provide a support network based on the *Alcoholics Anonymous* twelve-step program. Some of the alleged symptoms of this religious addiction were:

Compulsive and excessive church attendance

An inability to think, doubt, or question authority

The inability of people to work things out for themselves

A shame-based belief that you aren't good enough for God, or that you can't do things right

A magical worldview in which God will fix everything for you.

The addiction model needs to be taken seriously. Only this week, a priest wrote to me saying that while he had to work to make some people come to church, there were others that he had to wean off church, so that they could get on with their lives. "Using" religion, like using drugs everywhere, is a substitute for coping with real life and a toxin in the spiritual bloodstream. When this happens, church becomes not a place of sanctuary, but a retreat from reality; a source of sickness, rather than healing; a place of addiction, rather than abundance.

There is much to commend the addiction model, for we know that it fits pastoral as well as clinical experience, and it allows us to extend it to the co-dependency of whole families, if not congregations. There are, however, two things about it which should make us cautious of its legitimate application.

First, this is a model much loved by liberals, who see addictive religion as essentially fundamentalist or conservative Christianity. Father Leo Booth's book, *When God Becomes a Drug,* is an example of this approach. His solution to religious addiction is a course of therapy, the setting-up of a support group, and the gradual transposition of "closed" religion to an open-ended replacement.

Does Father Booth think, we might wonder, that political correctness causes harm? Can a liberal agenda abuse when it is imposed illiberally? May a liberal gospel itself be harmful if it promises false hopes? When the people ask priests for spiritual bread and they are given therapeutic prescriptions, what will be the effects of these medicinal approaches: the loss of faith as well as an end to addiction?

Secondly, as useful as the addiction model may be in some cases, it runs the risk of turning the spotlight of religious abuse onto the individual lay person as victim, and away from the abusers: priests, elders, those invested with authority, or those who simply take authority upon themselves. If the co-dependency model of addiction holds true, it does so more often than not because people unwittingly or wittingly are manipulated in authority over them.

This leads us to the second model of harmful religion to come out of America. (It is the model that underpins the conference on religious abuse to be held at King's College London.) This model concentrates on the abuse of power and the misuse of authority.

The model has three features to recommend it. First, it is consonant with a thoroughly Christian theology. When Tom Smail, Nigel Wright, and I held our workshops in Britain on the charismatic movement, we did so under the title of "the love of power and the power of love." We were at pains to stress the vulnerable and sacrificial nature of Christian discipleship over and above triumphalism, messianic delusion, and rank power.

We wanted to show that the Christian way is always the way of the cross. Not that obsession with power, and the abuse of power, is by any means an exclusive charismatic temptation. It is the way of the devil, who wants to be God. It is the abuse of others for self-glorification or self-gratification. It is the way of fallen humanity that would "lord it over" others if only it could.

The second advantage of the abusive model is that it forces us to look at denominational Christianity, instead of imagining that harmful religion is the exclusive province of fundamentalist religion or cults. Cultish behavior can occur in the heart of the mainline churches too. This holds true for *Opus Dei* in the Roman Catholic Church and possibly for a short-time in the life of the Nine O'clock Service. In my opinion, in many a church and chapel, as well as in the cult and the coven, widespread and occasionally systematic abuse occurs, which can properly be called "harmful religion."

This can, of course, be deliberately orchestrated by unscrupulous persons, or what George Tarleton, a former "apostle" in the house church movement, once called "wrong uns"; it is likely, however, that such abuse is rare. More typically, it will result from well-meaning, misguided, or deluded authority figures, or simply through the unreflective practice of sedimented traditions and conventional wisdom. Endemic religious harm, such as incipient racism or sexual discrimination, can exist through institutional practices so long-standing as to seem hallowed by time.

Systematic religious abuse, on the other hand, more typically occurs in structures that lend themselves to manipulation and authoritarian control, rather than in structures where authority is diffuse, or where it is clearly delineated in a sensible, rational, and yet personal way. Communities that are geographically or socially isolated, and which are under an authoritarian leader, are prime candidates for abuse. However, we must realize that if this holds true for cults and exclusivist sects, it also applies to monasteries and covenanted communities. The line between saints and fanatics can be very thin.

We should also recognize that mainline churches can suffer from what we might call "*sectarian implants.*" "In-crowds" or "ginger groups" that are secretive, and are therefore not openly accountable, are breeding grounds for abuse. They hatch elitist mentalities and delusional qualities, authoritarian controls and ideologies of power. Ginger groups can pep people up, but they can also force people out.

There is a third positive feature of the abusive model of harmful religion. By concentrating more on the institutional structures and its officers, and less on individual members of lay congregations, we encourage the moral virtues of stewardship, responsibility, and accountable leadership. In addition, the model looks to the spiritual fruits of repentance and restitution, which may be more faithful to the gospel than therapeutic and counselling methodologies in combating addiction.

Nevertheless, the abusive model has its own dangers. First, when applying it to others, especially of those who are in authority, it is important not only to get our facts right, but also not to flout a judgmental spirit that in reality hides our own wrongdoing. Motes in other people's eyes always seem bigger to us because of the beams in our own.

A second danger with the model is the possibility that we will let our genuine concern to protect others from harm to interfere with legitimate religious freedom. Harmful religion is a religious belief or practice which damages or hurts somebody spiritually, mentally, or physically. Harmful religion is not religion that is not to our taste, or which we think may be mistaken in its beliefs—although as we saw earlier, for an orthodox believer heresy *is* spiritually harmful.

For those who want to limit the notion of religious harm to psychological or physical damage they will find that much reflection and discernment will be needed to define the problem. They will need to distinguish between harmfulness *per se,* and community practices that may strike the outsider as inflicting pain of some kind, but which are considered normative by members. Religious physical abuse, for example, covers the spectrum of harm from immolation to torture, from emasculation to circumcision, and even from tattooing to corporal punishment and the deprivation of food and sleep. Many Christian traditions encourage fasting. North African Christians tattoo their bodies. Jews, Arabs, and many Christian circumcise their boys.

Christians will not condone immolation, torture, and female "circumcision," but they will be divided over the other examples given above. We can see, at the very least, that harmfulness will range from strong to weak, high to low levels, the horrific to the painful, the unacceptable to the tolerable. In some cases, we may want to say that the language of harm is inappropriate.

The abusive model of harmful religion will appeal to those who are strongly committed to justice and reparation for the damage caused to others. The addiction model will appeal more to those who are committed to healing and holistic approaches. But both models are really complementary, rather than contradictory or competitive. In the New Testament, Jesus heals the sick and binds up the broken-hearted, but he also condemned the oppressive religious leaders of his day.

As for us, we are told by Jesus in terms of uncompromising severity what will happen if we harm the weak, the innocent, and especially, the children: "Whosoever shall offend one of these little ones which believe in me, it would better for him that a millstone were hanged about his neck, and that he were drowned in the depth of the sea. Woe unto the world because of his offenses, for it must need be that offenses come, but woe to that man by whom the offense cometh!" (Matt 18:6–7).

19

THE THIRD SCHISM

The Great Divide in Christianity Today[1]

(1986)

W
hen I was asked to contribute an article to *In Search of Christianity*, two images or metaphors came to mind. Firstly, I pictured an expedition organized by the Royal Geographical Society desperately seeking to find the remnants of a fast-disappearing species. No doubt some modern-day Stanley, having been misdirected to the Greater London Council's Mr. Livingstone, would press on into darkest Hertfordshire in hope (this time) of a genuine sighting of the rare genus *homo christianus*.

But while such an image is not entirely idle—in the face of the reality that less than 10 percent of the British population attend church—I found it soon superseded by a second picture. This time what came to mind was not an adventure nor quest, but a search for a good bargain.

---

1. I wrote this article in a journalistic style and with polemical intent. It was an exercise aimed at the West and was not intended to be an accurate historiography of the Christian church. To do this I would have to go into the Nestorian Schism following the Council of Ephesus in 413 AD and the rise of the so-called oriental (or non-Chalcedon) churches following the Council of Chalcedon of 451 AD—notably the Coptics of Egypt. We would also have to include the Armenian Church and the Assyrian Orthodox in this category. But as far as the West is concerned, the Schisms that have most effected the West are the Great Schism of the eleventh century, with the break between Rome and Byzantium and the Protestant Reformation of the sixteenth century, and the Third Schism, which is happening now.

Christianity is now on sale in multiform shapes and sizes. Competing in the open market with other religions, there is a bewildering yet broad choice of "real" and "best" Christianities for anyone who wants to buy. No doubt someone will soon publish "The Consumer Guide to God" so that people can pop in and out of churches with the same ease and comfort as they visit their favorite restaurants.

"You pays your money and takes your choice" surely exemplifies the "spirit of the age"; for in our culture religion is not seen as the *raison d'être* of our society and life: it is a series of options which we choose—or goods that we buy—if we feel so inclined. This plurality of religious belief and practice is often applauded as evidence of cultural maturity and tolerance. Nobody forces a version on us anymore. There are many varieties on sale vying for our attention, but we, the consumers, have the absolute power of either buying one version in preference to another or withholding payment altogether.

This present collection of essays is itself a demonstration of consumer religion: you (the broad reading public) are being offered a variety of "goodies" (perspectives) on Christianity. And we (the authors) are selling you our "lines" like so many religious peddlers in the market place. (Like the BBC's "Thought for the Day" you are being offered not the gospel but the gospel according to the Reverend so-and-so, the personal views of Ms. Suburbia, and the subjective impressions of Dr. X.)

In this sense, of course, I have to admit to being one-of-the-crowd like everybody else. While I accept the inevitability of this, and while I run the logical risk of being hoist by my own petard, I want to assert in this paper that the Christian gospel has a central core of truth that has an objective character about it. To put it in aphoristic form: Christianity is not this or that, but it can be said to be this and not that.

The purpose of this assertion, however, is not so that I can demonstrate this objectivity in a logical way, but in order that I can make out a case that the Christianity of the historic church, of the ancient creeds and sacred scriptural canons, is in danger of being swallowed by something else in the name of religious progress.

To say this is to come clean and admit two things. First, I am a traditionalist or primitive of sorts, and believe that the Christian faith is founded on biblical revelation concerning a loving God and his incarnation in the world through the historical person of Jesus Christ. Such a belief takes some swallowing today, or in any age, and cannot be demonstrated as factual in a scientific or empirical way. This is not to say, however, that such a belief is false, and certainly it is not to say that it is irrational.

The second thing to admit is that I am neither approaching this article from an Empyrean vantage point nor with the logical disinterest of a mathematical calculator. Christianity, the religion of the apostles, now tattered and divided by schism and heresy—but still bearing the marks of God's grace—has entered the most serious crisis of its two-thousand-year history. I passionately want to see that faith both survive and strengthen in the face of modern Christian alternatives.

I have chosen, therefore, polemic rather than a careful historical analysis as the medium to express both passion and conviction. The polemic—that Christendom has entered its third and most serious schism—is, I believe, true, and is based on historical argument that is rational and open to refutation. As to whether the schism is a good or a bad thing depends on which side of the present divide you stand.

To say that we have entered a crisis in Christendom, which can be characterized as a third schism, necessitates a brief mention of the first two divides, and something about the meaning of schism. "Schism" is a word that we usually associate with a breach in the unity of the visible church. The so-called Great Western Schism of 1378–1417, for example, was a break in the unity of the (Western) Catholic Church due to disputed elections to the papacy in which, until the schism was healed, there were competing popes.

As serious a schism as this was, however, it was not of the magnitude of the really great divides of Christendom. Furthermore, the word "schism" means to divide, cleave, or rend. It is this sense of major division with which I am concerned rather than the idea of a visible split. The first two great schisms of Christianity, between the Eastern and Western Churches, and the Western Reformation, were indeed visible divides. The Third Schism, because it cuts across denominations rather than between them, is not invisible (we can see it happening), but it is not yet denomination against denomination, creating visible and separate camps within Christendom.

THE FIRST SCHISM: THE DIVIDE BETWEEN THE WESTERN AND EASTERN CHURCHES

It says a great deal for our parochial worldview that Christianity is seen as a Western religion. British students of theology take some time to adjust to the fact that the Western Reformation is only part of a far more fundamental divide of the Christian church. This division has its origins in the inability of the Greek East and Latin West to cohere.

Although the official date of the Great Schism is 1054, in reality the two halves of Christendom had been pulling apart for centuries. The addition by the Latin West of the word *filioque* ("and the Son") to the Nicene creed, which now said of the Holy Spirit "who proceeds from the Father *and the Son,*" and the decision by the Roman See that the bishop there was to be seen no longer as *Primus inter pares,* but as possessing superior and unique authority in the Christian church, are the main reasons cited by Eastern Catholics (the Orthodox) for the Great Schism.

This is not untrue, but it is also the case that the nature of spirituality, liturgy, and theology increasingly developed along separate lines as Eastern and Western cultures evolved and diverged.

Henceforth, the Orthodox continued without a pope and without a reformation (to this day), and the Catholic Church—cut off from the collegiality of the Eastern sister churches—went it alone in an increasingly centralized and Westernized way. The essential tragedy of the schism was that the universal catholicity of the "one undivided church" was broken.

THE SECOND SCHISM: THE REFORMATION

The second great divide in Christendom shares with the first schism the characteristic of a gradual breaking down of catholicity. While it may be true that the Roman Catholic Church maintained a powerful hegemony throughout the early Middle Ages, its influence began to wane as Renaissance humanism, the emergence of a natural philosophy that owed little to revelation, and the rise of an embryonic capitalism, weakened the omnipresent authority of the church. The fact that Martin Luther nailed his famous principles of the Reformed faith to the door of the church at Wittenburg in 1517 is only an historical landmark in the greater reformation of medieval society.

Protestants like to see the Reformation as a great recovery: a return to New Testament Christianity. Undeniably, Protestantism has shown itself to be full of life and vigor, but it has also demonstrated that by its very nature it is schismatic. The Reformation became reformation *ad nauseum*: and modern denominationalism was born. This was inevitable while the reformers saw Protestantism as replacing the authority of the pope by the authority of the Bible. It was also the case that now every person was a "pope" who could—and did—interpret the Bible according to his own lights.

Furthermore, religious Protestantism paved the way for its own demise and the Third Schism of recent years. Once it was accepted that Scripture stood alone outside tradition, and could be interpreted correctly by anyone with a pure heart and God-given rationality, it was not too big a step to suggest that the same could be said of nature. The emergence of reasoning independent from the church, begun in the Renaissance, was accelerated under Protestantism, and heralded both the rise of the scientific method and the birth of the philosophical Enlightenment of the eighteenth century.

With the first Great Schism, the West separated from the East; the second schism, the Reformation, saw Protestantism freeing itself from the authority of the church. The Enlightenment, like Prometheus unbound, tore Western culture away from the authority of the Bible. This not only marked the beginning of modern secularism, but it also began the slow process of the Third Schism.

Since that time, Protestantism has become increasingly naked and vulnerable, as its progeny (the secular doctrines of the Enlightenment) has turned on its parent with all the fury of its Oedipal Rage.

THE THIRD SCHISM

Christianity in the Third World, and in Eastern Europe, is clearly both grow-ing and growing in a more orthodox fashion than in Western Europe and North America. It is the West where what I call the Third Schism has be-come endemic. As institutional religion has been in decline for one hundred and fifty years, and religious categories of thought have been under constant attack for the same period, this is not very surprising. It is impossible, living in the Western world, not to be influenced by the modern worldview and the mores and habits of the secular culture.

In the last twenty years, since the publication of John A. T. Robinson's *Honest To God*, the endemic nature of the Third Schism has become acute; so that today we find that a significant number of ecclesiastical leaders, theologians, and many ordinary men and women, can no longer relate to the central tenets of Christianity as traditionally understood. That is to say, growing numbers (perhaps already the majority) of people want to remain Christian in some way, despite the fact that they can no longer assent to many of the doctrines of the creeds, believe in the Bible as a reliable record of historical narratives, which includes the virgin birth and resurrection of Christ, or find credible the possibility of miracles in either the past or the present.

Despite the first two great schisms of Christianity, there was enough common ground to assert that there was a family resemblance of Christians, even though the family was separated and relationships impaired. This re-semblance was related to a certain "orthopraxis"—a way of living and acting that was seen as being connected in some way with orthodoxy, or right faith or right believing. In practice the link between these two has always been tentative. It cannot be said with certainty that ordinary Christians with little theological training have always grasped the nuances, paradoxes, and presuppositions of the theologians and doctors of the church. Indeed, it would probably be more accurate to assert that orthodoxy, insofar as it existed, was learned more through the medium of liturgy and rite than through sermons or formal treatises. It is an interesting point, for example, that the Eastern Orthodox often translates "orthodoxy" not as true *beliefs*, but as true *worship*.

Nevertheless, however true it may be that behavior and worship tell us more of the nature of Christianity than do its beliefs taken in isolation from practice, it has always been the case that the Christian faith (far more than Islam or Judaism) has been predicated upon certain beliefs that have been held to be true. Michael Goulder, now an atheist who has resigned from holy orders, makes this telling point against his friend John Hick, who remains a "Christian" yet without believing in either a Holy Trinity or a personal God.

To put the word Christian in inverted commas in this way is not in order to say something unpleasant about John Hick, but in order to register certain uncomfortableness about the use of the word Christian when applied in this way. I recall a similar lack of ease when Professor Ayer took issue with Don Cupitt's rather cavalier use of the word "God" in a discussion following the BBC television series, "The Sea of Faith." God is not a word to be used in any way we please; it has a meaning that has been sanctioned by usage. Indeed, traditional Christians would want to say that it has a content—a being-in-itself.

Or again, when a former Bishop of Durham, David Jenkins, says that he does not believe in a literal physical resurrection of Jesus from the dead, but thinks that we should understand and believe resurrection in some (unspecified) other way, what does he mean? Is his way of seeing, which is clearly not the way of orthodoxy, a different perception of the same event? A mere question of semantic differences, or is it a different gospel?

It would be absurd for a member of the Communist Party to declare to his comrades that he no longer accepted the basic tenets of Marxist-Leninism, but that he would stay in the Party. It would be simply odd for a Tory Member of Parliament to stay in office having publicly renounced free enterprise altogether. At the very least, we would want to insist that, if a woman tells us that she is a radical feminist and yet believes in the desirability of patriarchy, her position is inconsistent and logically untenable. We may, of course, think that she is just plain daft, like the man who proclaims that he is Napoleon when we know that his name is John Smith.

And yet, we find these not unreasonable common-sense observations are so often not applied to Christianity. This may be in part because

Christians these days are wary of intolerance and bigotry. Heretic-hunting is unfashionable, and certainty and truth are subservient words to authenticity and lovingness. It may be that the strange language of many modern Christians, who seem unable to feel at home with the old language (but do they believe in the same realities to which that language pointed?), is itself strong evidence that a major shift in consciousness has occurred. Perhaps, though I use this only analogously, we are witnessing a paradigm shift, a major change in worldview, from the old theological universe to a new one; rather like Newton's cosmology radically shifted to the new scientific worldview of Einstein.

I think that we are undergoing a revolution in thinking and perception that, far from being really new, is in fact the eventual triumph of Enlightenment consciousness over orthodox Christian thinking and experience—in practice, simply, a capitulation to the forces of rationalism and subjectivism. These forces have ushered in forms of Christianity entirely at odds with Christian tradition.

At times it seems that to stand on the modernist side of the divide is to see oneself as the progressive, the reformer; and the orthodox side as the counter-revolutionary, or, more appositely, the counter-reformer.

From the orthodox side of the Third Schism, the new Christianity (but not the Christians who make up this new constituency) is the enemy. To stand against it is not reactionary conservativism; it is the stance of the resistance fighter.

Battle lines are by no means firmly drawn, not least because many orthodox Christians are still busy fighting the divisions of the first two schisms. Many of them do not seem to know where the new, and crucial, barricades are. I shall return to this theme in my conclusion. But now I want to outline briefly how the Enlightenment and its consequences brought about the Third Schism.

THE ENLIGHTENMENT

It is the philosophical Enlightenment of the eighteenth century, however, that was the dawn of modern optimism, idealism, and intellectual illumination. It was the morning star of modernity without which modern democracy and republicanism would not have been born, and scientific and technological progress would not have been possible. And yet, paradoxically, the Enlightenment had its darker side: the morning star in biblical imagery is, after all, another name for Lucifer.

And yet, Protestants, as if suffering from an incurable "death wish," have not only attempted to make peace with the darkling child (their offspring), but have grasped him to their bosoms with joy. "Perhaps," they have said, "he may destroy the old religious order, but he will bring new life and make Christianity more authentic, and set it—and society—free."

But perhaps the new progeny of Protestant society had no natural filial relationship to Christianity. The child of hope seemed angelic, but was in fact a changeling: an incubus whose purpose was to draw out the lifeblood of its progenitor until it was dead.

We have all seen enough horror movies to know that the vampire first sucks the blood of his victim while she is beguiled or sleeping. After a gradual weakening and loss of blood—with only a few telltale marks to show what is really happening—the entranced somnambulist, with her lifeblood literally draining away, offers her jugular in a final abandonment to her demon lover. She then joins him, keeping the semblance of her former life, but in reality living (if we can call it living) the life of the undead.

Modern Western Christianity may not be undead yet! But a near-fatal incision began with the Enlightenment. From the eighteenth century onwards the world of the senses takes precedence over not only the supernatural world, but also the world of ideas. Newton's great synthesis of natural sciences and cosmology made allowance for a creator, but this God, having made the universe as a clockmaker constructs a clock, withdraws from his creation and leaves it running by its own inviolable laws.

The empirical world, without God, increasingly took the attention. And if there was a tension between the abstract rationality of German philosophers such as Kant and Hegel, and the more pragmatic and empiricist French and British thinkers, there was a common commitment to the primacy of self-knowledge. In Pope's words: "Know then thyself, presume not God to scan, The proper study of mankind is man."

As eternal verities were translated into rationalistic philosophy, and miracles were interpreted in the light of the new physics, orthodox doctrines of Christ's divinity and the conundrum of the Holy Trinity came under attack.

Capitalistic economic theory, utilitarianism (that old pagan hedonism in disguise), Kant's progressivism (not to mention Hegel's), and the material and phenomenal world outlook of the philosophers became embodied in the social, economic, and political structures of nineteenth-century Europe.

Modernity was born, and the ideas of the Enlightenment became the stuff of everyday life. In themselves the doctrines of the eighteenth-century philosophers carried conviction, but lacked potency. The massive social upheavals of the nineteenth century, with the move from the country to the

towns, the explosion of cities, the dazzling success of science and technology, and the growth of industrialism and bureaucracy, provided the muscles
and sinews that enabled the Enlightenment to come fully to life: it insinu-
ated itself into the consciousness of Victorian men and women, found its
way into the language and syntax of both specialist and mundane speech,
and created a new culture.

This is not to say that the nineteenth century was not a religious success
in some ways. There was the significant growth and influence of conservative evangelicalism, the rise of tractarianism, a new outcrop of enthusiastic
sectarianism, and a gradual increase in the significance of Catholicism. But
the Christian religion, despite these obvious successes, was beginning to
show the early signs of anemia.

This happened in two ways. Firstly, the churches and their doctrines
came under direct attack. Secondly, as the century progressed, many of the
churches internalized more and more of the modern scientific worldview
and the methodology of science itself. Darwinism, and the direct assault
on the authority of the Genesis account of creation and *inter alia* the whole
authority of Scripture is well known. But, in fact, the doctrines of positivism and science espoused by Auguste Comte since the 1830s, had already
declared that both religion and metaphysics were the enemy of progress and
reason.

Victorians, including the young John Stuart Mill, were so overcome by
the success of the physical sciences that many believed with Comte that it
was only a matter of time before morality and religion would be explained
by science. This optimism gave rise to scientism: a doctrine that insisted that
all reality and truth were now circumscribed by science. Indeed, for Comte,
the young Mill, Spencer, and to a certain extent the mature Karl Marx, science took on the character of true knowledge, while religion was reduced
to mere opinion.

I think that C. S. Lewis was right when he asserted that Darwinism
provided the scientific underpinning for the progressive idealism of Kant's
rationality. Once it was believed that progress had a scientific basis, this
spilled over into another ideology: the political-Darwinism that no longer
saw itself as a biological theorem, but as a principle of progress in the universe itself. This political-Darwinism is found in Marx, Spencer, and Fabi-
anism, and was later to spawn twentieth-century Fascism.

If the incestuous vampire of Protestantism took time off from his re-
lentless meal throughout the nineteenth century, it was to whisper "progress, progress" into the ear (so close to the neck) of his victim. "There will be
no apocalypse," he breathed: "no archangel to sound the last trump; heaven

is to be built on earth, and the kingdom of God is to become the kingdom of man."

Towards the end of the nineteenth century there was a Romantic backlash against the certainties of positivism and scientism. Protestantism partly embraced positivism, and partly tried to disengage itself. Two theological thinkers—and trends—stand out as markers towards the Third Schism.

Right at the beginning of the century, Schleiermacher, "the father of modern theology," convinced that Kant had proved the impossibility of approaching God through rationalistic philosophy, and anxious to avoid both sterile rationalism and dogmatic revelation, opted for experience as the touchstone of certainty in faith.

Schleiermacher's influence on Protestant theology has been colossal, and is directly linked with sophisticated and ingenious interpretations of Scripture. His experiential theology is not essentially tied to the "dogmatics" of revelation, and the Jesus experienced in faith is not necessarily "the Christ of Scripture." Schleiermacher and his many followers today—not least the sociologist Peter Berger—want to resist rationalism and scientism. Berger thinks that experientialism is an antidote to modernism. He must also face the fact that it may be a capitulation to subjectivism.

The emphasis on authentic faith, and careful interpretative understanding of Scripture, was added in a more scientific way by the Ritschlean School of liberal Protestantism in the last quarter of the nineteenth century. Here, we see the beginnings of modern criticism, so dominant in university departments today. The German scholars began to look at the Scriptures not as sacred canon, but as scientific object. They felt that they wanted to go beyond the overlay of theological understanding imposed on the New Testament to the primary data of the historical Jesus.

But the quest for the historical Jesus led to a wedge being driven between the Christ of faith and the first-century Jew from Palestine. Since that time, modern theology has oscillated between a view of Christ as almost all Spirit, bereft of the humanness of Jesus, or as a mere historical figure empty of divinity.

More generally, the beginnings of historical and textual criticisms in their many forms turned the theological enterprise away from expounding the "dogmatics" of revelation to a scientific or interpretative viewpoint. Henceforth, the unexamined presuppositions of modern theology were the acceptance of the primacy of rational understanding. The authority of church or Bible was no longer an axiom from which one starts: it was simply data to be examined critically.

Much could be said of twentieth-century developments. When, in the 1940s and 50s, C. S. Lewis warned against the consequences of Christianity

absorbing rationalism and scientism and people smiled at the unlikely success of Bultmann's demythologizing program for freeing the "real" Jesus
from a first-century worldview, few orthodox Christians realized that the
demon lover had nearly drained the progenitor dry.

In just the last few years, the pace of change has overtaken us. As Goulder puts it: "We are driving over the same course as our eighteenth-century
fore-bearers only now at four times the speed." The tremendous interest in
the last few years in political and social issues could be grounds for hope;
for it is a poor gospel that has nothing to say about oppression, racism, and
social evils. Yet so often we find secular gospels with theological dressings.
Feminist theology, liberation theology, the theology of peace studies or
Christian socialism can become what I call "constituency theologies" where
the social or political concern simply swallows the theology.

But if only Western Christianity—and we are now talking about all of
us, not just Protestants—could wake up before the engorgement of the demon is complete, it would discover a remarkable thing: while it lay sleeping
and dreaming dreams of authentic and mature religion (no longer innocent
after feeding from the critical tree of knowledge) the incubus that was drawing its life force so steadily yet so sweetly had already turned Enlightenment
"man" into a living corpse.

This is the truth for which the gospel of Jesus Christ and his apostles is
literally salvation. Modernity, the Enlightenment's child, has brought material wealth and medical aid in a manner undreamed of two hundred years
ago. But it has also brought us to the verge of extinction through nuclear
war and ecological folly. The West has hoarded most of the wealth for itself,
and divides it in a way that is unjust. Materialism and the reality of the phenomenal world have all but drowned out the still small voice of the heart.
At the very moment that systems analysis in government and microchip
technology in business and education take us yet further into a rationalistic
society, our moral structures are falling apart.

The flip-side of scientism so easily becomes nihilism. At the moment
that the certainty of science is praised to the skies, traditional morality and
orthodox religion are dismissed as "mere conventions," "wish-fulfillment,"
or "subjective delusions." Enlightenment man has undoubtedly been a man
of power, but he has also been a barbarian. Now he is stumbling.

The church should not be helping him up, but helping him over: false
optimism does not need a helping hand; it needs firstly the truth, and secondly love to salve the lost illusions and move on to a fuller humanity.

People in the inner cities, the unemployed, those living in fear of annihilation from nuclear war, no longer believe the empty words of progress.
But can the new Christianity, the Christianity that has become so synergistic

with the modern world—so infused with the life-force of the incubus—preach a gospel of hope to heal the despair? The short answer is *no*, not until it exorcises its own demon, and ceases to live its undead existence.

But will the orthodox Christians, scattered and divided by the first two schisms of Christendom, fare any better? Do they have a gospel for a fallen culture? The short answer is that they do, though it is not a new gospel.

RETELLING THE STORY

The old story needs retelling and reformulating in the idioms of a modern world, weaned on the realities of technologies and consumerism. But the truths of the story remain the same. God is love, and it is in the nature of love that it offers itself to others. But others, in order to receive love, must be free to reject it, and free to choose for themselves whether they will return it. Since the creation of the world people have chosen to reject God and love, and have preferred selfishness and self-knowledge. The old-fashioned word for this is sin. But sin, written large in the cultures and nations of our planet, has wrought divisiveness, war, and separation.

Although we wonder whether the suffering and evil of existence is too high a price to pay for freedom, God takes the initiative in our agony and confusion, and, divesting himself of his power and glory, enters into solidarity with us in the person of Jesus. We read in the Gospels that Jesus healed a leper by touching him and yet did not become leprous himself. Similarly, as God-man, Jesus entered truly into our human condition and yet was not overcome or contaminated by the unlovingness and destructiveness of human evil.

He conquered and redeemed us from within our own humanity, and then finally this man of love was taken "without a city wall" and crucified. Love, however, also conquered death, the final enemy that separates us from each other and destroys hope and joy. The risen Christ returned to God the Father having established a bridgehead between fallen humanity and perfect love, which is God himself. Jesus, having left the world, sent the Holy Spirit—that aspect or "person" of God's nature that heals and comforts and pleads—to re-establish communion and unbroken love between God and man. To become a Christian is to become not only a believer and follower of Christ, but to be supernaturally or spiritually joined to him through the enabling power of the Spirit. In that sense the church is one body of Christ.

Jesus, who is the head of the church, which is the body, not only shows the way of love and reconciliation. He is the way: the path from our broken and fallen humanity to a new humanity, which acquires the stature of Love itself.

The history of salvation is essentially an unfinished love story. It begins simply, in the words of John's Gospel, "For God so loved the world . . . ." The story never ends because love never ends; love is limitless. But we are a long way from limitless love, and the modern world with all its mastery of nature and self-knowledge seems incapable of finding it. I do not believe that the new Christianities, predicated as they are upon either rationalism or subjectivism, really believe any more that God is love, nor do they knew how to tell his story.

But orthodox Christians, who can tell God's story in many different ways, and with different though complementary emphases, are not preaching this message with any prophetic power because they are too busy still fighting the first two schisms. It is difficult to convince a fallen culture that there is an ultimate and saving love in the universe when Christians squabble and fight like any other human family. There is no doubt that the message of God's love is simple, perhaps deceptively simple for modern man, but the way of love is unbearably hard.

In order to show that love, and in order to prevent the Third Schism becoming Christianity's final divide, orthodox Christians will have to come together and put aside their differences (except when conscience absolutely forbids it).

A radical realignment of forces, however, is useless as a pious hope. It needs concrete action. Evangelicals must open themselves to Catholics and Orthodox. The Roman Catholic Church must enter the British Council of Churches (despite the very real risk that this could exacerbate the old second schism and even worsen the Third Schism). Anglo-Catholics and evangelicals within the Church of England will have to come out from their separate corners and join hands. The Church Society must decide whether it is still defending the sixteenth-century Reformation or fighting today's war. West Indian Pentecostals and Greek and Russian Orthodox will have to come out of their ghettos and remember that they are in Britain as missionaries. The Catholic and Protestant Truth Societies will need to form a Christian Truth Society.

All of this, of course, sounds like a sort of madness, certainly a kind of desperation. But believing in love and proclaiming a gospel of hope is not a sort of fatalism that says "it will all come right in the end." Paradoxically, love has to be fought for. Christianity is being subverted by the forces of darkness (however reasonable and rational they seem). This calls for warfare. Nothing less.

20

THE GOSPEL IN A CULTURE
OF FALSE GODS
Interview with Bishop Leslie Newbigin
(1988)

Andrew Walker: Bishop Newbigin, in recent years you have turned your attention particularly to problems of Western culture. Would it be correct to say that you think that advanced Western industrial societies took a wrong turn with the Enlightenment?

Leslie Newbigin: I became involved in these questions basically because I was a foreign missionary in India and have been through the experience of seeking, as an Englishman, to communicate the gospel across the cultural divide that separates our countries. And therefore I have had to reflect about the way that one communicates the gospel in a culture whose presuppositions simply make it incredible.

Having spent most of my working life in India and then coming back, I have discovered—in a way, to my own astonishment—that one faces the same problem here, and that one is again in a culture where, when you attempt to communicate the gospel, you are going completely against the stream.

What has troubled me greatly is that the response of the churches on the whole has been so timid—that there is a tendency to feel that when somebody says, "But I can't believe that!" then you hoist the white flag and say, "Well of course we can't expect you to!" As a foreign missionary, on the other hand, one is accustomed to the situation where you know that what you're saying runs counter to the dominant culture, but nevertheless you have to say it.

Walker: Let me be clear about this: are you saying, in effect, that when you came back to "the mother country" that sent you out to missionize "the heathen," that you came back to a land of heathens?

Newbigin: Well, yes, in a sense. By which I mean that I had been accustomed, like all of us in the 1960s, to talking about the secular society and its great values and so on. I was to a considerable extent conned by the dominant theology of the 1960s and thought that secularity was one of God's great gifts—and there is a real truth in that. But it didn't take long to discover that we are really not in a secular society, but in a pagan society—not in a society which has no gods, but a society which has false gods. I came to feel that more and more.

Walker: If you think, then, that we're in a society that has false gods as opposed to no gods, what are these false gods?

Newbigin: Well, very obviously, at a superficial level they are money, sex, prestige, power—all those things. But at a more fundamental level, I think there hides a concept of reality which is supposed to be beyond question. As you know, the sociologists like Peter Berger talk about "plausibility structures." In any society, there is a plausibility structure—things within that are immediately believed; things that contradict it are simply not believed.

Now we have a plausibility structure which, broadly speaking, is the result of the whole immense shift of thought that took place in the Enlightenment, with all its positive elements. But what people fail to see, of course—and one does fail to see it if one has never moved outside of it—is that every plausibility structure rests upon faith commitments.

What I find so difficult is that we're in a society here where if you make statements that are within that plausibility structure, you're OK—no questions are asked, you can say what you like. But if you make, for example, a Christian statement, then that's not acceptable in public life—it's not acceptable in politics, it's not acceptable in the university essay—because that represents a particular faith commitment and therefore it is ruled out . . . omitting to note that our accepted plausibility structure also rests on faith commitments.

What I feel, and have felt, is the need to encourage my fellow church leaders to be less timid in challenging the plausibility structure that dominates our society, to be ready to say, "Yes, what I'm saying rests upon other faith commitments, but that doesn't make it untrue."

Walker: Well, let's take this up, then. What are these faith commitments?

Newbigin: I think it is the belief that the scientific method, which has been so enormously fruitful for human life, is the only reliable way of understanding the total human situation. That's what I think one has to challenge.

The difficulty I feel is that when Christians are unwilling to challenge that, then the gospel becomes either (a) just something that is helpful—you know, "It helps me in my personal life"; or (b) something which degenerates into mere moralism—"This is what you ought to do"—so that preaching becomes either telling people what they ought to do, or lambasting people because of what they do not do; or (c) something which just offers people some kind of personal "'spiritual' consolation," but does not challenge people's understanding of what is the real world they have to deal with.

Walker: I know that Jim Packer has sometimes used the phrase "scaled-down Christianities," by which he seems to mean that we cut our gospel down to fit the secular climate in which we find ourselves. Is that what you think is the most negative aspect of modern Christianity?

Newbigin: Yes. And you see this is the kind of issue that one faced in trying to communicate the gospel in India. You obviously had to take seriously the whole Hindu worldview, with its great elements of rationality and strength, which I found enormously impressive. In that kind of situation you have to ask yourself, not "How can we fit the gospel into this?" but, "At what points does the gospel illuminate this, at what points does it question it, at what points does it contradict it?"

But one has to express those things in a way that the listening Hindu will recognize as his own language. That's the crucial thing. And that I think was the difficulty, because if you're going to use another language, you're at least provisionally accepting the way of understanding the world which that language embodies, and you therefore have to commit yourself to the other worldview, at least up to that point—but in order to challenge it.

Walker: How do you answer people when they say to you, "Why, Bishop Newbigin, do you believe in the incarnation and the resurrection of Christ?" I mean, how would you suggest to a modern world that such a belief is credible?

Newbigin: Well, ultimately, of course (and here we see my Reformed background), I come to the doctrine of election. I mean that by his mysterious grace God took hold of me, an unbelieving, pondering person, and put me in a position where the reality of Jesus Christ, crucified and risen, became for me the one clue that I could follow in making sense of a very perplexing world.

The test, of course, can only come at the end. I would want to claim that that clue ultimately gives one a kind of rationality that is more inclusive of the whole of human experience than the real, though limited, rationality of the reductionist and rationalist scientific point of view. But at the end of the day, we have to wait for the day-of-judgment. There is an element of risk, there is an element of commitment involved, where you don't pretend to *have* something—that is, if there were some way by which I could prove the authority of Jesus Christ from outside, then *that* would be my authority and not Jesus Christ. I can only point to him.

Walker: Given that you can point to him, do you think it reasonable or unreasonable to suggest that to be a Christian does involve some minimal amount of beliefs?

Newbigin: Oh yes, surely it does.

Walker: I mean, if somebody was to come here, put you into a corner and say, "Now look here Bishop, what have you got to believe to be a believing Christian?" What would you say are the basics?

Newbigin: I would simply say, "Jesus Christ, the final and determinative center around which everything else is understood." If that is there, I am not enthusiastic about drawing exact boundaries. I think you can define an entity by its boundaries or by its center. I think that Christianity is an entity defined by its center. So provided a person is, as it were, "looking to Jesus," and seeing him as the central, decisive, determinative reality in relation to which all else is to be understood, then even if his ideas are weird or offbeat, I would regard him as a brother in Christ.

But once you start trying to define Christianity by its boundaries, you'll always come up against some kind of legalism. You know: "Has he been baptized? Has he been confirmed? Was the bishop who confirmed him in the right apostolic succession?" and so forth. Or: "Has she had the right kind of religious experience? Was her conversion datable? Did she have those kinds of feelings at that time?" and so on. You always finish up with some kind of legalism, whereas I think Christianity is to be defined by its center.

Walker: If we're going to define Christianity by its center, in what ways can you say that Jesus Christ is still good news for "modern man?"

Newbigin: Because death is conquerable; because the crucified is risen; because not just anyone rose from the dead, but this one who went down to the very depths of the human situation; because he is raised. I see Christianity as a kind of fall-out from an original explosion of joy. But of course you don't just communicate it simply by arguments. It's an existential reality present in a believing, worshipping community, and the only ultimate "hermeneutic for the gospel" is a believing community.

Walker: What are your hopes for the future as far as the church is concerned? What do you look for generally and hope for as the way forward?

Newbigin: You may think that I'm evading your question, but I do believe fundamentally that the horizon for the Christian is not some prospect, some bit of futurology—either for his own personal life or for the life of his society. The horizon for the Christian is "He shall come again" and "We look for the coming of the Lord." It can be tomorrow or any time, but that's the horizon. That horizon is for me fundamental, and that's what makes it possible to be hopeful and therefore to find life meaningful.

As regards what we can in our fallible human guesswork anticipate, I don't know. The one thing that strikes me about all the futurological essays one reads is that after ten years we realize that they were wrong. Our capacity to forecast the future is very limited. All I can say is that one sees signs of hope, one sees signs of growth. I often liken the church to a bush that's been very hard pruned: I think there are buds, and though they are very small I think they are signs of hope.

SHORTER PIECES

21

THE CRISIS OF CHRISTMAS

(2003)

Most of us know that in significant ways Christmas is a pagan invention. European "Father Christmas" can perhaps claim a longer life than the American "Santa Claus," but both these jolly creatures are a bastardization of fourth-century Saint Nicholas, Bishop of Myra, whom legend has it, gave gifts to children and also contended for the full divinity of Christ at the Council of Nicea in 325 AD. Christmas trees are a nineteenth-century recreation of a German pagan tradition, and mistletoe and holly-harp go back to the folk fertility of Druidic religion.

We tend to accept such pagan importations into the Christmas story because they all seem to be part of the "spirit of Christmas"—a time of giving, family, merriment and mulled wine, carols, decorations, and snowflakes. This is "quality time" for us, conjured up by residual images of a Victorian Christmas strained through repeats and rehashes of Dickens' *A Christmas Carol*. It is a world of humanitarian decency which allows a sanitized and sentimental baby Jesus to slip-in with barely a rustle of discomfort from either the religiously indifferent masses or the cohorts of interfaith watchdogs.

Indeed, Jesus is welcomed into the festive season, not so much because it is his birthday, but because he is a symbol of the Christmas spirit. Witness the tableau of the holy family with adoring mother fawning over adorable child while an elderly Joseph looks on, pleased as punch. See the gift-bearing kings from exotic lands. Watch rough-hewn shepherds with their fleecy baby sheep. Add cows and donkeys for good measure, perhaps a hovering angel or two, and together it all adds color to the Christmas spirit, which is arguably not even Dickens any more but a hazy warm feeling—an "atmosphere"—created by market forces and unrestrained hedonism.

If we are committed Christians, we are quick to blame the corruption of Christmas on pagan innovations—not to mention commercial interests—but we are slow to concede that we too have corroded the Christmas story through the sugary acids of sentimentality. And sad to say, it may have begun in the fourteenth century with Francis of Assisi.

A great preacher and popularizer, as well as self-elected pauper, Saint Francis embellished the Gospel stories in order to make them fresh and vivid to ordinary people: the dark cave of the outcast God-child, for example, took on the glow of a rural idyll as sweet hay and wooden manger turned the landlord's outhouse into a country stable. Franciscan spirituality was also expressed through homely iconography so that the stories were imaged in frescoes and church windows. By the time of the Renaissance, Christmas scenes were skillfully animated by artists who increasingly saw religious art as a triumph of technical flair and imaginative creation over dogmatic content.

Lest Protestants lay all blame at the pierced feet of Saint Francis, or the decadence of Italian art, we should perhaps recall Martin Luther's carol, "Away in a Manger," where lowing cattle and the laid-down oh so sweet head of Jesus almost switches off the true light which has come into the world.

All of this is perhaps the more sobering when we realize that we don't even know whether the early church celebrated Christmas at all. We do know that by the third century the Eastern Churches had added Epiphany to the great liturgical feasts of Easter and Pentecost. This great theophany— this public announcement of God's intentions—remains to this day in the Orthodox Church as an event as important as Christmas. Epiphany is not understood as the celebration of the Magi, as it has become in the West, but a celebration of the baptism of Jesus, some thirty years after his birth. The Eastern Epiphany is seen as a Trinitarian declaration on the banks of the river Jordan that in Jesus what you see is none other than the revelation of God to the world.

The Christmas celebration itself emerges from the shadow of Easter in Western Christianity sometime after the imperial Edict of Toleration in 311 AD, when the date of December 25th was chosen as the official birthday of Jesus. In itself this date is quite arbitrary, as the Bible gives no hint as to what time of year Jesus was born. The scholarly consensus is that December was chosen to celebrate the birth of the "sun of righteousness" as an evangelistic marker against the pagan celebration of the winter solstice.

For those of us living in colder climes, the solstice is now so inter-twined with Christmas that the festive season is a veritable Yuletide with all the gloss of chocolate logs, snowmen, chestnuts roasting on an open fire, reindeer, frosted window panes, Santa and elves in Lapland, and even shepherds wrapped up against the cold on a billion Christmas cards. In the United States, you can even visit Christmas shops in the Deep South at the height of summer, as you walk in a winter wonderland like Lucy pushing through the coats of the wardrobe only to find her feet scrunching in the snows of Narnia.

The pagan accoutrements of the Christmas story—of Santa, trees, red berries, and winter pleasures—are not in themselves evil, and they are, in their own way, delightful. The problem lies elsewhere: the true meaning of Christmas has been buried beneath an avalanche of nostalgia, a "feel good" experience—a remembrance of a childhood past, of magic, of reconstituted joy. That's the problem.

But there's more. Christmas should be the season when the church calls us to remember the inauguration of God's rescue mission for human-kind. Jesus the Word of God, Son of the Father, in obedience to the divine love, divested himself of his power and glory, and in the power of the Spirit joined himself irrevocably to human flesh. The at-one-ment of God with the world may have culminated at Calvary, but it began in Nazareth with God's wooing of Mary through the angelic messenger and her voluntary ac-ceptance of the divine proposal. The birth of Jesus in Bethlehem was God's initiative, but one that was in full co-operation with the chosen maiden of Israel.

Christmas, in other words, is the recollection and retelling of salva-tion history: it is the crisis event in the story of the world that changes it forever. Time itself, as C. S. Lewis reminded us, turned a corner with the incarnation.

Therefore, let us, by all means, buy our family presents, and eat our mince pies, wallow in sentiment if we must, and even sail close to the pagan winter wind. But let us also, by no means, fail to announce to the world that Jesus the son of Mary is none other than Immanuel—God with us.

22

GALLOPING CONSUMPTION

(1996)

The defining moment in modernity, when it passed from its early to its late phase, was not the permissive 1960s, or the micro-chip wizardry of the 1990s, but the burgeoning consumerism of the 1950s.

Beginning in the United States, and heralded in the 1940s by Henry Ford, consumerism has become the dominant cultural force of the last half of the century. "Fordism" was the application of mechanical mass-production methods to create consumer durables for a mass public at affordable and competitive prices. This "Fordism," with its skilled and semi-skilled workforce, paved the way for the first phase of the consumer society.

In the eighteenth century, consumption was restricted to the aristocracy, and production was in cottage industries. Nineteenth-century production methods changed all that, yet the earliest mass markets were not consumer-led, but driven by industry and government. After the Second World War, rising standards of living, full employment, technological advance, and innovative marketing spearheaded the American revolution that has led to its cultural dominance and imitation ever since.

The 1950s was the American dream in a bubble. It was a dream of innocence and naughtiness rolled up together, like Pinocchio and his friends "letting rip" on Pleasure Island before the fun turned sour and they turned into braying asses.

It was not a dream that included African Americans or independent women. For white, married women, the dream was of "the dream kitchen," with its stainless steel and Formica surfaces, built-in ovens, refrigerators, and dish-washers.

For white men, the dream was of a niche in the corporation, expense accounts, and the car, complete with gleaming chromium. For the nuclear family of mom, dad, and 2.4 children, it was the dream of a crime-free environment, motoring holidays, and barbecues in the great outdoors.

It was a dream of the middle-class "okay religion"; a middle-America at home with itself and on top of the world. This dream of the modern home in a civilized society was reinforced by the establishment of supermarkets where the shelves groaned under the weight of pre-packaged food. Even the perishable goods could be purchased to store in the freezer back home.

Purchasing was enhanced by the credit card, which was invented to make spending simpler. If cash was not available, this could be taken care of by hire-purchase agreements.

Such rational simplicity, however, also pandered to a hedonistic "impulse buying," as the 1950s witnessed the beginning of the "live-now-pay-later" era of late modernity, registering the dream-like quality. It demonstrates that right from the beginning the consumer revolution was predicated not only upon a built-in obsolescence of consumer durables, but also on the fact that selling goods was the selling of a lifestyle. Consumer products were not value free, but came packed with an association of ideas. Middle conservative Americans in particular were receptive to suburban "wish-fulfillments." Ascetic individualism still lingered on in those days, and in the "burbs," with their gleaming cars and shining respectability, seemed a fitting, albeit secular, fulfillment of the earlier Puritan vision of America as the "city set upon a hill." However, dreams are determined by desires, and desires are legion. Modern consumerism soon discovered that blue collar workers and young people had dreams too, and these were different to those of suburban housewives and corporate executives.

Jeans and t-shirts, rock and roll, and aviation sun glasses were also the inventions of the American 1950s. So too was the "beat generation," with its "reefers," and the subterranean counter-culture of Jack Kerouac's drifters "on the road."

Relying on new theories, themselves often derived from psychological hedonism, Madison Avenue and the admen became a force to be reckoned with in the modern world. To be sure, Vance Packard warned of the *Hidden Persuaders*, and Reyner Banham as early as 1955 bemoaned the establishment of "a throw-away economy," but the new consumerism was sanitized by commercialism, which on the whole was jolly, rather than sinister.

In the United States, advertising, especially in the Midwest, meant outsized billboards in the great outdoors. America became quite literally the place of signs. Even today, although, states such as Vermont ban billboards, commercial signs dominate the skyline across America. Driving along the highways, or entering the smallest Midwest town, is to be confronted—"in your face," as Americans say—by the towering signs of fast food joints, motel chains, liquor stores, and evangelistic promise. The small towns change, but the signs remain the same, like a familiar and reassuring skyline: MacDonald's, Arby's, Waffle House, Motel 6, Holiday Inn, Word of Faith, and Best Western.

But advertising in the 1950s also moved into the home, where a captive audience sat goggle-eyed in front of the technological marvel of the modern age: the TV. The television commercial was an opportunity to link products to lifestyle and front them with famous personalities. Tobacco companies took advantage of this, using for example the comedian Phil Silvers—from the TV sitcom *Bilko*—to sell Camel cigarettes. Once TV, film, and consumer products were linked together, merchandising took a new turn: fads became fashions that sometimes turned into a craze. One of the earliest revolved around Walt Disney's film *Davy Crockett,* which spawned a host of imitation raccoon hats, plastic muskets, and Red Indian knives. Before the 1950s were over, people had learned to buy products because they were thought to be good in themselves, enhanced a desired lifestyle, and were associated with a favorite film, television program, or famous personality. It was as if the glamour and fame of the "stars" could rub off on you like pixie dust when you bought products tagged to their names.

Eventually, this process was also made to work in reverse. Some of today's films are now carried on the back of merchandizing. Children's toys such as "Care Bears" and "Transformers" were products first—with televised cartoons acting like the promotional videos of pop stars—before they became movies. The Hollywood films *Mario Bros, Street Fighter,* and *Mortal Kombat* all first existed as interactive computer games.

Piggy-back selling also works through televised advertising. One of the most extraordinary examples in recent times was the selling of the coffee product Gold Blend. This was promoted through an extended advertising campaign on British television, where the adverts became a serialization of a couple's developing a romantic relationship over their shared love for Gold Blend. On the back of this much-watched and admired advertising "soap," came the book *Love Over Gold* in 1993, which became a bestseller! Modern admen have gone one stage beyond this approach and now talk of "synergy," as they seek to produce a film with a bestselling soundtrack that generates a video with clips from the film and that helps sell the album, which is promoted on MTV. This is precisely how the film *The Bodyguard* was developed as the central core of a multimedia extravaganza, which netted over $80 million.

In the 1950s, however, before the bubble-burst in the late 1960s, there was a certain kind of innocence in the new dream toys of consumerism. They were fun and they were material compensation for the hardships of depression and war. They proved you were somebody. A television series such as *I Love Lucy*, and in successive decades *The Dick Van Dyke Show* and *The Brady Bunch*, were all part of the "good clean fun" and joyous celebration of having found a niche in the American dream.

However, we now realize that there was never any innocence, goodness, or moral cleanliness in the promotion of commercialism. American entrepreneurs, and their Madison Avenue "shrinks," had discovered that people could be made to want "things." As J. K. Galbraith pointed out in his *The Affluent Society*, consumerism meant the replacement of basic needs with the implantation of "wants" that you did not even know you had until the advertisers told you so. Keeping up with the Joneses, for example, was a deeply-felt anxiety of Americans who were jostling for their place in the sun. Advertising both plays on this created anxiety and offers promises of self-esteem and pleasure to those who purchase the goods.

It was a long time before Europe caught up with American advertising techniques and products. In Great Britain at the end of the 1950s, for example, half the cosmetics, most of the foundation garments, two out of every three cars, and nine out of ten razor blades were supplied by American-owned firms. Since that time, however, we have imported, adopted, and adapted American music, game shows, TV sitcoms, and teenage fashions of dress and behavior. France has resisted the colonialization of American culture better than Britain, but like everyone else, even France has submitted to the takeover of the consumer society as the designer culture of the modern world.

Consumerism has proved itself insatiable. It is forever seeking new markets for new products and, more insidiously, imposing its mind-set upon high culture and religion. As early as the 1960s, it was clear that consumerism was politically open. It did not object to any particular political dream, as long as it did not threaten to interfere with the market.

Even the revolutionary and anarchic potential of 1960s counter-culture was domesticated by mass-produced music and fashion. Real revolutionaries such as Che Guevara became cultural icons of radical chic. With his red beret and Jesus Christ beard, Che's iconic representation on a million t-shirts murdered the real image. Today's cultural icons, scattered across the world on billions of t-shirts, are rarely political figures cut down to size. They are more likely to be cartoon figures brought to life, like the "toons" in

Walt Disney's *Roger Rabbit*, or *Wicked City* and *Akira* from Japanese Manga videos vie for attention with *Batman, Beavis and Butthead,* and *Lion King.*

Whereas Che was made to look like a pop idol, pop idols have now become the revolutionary symbols of "cool" culture. Madonna is not just a soft-porn queen, she is a post-feminist; rap bands are not sexist or racist, they are the authentic voice of oppression; Seattle grunge is not drug addicted, down-dressing, it is "real people."

There is no longer a leader of the pack, but merely lost leaders in a consumer market of hits and misses. This is so because over time consumerism has become multifaceted, a mosaic, as it seeks to reflect the cultural fragmentation it helped create. Any fears by High Tories that consumerism would create a uniform popular culture of the lowest common denominator has been proved wrong; high culture can no longer be clearly distinguished from popular culture, because both have been commercialized. Niche marketing—from the National Rifle Association for patriots and bigots in America to the yuppie concerts of Pavarotti in Great Britain—are recognitions in late modernity that "you pays your money and you takes your choice."

There is now only one market, but this one market has become like the supermarket of the 1950s: virtually everything is on sale for anyone who will buy. The recognition by the producers in the 1990s, however, is that buyers are fickle, personality types are legion, wants and wishes are whimsical, and cultural times keep changing. Once, the market sold us novelties to keep us buying the old products and to keep us loyal to established brands. Now, the idea of novelty itself has become so successfully implanted in consumers that it drives us towards difference for its own sake. Brand loyalty is notoriously difficult to maintain. We demand ever new products. So demanding have we become that in some areas of economic life—popular music, for example—that it is the consumer and not the producer who calls the tune.

Thus the rapaciousness of modern consumerism in generating new markets, technologies, and lifestyles has arguably altered the structure of capitalist production. Desktop publishing, for example, blurs the boundaries between production, producer, and consumer. More obviously, consumerism has shifted the balance from traditional industries to new ones. Coal, steel, and shipping have declined, while technologically "light" and electronically-driven production forces have become dominant.

The service sector of late capitalism in many countries now outweighs the significance, in terms of GNP, of manufacturing production. Charles Handy tells us that between 1960 and 1985, employees in the service sector of the United States economy rose from 56 to 69 percent and in Italy from 33 to 55 percent.

Of course, giant manufacturing corporations are not a mirage. Companies such as Sony, IBM, and General Motors are real enough, but they do not single-handedly hold countries to ransom, or control the private social reality of citizens in the modern world. Furthermore, the giant corporations of the 1950s are in retreat. ICI, for example, has voluntarily divided.

More pertinently, we are witnessing the descaling, restructuring, or "downsizing" of bureaucracies. With the advent of new technologies and tighter fiscal controls, the middle management of industrial and government corporations are being stripped away. *Company Man,* as Anthony Sampson has shown, belongs to the first great boom of consumerism in the 1950s, but is now destined for rapid decline in the twilight of modernity.

Marxists may still be able to argue that capital is concentrated in the hands of oligarchies—indeed, increasingly so—but monopoly capitalism in its institutional form is being deconstructed before our eyes. Deregulation means the end of corporate loyalties and the breakdown of differences between ownership, managers, and workers. Symbolic analysts, computer programmers, and the technologically literate are emerging as a new "class," divorced from the old loyalties of workers and unions, middle-class, and management.

Perhaps a more telling symbol of late modernity than the giant national or super-national economic conglomerate is the shopping mall of America. Malls have not merely replaced smaller stores and former supermarkets, but have become America's prime leisure contexts. American teenagers, for example, spend more time in malls than any other cultural space outside the home. Malls are the cathedrals of late modernity where people come to gaze and wonder in the sacred space to offer homage and pay their dues to the gods of mammon. In Dallas, Texas, one major Baptist Church has been built to look like a mall and has created space to "hangout" and shop as well as providing sanctuaries for worship.

23

THE TRUE TRAGEDY OF
CREATIONISM

(2001)

A couple of weeks ago I took part with biologist Steve Jones in a live debate on BBC Radio 3's program "Night Waves" on the subject of creationism. The debate was scheduled in response to the news that Alabama State schools were issuing new scientific textbooks with a warning sticker claiming that evolution was a "controversial theory" that should be questioned.

A recent article in *Nature* has also claimed that creationism is actually on the increase globally—and apparently more than half of Americans don't believe in scientific evolution.

In the event, the whole thing turned-out to be a damp squib. The program's introduction was a recorded interview with creationist Philip Johnson. Steve and I expected him to kick off by vigorously putting the boot into evolution, but he failed to deliver, which left the poor presenter scrambling to get the debate back on track.

But even if Radio 3 had started off with a bang, it is doubtful if Steve Jones and I would have really clashed on air, for the truth of the matter is that many Christian scientists and theologians have had to come to terms with the idea of evolution. This is not only obviously true for liberal scientist/theologians like Arthur Peacocke and John Polkinghorne, but also evangelical geneticists like Sam Berry of University College, London.

Even in what we might have expected to be the heart of theological conservatism, the charismatic new churches, we find people like Roger Forster of London's Ichthus Fellowship reflecting in his book, *Reason, Science and Faith*, a view of science that can find room for theistic evolution without seeing it as an attack of science on the Bible.

What I believe binds together many people who would widely be considered conservative theologians and scientists, is a recognition that creationism is a basic category mistake.

C. S. Lewis led the way in the 1940s, by arguing cogently and convincingly that Genesis chapters 1 and 2 were not written as science, but as myth (in the high sense following Coleridge and George MacDonald). Such a view is itself a reflection of a very early Christian tradition exemplified by Jerome in the West and Origen in the East.

It would probably be true to say, however, that before the advent of modernity, most divines would have been more likely to hold to a pre-scientific literalism regarding the creation story; and this still holds true today for many Christian believers in the Third World as well as in enclaves of Christian sectarianism in the West.

At Princeton Seminary in America during the early days of the last century, Protestant theologians such as B. B. Warfield and Archibald Hodge recast the Genesis creation story from a literary-historiographical account into a scientific one.

One of the consequences of this was that by the time the intellectual foundations of fundamentalism were laid, with the publication of the twelve volumes of *The Fundamentals* (printed 1910–15), American evangelicalism had identified itself not only with a principled stance against the new "higher criticism" of biblical scholarship, but also with a radical rejection of Darwinism. Both these positions were seen to be logically connected and together they have been imprinted on evangelical memory as a major offensive in "The Battle for the Bible."

However, the reality is that today's creationists are not battling for the Bible, but defending a pseudo-science. The overriding paradigm to which most of them are committed is that the world is only 5,000–6,000 years old (based on an arithmetical or actuarial addition of all the recorded ages of people and times in the Bible).

Consequently, with the assurance that they are following *The Biblical Basis for Science* (to quote a book title by creationist Henry Morris), creationists have launched a program to demonstrate the newness of creation, which ranges from denying the efficacy of carbon dating, doubting (or reinterpreting) the fossil records, insisting that dinosaurs walked with humans and accumulating evidence to prove the global effects of the biblical flood.

The upshot of all this is that, despite the rhetoric, creationists actually fail rigorously to engage with evolutionists because they do not have the intellectual tools to rattle their cage. In fact, were they to know it (and Philip Johnson certainly has an inkling), the cage is already being rattled from within: Professor Stephen Jay Gould, for example, thinks that natural selection is as much a matter of luck, random mutation, and happenstance as inexorable genetic processes.

Other scientists, such as Robert Wright, are outraged at Gould's "heresy" because they stress that the propensity for complexity that is built into a living organism leaves no room for gaps—perhaps the fear is that they will be filled by God!

There is also a long-standing debate in the philosophy of science as to whether, strictly speaking, Darwinian evolutionary theory is a science at all. Karl Popper, for most of his life at least, felt that evolution was really a "metaphysical research program," because although he found the accumulated evidence overwhelmingly supported Darwin, he could not think of a way in which the theory could be falsified. For Popper, it is falsification rather than verification that is the logic, or the method, of scientific enquiry.

What creationism has supremely failed to do, therefore, is to nail evolution when it climbs out of its biological cage and roams into territories beyond its proper jurisdiction. It is political-Darwinism, rather than Darwinism itself, which has let mischief loose into the world. It has been on the loose since the nineteenth century when the Enlightenment doctrine of progress was joined in unholy matrimony to evolution.

Once Darwin's *Origin of Species* was published in 1859, it was plundered by intellectuals, of right- and left-wing persuasions, to add weight to their political predilections. It was Herbert Spencer, the sociologist, for example, who first coined the phrase "the survival of the fittest" and spuriously suggested that superior civilizations and societies (he meant Western ones) were determined by those best-suited intellectually and racially to rule.

On the other wing, it was Engels who took the earlier idealistic Hegelianism of Marx and spliced it together with his imperfect understanding of Darwin and created "scientific socialism," which ended up as official Soviet ideology.

Political-Darwinism also found its way into Italian fascism, directly in the writings of Mussolini, but also in the theories of two of his most enthusiastic supporters, the sociologists Pareto and Mosca. And if this was not enough, it wandered into the Nazi ideology of miscegenation and eugenic policy which ran its course in the ovens of Auschwitz.

And in addition, I'm also afraid we cannot let feminist Mary Stokes off scot-free either, for although she championed contraception for women, she also wanted to tinker with the genes of the proletariat in order to weed out the weak and the wanton, the deformed and the depraved.

Political-Darwinism is still out of its cage today: in its benign guise it continues to underpin Fabian socialism and has informed the thinking of Peter Wilson in his magnificent study of the twentieth century, *A Terrible Beauty*. In a more strident, seemingly scientific form, we can also find it in Edward O. Wilson's sociobiology. In its demonic guise a pseudo-Darwinism stalks the halls of scientific sorcery where the gathered covens are hell-bent on putting an end to natural selection and replacing it with biotechnological cloning and genetically-engineered spare-part replacements for malfunctioning humanoids.

And so, instead of joining forces with the broad stream of Christian orthodoxy in order to battle with the pressing theological, scientific, and ethical issues of the day, creationism is squandering its intellectual and financial resources up a Texas creek looking for the footprints of a latter-day dinosaur running side-by-side with early man.

That is the true tragedy of creationism.

24

Obituary for Metropolitan Anthony of Sorouzh

(2003)

Metropolitan Anthony of Sorouzh, the senior bishop in the Russian Orthodox Patriarchal Church and the head of the Russian Church in Great Britain and Ireland, was the single most influential voice of the Orthodox tradition in the British Isles.

A charismatic figure, with a palpable spiritual presence, he was cast more in the mold of a Staretz (a holy man of great spiritual insight and wisdom) than a career bishop responsible for the administration and pastoral oversight of a diocese. With his striking dark looks, and beautifully spoken English—reprised through a French, rather than a Russian accent—he would hold an audience in the palm of his hand. His gifts of communication were legendary: he never used notes or prompts, and whether he was preaching in the Russian Cathedral at Ennismore Gardens in London, giving a lecture on the Orthodox tradition at a conference, discussing Christianity with a group of students, or giving spiritual direction to an individual, he always radiated a sense of personal depth and boundless faith.

He could also be disarming. His conversation on BBC television in 1970 with the atheist Marghanita Laski would have been memorable enough for his respect of her intellectual integrity, and his undeniable charm. But it was the more remarkable for his wit, intellectual toughness, and his unconventional arguments. Instead of trying to justify his faith, for example, he told Laski that he knew that God existed, and was puzzled how she managed not to know. This unexpected turn in the conversation was typical of him and it threw her off guard.

The hallmarks of his ministry throughout his fifty years in Great Britain were pastoral sensitivity, penetrating insight as a spiritual director, and an irenic missionary outlook. He took the view that everyone was welcome in the Church—Russian, African, or indigenous Briton. And, while he was congenitally opposed to proselytizing, he attracted hundreds of English converts over the years. More significantly, he indelibly stamped the spirituality and theology of the Orthodox tradition upon the British religious consciousness, influencing many thousands of British lives through personal contacts and his writings, chiefly on prayer. At the height of his fame, Gerald Priestland, the renowned BBC religious correspondent, called him "the single most powerful Christian voice in the land."

Metropolitan Anthony had strong aversions and predilections. Despite making a significant contribution to the World Council of Churches at Delhi in 1961, he was allergic to institutional ecumenism. And while he deeply respected individual Catholics, he was less than enthusiastic about Roman Catholicism. Conversely he warmed to evangelical religion. In the early 1980s he requested a meeting with the Evangelical Alliance and on arrival stunned them right from the start, in the argot of evangelicalism, by "giving his personal testimony." He told them that when he was a young teenager living in France, and a convinced atheist, he was reading Mark's Gospel in his room when he was aware of a personal presence which he was convinced was Christ.

This dramatic story of conversion highlights Metropolitan Anthony's existential approach to faith. He said in a published interview in 1988, "I don't know anything of metaphysical language. What we [the Orthodox] say about Christ is experiential." While many labelled him as a mystic, he eschewed this designation, and preferred to talk of Christianity in the language of *ascesis* and disclosure. He genuinely believed that Eastern Orthodoxy was the simplest way to faith. The combination of simplicity in his personal life (he was completely indifferent to money and ecclesiastical *haute couture*) and his passionate commitment to the gospel were the inner springs of his spirituality. He once said that he had never preached Russian Orthodoxy in his life, but only Christ.

This Christian for all Christians was nevertheless strongly attached to Russia. During the Soviet era, his BBC Radio talks, and his books and sermons, penetrated deep into Russian culture and were proudly accepted as the authentic voice of "Holy Russia." When he visited the Soviet Union in person, he was overwhelmed by excited crowds eager to hear his words and just to see him. Metropolitan Anthony's stature among the people of Soviet

Russia was enhanced by the fact that he remained loyal to the Patriarchate, but maintained total political independence. This unique position of a see in the Russian diaspora was the lynchpin of the Metropolitan's *realpolitik* throughout the Soviet years.

The end of the Soviet empire in the early 1990s opened a new chapter in his relationship to Russia: with the easing of travel restrictions by President Boris Yeltsin, a fresh influx of émigrés found their way to his door. He welcomed them with open arms and devoted the last few years of his life trying to facilitate these post-Soviet Russians into the diocese as best he could.

One of Metropolitan Anthony's favorite quotations was Nietzsche's aphorism that chaos gives birth to a star. It could stand as a summary to his life. He was born André Bloom, at Lausanne in Switzerland in 1914. His father was a Russian imperial diplomat of Dutch extraction and his mother was the half-sister of the modernist composer Alexander Scriabin (and also related to Vyacheslav Molotov). While the young André admired his father, they were not really close. His mother, on the other hand, was the dominant influence in his life until her death when he was forty years of age and already well-established in Britain.

The young André missed the cataclysmic events of 1917, for at that time he was living with his parents in Persia. After sundry adventures and hardships they ended up living in Paris. His experiences as a refugee were mainly negative: his parents were living separate lives and he was the victim of bullying at school. After his dramatic conversion it was not to the priesthood he first turned, but to medicine. He trained initially at the Sorbonne and then in the French Medical Corps with the outbreak of war.

During the German occupation he worked as a doctor, but joined the Resistance. He took secret monastic vows and was first professed as a monk in 1943, when he adopted the name of Anthony after the founder of monasticism. And then, quite unexpectedly, he was ordained priest in 1948 and came to Britain to pastor the predominantly White Russian émigrés in London. His rise through the ecclesiastical ranks was meteoric. He became a bishop in 1957, archbishop in 1962, and the Patriarch of Moscow's exarch of Western Europe in 1963; and in 1966 was elevated to Metropolitan— the highest-ranking bishop in the Russian tradition outside the office of Patriarch.

But, like most people of genuine charisma, Metropolitan Anthony was a powerful and perplexing figure. Conservative in theology and politics, he was nevertheless totally free of sexism, even to the point of daring to question the theological warrant for an exclusively male priesthood. A personalist through and through, he was an inspired visionary, but had a poor grasp of administrative detail and diocesan strategy. He liked to be in control, but ideologically was deeply committed to lay participation in the Church and always talked of hierarchy in terms of service, rather than power. He put his money where his mouth was too and set-up a democratically elected Assembly and Council to run the affairs of the diocese of Sourozh in Britain which, in concert with him, it has done so until the present time.

Charismatic leaders, however, whether saints or savants, grow old and inevitably judgment falters as health and vigor fade. Towards the end of his life, Metropolitan Anthony simply had more on his plate than he could manage and people expected too much of him. But one thing remains clear: he once said that no one could turn towards eternity if he has not seen in the eyes or in the face of at least one person the shining of eternal life. Metropolitan Anthony was not infallible, despite what the hagiographers will say, but he shone.

25

CHUCKLING IN *THE SHACK*

(2008)

INTRODUCTION

By now, last year's sudden and unheralded appearance at the top of the *New York Best Seller List* of a privately published religious novel *The Shack* is no longer news. The fact remains, however, that it is still selling in the millions and has become one of those books you either love or hate. Its depicting the Trinity as central characters in a novel is "novel" enough, but more so when the Father is a Black African American woman (who answers to Papa) and Jesus, of obvious Middle Eastern features, is an odd job man, and the Holy Spirit (who answers to Sarayu) is slim, female, and Far Eastern in appearance.

The novel not only deals with the Trinity, but also with the problem of evil, forgiveness, salvation, and much more. Liberal Protestants eulogize it, as do "open evangelicals," and the movement known as the emerging church. Conversely, the fundamentalist Protestant right and conservative Christians everywhere in America have hailed it as heresy, harmful religion, and corrupting. I have lectured on the theology of *The Shack* at King's College, London, but I have not expressed a personal view in print until now.

REVIEW

I've tried very hard to like *The Shack,* especially having read some of the nonsense that its traducers have written about it. The claims by some evangelicals, for example, that the book is riddled with heresies are simply wrong. William Paul Young, the author, may be unorthodox, but he is not on the whole heterodox. In my view, the book is more personal catharsis and therapy than Christian doctrine, despite Young's claim that he wrote it as a testament of his religious beliefs for his children and grandchildren.

It must seem churlish of me to criticize a book which hundreds if not thousands of people claim has changed their lives. At the very least, you'd think I could have the decency to acknowledge that *The Shack* has brought Christian ideas out of the ghetto and into the heart of the secular market-place. And yet, despite these caveats, I cannot quite shake off my irritation with the book. I'll begin with a small issue that has snowballed in my mind to become a river I cannot cross. The word "cross" brings me to Jesus, and after a snippet of theology and a snatch of Scripture, I'll show why I had trouble with *The Shack*.

We learn about God's love for the world and are able to love him in return by grasping the fact that the incarnation of His Son had serious con-sequences for Jesus as well as for us. He assumed our flesh so we could be restored to our own good selves, but in taking into his divine person our human nature and sharing it with his own, he became a "man of sorrows and acquainted with grief." For us, restoration entailed reconciliation with God; but for Jesus it entailed death on a Roman gibbet.

This Son of God become Son of Man is at his most poignant and vul-nerable in the Garden of Gethsemane, when, afraid of dying and in great distress, he calls on his heavenly Father to rescue him from his anticipated torture. His prayer is in a language that touches our hearts; he addresses his Father as "Abba," an Aramaic term of intimacy close to the English word "Daddy," but closer still to the French thou or *tu*. But we also have a foretaste of the vulnerable and frail humanity of Jesus from the shortest verse in the Bible, "Jesus wept" (John 11:35). A holy God demands our obedience and earns our respect, but a weeping Jesus commands our love and wins our allegiance.

By contrast, in *The Shack,* Jesus seems to be done with weeping. We learn in the shortest trope of the novel that "Jesus chuckled." This chuckling Jesus chortles and giggles his way through the book, but it is hard to believe that like the first disciples we would give up our lives and follow him, let alone love him. Why not simply play with him?

After all, Young's Jesus is a down-to-earth sort of guy, plain as a pike-staff, but nevertheless a man who likes a bit of fun. So, not to be left out, do the other members of the Trinity: together they are a chorus of chucklers. I don't know when Young decided to let the Holy Trinity chuckle—not least because the word means to titter, or snigger; at best it means suppressed laughter, or laughing so quietly it's barely laughing at all. It seems appropriate, however, that Papa laughs first. Jesus first chuckles on page 111, the second to laugh in the sequence of Father, Son, and Holy Spirit.

Once Jesus starts to chuckle there is no stopping him, and the second time he does it the chuckling gives way to spasms of mirth. Young is in mimetic biblical verse again a few pages on in the narrative with a simple, "Jesus chuckled." A few pages later there is more of the same. Keep turning the pages and the tittering trope is extended when Young adds the filler, "Jesus said with a chuckle."

We are given a little respite from the chuckling Jesus a couple of chapters on because Papa chuckles for a change. But before the next chapter is out, Jesus is back chuckling for all he's worth. The only member of the godhead who shows some measure of self-control is Sarayu, who only chuckles once.

Chuckling is, of course, contagious, so it is no surprise that the main character of the book, Mack, who had already expelled an awkward chuckle on discovering that God the Father was in fact a black mom, chuckles along with the laughter of the mysterious Sophia, "not even knowing or caring why." He also has one final chuckle with Jesus about Sophia, whom Mack had initially thought might be the unknown member of the godhead.

It might seem unreasonable to pick on Young for making God chuckle; perhaps it is just a case of a restricted vocabulary or a subliminal response to his own chuckling, which he must have experienced when a book that started out as a private initiative went on to sell millions of copies. But Young's chuckling is more than a linguistic stammer, more than evidence that he is not a wordsmith or literary craftsman: it is also indicative of his tendency to equate laughter with holiness, as natural and good as organic food.

In contrast, the desert fathers of the early church period considered laughter to be demonic and evidence of a lack of sobriety, not a characteristic of a loving God. Admittedly, the fathers were not right about everything, and there is no reason to believe that God has no sense of humor. The patristic doctrine of *perichoresis* (the co-inherence of the persons of the Trinity) might seem to lend credence to a shared humor, as the Greek term evokes a sense of perpetual motion, or a never-ending dance routine, but I know of no mention of eternal chuckling.

The trouble for me with the tittering Trinity is best demonstrated by the Jesus character in *The Shack*. He does not resonate with the Jesus who wept in the Gospel. With Thomas, I am prepared to call Jesus "Lord and God," but the Jesus of *The Shack* is another matter. When he is out fishing with Mack, he rebuts his suggestion that he could use his power to catch fish with a surprising reply: "'What would be the fun in that then, eh?' He looked up and grinned." At this point, I am compelled irreverently to call Young's Jesus a "chucklehead"—not a divine title, admittedly, not even a surrogate for a "holy fool," but according to most dictionaries, "a stupid person or a dolt."

I guess my real irritation is with Young himself. I felt it was tawdry to write a sentimental book about a murdered girl (Missey) whose father (Mack) is eventually able to forgive her murderers, and just for good measure is also able to forgive his own father for abandoning him when he was a boy. Sentimentality robs forgiveness of its redemptive shine—"Daddy, I'm so sorry! Daddy, I love you . . ."—and steps over the line of self-restraint and appropriate show of emotion into silliness. Sentiment, when sugar-coated, rots the teeth of their creative bite and can be malevolent, if not malignant.

I am less than sanguine, for example, about the invitation at the end of the book for readers to join the Missy Project, as this is clearly intended as a money-raiser: "If you've been touched by the wonder of this book and want to make it available to others."

Young comes across in the book and on numerous Christian talk shows as folksy and as an alternative to mainstream Christianity, but also disingenuous—a Christian who does not go to church and one who believes in universal salvation, but was persuaded by colleagues, according to several sources, not to commit these thoughts to paper. He has allegedly suffered sexual abuse by Natives of New Guinea and unspecified persons in an American Boarding School. He admits to cheating on his wife with one of her best friends, but when he was "found out" it was not to the pastor's door he beats a path, but to the therapist's couch! Ostensibly, then, Young wrote *The Shack* for his grandchildren, but he was "street wise" enough to gather round him Lutheran pastors who, working from his garage, turned *The Shack* into "America's self-publishing miracle," hitting the bestseller lists around the world.[1]

Eugene Peterson, who is as good as any scholar with an open Bible, seems less at home in deciphering the merits of a modern text. To think, as he does, that *The Shack* is so good it will do for our generation what John Bunyan's *The Pilgrim's Progress* did for his, beggars the imagination. Bunyan's

---

1. Guardian.co.uk (July 17, 2008).

book is an allegory steeped in the language of the King James Bible, Shakespeare, and John Milton. It has been hallowed by time and become a classical text that is required reading in homes and schools all over the world. *The Shack,* on the other hand, is not an allegory, but a work of the imagination and written in an eclectic style that stumbles from didactic theologizing to counter-culture mysticism, Narnia pastiche, and colloquial Americanisms.

It does not have the literary merit or the mainstream appeal to become a literary icon such as Steinbeck's *The Grapes of Wrath* or the moral strength and simplicity of Anne Tyler's *Dinner at the Homesick Restaurant* or *Searching for Caleb.* It is a significant book, but *The Shack* is too religiously divisive and intellectually quirky to give it the status of that other American shack, *Uncle Tom's Cabin.* Maybe it will become a cult book like Pirsig's *Zen and the Art of Motorcycle Maintenance,* to be deposited in charity shops and squirreled away in boxes marked "Do not open."

26

RE-SEXING THE TRINITY

The Spirit as Feminine?[1]

(1990)

In her editorial in the autumn issue of *Theology* Grace Jantzen is surely right when she insists that feminist theology cannot be dismissed as merely trendy; the high level of scholarship belies this prejudicial characterization.[2]

But Jantzen is also surely right when she admits "that there are considerable differences amongst feminist theologians."[3] Daphne Hampson, for example, could properly be called a "post-Christian theist."[4] Perhaps Sarah Coakley's work could be understood to be a "radical orthodoxy,"[5] while Alwyn Marriage's is really a "reformed orthodoxy."[6] We can detect in Marjorie Suchocki's work an attempt to marry radical feminism with process theology.[7] And in the marvelously eclectic Rosemary Radford Ruether we can witness a liberationist/ deconstructionist/reconstructionist at work. It is Ruether who has convincingly demonstrated the various responses of femi-

---

1. This paper was originally read to a seminar group on September 26, 1990 in the short-paper section of the Trinity Conference organized by the Institute of Systematic Theology, King's College, London.

2. Cf. Janzen, "What is Feminism?"

3. Ibid., 339

4. Cf. Hampson, *Theology and Feminism.*

5. Coakley, *Creaturehood before God*, 343ff.

6. Marriage, *Life-Giving Spirit.*

7. Suchocki, *God, Christ and Church.*

nists to God and anthropology, ranging from liberalism to conservative and radical romanticism (and beyond).[8]

To begin, I would like to look at one strand of feminism that, in Ruether's terminology, would be best described as "conservative romanticism."[9] It seeks to improve the dignity and self-worth of women by identifying the feminine in the Trinity. This is more than an attempt to switch labels so that we may call God "Mother" as well as or instead of "Father." Rather, the conservative romanticism I wish to identify concerns the attempt to identify the Spirit, as person, in terms of the feminine gender. The Spirit is then read back into womankind in terms of divine image. In this way, it is hoped, women can be properly included—by the nature of things—in the Godhead and also find their proper personal identity and station in society.

It is, of course, not the case that many feminists take this particular approach. The more radical track is to transcend gender concepts completely and with them also personal categories. The seminal work here is Mary Daly's *Beyond God the Father*,[10] where we are presented with a God of Power, Justice, and Love. Indeed, Daly's predilection for substituting non-personal nouns for personal ones is compounded by her preference for substituting verbs for nouns. Janet Morley's Trinitarian blessing exemplifies a full-blown Dalyesque: May the God who dances in creation, who embraces us with human love, who shakes our lives like thunder, bless us and drive us out with power to fill the world with her justice.[11]

I personally do not find the radical feminist approach an improvement on the traditional doctrine of the Trinity, but I do not want to quarrel with it here.[12] To recapitulate, I wish to concentrate on the "romantic feminism" that seeks to understand the Holy Spirit as feminine. While I believe this

---

8. Ruether, *Sexism and God Talk*.

9. It may be stressed that Ruether's romanticism may be understood negatively and is in no sense related to the Romantic Movement, which would be more sympathetic to the intuitive and the feminine archetype.

10. Daly, *Beyond God the Father*, 127.

11. Included in comments sent (updated) to the B.C.C.'s draft of the study guide on the Trinity.

12. Suffice is to say that it suffers similar problems to those reformist approaches that seek to replace persons with functions. In many of our liturgies today it has become commonplace to replace Father, Son, and Holy Spirit, with Creator, Redeemer, Sustainer. This schema is not only overly modalistic, which in itself is common enough in the Western theological tradition, but it fails on a basic level of biblical adequacy. To say, for example, that the Spirit is sustainer is hardly a comprehensive description of attributes or economic functions. Is not the Spirit the Lord and giver of life, the mover upon the waters, the one who overshadows the maiden of Israel, endows Jesus with power, raises him from the dead, and baptizes the church with fire?

approach to be unfortunate, I think it important to recognize that in some ways the attempt to feminize the Spirit is both admirable and understandable. A short gloss on theological anthropology in the early church will demonstrate the way in which women have not always been seen to be full partakers of the *imago dei*.[13]

Gregory of Nyssa, for example, when talking of the creation of men and women speaks of a double creation. First, there is a spiritual creation where both men and women partake of the divine image and equally so. In anticipation of the fall, however, God (whom Nyssa depicts as canny, if not downright cunning) calls into existence a second creation where material form is manifested in the sexual natures of male and female.

In principle, however, men and women, for Gregory, are equal partakers of the divine image, moving from what Sarah Coakley calls a sort of humanoid state into fallen humanity—where the woman is the helper of and submissive to the man—and eventually by grace men and women become adopted into God's androgynous nature, thus transcending the sexual differentiation of the fall.[14]

(Recent statements from the Vatican have insisted that the resurrected and ascended Christ remains male, but I am not sure that Gregory would have said that. This is no small matter in the fierce debate over the ordination of women if, as the Epistle to the Hebrews would seem to suggest, Christ as High Priest is understood eschatologically rather than incarnationally.)

Augustine in contrast—and on this issue John Chrysostom is closer to him than Gregory—rejects the splitting of androgyny into male and female natures, for he believes that sexual differences are intrinsic to creation. Furthermore, he sees the man as the true embodiment of the divine image though he talks about image in terms of properties in contradistinction to Chrysostom's *imago dei,* which is viewed in terms of the man's superior spiritual and natural authority.

In many schemas of the early church, even where men and women are held to be created equal (in the sense of both possessing the divine image as in Genesis 1:27), two factors combined to place the woman in a position of inferiority.

1. The fathers understood the begottenness of the Logos in eternity not to denote an "event," but to highlight the one nature and being of Father and

---

13. Two useful surveys on attitudes to women in the early church are Peter Brown, *The Body and Society*, and Elizabeth Clark's, *Women in the Early Church*.

14. See her remarks in *Theology,* 349–50. Nyssa's view is colored by his Platonism whereby the divine image cannot be seen in any corporeal sense. More positively, unlike Augustine, Nyssa sees nothing intrinsically wrong with the natural passion of sexual intercourse.

Son. When they came to Eve's begottenness in space and time, they tended to say, to parody Arius, "there was a time when Eve was not." In good Arian fashion, they saw the subsequent nature of women to mean secondary or less than the fullness of the male prototype.

2. Eve is the first to sin in the Genesis narrative and this is taken to mean that she is more culpable than Adam. The perfidiousness of Eve is then projected on to all women. Tertullian's hounding of the second sex is well illustrated by his infamous remarks, "you are the devil's gateway; you are the 'un-sealer of the tree'; you are the one who persuaded him whom the devil was not brave enough to approach; you so lightly crushed the image of God, the man Adam; because of your punishment, that is death, even the Son of God had to die . . ."[15]

Women as the second and therefor secondary sex were doubly cursed, then, because the second sex sinned first. Women were often viewed in terms of this doubly-dimmed divine image so that an antinomy was created between the male as rational (*nous*) and therefore more like God's image and the female as carnal, lower, bodily, subordinate, dependent, and there-fore less like God's image. Bodily materials, superabundant in women, were potentially dangerous, if not treacherous.

Women, however, could become more spiritual (though more so in terms of *pneuma*, rather than *nous*) and more like men (and *ipso facto* God) if they overcame their bodies in ascetic endeavor.[16] This became an increas-ingly acceptable form of spiritual and social advancement for women in the early Middle Ages (though even in the third century there were Syriac women ascetics—heads shorn to show their at-one-ment with men).

But motherhood (and more so martyrdom) was the pathway to honor God in the early church, for women and the positive values of the helper/ server as well as the inferior qualities of womanhood developed into their own archetype. No doubt influenced by the example of his saintly sister, Macrina, Gregory of Nyssa stressed in his writings the virtues of feminine supportiveness, intuition, and altruism. No woman could match the match-less majesty of the *Theotokos*, ever virgin and mother, but nonetheless a secondary spiritual archetype of femaleness emerges militating against the baseness and lewdness of the bodily female archetype.

It is the unquestionable acceptance of a spiritual feminine archetype that binds together those writers who wish to identify the Spirit as in some way feminine. This holds true for Alwyn Marriage and Naomi Goldenberg,

15. Quoted in Elizabeth Clark's *Women in the Early Church*, 39.

16. The identification of women's spirituality with intuition, caring, and altruism, helped facilitate, I suspect, the idea that women could be icons of the Spirit, who is Comforter, the go-between Father and Son (*vinculum amoris*).

but also for Leonardo Boff and the Orthodox writer Father Thomas Hop-ko.[17] Admittedly, the archetype is not always conceived in the same way and only Boff, of the above writers, has tried to link the *Theotokos,* womenkind, and the Spirit ontologically. Nevertheless, it is the acceptance of a female archetype on the one hand and the belief that this is linked to the Spirit as personal on the other that creates a family resemblance between these writers.

In the case of Father Hopko, whose thesis I shall evaluate a little later on, it is to his credit that he rejects the base and lewd version of femaleness for positive spiritual and human values. Radical feminists will identify, how-ever, Hopko's feminine archetype, which is altruistic, supportive, intuitive, peaceful, etc., as designed to ensure that women in society are destined for the wooden spoon. (In fact, Hopko's article is an attempt to demonstrate that women are equal to men, but distinct in function: this distinctiveness, for him, excludes them from the priesthood.)

Hopko suffers, like Marriage, in convincing us, whether we are radical feminists or not, of the legitimacy of the spiritual feminine archetype (or the masculine archetype, for that matter). Empirically, most neurological investigations of men and women recognize only minor differences in intel-ligence and aptitude. Cross-cultural studies demonstrate that the givenness of biological distinction between the sexes does not match gender roles in an isomorphic way.

In anthropology it is clear that to talk of the feminine and masculine is to talk of a cluster of attributes archetypically understood but scattered throughout the human population, both male and female. This is somewhat analogous to the fact that no one human race contains unique blood groups that cannot be found in all races.[18]

Typically, however, empirical counter-evidence does not seem to cut much ice with archetype thinking, whether it comes in neo-Platonic forms (such as Hopko's and Marriage's), Jungian depth psychology, or Husserlian pure consciousness. Such evidence is always put down as distortion, perver-sion, a-typicality, or merely surface evidence. This is not to say that there are no deep structures (of language, for example) or transcendental realities beyond sense data, but it is to say that in the case of feminine archetypes we

---

17. Cf. Marriage, *Life-Giving Spirit;* Goldenberg, "Dreams and Fantasies as Sources of Revelation: Feminist Appropriation of Jung"; Boff, *The Maternal Face of God;* Hopko, "On the Male Character of Christian Priesthood."

18. Though admittedly, there are distinct clusterings and oddities. For example, the people with the most similar blood groups to Great Britain—in terms of statistical scat-ter—are the Aborigines of Australia.

should at least posit the possibility that they are social constructions and culturally determined realities.

To depict the so-called feminine attributes as having their ultimate identity in God the Holy Spirit may satisfy a Christianized Platonic framework, but it is hardly commensurate with the biblical witness. As we have already seen, the Holy Spirit may be Comforter and Facilitator of Relationships, but the Spirit is also Lord, Creator, Mover, and Baptizer. Conversely, the *kenosis* of the Son, both in terms of the "divine condescension" of the Logos and Jesus' road to Calvary, cannot be read off as an iconic faithfulness to some archetypical notion of divine maleness.

And yet, as problematic as the role of archetypes may be in linking women with the Spirit, the real difficulty lies elsewhere. The question is this: how is the ontological link to be made between the Spirit as person (yet functionally conceived as the *vinculum amoris*) and womankind? Alwyn Marriage in her book *Life-Giving Spirit* is not altogether clear about this, but Hopko is. While he would not wish to be called a feminist, even of a conservative kind, his methodology is designed precisely to show that there is a kind of "symmetry" between womankind and the Spirit of God. Let us see if he succeeds.

Hopko presents his view of the Holy Spirit as Orthodox, and he disavows any association with sophiology, for he rightly sees that any identity between Wisdom and Spirit has a bias towards Gnosticism. Hopko also insists, though only in a footnote: that there is nothing "feminine" in divinity, as there is nothing "masculine." Divinity is beyond sexuality as it is "beyond being itself."[19] Having espoused apophaticism, however, Hopko then goes on to say a great deal about sexuality in the Godhead, but in a most curious way.

In Hopko's scheme the Father follows the Cappadocian tradition in being not only *primus inter pares,* but also the source, or cause, of the Trinity. But in his essay, unlike the tradition, the Father is strangely absent as a person. He is rather like Irenaeus' Father, whose two arms comprise the Son and the Spirit, except for the fact that Hopko's Father has little function other than to be the trunk that holds them together. (I am not suggesting for a moment that Hopko has an inadequate doctrine of God; only that in *this* essay God as Father is of no great consequences to his argument.)

I am sure that Hopko believes that neither the Father nor the Son can be said to be male in their eternal persons any more than the Spirit can be said to be of the feminine gender.[20] I assume he believes that gender is an

19. Cf. Hopko, "On the Male Character of Christian Priesthood," 108.

20. Of the B.C.C. Study Guide, *The Forgotten Trinity,* it states on page 32: "To project

inappropriate concept for divine persons.[21] Nevertheless, what he does is this: leaving the Father as an androgynous but all-pervading backdrop, he brings into focus the Son and Spirit. He says that there is "a direct analogical, symbolic and epiphanic relationship between Adam and the Son of God and between Eve and the Spirit of God . . . ."[22]

He is not talking about an isomorphic equivalence between Son/Adam and Spirit/Eve as historical hypostases. He means that there is an interplay or synergy, an epiphany—to use his own word—between the divine persons of Son and Spirit and male and female nature.

The equivalence between divine persons and created natures is a fundamental category mistake on which the whole of Hopko's thesis falls. The coherence of the Trinity in Orthodox theology is the *perichoesis* of persons unified by love as one being, or, as John Ziziouslas puts it, their "being is communion."[23] There are no complementary natures that coinhere in the Trinity. To suggest that created human natures reflect the coinherence of uncreated divine personhood is meaningless.

The *imago dei* in humankind is not a reflection of divine personhood mediated through created nature unless created nature shares in divine personhood. To put it less aphoristically and tautologically: you cannot read off human natures from divine persons if you are going to employ a patristic taxonomy of *hypostasis, ousia,* and *physis.* In short, to claim that male nature reflects eternal sonship or that female nature bears an *epiphanic* relationship to the Spirit as feminine archetype is not warranted by patristic methodology.

But Hopko's thesis does not stop there. Having told us that there is no sex in the Trinity but that there is an *epiphanic* relationship between divine Son/masculine nature and divine Spirit/feminine nature, he goes on to tell us "there is a taxis in the divine Trinity according to traditional Orthodox theology—an order, and one might even say a hierarchy, if one does not interpret this as some sort of ontological and essential 'subordinationism'—so there is a taxis in humanity, an order and hierarchy."[24]

There are two things here. First, as we have already seen, you cannot equate the taxis of divine persons with a hierarchical order of created

maleness into the Trinity is a dangerous and ultimately a blasphemous exercise."

21. It cannot be said that the Father is male in the usual anthropomorphic sense. He is called "Father" in the tradition because Jesus calls him Father and this scriptural warrant for the relationship is theologically reinforced by the fact that we are all, men and women who "have put on Christ," the *totus Christus.*

22. Hopko, "On the Male Character of Christian Priesthood," 106

23. Ziziouslas, *Being as Communion.*

24. Hopko, "On the Male Character of Christian Priesthood," 123.

nature so that maleness is to be given greater honor over femaleness. To risk repetition *ad nauseam:* person and nature are not equivalent categories in patristic thought.[25]

Second, non-essential subordinationism in the Trinity cannot mean a descending order of Father, Son, and Holy Ghost in the sense that the Spirit willingly self-effaces Herself before the Son in the proper and unique sense that the Son willingly submits to the Father's will. At its crudest, Hopko's model begins to look like patriarchal father, dutiful son, and submissive daughter who also defers to her brother. It is perfectly proper to say that the Spirit does eternally defer to the Son, but then so do all divine persons defer to each other in mutual reciprocity.

It is not Hopko's intention, but through his identification of the Spirit archetypically as the discreet and veiled hand-maiden the Trinity begins to take on an ominous lopsidedness. The Spirit, as person, is hemmed in, cramped, and fleeting like an eternal Cinderella. Functionally, though not ontologically, the Spirit begins to fade into the background, like a good servant girl, which is precisely what the *filioque* achieved for the Western theological tradition.

Father Hopko does not mention it, but the ancient order of deaconesses would appear to come to his support, for the women deacons were declared to be the icons of the Holy Spirit. This, however, begs more questions than it answers. Was it womanhood that was iconic, or lay personhood? If it was the former, this falls into the category mistake already discussed in this article. If the later, then presumably both men and women could be icons of the Spirit. (Can only men be icons of the Son?) Suffice it to say, it is clear from the Apostolic Constitutions of the fourth century that the order of deaconesses came into existence as a measure of economy, and it has not been normative in the Eastern Orthodox churches since the early Middle Ages.[26]

The purpose of this paper has been to examine some of the attempts to identify the Holy Spirit as archetypically feminine, which then try to read this "femininity" into womankind. I have attempted to show that the adoption of the altruistic feminine archetype has the merit of seeing positive spiritual value in women's lives, but the demerit of disenfranchising women from positions of power and authority. This is analogous to Auguste Comte's attempt in his now forgotten "Positivist Religion of Humanity" to award

25. It is surely the great achievement of the Cappadocians that they pioneered the usage of *hypostasis* as a distinct reality in contradistinction to its earlier usage as a virtual synonym for *ousia*. (This was made necessary because of the conceptual inadequacy of the dramaturgical *prosopon*).

26. Cf. Elizabeth Clark, *Women in the Early Church*, chap. 4.

women the highest honor in terms of spiritual development (remembering that it was Comte who coined the word "altruism"), but refusing them any place in either the market place or the academy.

For the romantic and conservative feminist the problem exemplified by Hopko's work is that even if it were possible to identify in some way the Spirit as feminine, we cannot adequately show, either ontologically or analogously, how the taxis of divine personhood equates to a hierarchy of human natures or to a distinctive complementarity of the sexes.

AFTERWORD

I would like to thank Wipf & Stock for publishing a collection of my academic and journalistic pieces, and to Andy Kinsey for editing the work. It is rewarding to see.

There are three things I would like to comment on that I think will facilitate an understanding of this book. The first is to remind readers that it is work that covers publications over forty-five years. Many of the pieces reflect a multidisciplinary approach to Christianity, and my aim during this time has been to write in a way that is as accessible as possible. During the past forty-five years I have changed my mind on a number of issues, and rather than present a corpus of work that is consistent and without contradiction, I have let the ragged and sometimes disjointed aspects of my publications remain (having always insisted that the New Testament is also replete with "loose ends"; the least I can do is to apply that insight to my own work—although, unlike sacred texts, my musings have no canonical status).

The second thing I would like to state is that all the publications included in this volume are motivated by the one big idea that has dominated my thinking since the early 1980s: there is a broad alliance of Christians across the divides of Christendom that should and can stand together on the essential truths of the gospel. It was this idea that led me to establish the C. S. Lewis Center for the study of religion and modernity in 1987. That venture enabled me to lecture and write on issues of "mere Christianity," but it also became a burden because many Lewis aficionados only wanted me to talk about Lewis, and not continue his penetrating work on the paucity of modernism or defend the central tenets of the gospel. Any criticism I made of Lewis—of his Platonism, for example—was treated as treachery. I love Lewis and his writings enormously, but they are not in themselves the gospel.

Nevertheless, I have not abandoned Lewis' belief that there are essential features of Christianity that we all must affirm if we are to call ourselves

Christians. I continue to write and speak about the core Christian Tradition, and it is why I have championed Lewis' phrase "Deep Church" to encapsulate basic Christianity, although I am not sure Lewis would have approved of my extended use of it.

The third and final thing I would like to make clear is that I have had only two denominational affiliations in my life: Pentecostalism, by virtue of the fact that I was the youngest son of a Pentecostal pastor, and Eastern Orthodoxy, with a distinctive, though not exclusive, debt to the Russian Diaspora. It was abandoning Pentecostalism that led me to the sociology of religion, and it was the discovery of Orthodoxy that immersed me in theology. I hope that I have written about Pentecostal/Charismatic Christianity with affection and sympathy; I remain indebted to its experiential encounters with God. Equally, I trust that my Eastern Orthodox commitments have not made me blind to its many faults, but remain confident that in rediscovering the patristic heritage the Western churches will also find the depth that many Christians are seeking.

TIMELINE

Andrew G. Walker

Born in 1945, as the youngest son of a Pentecostal pastor, Andrew spent most of his junior schooling in South Wales and Worthing in West Sussex; he then completed his High School education in Worthing.

After an abortive attempt at Bible College in 1964, and after losing his Christian faith, Andrew attended Hull University, where he graduated in 1968 with a degree in social science. A second degree followed at Salford in 1969 (Masters of Science in Sociology), after teaching one year at Manchester University. Andrew then moved to London and completed a part-time doctorate at Goldsmiths in 1979 in sociological/philosophical anthropology.

Andrew's first publication was in *Sociological Review* in 1971, with an article in collaboration with James Atherton on a Pentecostal Convention. After philosophical pieces in journals such as *Theory and Society* (1975) and *Philosophy of the Social Sciences* (1979, 1983), Andrew turned his attention to religion—sociologically and then theologically.

In 1985, Andrew published his first book, *Restoring the Kingdom*—available in four editions from 1985 to 1998. From this point on Andrew wrote pieces exclusively from a Christian perspective, most of which are listed in the bibliography.

THEOLOGICAL, PERSONAL, AND CAREER CHANGES

In 1973, after recovering his Christian faith, Andrew joined the Eastern Orthodox Church, becoming a committed ecumenist, bringing people together, and trying to restore confidence in the gospel among various Christian communities.

In 1987, Andrew founded and served as the director of the C. S. Lewis Center for the study of religion & modernity. This was a charitable trust and venture supported by many leading theologians from a wide-range of churches, under the patronage of the Archbishop of Canterbury and the chairmanship of Orthodox bishop, Metropolitan Anthony of Sourozh.

Under the auspices of this trust, first with Hodder & Stoughton and then with SPCK, the Center published eighteen books, some of which were collections reflecting on the relationship between the gospel and culture (e.g., *Different Gospels,* 1988) and others of which were collaborations (e.g., Tom Smail, Andrew Walker, and N. G. Wright, *Charismatic Renewal: The Search for a Theology,* 2nd ed. 1993). Solo works included Andrew's *Enemy Territory,* which Andrew believes is his best book out of this period.

In 1990, Andrew left the College of Higher Education to become lecturer in Theology and Education at King's College, London, where he was promoted to Senior Lecturer in 1994 and Professor of Theology and Education in 1999. From 1993 to 2003, Andrew served as Visiting Professor in Evangelism at Southern Methodist University, Dallas, Texas.

In 1993, the C. S. Lewis Center started publishing a quarterly journal, *Leading Light.* In 1995, as a result of a request from Bishop Leslie Newbigin, the Center merged with the Gospel and Culture Network. The group disbanded in 1997, ending the publication of the journal (though the Gospel & Culture Network lives on under different auspices).

Also in 1997, the Center for Theology, Religion & Culture at King's College—which was based in the Department of Education, but supported by the Dean's Office and the Department of Theology—was established. With increasing concentration on training for church leadership, Andrew became increasingly involved in collaborative enterprises, ranging from conferences on "Harmful Religion and Worship" at King's to supporting ordination courses in the Church of England, as well as teaching patristics to the Ichthus New Church Network

In 2002, Andrew was installed as an Ecumenical Canon of Saint Paul's Cathedral in London, becoming instrumental in supporting the "Deep Church" movement. Recent publications, which reflect this emphasis, are *Remembering Our Future,* co-edited with Luke Bretherton (2007), and *Deep Church Rising,* co-authored with Robin Parry (2014). Two other books are also dedicated to Andrew in regards to his work in "Deep Church" and his career in theology and sociology: *The Wisdom of the Spirit* (2014) and *The Great Tradition—A Great Labor* (2011).

BIBLIOGRAPHY

Abraham, William J. *Canon and Criterion in Christian Theology: From the Fathers to Feminism*. Oxford: Clarendon, 1998.

———. *The Logic of Evangelism*. Grand Rapids: Eerdmans, 1989.

———. *The Logic of Renewal*. Grand Rapids: Eerdmans, 2007.

Allen, David. *The Unfailing Stream: A Charismatic Church History in Outline*. Tonbridge, UK: Sovereign Word, 1994.

Allen, Gustav. *Christus Victor*. Translated by A. G. Herbert. London: SPCK, 1965.

Allen, Joseph, ed. "The Thoughts of Metropolitan Philip on Missiology." April 2008. Online: http://www.antiochian.org.

Anderson, Ray S. *On Being Human*. Grand Rapids: Eerdmans, 1983.

Anderson, Robert Mapes. *Vision of the Disinherited: The Making of American Pentecostalism*. Oxford: Oxford University Press, 1980.

Atherton, J. S. "An Easter Pentecostal Convention: The Successful Management of a 'Time of Blessing.'" *Sociological Review* 19.3 (1971) 367–87.

Augustine. *De Doctrina Christiana*. Translated by D. W. Robinson. Indianapolis: Bobbs-Merrill, 1984.

Ayer, A. J. *The Concept of a Person and Other Essays*. New York: Vintage, 1983.

———. *Philosophy in the Twentieth Century*. New York: Vintage, 1984.

Bailey, Edward. "The Religion of a Secular Society." Ph.D. thesis, University of Bristol, 1976.

Balmer, Randall. "The Princetonians and Scripture: A Reconsideration." *Westminster Theological Journal* 44.2 (1982) 352–65.

Banks, J. A. *The Sociology of Social Movements*. New York: Macmillan, 1972.

Baptism, Eucharist and Ministry. Faith and Order Paper No. 111. Geneva: World Council of Churches, 1982.

Bar-Hillel, Yehoshua. "Indexical Expressions." *Mind*, New Series 63.251 (1954) 359–79.

Barker, Eileen. *New Religious Movements: A Practical Introduction*. London: HMSO, 1989.

Barrett, David B. "Global Table 1: Global Expansion of the Renewal across the 20th Century—Column 4." In *Dictionary of Pentecostal and Charismatic Movements*, edited by Stanley M. Burgess and Gary R. McGee, 812. Grand Rapids: Regency, Zondervan, 1989.

Basham, Don. "Spiritual Warfare." Audiotape. Mobile, AL: Integrity, 1983.

Basil, Saint. *Treatise on the Holy Spirit*. Crestwood, NY: Saint Vladimir's Seminary Press, 1980.

Behr-Sigel, Elizabeth. *Lev Gillet: A Monk of the Eastern Church*. Oxford: Fellowship of Saint Alban and Saint Sergus, 1999.

Bell, Daniel. *The Cultural Contradictions of Capitalism*. London: Heinemann, 1976.

Bellah, Robert N. "Civil Religion in America." In *Beyond Belief: Essays on Religion in a Post-Traditional World*, edited by Robert N. Bellah, 168–89. New York: Harper & Row, 1970.

Benn, Wallace, and Mark Burkhill. *A Theological and Pastoral Critique of the Teachings of John Wimber*. Harold Wood Booklets, No. 1. Saint Peter's Church, Romford, Essex, RM3 oQB, n.d.

Bennett, David Malcom. *Edward Irving: The Man, His Controversies, and the Pentecostal Movement*. Eugene: OR: Wipf & Stock, 2014.

Berdyaev, Nicholas. *The Fate of the Modern World*. London: SCM, 1935.

———. *Freedom and the Spirit*. Charlottesville, VA: University of Virginia Press, 1972.

———. *Truth and Revelation*. London: Bles, 1953.

Berger, Peter. *Facing Up to Modernity*. New York: Basic, 1979.

Berger, Peter, and Thomas Luckmann. *The Social Construction of Reality*. New York: Anchor, 1966.

Battenson, Henry. *Later Christian Fathers: A Selection from the Writings of the Fathers from Saint Cyril of Jerusalem to Saint Leo the Great*. Oxford: Oxford University Press, 1972.

Behr, John. "On the 1600th Anniversary of Saint John Chrysostom's Death." Talk delivered at the Orthodox Church of America, parish of Saint John Chrysostom. Home Springs, MO, September 29, 2007.

Beversluis, John. *C. S. Lewis and the Search for Rational Religion*. Grand Rapids: Eerdmans, 1985.

Bloom, Alan. *The American Religion: The Emergence of the Post-Christian Nation*. New York: Simon & Schuster, 1992.

Bloom, Harold. *The Closing of the American Mind*. New York: Simon & Schuster, 1987.

Boff, Leonardo. *The Maternal Face of God: The Feminine and Its Religious Expressions*. San Francisco: Harper & Row, 1979.

Brown, Peter. *The Body and Society*. London: Faber & Faber, 1990.

Bruce, Steve. *Pray TV: Televangelism in America*. New York: Routledge, 1990.

Buber, Martin. *I-Thou*. Translated by R. G. Smith. Edinburgh: T. & T. Clark, 1959.

Bultmann, Rudolph. "New Testament and Mythology." In *Kerygma and Myth*, edited by H. W. Bartsch, 1–43. London: SPCK, 1955.

Bulgakov, Sergius. *The Bride of the Lamb*. Grand Rapids: Eerdmans, 2001.

Bugeon, John Williams. *Byzantine Texts*. Rev. ed. Edited by M. L. Chadwick and V. A. Chadwick. London: Murray, 1883.

Butler, Joseph. *Awash in a Sea of Faith: Christianizing the American People—Studies in Cultural History*. Cambridge: Harvard University Press, 1990.

Carrithers, Michael, Steven Collins, and Steven Lukes, eds. *The Category of the Person: Anthropology, Philosophy, History*. Cambridge: Cambridge University Press, 1985.

Carpenter, Humphrey. *J. R. R. Tolkien: A Biography*. London: Allen & Unwin, 1977.

Carr, Wesley. *Angels and Principalities*. Cambridge: Cambridge University Press, 1981.

Catechism of the Orthodox Church of Saint Philaret. Liberty, TN: Saint John of Kronstadt, 2009.

Christensen, Michael J. *C. S. Lewis on Scripture: His Thoughts on the Nature of Biblical Inspiration, the Role of Revelation and the Question of Inerrancy.* London: Hodder & Stoughton, 1979.

———. *C. S. Lewis on Scripture.* 2nd ed. London: Hodder & Stoughton, 1990.

Cicourel, Aaron V. *A Cognitive Sociology: Language and Meaning in Social Interaction.* New York: Free, 1974.

Church of England Yearbook. London, Church House, 1991.

Chrysostom, John. *Adversus Judaeos.* Homily V. The Fathers of the Church, vol. 68. Translated by P. W. Hartings. Washington, DC: Catholic University Academic Press, 1979.

Clark, Elizabeth. *Women in the Early Church.* Wilmington: Glazier, 1983.

Clark, S. B. *Redeemer.* Ann Arbor, MI: Servant, 1992.

Coakley, Sarah. "Creaturehood before God, Male and Female." *Theology* 93 (1990) 343–53.

Coates, Gerald. *Divided We Stand.* Eastbourne, UK: Kingsway, 1986.

———. *What on Earth Is This Kingdom?* Eastbourne, UK: Kingsway, 1983.

Cooley, Charles H. *Human Nature and the Social Order.* New York: Scribners, 1902.

Congar, Yves. *I Believe in the Holy Spirit.* New York: Crossroads, 1997.

Cotton, Ian. *The Hallelujah Revolution: The Rise of the New Christians.* London: Little Brown, 1995.

Cox, Harvey. *Fire from Heaven: Pentecostalism, Spirituality, and the Reshaping of Religion in the Twenty-first Century.* New York: Addison-Wesley, 1994.

Cupitt, Donald. *Creation Out of Nothing.* London: SCM, 1990.

Dahrendorf, Ralf. *Homo Sociologus.* New York: Routledge and Kegan Paul, 1973.

Daly, Mary. *Beyond God the Father.* Boston: Beacon, 1985.

Dayton, Donald. *Theological Roots of Pentecostalism.* Grand Rapids: Zondervan, 1987.

Derrick, Christopher. *C. S. Lewis and the Church of Rome.* San Francisco: Saint Ignatius, 1981.

Ditton, Jason. *The View from Goffman.* New York: Macmillan, 1980.

Dixon, Patrick. *Signs of Revival.* Eastbourne, UK: Kingsway, 1994.

Dobblelaere, Karel. "Secularization: A Multi-Dimensional Concept." *Current Sociology* 29.2 (1981) 15–22.

Doerkse, Brian. *Isn't He/Eternity: Intimate Songs of Praise and Worship.* Anaheim, CA: VMI, 1995.

Dostoevsky, Fyodor. *The Brothers Karamazov.* New York: Farrar, Straus and Giroux, 2002.

Drew, Paul. *Erving Goffman: Exploring the Interaction Order.* Cambridge: Polity, 2000.

Douglas, Mary. *Purity and Danger: An Analysis of Concepts of Pollution and Taboo.* New York: Routledge, 2002.

Douglas, Jack D. *Understanding Everyday Life.* Chicago: Aldine, 1970.

Durkheim, Emil. *The Division of Labor in Society.* New York: Macmillan, 1984.

———. *The Elementary Forms of Religious Life.* New York: Free, 1995.

———. *The Rules of Sociological Method.* New York: Free, 1982.

Eco, Umberto. *Travels in Hyperreality.* Translated by William Weaver. London: Picador, 1987.

Edwards, Jonathan. *Religious Affections.* Edited by J. Smith. New Haven: Yale University Press, 1979.

Engels, Frederick. *Anti-Druhring.* New York: International, 1966.

Evans, C. Stephen. *Preserving the Person*. Downers Grove, IL: IVP, 1977.

Farah, Charles. "America's Pentecostals: What They Believe." *Christianity Today*, October 16, 1987, 22–26.

Feuerbach, Ludwig. *The Essence of Christianity*. New York: Continuum, 1957.

Festinger, Leon. *When Prophecy Fails*. Minneapolis, MN: University of Minnesota Press, 1956.

Fletcher, Colin. *The Person in the Light of Sociology*. New York: Routledge and Kegan Paul, 1975.

The Forgotten Trinity. Study Guide of British Council of Churches. London: British Council of Churches, 1989.

Garfinkel, Harold. *Studies in Ethnomethodology*. New York: Prentice Hall, 1967.

Gelpi, Donald. *Pentecostalism: A Theological Viewpoint*. New York: Paulist, 1971.

Gilquist, Peter E. *Metropolitan Philip*. Nashville, TN: Nelson, 1991.

Goffman, Erving. *Asylum: Essays on the Social Situation of Mental Patients and Other Inmates*. New York: Anchor, 1961.

———. *Frame Analysis: An Essay on the Organization of Experience*. Boston: Northeastern University Press, 1986.

———. *Interaction Ritual: Essays on Face to Face Behavior*. New York: Pantheon, 1982.

———. *The Presentation of the Self in Everyday Life*. New York: Anchor, 1959.

———. *Stigma: Notes on the Management of Spoiled Identity*. New York: Simon & Schuster, 1963.

Goldenberg, Naomi R. "Dreams and Fantasies as Sources of Revelation: Feminist Appropriation of Jung." In *Womanspirit Rising: A Feminist Reader in Religion*, edited by Carol P. Christ and Judith Plaskow, 219–27. San Francisco: Harper & Row, 1979.

Gunton, Colin E, *Enlightenment and Alienation: An Essay Toward a Trinitarian Theology*. New York: HaperCollins, 1984.

———. "The Spirit as Lord: Christianity, Modernity and Freedom." In *Different Gospels*, edited by Andrew Walker, 74–85. London: SPCK, 1993.

Graham, Billy, "Foreword." In *Betraying the Gospel*, edited by Andrew Walker, 15–19. Wilmore, KY: Bristol, 1988.

Guiness, Os. *The Gravedigger File*. London: Hodder & Stoughton, 1983.

Hammond, Frank, and Ida Mae Hammond. *Pigs in the Parlor*. Kirkwood, MO: Impact, 1973.

Hampson, Daphne. *Theology and Feminism*. Oxford: Blackwell, 1990.

Harper, Michael. *Charismatic Crisis: The Charismatic Renewal—Past, Present and Future*. London: Hounslow, 1980.

———. *None Can Guess*. London: Hodder & Stoughton, 1971.

Harrold, Philip, and D. H. Williams, eds. *The Great Tradition—A Great Labor: Studies in Ancient-Future Faith*. Eugene, OR: Cascade, 2011.

Harvey, David. *The Condition of Postmodernity: An Enquiry into the Origins of Cultural Change*. Oxford: Blackwell, 1989.

Hatch, Nathan. *The Democratization of American Christianity*. New Haven: Yale University Press, 1989.

Heidegger, Martin. *Being and Time*. New York: Harper & Row, 1962.

Hick, John, and Paul Knitter, eds. *The Myth of Christian Uniqueness*. Maryknoll, NY: Orbis, 1987.

Hilborn, David. "Interview with Professor Andrew Walker." In *The Wisdom of the Spirit*, edited by Martyn Percy and Pete Ward, 173–93. Farnham, UK: Ashgate, 2014.

Hill, Michael. *A Sociology of Religion*. London: Heinemann Education, 1973.

Hocken, Peter. *Streams of Renewal: Origins and Early Development of the Charismatic in Great Britain*. Exeter, UK: Paternoster, 1986.

Hopko, Thomas. "On the Male Character of the Christian Priesthood." In *Women and the Priesthood*, edited by Kalistro Ware, Gerald Barrois, Thomas Hopko, 97–134. New York: Saint Vladimir Seminary Press, 1982.

Hollenweger, Walter. "The House Church Movement in Great Britain." *The Expository Times* 92 (1980) 45–47.

———. *The Pentecostals*. London: SCM, 1972.

Hooper, Walter, ed. *C. S. Lewis: Selected Literary Essays*. Cambridge: Cambridge University Press, 1969.

———, ed. *Letters of C. S. Lewis*. London: Collins Fount, 1988.

———. "Preface." In C. S. Lewis, *Fern-seed and Elephants and Other Essays on Christianity*, vii–ix. London: Collins Fount, 1977.

———. ed. *They Stand Together: The Letters of C. S. Lewis to Arthur Greeves, 1914–1963*. London: Collins, 1979.

Horne, Brian. "A Peculiar Debt: The Influence of Charles Williams on C. S. Lewis." In *A Christian for All Christians*, edited by Andrew Walker and Patrick James, 83–97. London: Hodder & Stoughton, 1990.

Howard, Roland. *The Rise and Fall of the Nine O'Clock Service*. London: Mowbrays, 1996.

Hunt, Stephen. "Giving the Devil More Than His Due: Some Problems with Deliverance Ministry." In *Harmful Religion: Studies in Religious Abuse*, edited by Andrew Walker and Laurence Osborn, 43–64, London: SPCK, 1997.

Hunter, James Davidson. *American Evangelicalism: Conservative Religion and the Quandary of Modernity*. New Brunswick: Rutgers University Press, 1983.

Irving, Edward. *The Day of Pentecost, or the Baptism with the Holy Ghost*. London: Ellerton and Henderson, for Baldwin and Cradock, 1831.

Janzen, Grace. "What is Feminism?" *Theology* 755 (Sept/Oct 1990) 339–43.

Kamenka, Eugene. *Marxism and Ethics*. New York: Macmillan, 1969.

Kant, Immanuel. *The Moral Law: Groundwork of the Metaphysics of Morals*. New York: Routledge, 1948.

Kerr, Hugh. *Preaching in the Early Church*. New York: Revell, 1942.

Kim, J. H. "Sources outside of Europe." In *Spirituality and the Secular Quest,* edited by Peter Van Ness, 53–71. London: SCM, 1996.

Khomiakov, Alexei S. *The Church Is One*. Liberty, TN: Saint John of Kronstadt, 1863.

Khodr, Georges, "Christianity in a Pluralist World: The Economy of the Holy Spirit." *The Ecumenical Review,* 23.2 (April 1997) 118–28.

Kuhn, Thomas S. *The Structure of Scientific Revolutions*. Chicago: Chicago University Press, 1970.

Laing, R. D. *The Divided Self: An Existential Study in Sanity and Madness*. New York: Penguin, 1965.

Lampert, Evgeniil. *The Divine Realm: Towards a Theology of the Sacraments*. London: Faber & Faber, 1944.

Lewis, C. S. *The Abolition of Man*. London: Collins Fount, 1978.

———. *Broadcast Talks*. London: Bles, 1942.

———. "De Descriptione Temporum." In *Selected Literary Essays,* edited by Walter Hooper, 1–15, Cambridge: Cambridge University Press, 1969.

———. *The Discarded Image: An Introduction to Medieval and Renaissance Literature.* Cambridge: Cambridge University Press, 1967.

———. *An Experiment in Criticism.* Cambridge: Cambridge University Press, 1992.

———. *Fern-seed and Elephants and Other Essays on Christianity.* London: Collins Fount, 1977.

———. *The Four Loves.* London: Collins Fount, 1963.

———. *The Great Divorce.* London: Bles, 1942.

———. *The Last Battle.* London: Collins Lions, 1980.

———. *The Lion, the Witch, and the Wardrobe.* London: Bles, 1950.

———. *Mere Christianity.* London: Collins Fount, 1977.

———. *Miracles: A Preliminary Study.* London: Collins Fount, 1977.

———. "Myth Became Fact." In *God in the Dock: Essays on Theology,* edited by Walter Hooper, 63–67. London: Collins Fount, 1979.

———. "On the Reading of Old Books." In *First and Second Things,* 25–33. London: Collins Fount, 1985.

———. *The Pilgrim's Regress: An Allegorical Apology for Christianity, Reason and Romanticism.* London: Collins Fount, 1977.

———. *The Problem of Pain.* London: Collins Fount, 1957.

———. *Prayer: Letters to Malcolm.* London: Collin Fount, 1977.

———. *Reflection on the Psalms.* London: Collins Fount, 1977.

———. *The Screwtape Letters.* London: Bles, 1942.

———. *Surprised by Joy: The Shape of My Early Life.* London: Harcourt, 1955.

———. "Transposition." In *Screwtape Proposes a Toast and Other Pieces,* 9–27. London: Collins Fount, 1977.

———. *Voyage to Venus (Perelandra).* London: Pan, 1953.

———. "The Weight of Glory." In *Screwtape Proposes a Toast and Other Pieces,* 94–110, London: Collins Fount, 1977.

Lindsay, A. D. "Individualism." *Encyclopedia of the Social Sciences,* 7 (1930–33) 674–80.

Lloyd Jones, Martyn. *Romans: An Exposition of Chapters 7:1—8:4. "The Law: Its Function and Its & Limits."* Edinburgh: Banner of Truth, 1974.

———. *Romans: An Exposition of Chapter 8:5–7. The Sons of God."* Edinburgh: Banner of Truth, 1974.

Lossky, George. *The Mystical Theology of the Eastern Church.* Crestwood, NY: Saint Vladimir's Seminary Press, 2002.

Lukes, Steven. *Emil Durkheim: His Life and Work.* Stanford: Stanford University Press, 1973.

———. *Individualism.* New York: HarperCollins, 1974.

MacIntyre, Alasdair. *After Virtue: A Study in Moral Theory.* London: Duckworth, 1985.

———. *Marxism and Christianity.* Notre Dame, IN: University of Notre Dame Press, 1984.

———. *Whose Justice? Which Rationality?* London: Duckworth, 1988.

MacMurray, John. *Persons in Relation.* London: Faber & Faber, 1961.

MacRobert, Ian. *The Black Roots and White Racism of Early Pentecostalism in the USA.* London: MacMillan, 1988.

Malinowski, Bronsilaw. *A Scientific Theory of Culture.* Chapel Hill, NC: University of North Carolina Press, 1944.

Marriage, Alwyn. *Life-Giving Spirit: Responding to the Feminine in God.* London: SPCK, 1989.

Marsden, George. *Fundamentalism and American Culture: The Shaping of Twentieth-Century Evangelicalism, 1870–1925.* Oxford: Oxford University Press, 1980.

Martin, David. "Latin America Pentecost." In *Leading Light: Christian Faith and Contemporary Culture* 3.1 (Summer 1996) 11.

———. *Tongues of Fire: The Explosion of Protestantism in Latin America.* Cambridge: Blackwell, 1990.

Marx, Karl. *Early Writings.* New York: Vintage, 1975.

McDonnell, Daniel. *The Promise of Health and Wealth: A Biblical and Historical Analysis of the Faith Movement.* London: Hodder & Stoughton/C. S. Lewis Center, 1990.

McConnell, Kilian. *The Charismatic Renewal and Ecumenism.* New York: Paulist, 1978.

McGrath, Alister. *C. S. Lewis—A Life: Eccentric Genius, Reluctant Prophet.* Carol Stream, IL: Tyndale House, 2013.

Mead, George Herbert. *Mind, Self and Society.* Chicago: University of Chicago Press, 1967.

Metropolitan Philip. "Address to the Episcopal Church." May 2010. Online: http://www.antiochian.org.

Mill, John Stuart. *August Comte and Positivism.* London: Longman, 1865.

Missen, Alfred. "The Pentecostal Movement in the Eighties." Address at the Elim and Assemblies of God Churches Conference, November 16, 1979.

Mitchell, Basil. *The Justification of Religious Belief.* New York: Oxford University Press, 1981.

———. *Morality: Religious and Secular—The Dilemma of the Traditional Conscience.* Oxford: Oxford University Press, 1980.

Mohabir, Philip. *Building Bridges: Dramatic Personal Story of Evangelism and Reconciliation.* London: Hodder & Stoughton, 1989.

Moore, John. "The Catholic Pentecostal Movement." In *Sociological Yearbook of Religion,* edited by Michael Hill, 73–90. New York: SCM, 1973.

Moynihan, Martin. *Letters: C. S. Lewis and Don Giovanni Calabria: A Study in Friendship.* London: Collins, 1989.

Moltmann, Jürgen. *The Crucified God.* New York: Harper & Row, 1974.

———. *God in Creation.* New York: Harper & Row, 1985.

———. *The Trinity and the Kingdom of God.* New York: Harper & Row, 1981.

Neibuhr, H. R. *Christ and Culture.* London: Faber & Faber, 1952.

Neurath, Otto. "Sociology in the Framework of Physicalism." In *Philosophical Papers, 1913–1946,* edited by Cohen and Marie Neurath, 158–90. New York: Reidel, 1983.

Newbigin, Leslie. *The Gospel in a Pluralist Society.* London: SPCK, 1989.

Noll, Mark A, ed. *The Princeton Theology, 1812–1921: Scripture, Science and Theological Method from Archibald Alexander to Benjamin Breckinridge Warfield.* Grand Rapids: Baker, 1983.

Nowak, Kurt, et al., ed. *Adolf Harnack: Christentum, Wissenschaft und Gesellschaft.* Gottingen: Vandenhoeck and Ruprecht, 2001.

O'Connor, Edward D. *The Pentecostal Movement in the Catholic Church.* Notre Dame:, IN Ave Maria, 1971.

Oleska, Michael. *Another Culture/Another World,* Juneau, AK: Association of Alaska Schools, 2005.

Otto, Rudolph. *The Idea of the Holy.* 2nd ed. Translated by John W. Harvey. London: Oxford University Press, 1958.

Packer, J. I. "Theological Reflections on the Charismatic Movement." *Churchman* 94.2 (1980) 1–2.

Papas, George S. *Berkeley's Thought.* Ithaca, NY: Cornell University Press, 2000.

Parry, Robin A. *Worshipping Trinity.* 2nd ed. Eugene, OR: Cascade, 2013.

Patrick, James. "C. S. Lewis and Idealism." In *A Christian for All Christians: Essays in Honor of C. S. Lewis,* edited by Andrew Walker and James Patrick, 156–73. London: Hodder & Stoughton, 1990.

———. *The Magdalen Metaphysics: Idealism and Orthodoxy at Oxford, 1901–1945.* Macon, GA: Mercer University Press, 1985.

Peacock, Arthur, and Grant Gillet, eds. *Persons and Personality.* Malden: MA, Blackwell, 1987.

Pelikan, Jaroslov. *Christianity and Classical Culture.* New Haven: Yale University Press, 1993.

Penn-Lewis, Jessie. *War on the Saints.* Reprint. New York: Lowe, 1973.

Percy, Martyn. "Sweet Rapture: Subliminal Eroticism in Contemporary Charismatic Worship." Unpublished Paper.

Percy, Martyn, and Pete Ward, eds. *The Wisdom of the Spirit: Gospel, Church and Culture.* Farnham, UK: Ashgate, 2014.

———. *Words, Wonders and Power.* London: SPCK, 1996.

Peretti, Frank. *This Present Darkness.* Chicago: Crossway, 1986.

Petipierre, Dom Robert. *Exorcism: The Findings of the Committee Convened by the Bishop of Exeter.* London: SPCK, 1972.

Persig, Robert. *Zen and the Art of Motor Cycle Maintenance: An Inquiry into Values.* New York: Bantom, 1974.

The Philokalia. Translated by G. E .H. Palmer. 3 vols. London: Faber & Faber, 1981–84.

Popper, Karl. *The Open Society and Its Enemies.* Princeton: Princeton University Press, 1945.

Popovic, Justin. *Notes on Ecumenism.* Alhambar, CA: Sebastian, 2013.

Porter, Stanley E., and Philip J. Richter. *The Toronto Blessing, Or Is It?* London: Darton, Longman, and Todd, 1995.

Powell, Graham, and Shirley Powell. *Set Yourself Free.* Chichester, UK: New Wine, 1983.

Prince, Derek. *Blessing or Curse: You Can Choose.* Milton Keynes, UK: Word, 1990.

———. "Principalities and Powers." Anchor Bay, MI: Ministry Messages, n.d.

Rapp, Christoff. "Aristotle's Rhetoric." In *Stanford Encyclopedia of Philosophy,* edited by E. N. Zalsa. 2010. Online: http://www.plato.stanford.edu/entries/aristotle-rhetoric/.

Rex, John. *Key Problems of Sociological Theory.* New York: Routledge, 1961.

Richards, W. T. H. *Pentecost Is Dynamite.* Lakeland, FL: Cox and Wyman, 1971.

Roberts, Dave. *The Toronto Blessing.* Eastbourne, UK: Kingsway, 1994.

Rorty, Amelie Oksenberg. *The Identities of Persons.* Oakland, CA: University of California Press, 1976.

Ruether, Rosemary. *Sexism and God-Talk: Towards a Feminist Theology.* London: SCM, 1983.

Sacks, Harvey, Emmanuel A. Schegloff, and Gail Jefferson. "A Simplest Systematics for the Organization of Turn-Taking for Conservation." *Language* 50.4 (1974) 696–735.

Scott, Nathan A., and Ronald A. Sharp, eds. *Reading George Steiner*. Baltimore: John Hopkins University Press, 1994.

Schmemman, Alexander. *Church, World, Mission*. Crestwood, NY: Saint Vladimir's Seminary Press, 1979.

———. *Of Water and the Spirit*. Crestwood, NY: Saint Vladimir's Seminary Press, 1995.

Schutz, Alfred. "Common Sense and Interpretation of Human Action." *Philosophy and Phenomological Research* 14.1 (1953) 1–38.

———. *The Phenomenology of the Social World*. Evanston, IL: Northwestern University Press, 1967.

———. "The Problem of Rationality in the Social World." *Economica* 10.38 (1943) 130–49.

Seel, John. "Modernity and Evangelicals: American Evangelicalism as a Global Case Study." In *Faith and Modernity*, edited by Philip Sampson, Vinay Samuel, Chris Sugden, 287–313. Oxford: Regnum, 1994.

Sills, David. *International Encyclopedia of the Social Sciences*. New York: Macmillan, 1968.

Signs of the Spirit: Official Report, Seventh Assembly, Canberra, Australia, 7–20, February 1991.

Smail, Tom. *The Giving Gift*. London: DLT, 1995.

Stackhouse, Ian. *The Gospel-Driven Church: Retrieving Classical Ministries for Contemporary Revivalism*. Milton Keynes, UK: Paternoster, 2004.

Steiner, George. *Real Presences: Is There Anything in What We Say?* London: Faber & Faber, 1989.

Subritzky, Bill. *Demons Defeated*. 2nd ed. Chichester, UK: Sovereign World, 2004.

Suchocki, Marjorie. *God, Christ and Church*. New York: Crossroads, 1986.

Sullivan, Emmanuel. *Can the Pentecostal Movement Renew the Churches?* London: British Council of Churches, 1971.

Swinburne, Richard, and Samuel Shoemaker. *Personal Identity*. Malden, MA: Blackwell, 1984.

Symeon the New Theologian. *The Practical and Theological Chapters & The Three Theological Discourses*. Kalamazoo, MI: Cistercian Publications, 1982.

Taliaferro, Charles. "A Narnian Theory of the Atonement." *Scottish Journal of Theology* 41.1 (1988) 75–92.

Tarleton, George. *Birth of a Christian Anarchist*. Private Publication. Hillsdale, NY: Pendragon, 1993.

Taylor, Mark C. *Erring: A Postmodern A-Theology*. Chicago: Chicago University Press, 1987.

Thurman, Joyce. *New Wineskins*. New York: Lang, 1982.

Troparian of the Feast of the Annunciation, Orthodox Liturgy.

Trubetskoi, Eugene. *Icons: Theology in Color*. Crestwood, NY: Saint Vladimir's Seminary Press, 1973.

Walker, Andrew G. "After the Monarchy." *Leading Light: Christian Faith and Contemporary Culture* 1.2 (1993) 11–14, 26.

———. "The Angel of Regent Square." BBC Radio 4 Broadcast, December 1984. Repeated January 1985.

———. "The Ark." *Ship of Fools Blog*. Online: http://shipoffools.com/features/2003/holy_fools.html.

———, ed. *Betraying the Gospel: Modern Theologies and Christian Orthodoxy*. Wilmore, KY: Bethany, 1990.

———. "Between Scylla and Charybdis: 'Analysis' and Its Heroic Quest for That Which is No-Thing." *Philosophy of the Social Sciences* 13 (1983) 73–85.

———. "Beware a New Crusade." *Ship of Fools Blog*. November 2001. Online: http://www.shipoffools.org.

———. "Charismatic and Pentecostal Religion." In *The Blackwell Encyclopedia of Contemporary Christian Thought*, edited by Alistair McGrath, 428–34. Oxford: Blackwell, 1993.

———. "Charismatics on the March, Part One." *Journal of Contemporary Religion* 6.1 (1991) 11–13.

———. "Charismatics on the March, Part Two." *Journal of Contemporary Religion*, 7.1 (1992) 13–15.

———. "Chuckling in *The Shack*." *Ship of Fools*. January 2008. Online: http://www.shipoffools.com.

———. "The Concept of Person in Social Science: Possibilities for Theological Anthropology." In *The Forgotten Trinity: A Selection of Papers Presented to the BCC Study Commission on Trinitarian Doctrine Today*, edited by Alasdair I. C. Heron, 137–57. London: British Council of Churches, 1991.

———. "The Crisis of Christmas." *Ship of Fools Blog*. December 2003. Online: http://www.shipoffoolscom.

———. "Crossing the Restorationist Rubicon: From House Church to New Church." In *Fundamentalism: Church and Society*, edited by Martyn Percy and Ian Jones, 53–65. London: SPCK, 2002.

———. "Deep Church as *Paradosis*: On Relating Scripture and Tradition." In *Remembering Our Future: Explorations in Deep Church*, edited by Andrew Walker and Luke Bretherton, 59–80. Milton Keynes, UK: Paternoster, 2007.

———. "The Devil You Think You Know: Demonology and the Charismatic Movement." In *The Love of Power and the Power of Love: A Careful Assessment of the Problems within the Charismatic and Word-of-Faith Movements*. Tom Smail, Andrew Walker & Nigel Wright. 53–72. Minneapolis, MN: Bethany, 1994.

——— ed. *Different Gospels: Christian Orthodoxy and Modern Theologies*. London: SPCK, 1993.

———. *Enemy Territory: The Struggle for the Modern World*. London: Hodder & Stoughton, 1987.

———. "Facing the Future." *Gospel & Culture Network Newsletter* 23 (November 1996). Online: http://www.gospelculture.uk.org.

———. "Faith in Fatima." *Ship of Fools: Epistles of Straw*. May 2000. Online: http://www.shipoffools.com.

———. "The Faith Movement and the Question of Heresy." In *The Love of Power or the Power of Love*, edited by Tom Smail, Andrew Walker, Nigel Wright, 73–92. Minneapolis, MN: Bethany, 1994.

———. "Foreword." In William J. Abraham, *The Logic of Renewal*, ix–xii, London: SPCK, 2003.

———. "Foreword." In James H. S. Steven, *Worship in the Spirit: Charismatic Worship in the Church of England*, xiii–xiv, Eugene, OR: Wipf & Stock, 2002.

———. "Front Room Gospel." BBC Radio 4 program broadcast in 1984.

———. "Fundamentalism and Modernity: The Restoration Movement Britain." In *Studies in Religious Fundamentalism,* edited by Lionel Caplan, 195–210. London: MacMillan, 1988.

———. "Galloping Consumption." *Leading Light: Christian Faith and Contemporary Culture,* 3.1 (1996) 19–21.

———. "Harmful Religion." *Leading Light: Christian Faith and Contemporary Culture* 2.2 (1995) 5–7.

———. "Homiletics and Biblical Fidelity: An Ecclesial Approach to Orthodox Preaching." In *Text Message: The Centrality of Scripture in Preaching,* edited by Ian Stackhouse and Oliver D. Crisp, 117–30. Eugene, OR: Pickwick, 2104.

———. "The House Church Movement." *Journal of Contemporary Religion* 1.1 (1984) 6–7.

———. "Into the Future." *Leading Light: Christian Faith and Contemporary Culture* 4.1 (1997) 10.

———. "Interview with Basil Mitchell: Reflections on C. S. Lewis, Apologetics, and the Moral Tradition." In *A Christian for All Christians: Essays in Honor of C. S. Lewis,* edited by Andrew Walker and James Patrick, 7–26, Washington, D.C.: Regnery Gateway, 1992.

——— ed. "Interview with Cardinal Leon-Joseph Suenens." In *Betraying the Gospel,* edited by Andrew Walker, 73–81. Wilmore, KY: Bristol, 1990.

———. "Interview with Leslie Newbigin." In *Betraying the Gospel,* edited by Andrew Walker, 48–59. Wilmore, KY: Bristol, 1990.

———. "Interview with Metropolitan Anthony of Sourozh." In *Betraying the Gospel,* edited by Andrew Walker, 41–47, Wilmore, KY: Bristol, 1990.

———. "Introduction." In *Betraying the Gospel: Modern Theologies and Christian Orthodoxy,* edited by Andrew Walker, 19–38. Wilmore, KY: Bristol, 1990.

———. "Introduction: Exploring Harmful Religion." In *Harmful Religion: An Exploration of Religious Abuse,* edited by Andrew Walker and Lawrence Osborn, 1–11. London: SPCK, 1997.

——— "Introduction." In *On Revivalism: A Critical Examination,* edited by Andrew Walker and Kristin Aune, xxi–xxviii. Carlisle, UK: Paternoster, 2003.

———. "Knowing God Personally: Reflections on the Feminist Concept of Patriarchy." In *Different Gospels,* edited by Andrew Walker, 173–93. London: SPCK, 1993.

———. "Learning to Love America." *Ship of Fools: Epistles of Straw.* October 2001. Online: http://www.shipoffools.com.

———. "A Little Too Much Plato." *Church Times,* November 27, 1998.

———. "Miracles as Holy: The Spirituality of the Unexplained." In *The Love of Power or the Power of Love,* edited by Tom Smail, Andrew Walker, Nigel Wright, 113–24. Minneapolis, MN: Bethany House, 1994.

———. "Notes from a Wayward Son." In *The Love of Power or the Power of Love,* edited by Tom Smail, Andrew Walker, Nigel Wright, 153–67. Minneapolis, MN: Bethany House, 1994.

———. "Obituary for Metropolitan Anthony." *The Independent,* August 9, 2003.

———. "Open or Shut Case? An Orthodox View on Inter-Communion." The Saint Andrew Constantinople Lecture, 2002.

———. "The Orthodox Church and the Charismatic Movement." In *Strange Gifts?,* edited by David Martin and Peter Mullen, 163–71. Oxford: Blackwell, 1984.

———. "The Other Zionism." *Ship of Fools: Epistles of Straw.* November 2000. Online: http://www.shipoffools.com.

———."Pentecostal Power: Charismatic Movements and the Politics of Pentecostal Experience." In *Of Gods and Men: New Religious Movements,* edited by Eileen Barker, 89–108. Macon, GA: Mercer University Press, 1983.

———. "Pluralism and the Privatization of Religion." In *20/20 Visions: The Futures of Christianity in Britain,* edited by Haddon Wilmer, 46–64. London: SPCK, 1992.

———. "Preface." In *A Christian for All Christians: Essays in Honor of C. S. Lewis,* edited by Andrew Walker and James Patrick, ix–xii. Washington, D.C.: Regnery Gateway, 1992.

———. "The Prophetic Role of Orthodoxy." In *Living Orthodoxy in the Modern World,* edited by Andrew Walker and Costa Carras, 217–35. London: SPCK, 1996.

———. "Recovering Deep Church: Theological and Spiritual Renewal." In *Remembering Our Future: Explorations in Deep Church,* 1–29, Milton Keynes, UK: Paternoster, 2007.

———. "Resexing the Trinity: The Spirit as Feminine." *King's Theological Review* 13 (1990) 41–44.

———. *Restoring the Kingdom: The Radical Christianity of the House Church Movement.* London: Hodder & Stoughton, 1989.

———. *Restoring the Kingdom: The Radical Christianity of the House Church Movement.* 4th ed. London: Guildford Eagle, 1998.

———."Report on House Churches." *The Dales Bible Week.* Sunday Program: BBC Radio 4. Broadcast August 8, 1982.

———. "Scripture, Revelation and Platonism in C. S. Lewis." *Scottish Journal of Theology* 55.1 (2002) 19–35.

———. "Second Time Around." *Ship of Fools: Epistles of Straws.* June 2000. Online: http://www.shipoffools.com.

———. "Sectarian Reactions: Pluralism and the Privatization of Religion." In *20/20 Visions: The Futures of Christianity in Britain,* edited by Haddon Wilmer, 46–64. London: SPCK, 1992.

———. "Suffering from PMT." *Leading Light: Christian Faith and Contemporary Culture,* 1.1 (1993) 5–6.

———. *Telling the Story: Gospel, Mission and Culture.* London: SPCK, 1996.

———. "The Theology of the 'Restoration' Churches." In *Strange Gifts?,* edited by David Martin and Peter Mullen, 192–207. Oxford: Blackwell, 1984.

———. "The Third Schism: The Great Divide in Christianity Today." In *In Search of Christianity,* edited by Tony Moss, 202–17. London: Waterstone, 1986.

———. "Thoroughly Modern: Sociological Reflections on the Charismatic Movement from the End of the Twentieth Century. In *Charismatic Christianity: Sociological Perspectives,* edited by Stephen Hunt, et al., 17–42. New York: Macmillian, 1997.

———. "A To-Die-For Sort of Faith." *Ship of Fools: Epistles of Straw.* July 2001. Online: http://www.ship offools.com.

———. "The True Tragedy of Creationism." *Ship of Fools: Epistles of Straw.* December 2001. Online: http://www.shipoffools.com.

———. "Two Versions of Sociological Discourse: The Apophatic and Cataphatic Grounds of Social Science." PhD, Goldsmiths College: University of London, 1979.

———. "Under the Russian Cross: A Research Note on C. S. Lewis and the Eastern Orthodox Church." In *A Christian for All Christians: Essays in Honor of C. S. Lewis,* edited by Andrew Walker and James Patrick, 63–67. Washington, DC: Regnery Gateway, 1992.

———. "A Word of Welcome." *Gospel & Culture Network Newsletter* 22, June 1995. Online: http://www.gospelculture.uk.org.

———. "Young Jack." Online: http://www.rejesus.co.uk/site/module/cs_lewis/P5/.

Walker, Andrew G., Jeff Astler et al., eds. *The Idea of a Christian University.* Carlisle, UK: Paternoster, 2004.

Walker, Andrew G, and Kristen Aune, eds. *On Revival: A Critical Examination.* Carlisle, UK: Paternoster, 2003

Walker, Andrew G., and Luke Bretherton, eds. *Remember Our Future: Explorations in Deep Church.* Milton Keynes, UK: Paternoster, 2007.

———. "Introduction: Why Deep Church?" In *Remembering Our Future: Explorations in Deep Church,* edited by Andrew Walker and Luke Bretherton, xv–xx. Milton Keynes, UK: Paternoster, 2007.

Walker, Andrew G., and Costa Carras, eds. *Living Orthodoxy in the Modern World.* London: SPCK, 1996.

Walker, Andrew G., and Neil Hudson. "George Jeffreys, Revivalist and Reformer: A Reevaluation." In *On Revival: A Critical Examination,* edited by Andrew G. Walker and Kristin Aune, 137–56. Carlisle, UK: Paternoster, 2003.

Walker, Andrew G., and Laurence Osborn, eds. *Harmful Religion: An Exploration of Religious Abuse.* London: SPCK, 1997.

Walker, Andrew G., and Robin A. Parry. *Deep Church Rising: The Third Schism and the Recovery of Christian Orthodoxy.* Eugene, OR: Cascade, 2014.

Walker, Andrew G., and Mark Patterson. "Our Unspeakable Comfort: Irving, Albury, and the Origins of the Pre-tribulation Rapture." In *Christian Millenarianism: From the Early Church to Waco,* edited by Stephen Hunt, 98–115. Bloomington, IN: Indiana University Press, 2001.

Walker, Andrew G., and Martyn Percy, eds. *Restoring the Image: Essays on Religion and Society in Honor of David Martin.* Sheffield, UK: Sheffield Academic Press, 2011.

Walker, Andrew G., Tom Smail, Nigel Wright, eds. *Charismatic Renewal: In Search of a Theology.* London: SPCK, 1995.

Walker, Andrew G., and Andrew Wright. "A Christian University Imagined: Recovering *Paideia* in a Broken World." In *The Idea of a Christian University,* edited by Jeff Astley, Andrew G. Walker et al., 56–74. Carlisle, UK: Paternoster, 2004.

Wallis, Arthur. *Restoration.* Summer 1981.

Ware, Timothy. *The Orthodox Church.* New York: Penguin, 1963.

Weber, Max. *Basic Concepts in Sociology.* New York: Kensington, 1962.

———. *The Protestant Ethic and the Spirit of Capitalism.* New York: Scribners', 1958.

———. *The Sociology of Religion.* Boston: Beacon, 1993.

Willmer, Haddon, ed. *20/20 Visions: The Futures of Christianity in Britain.* London: SPCK, 1992.

Williams, D. H. *Evangelicals and Tradition: The Formative Influence of the Early Church.* Grand Rapids: Baker Academic, 2005.

Wilson, Bryan. *Religious Sects.* London: Weidenfield & Nicolson, 1970.

———. *Sects and Society.* London: Heinemann, 1978.

Wilson, E. O. *Sociobiology.* Cambridge: Harvard University Press, 1975.

Wimber, John. *Power Evangelism.* London: Hodder & Stoughton, 1985.

Wink, Walter. *Naming the Powers: The Language of Power in the New Testament.* Philadelphia: Fortress, 1984.

Wright, Nigel G. *The Fair Face of Evil.* London: Marshall Pickering, 1989.

Wybrew, Hugh. *The Orthodox Liturgy: The Development of the Eucharistic Liturgy in the Byzantine Rite.* Crestwood, NY: Saint Vladimir's Seminary Press, 1987.

Yoder, John Howard. "A People in the World." In *The Concept of the Believer's Church,* edited by H. L. Garrett, Jr., 252–83. Scottsdale, PA: Herald, 1969.

Yu, Anthony C. "A Meaningful Wager." *Journal of Religion* 70.2 (1990) 241–44.

Zernov, Nicholas. *The Russians and Their Church.* Crestwood, NY: Saint Vladimir's Seminary Press, 1997.

Ziziouslas, John D. *Being as Communion: Studies in Personhood and the Church.* London: Darton, Longman & Todd, 1985.

———. "The Doctrine of God Today." In *The Forgotten Trinity,* BCC Study Commission on Trinitarian Doctrine Today, 19–32. London: Interchurch House, 1991.

Lightning Source UK Ltd.
Milton Keynes UK
UKOW01f0708130516

274177UK00004B/120/P